32.95

W9-AVT-439

5/01

Flying Black Ponies

With a Foreword by Stephen Coonts

Flying Black Ponies

The Navy's Close Air Support Squadron in Vietnam

Kit Lavell

Naval Institute Press
Annapolis, Maryland

Naval Institute Press
291 Wood Road
Annapolis, MD 21402

MAY 2001   959.704

Library of Congress Cataloging-in-Publication Data
Lavell, Kit, 1944–
    Flying Black Ponies : the Navy's close air support squadron in
Vietnam / Kit Lavell.
        p.   cm.
    Includes bibliographical references and index.
    ISBN 1-55750-521-7 (alk. paper)
    1. Vietnamese Conflict, 1961–1975—Regimental histories—
United States. 2. United States. Navy. Light Attack Squadron
Four. 3. Vietnamese Conflict, 1961–1975—Aerial operations,
American. 4. Vietnamese Conflict, 1961–1975—Personal narra-
tives, American. I. Title.
DS558.4.L38 2000
959.704'3373—dc21   00-41136

Printed in the United States of America on acid-free paper ♾
07 06 05 04 03 02 01 00   9 8 7 6 5 4 3 2
First printing

Unless otherwise noted, all photographs are from the author's
collection.

To Loretta, Jack, and David

And to the memories of Peter Russell, Aubrey Martin, Roy Sikkink, Joel Sandberg, Carl Long, Jere Barton, Bob Lutz, and Adm. Elmo R. Zumwalt Jr.

Contents

Foreword

One of the essential points of American military history often missed by students is that the people in the critical skill positions in all our wars were volunteers.

The Americans who awaited the British soldiers at Lexington and Concord, gathered at Breed's Hill, wintered at Valley Forge, manned John Paul Jones's ships, and trapped Cornwallis at Yorktown were volunteers to a man. During the American Civil War, America had a draft of sorts, but the men who were responsible for victory or defeat were volunteers—U. S. Grant, Robert E. Lee, Joshua Chamberlain, the list goes on and on. Since the invention of the airplane, cockpits have been exclusively reserved for those who wanted to be there, those willing to put forth the effort and pay the price to earn their seat. Even in that most unpopular war, Vietnam, it was so.

The men you will meet in this book were not the sons of the privileged elite. Their fathers were not senators, officers of major corporations, or decorated with inherited fortunes. They were from blue-collar or lower-middle-class backgrounds. They usually hailed from small towns or farms, had good but not spectacular educations, had fathers and uncles who served in World War II or Korea, and—universally—were patriots. Those who survived combat had their patriotism and faith in their fellow Americans tempered like fine steel.

As you read this book, I invite you to speculate on the motivations that took these men to Vietnam, that put them in the cockpit of an OV-10 Bronco—diving into the dragon's mouth with cannons blazing and rockets rippling off the wings.

For some those days of combat were a grand adventure. No doubt testosterone was a part of the mix, but only a small part. Whatever the reasons that got them into that cockpit in Vietnam, once they were there, cold reality became impossible to ignore.

The job was killing the enemy. The bullets were real. The game was brutal and bloody, played for keeps, and the stakes were human lives. Inevitably Americans died or were maimed for life. No one was immune.

Life for them became very precious, tenuous; the men around them were killed with awe-inspiring regularity, and yet, almost to a man, these young American warriors hung in there, gutted it out, kept fighting until a bullet found them or the navy sent them home.

These aerial warriors were not unique. America sent tens of thousands of young men like them to Vietnam. To my mind, the fact that in times of crisis average Americans are willing to risk all they are and all they hope to be, fighting for their country, is one of the profound virtues of our Republic, a saving grace that redeems us from much of the pettiness, selfishness, and day-to-day greed that assault us at every turn. The stay-at-home, sunshine patriot has been with us always and, no doubt, always will. Yet America's continued existence as a free nation has always rested on its ability to produce men who would fight.

The story of VAL-4, the Black Pony Squadron, is so stereotypical of American military operations as to be almost trite. Born of military necessity, opposed by many in the establishment because it didn't fit doctrine or the grand plan, approved reluctantly, the squadron was parsimoniously equipped with obsolete, borrowed airplanes and manned with youthful inexperience and proverbial black sheep. Amazingly, these men learned to fight and gave an extraordinary account of themselves.

Kit Lavell puts you in the cockpit with the Black Ponies and takes you flying. It's a grand ride. Contained within these pages is the distilled essence of the American military experience. Regardless of what the establishment says or does with the billions of defense dollars that flow through Washington every year like a great river, *this* is the way America fights.

Stephen Coonts

Preface

What's past is prologue.

—William Shakespeare, *The Tempest*

Years after flying several hundred combat missions in Vietnam, Ed Sullivan sat at a bar in Suda Bay, Crete, spinning "sea stories," or war stories in his case, using his hands, of course—as naval aviators are wont to do. Suddenly a huge paw landed on his shoulder. When "Sully," who is six foot five, turned around, he was face to barrel chest with a huge stranger.

"Good God," Sully thought.

"Hey," the big guy grunted in a deep, gravelly voice, "Were you a Black Pony?"

"Yes—yes I was."

The big guy looked Sully over as if he were about to have him for dinner. Then he grinned and slapped Sully on the back.

"I can't tell you how many times you saved our lives."

The Black Pony pilot and the navy SEAL embraced and laughed and then talked about Vietnam. Not long into the conversation the SEAL mentioned a particular operation on which the bad guys had his platoon surrounded and the Black Ponies provided close air support that enabled the SEALs to safely extract and complete the op.

"I know the guy who was on that flight," Sullivan told him.

"You'll never buy another drink when you're in the same bar with me," the SEAL promised, and the two men talked into the night, strangers no longer, but brothers of a special kind.

This chance occurrence is not unique, for something similar has happened to almost every Black Pony pilot, at some time in his life: SEALs, crewmen from river patrol boats, soldiers in the army—fighting men who served in the Mekong Delta between 1969 and 1972—have run into Black Ponies, or sought them out. Their stories are similar in at least one respect. They all say they would not be alive had it not been for a Black Pony.

I have written this book because of these men.

This is the story of one of the most unique and colorful squadrons in naval aviation history, and arguably the most effective close air support unit in the Vietnam War: the Black Ponies of Light Attack Squadron Four. The navy's only land-based attack squadron, VAL-4 existed for little more than three years. But in that short time the Black Ponies saved more allied lives and destroyed more enemy with close air support than all of the Seventh Fleet squadrons combined. Yet few people even know that the squadron existed, let alone where it was located, what its mission was, and what it flew.

When I was a newly winged aviator, the man in charge of giving me my next set of orders—a detailer in the Bureau of Personnel (BuPers)—described Light Attack Squadron Four to me. I was not sure if he was trying to dissuade me from asking to be sent there, or encouraging me. He described VAL-4 as a combination of "McHale's Navy" —after the popular television program of the 1960s about an unorthodox but effective PT boat crew—and the "Black Sheep Squadron" of World War II fame. And as I found out, the Black Ponies certainly were an unorthodox, one-of-a-kind outfit. They did make up their own rules as they went along in that most unconventional of wars in Vietnam. They had to. There was no textbook for this kind of mission. The navy plunked a fixed-wing squadron in the middle of the Mekong Delta and gave it a mission to support the riverine patrol forces, SEALs, and allied units. As for being "black sheep," yes, many Black Pony officers either had been passed over for promotion and sent there to redeem themselves or had been sidetracked by the regular navy as falling outside a normal career pattern. For many, this posting was their last or only chance to make something of themselves. It held the promise of being a place to start over. It would attract some colorful characters.

Black Ponies fought with borrowed, propeller-driven aircraft in an era before smart weapons or computer gadgets, in an age before zero defects and political correctness, when warriors led and did not manage, and studied tactics, not strategic planning. Black Ponies flew a one-of-a-kind mission in the middle of the jungle, far from the traditional navy, a mission that placed a fixed-wing pilot in harm's way—down and dirty, low and slow.

In writing this book, my aim is to put the reader into the cockpit, and occasionally on the ground, to give him or her a feel for what it was like to fly close air support for men whose lives depended on their skills and daring as a pilot. I strive to have the reader experience and understand what the pilot is doing as he flies "by the seat of the pants," when whatever smarts in the aircraft were between the pilot's ears, not in the electronics.

And while *Flying Black Ponies* is a military history, it is also an action adventure about vivid characters, whose stories are told from various points of view. But the Black Pony story could not be told without also telling the stories of the others who served: the "brown water" sailors, the SEALs, the soldiers, advisors, and airmen the Black Ponies worked for. The stories in this narrative are not just about flying and combat. They are also about the lives of Black Ponies on the ground, at work and at play, the enlisted as well as the officers. Over a span of three years about 650 men served with VAL-4, only 20 percent of them officers. One secret behind the success of the Black Ponies was the incredible effort of the enlisted men who maintained the aircraft and ran the squadron. Most of them were young, some barely nineteen, and away from home for the first time. They came from all parts of the country, looking for adventure or a challenge, and wound up working harder than they ever had before or ever would in the future, as did all of the Black Ponies, who lived and worked in conditions that would seem primitive and dangerous to most people.

While life in the Mekong Delta was difficult, it could also be rewarding and at times funny—infused with the kind of black humor that arises when human beings face the trials of war. There is even a love story, poignant and tragic, as such wartime stories often are. Occasionally these stories may be controversial, the language coarse at times and the characters irreverent, but the image the Black Ponies project is positive, and I hope inspiring.

My feelings toward this group of men could only be described by writing this book. It was truly a labor of love. I am proud to have been a Black Pony. And while I participated in the Black Pony story, it is not my story. It is the story of a collection of colorful individuals who in the summer of their youth were called to an adventure that would test their skills, their characters, and their courage—an adventure that would test whether some men lived or some died. Few people ever get tested in this manner.

Dialogue and details of events have been reported to the best of my recollection. For those Black Ponies whose stories are told, I kept a diary while in Vietnam and sent letters and audiocassette tapes to my family and friends. I also installed an audiocassette recorder and movie camera in the cockpit of my aircraft for some combat missions. Other Black Ponies provided letters, tapes, and other materials for this book, sources that view events from various points of view. I also made use of historical documents and materials such as messages, spotreps (spot reports), after-action reports, transcriptions of skits, letters, citations, and official histories to reconstruct events. Using these resources, I have endeavored to render the truth as accurately and as graphically as possible. I alone take responsibility for the book's accuracy and content.

In writing this book I am indebted to scores of people, foremost among them the Black Ponies, SEALs, brown water sailors, army aviators, and other veterans of the Vietnam War in the Mekong Delta, whose stories are presented here and whose names appear in the text. I am honored to have worked with these people who gave so much to their country. I thank them for sharing their stories, memories, photos, letters, tapes, and other memorabilia. Many also helped with other aspects of the book's preparation; some are named in the text, some are not, and I would like to acknowledge these contributions. Among the Black Ponies, Larry Hone was the first to carry the torch and keep alive the squadron's story. He almost single-handedly tracked down all the pilots and organized the first reunion in 1990. Ron Pickett's advice and insight have proved invaluable. Through the efforts of Black Pony Webmaster Bob Peetz I was able to reach a number of veterans who worked with the squadron in Vietnam after they saw the Web page (http://www.blackpony.org) and contacted me.

I am indebted to the following people who provided information, contacts, or background that greatly helped me: Marty Schuman; John Butterfield; Mike Quinlan; T. Y. Baker; Ed Sullivan; Ken Williams; Jimmy Hanks; Tom McCracken; Jim Becker; Bill Robertson; and other Black Ponies. Thanks also to Dick Couch; Joe DeFloria; Barry Enoch; Darryl Young; Tom Boyhan; and other SEALs; as well as Dennis Cummings, author of books on SEALs. I wish to thank Jim Davy; Ed Pietzuch; Kerry N. Schaefer, president of the PBR Forces Veterans Association, Inc.; Ralph Fries of the Gamewardens Association; Max Popov, PBR FVA Webmaster; Ralph Singleton of the Swiftboat Sailors Discussion Group; Paul Gibbons; and others who served with the riverine patrol forces. For helping me understand the role that army aviation played in the Delta, I am grateful to Dave Fesmire of Darkhorse Control; William Robert Stanley; Mike Sloniker, historian for the Vietnam Helicopter Pilots Association; Mike Howe; Ernie Wells; and Brig. Gen. George Walker. I would also like to thank Tom Beard; Ken Jackson; Chuck Burin, historian for the OV-10 Bronco Association; and Dean Demmery of the Carolinas Aviation Museum, Charlotte, North Carolina.

I am especially grateful to Ken Russell and his wife Tudy for sharing memories and photos of Pete Russell, and to Reba Sikkink for sharing memories of her son, Roy.

Thanks also to Rosario "Zip" Rausa, editor, *Wings of Gold*, Association of Naval Aviation; Dick Knott; aviation artist Dan Witcoff; Roger Powell of Graphics Effects, Ltd; Bob Pace; and Naomi Grady.

I am particularly indebted to many who have helped in the research for this book at the Naval Historical Center: Dr. Edward J. Marolda, senior historian; Roy A. Grossnick, historian and head of the Naval Aviation History Office; Mike Walker, Operational Archives Branch; Mark Evans, historian, Naval Aviation History Branch; and Mark Wertheimer, archivist, curator, resident NavSpecWar/Vietnam specialist. I am also grateful to Dr. Bob Doyle; Dr. Ronald B. Frankum Jr. of The Vietnam Archive at Texas Tech University; Bill Doty at National Archives and Records Administration; and Jeanie Kirk at the Department of the Navy.

I owe a special debt to Wayne Cowie Clarke for his insight into riverine warfare and Duffle Bag operations, and for the invaluable research assistance he so graciously provided me. Finally, I wish to thank Paul Wilderson of the Naval Institute Press and Mark Gatlin of the Smithsonian Institution, whose enthusiasm and encouragement got this project started.

Flying Black Ponies

1

Setting the Stage

Let's meet, and either do or die.

—John Fletcher

"Whoa boy, I'm not looking forward to this."

Lt. Edward Smith liked his job as a naval intelligence officer. And the best part of it was riding in the back seat of the OV-10 Bronco. He got to fly and he got to take photos, two of his favorite pastimes. "Smitty" had an eye for spotting suspicious boat activity along the coast of the Mekong Delta. On this day, however, Smitty had difficulty holding onto the heavy, clunky 35-mm Pentax camera as Lt. Roy "Bubba" Segars, the pilot in the front seat, yanked the twin-engine turboprop aircraft around the sky. Smitty had spotted forty enemy soldiers on the beach just as Bubba made a low pass over them and pulled back on the stick, sending the aircraft skyward to the safety that altitude afforded, as the enemy soldiers raced to set up their antiaircraft guns.

Only moments before, a flight of two other OV-10s had spotted these enemy soldiers on the beach, near a jungle area on the coast of Vinh Binh Province. Naval Intelligence reports indicated the jungle canopy hid an ammunition factory that was supplied at night by North Vietnamese trawlers. That two-plane flight had tried to get a clearance to attack the soldiers, but was unsuccessful, so they left the scene. Smitty and

Bubba had heard them on the radios and flew to the area, arriving after the two-plane flight had left. Bubba and Smitty were flying a single-aircraft coastal surveillance mission. Although their aircraft was fully armed, the rules of engagement (ROE) prohibited single-plane air strikes; but a two-plane flight (like the one that had just left) could act as a "Fire Team" and attack the enemy. The primary mission of these OV-10s, known as "Black Ponies," was close air support of friendly troops on the ground. The Black Ponies were an attack squadron that also flew occasional single-plane reconnaissance missions. Smitty knew that Bubba hated these boring surveillance missions. He also knew that Bubba would always try to find and join up with another flight—a Fire Team—so he could shoot. "Never take good ordnance home," Bubba always told Smitty. Bubba had gotten so excited when he caught the bad guys out in the open that he set up for an attack while still calling out on "guard" emergency frequency for another aircraft to join him. Smitty realized that Bubba no longer was interested in taking photos. Bubba planned to take some enemy lives. But he needed a wingman.

Smitty watched in amazement as Bubba maneuvered the Bronco in tight circles over the bad guys while also dialing just the right radio frequencies, all from memory. Bubba knew so many allied units in the Mekong Delta that he had no trouble getting a clearance to fire on the enemy troops. Then Smitty began asking himself: "Did I hear Bubba right? Did he say we were a Fire Team? A two-plane? Okay, he's not lying, only jumping the gun. He will find himself a wingman. Yeah, but can he find one before he pees in his pants? I guess I'm merely along for the ride. And picture-taking time is over. Am I ready for this?"

"Okay, Bubba, I'm ready."

"Anybody have me in sight?" Bubba yelled into the UHF radio.

Lt. (jg) Ray Morris, on a single-aircraft naval gunfire-spotting mission on the other side of the Delta, heard Bubba and rushed to join him. Smitty frantically scanned the horizon for Morris's aircraft. Of course it was too far away to be seen.

"Do you see me yet?" Bubba impatiently radioed. The rules of engagement, along with other matters, required all four pilots in both aircraft to not only be in the same flight but to also agree on the location of the target and the nearest friendlies. Smitty knew that Bubba wouldn't deliberately break the rules of engagement—the ROE were unambiguous on this point—but at least Bubba would be . . . innovative.

Bubba aborted his roll-in a couple of times, and checked his weapons. "Got me in sight?" he radioed. The switches were all set. The bad guys were still on the beach. Bubba would begin an attack, and if he didn't find a wingman before he had to shoot, he would abort, climb back to altitude, and begin another attack. Smitty watchd Bubba perform this caper several times.

"I think I'm getting close," Ray Morris radioed back.

Bubba set his gunsight, selected his weapons stations, and charged his guns. "See me yet?" Bubba flipped the Master Armament Switch. Smitty craned his neck to look around the front ejection seat. Watching Bubba was like watching a cartoon. All frenetic motion. And Bubba was indeed a cartoon character to many who knew him. Not one-dimensional by any means, but larger than life, always doing the outrageous, on the ground and in the air.

Smitty heard the radio crackle, then Ray Morris's voice. "I'm about five miles out." Apparently that was all Bubba needed to hear, as the OV-10 rolled inverted and Smitty desperately tried to stow his camera before it banged him in the head.

"Okay, we're a Fire Team," Bubba declared over the UHF.

If Morris was five miles out, he must have Bubba in sight, Smitty thought. This was now a flight, wasn't it? A loose one, sure, but if an air force formation could stretch over two states, what the hell.

If Smitty had any doubts, Bubba by his actions surely did not. He made three tight rocket attacks, sending Zuni rockets exploding all along the beach, then pulled up and off to the right and immediately rolled the plane almost inverted into another dive. The Bronco lost altitude and energy on each pass. Smitty was barely able to keep his head upright as the G forces kept slamming him down into the seat, then against the side of the cockpit, then back down into the seat. Bubba flung the Bronco around into an ever-tighter pattern in the sky above the enemy soldiers caught in the open near the beach. The rockets' explosions appeared to Smitty to be getting closer and closer to them as the aircraft lost altitude on each attack. He could see the faces of the enemy as some of them stood their ground and fired back with AK-47s. They were like gunfighters at the OK Corral on speed. The Bronco was whirling around in a dervishly tight pattern just above the heads of the bad guys. Hey, this deserves a picture, Smitty thought. He pulled against the G forces and brought the camera up from his side, only to realize that he did not have a sidearm. Damn. I left my gun at home. Because of the cramped cockpit, Smitty had traded the pistol for the camera that day.

Bubba was out of rockets and began strafing the enemy with his machine guns, trying to gun down every last one as they scattered in all directions. Smitty's senses struggled to keep up with the plane and what Bubba was forcing it to do. The *rat atat tat, rat atat tat* of the M-60s echoed in the cockpit as the fleeing soldiers loomed large in the windscreen before falling in the sand. The echoes were then punctuated by static-filled radio exchanges that Smitty could barely comprehend . . . "You got 'em in sight?" "Negative Bubba". . . "Watch my tracers Ray". . . I'm coming around for another pass". . . *Rat atat tat* . . . "Christ, you see 'em now?"

The G forces telescoped Smitty's vision but he could see the ricochets splashing surf skyward before the Bronco banked into a tight turn to come around for another attack. He heard the groan of the engines as they fought to yield more power, the whine of the props biting the air as the Bronco struggled for altitude. Smitty's own manic rush to gather in all that was happening seemed to slam into an imaginary wall when he gaped helplessly, camera in hand, as Bubba pulled out of a shallow dive at very low altitude, just over the antiaircraft site. Almost in slow motion Smitty witnessed the aircraft he was in disintegrate before his eyes. Daylight opened up in front of Smitty as antiaircraft fire tore into the side and ripped open the bottom of the cockpit in a maelstrom of shrapnel and smoke.

The ejection seat's exploding rockets propelled Smitty's body through the fireball and debris more than 150 feet up with an initial force of twenty times the force of gravity. Ballistic devices fired, pulling the parachute out. The ejection seat ripped away from Smitty, who was violently snapped taut by the risers of his parachute. Smitty's body was pulled horizontal to the ground, now less than one hundred feet below, his head and eyes facing straight up into the blue sky—but he would see nothing. Before the parachute canopy filled with air, inertia had caused his head to accelerate faster than his brains which then smashed against the inside of his skull, the blow rendering him senseless. Later Smitty would recall getting half of a swing on his chute after it opened, then smashing into the ground and being violently dragged through the sand by the coastal winds. "Triple Sticks" (the aircraft's side number was 111) crashed only yards away on the enemy gun site, no doubt killing some of the surviving gunners.

Smitty landed on top of some sand dunes. A surge of adrenaline overtook the searing pain emanating from his battered and lacerated body and it momentarily cleared his mind: "I gotta get away from this parachute." Smitty released the Koch fittings attaching him to the parachute, pushed himself away from the orange-colored silk panels, and stumbled through the sand and brush. His mangled leg gave out, and he collapsed into the sand. "God, I can't go any further." He reached up to feel a large flap of scalp hanging over his face and the remnants of half his helmet still stuck to his bloody head. His eyeglasses were gone. "Gotta get away from here." A surge of energy. A lunge, and Smitty toppled over a sand dune. No sooner had he rolled over than he heard a muffled *plunk, plunk, plunk.* He didn't have to raise his head to know what it was. Plumes of sand puffed into the air as the AK-47 rounds tore into the parachute only yards away.

"Oh God, they're gonna get me." Images flashed through Smitty's mind. Only a few days before he had read a captured enemy document describing the interrogation by torture of a Naval Intelligence officer shot down on this very spot two years before. That intelligence officer, like Smitty, knew that yet another aircraft previously had been shot down on the same spot. "They sure as hell aren't going to get me." He reached for his sidearm before realizing all he had was a pocketknife and a pencil flare. "Damn, I'm going to buy it . . . I just know it." He pulled the pencil flare from his survival vest and aimed it toward where he heard the gunfire. Toward where the enemy's POW camp waited nearby. Toward where he knew—just knew—the bad guys would be coming for him. Before his fears could take him to that place, Smitty heard gunfire in the other direction. He peered over the sand dune, and through a blur saw Bubba struggling to get rid of his chute as, dragged by the wind, he barreled down the beach on his back. Those who fly by the seat of the pants . . . now being dragged by the ass. Smitty saw Bubba reach up and release the Koch fittings that were well above his head; then he watched Bubba tumble to a stop. The image of Bubba on his butt was that of a dime-store lead soldier that kids played with, a toy aviator sitting on the ground beneath his parachute. Bubba quickly got to his knees, ripped off his helmet, ran his hand to his head, and checked to see if his legs and other big parts were still attached. He then sprinted through the surf heading for the safety of the water—only to come face to face with two surprised enemy soldiers. They were carrying another soldier, whose leg was blown off, and had just emerged from the surf.

"If they get Bubba he'll die a slow death tonight."

Bubba ran past them at full throttle, kicking up a rooster tail of sand behind him, before the dazed enemy realized who that marathon man was. Bubba pulled his pistol out of his survival vest as he was sprinting, and just as he entered the water, he spotted another soldier emerging from the surf, only a few yards away. Bubba stopped, cocked his pistol, aimed it at the startled enemy, then apparently changed his mind and dashed for the water.

Smitty peered over the sand dune at Bubba as he struggled through the waves and dove into the water, furiously paddling against the tide and currents. He watched bullets plink in the water all around Bubba. Bubba then jettisoned most of his gear, which also included his radio and pistol. "Why is he doing that?" Smitty thought. Bubba must have believed he presented too big a target to miss, propped out of the water as he was by the buoyancy of his aviator's life preserver (an LPA-1 flotation device), even though it was not inflated. Bubba's body alternately swept out to sea and rushed toward the enemy with the ebb and surge of the surf and foam. Smitty's emotions ping-ponged until he witnessed his buddy break through the current and put distance between himself and his pursuers. Soon all that could be seen was Bubba desperately struggling to poke only his nose out of the water as the AK-47 rounds ringed his head.

With the enemy soldiers' attention focused on Bubba, Smitty realized that his and Bubba's fates were now in his hands. He yanked his survival radio from his vest and began making emergency calls.

Another flight of Black Ponies, having heard Bubba's frantic radio pleas for a wingman to join him, had returned to the scene just as Bubba's plane crashed. Smitty could not see them orbiting overhead. And he did not know that the pilots had seen the parachutes followed by pieces of Triple Sticks raining down on the beach and had heard the high-pitched wail of the emergency locator transmitter on "guard" frequency. The pilots had to orbit helplessly, for they could not positively identify the positions of Smitty and Bubba until—and if—they could make radio contact with them.

Smitty was also unaware that, back at the base in Binh Thuy, every available aircraft had launched to help out. The executive officer (XO) had arrived at the airfield in his jungle fatigues, and after hearing the frantic radio transmissions, ran out to the flight line where several aircraft were waiting to take off and pulled a pilot from his aircraft just as he was getting in. On the CO's wing the XO flew to Vinh Binh. When they arrived overhead the skipper heard Smitty's voice and quickly radioed.

"Bubba, is that you?"

Smitty looked skyward but could not see any aircraft. "No. No, it's 'Backseat' [Smitty's call sign]."

The next thing Smitty heard was, "Goddamn. It's only the backseat."

Fortunately, Smitty thought, this backseat had a radio and the presence of mind to use it. The Black Ponies overhead asked Smitty if he wanted them to fire at the enemy soldiers who had been shooting at his parachute. Smitty figured that if his orientation was correct, he was between these soldiers and a bunker that was the site of the antiaircraft fire. He was too close to the enemy and the Ponies would have to fire virtually into his position. Not a good idea.

An army helo flying down the coast, whose call sign was "Tailboard," responded to Smitty's "Mayday" and quickly established radio contact with him. From overhead, the Tailboard crew asked him to fire his flare for identification.

"Shit, that's the only thing lethal I got on me," Smitty thought.

"Pop a smoke."

"Now they're really going to find me."

And it wasn't the helo crew that Smitty was thinking about at that moment. He listened, then looked around. The machine gunfire had stopped. Are they waiting for me to stand up? Are they waiting for the helo? Well, it's now or never.

Smitty pulled out a marking smoke and popped it. Before he knew it, the helicopter had swooped down with the side-door gunner's machine gun blazing away. The helo settled into a cloud of sand and after what seemed to be an eternity the image of a Tailboard crewman emerged from the whirlwind . . . firing toward Smitty. The tracers sailed over Smitty's head. Smitty struggled to get into the hovering helo as a hail of enemy fire snaked its way through the sand to find him.

"Shit, they're going to nail me in the back."

A hand grabbed Smitty and yanked him aboard.

Snatched and safely onboard, Smitty then directed the Tailboard crew out to sea, to the place where he had last seen Bubba. The helo lifted off and twisted away from the enemy gunners as it headed for the water. It nosed over, descending for the foaming surf, and abruptly pulled up and hovered, the waves lapping at its skids while withering machine-gun fire from the enemy on the beach inched its way out to meet it. Bubba by then was so exhausted he had to be pulled out of the water by a crewman, who hung over the side while scooping Bubba onto the skids. Smitty wrapped his good leg around a stanchion and gave them a hand. When Bubba flopped onto the helo's floorboards, Smitty thought he looked like a beached whale leaking yellow dye.

For thirty-three minutes Bubba and Smitty had evaded death on the ground. The helo medevacked the Black Pony pilot and the rear-seat observer to My Tho, then to the Binh Thuy dispensary where Lt. Steve Rodgers— "Doc" Rodgers—the Black Pony flight surgeon, was waiting to work on them. The skipper and others debriefed Bubba, who was in a very agitated state, despite several shots that Doc gave him without apparent effect. A couple of corpsmen helped Bubba back to the bachelor officers quarters (BOQ), where Lts. Jim Arthur and Kit Lavell met him at the trailer, poured Scotch into him, and tried to calm him down. They ended up walking him up and down the dirt road, dumping booze into him while he kept babbling, "They almost got Bubba . . . they almost got Bubba," until he finally passed out. The skipper got Bubba into a plane the next day, with Bubba flying in the CO's back seat—the theory being the familiar one that, once thrown from a Bronco, it's best to get right back on one. Smitty's camera obviously had gone down with the OV-10. About a month later, he got a dunning notice from Saigon requesting that he return the broken camera to them or pay for it. He sent them back a short message saying that he would give them the exact coordinates and they could go get the damn thing themselves. So ended "Bubba's Misadventure."

The Setting

The Mekong begins its twenty-five-hundred-mile quest for the South China Sea in northern Tibet. The river flows south from China, separating Burma from Laos. It cuts a swath through the jungle as it transverses Cambodia and begins to branch out as it crosses the border of Vietnam into the Song Tien-Giang ("upper river") and the Song Hua-Giang ("lower river"). The two branches of the Mekong spread themselves out and shape the wide, flat, expansive tropical savanna of the Mekong River Delta. The upper river splits into the My Tho, Ham Luong, and Co Chien branches. The lower Mekong, only a few miles separated from its kin, is known by its French name, the Bassac River. These four branches, flowing parallel, then divide again just before reaching the end of their journey. So much soil is transported that the once crystal clear water bleeds a rich red-brown as it pours its silt, sediment and soul into the gray-green sea from its eight mouths. The entire river system is known as the Mekong. The Vietnamese call the system Cuu Long Giang—the "River of the Nine Dragons," adding one more imaginary mouth for good luck.[1]

The Mekong River Delta was one of the most strategically important areas of the Republic of South Vietnam. Along the western, or Gulf of Thailand, coast, dense, dark forests formed a demarcation between what the government of South Vietnam on a good day (but not at night) might try to lay claim to and what was indisputably usurped by the enemy. Between the sylvan thicket of tram trees and duoc trees, and the warm waters of the Gulf, mangrove forests grew haphazardly along coastal swamplands. Like a giant patchwork in a give-and-take between man and nature, mangrove forests coexisted with small fishing villages and settlements surrounded by brushwood, bamboo, weeds, and tall grasses. To the east and south of the forests, farmers grew primarily rice, but also some rubber and in small plantations, bananas, oranges, mangos, pineapples, jackfruit, coconut, and sugar cane. Within the hamlets and villages, kapok trees grew and villagers kept bees for their honey. Villagers also cultivated areca palms and betel peppers for their leaves and nuts, as well as oil palm and tobacco. The land was exotic to most Westerners and home to tigers, leopards, panthers, wild boars, mongooses, macaques, gibbons, and rhesus monkeys. Along the edges of lakes and on river and canal banks, one might regularly encounter lizards of all shapes and sizes and be startled by crocodiles, pythons, and cobras.

The Vietnamese under French colonial rule had built in the Delta a system of canals, one of the most intricate and elaborate inland waterways in the world. Only one paved highway transversed the region and most of the commerce took place on canals, streams, and rivers—as rice made its way to the major waterways leading to Saigon. The Delta was home to more than half the country's population, and 80 percent of its rice crop was harvested there. Much of the rice grew in the "floating rice" region, between the forests of the northwest and the mouths of the Mekong to the southeast, between the Cambodian border on the north, and Can Tho to the south, the largest town in the Delta. Here the floodwaters of the Mekong and the Bassac on their inexorable transmigration began to overflow their banks in April and May, reaching a height during October and November about fifteen feet above the dry season's level. To pilots flying over them, shimmering rice paddies sparkled from the air. Willowy wisps of green rice stems waved in the breeze, having elongated as the floodwaters rose, thus keeping their leaves above water to avoid drowning. Millions of people depended on the rice crop as a major source of sustenance and salvation.

Despite more than a decade of low-intensity guerilla warfare, South Vietnam in 1964 was one of the world's major rice exporters. But the amount of rice available to the government fell by 25 percent between 1965 and 1966 as the Vietcong increased their control over the Mekong Delta. By 1967 South Vietnam imported almost a million tons of rice as the Delta became virtually an enemy stronghold, providing rice, taxes, and recruits for the Vietcong war effort.

The Mekong River Delta's hundreds of miles of coastline, stretching from the Gulf of Thailand to the South China Sea, also provided the North Vietnamese with numerous routes to infiltrate weapons and supplies.

Likewise, the long border with supposedly neutral Cambodia provided the enemy with relatively safe land infiltration routes over which tons of supplies, as well as soldiers from the north, could migrate.

The Mekong Delta thus became a staging area for assaults on Saigon, and the South Vietnamese government. But even more significantly, it became—to the North Vietnamese—the prize itself.

2

For the Want of a Pony

O! for a horse with wings!

—William Shakespeare, *Cymbeline*

The young men who fought in the Vietnam War grew up reading history books in which the saga of the United States Navy unfolded against a backdrop of blue ocean. From John Paul Jones to John Fitzgerald Kennedy, naval heroes sailed into battle in the deep waters of the world's oceans and seas. Whether in sailing ships like the *Bon Homme Richard,* or PT boats like the 109, in aircraft carriers like the *Yorktown,* or in battleships like the *Missouri,* the men who became legends of naval history did so on waters far from land, and sometimes out of sight of their enemy. The Virginia Capes, the Barbary Coast, the battles of Midway and Leyte Gulf evoke images of hissing cannon balls cracking through ship's rigging, of huge salvos of 16-inch guns, of roaring engines from carrier-deck-launched fighter planes.

The young men who came of age in the fifties and sixties, who joined the navy and volunteered for Vietnam duty in-country, found a navy much different from the textbook image they had grown up with. Instead of blue ocean they found brown water, instead of large, steel-encased virtual cities plying deep waters they found small, cramped, plastic boats skimming narrow rivers and canals. And instead of war at a distance, technical and impersonal, they would slug it out with an enemy using small arms, at close range, like infantrymen.

The young men who fought in Vietnam also grew up in a world of cars and personal freedom, of movies and rock and roll, of great expectations and limitless opportunity. For the young officers and noncoms who led the brown water navy, fast boats were like fast cars, and while thirty knots may not seem fast, speed is relative. But for young men who expected much, they also adapted quite well to a brown water navy where much was expected of them. The sounds, the images, the increasingly frenetic pace of the rock and roll generation would also color the style, the tempo, and even the tactics of these young guns at war.

Until 1965 the U.S. Navy had only a small number of advisors in Vietnam. In order to control the infiltration of Vietcong (VC) craft from among the fifty thousand civilian boats operating in the coastal waters, and to prevent the twenty-five known enemy steel-hulled trawlers from shipping weapons and ammunition into the Delta, the navy began Operation Market Time in July 1965. They organized it as Task Force 115. The world's greatest open ocean, blue water naval power had to create a brown water navy—complete with boats, strategy, tactics, and trained men—almost overnight. Scores of PCF (patrol craft, fast), called "Swift boats," built from commercially available hulls in a very short time especially for this mission, joined seventeen eighty-two-foot Coast Guard cutters, known as WPBs, and several LSTs (landing ship, tanks) that anchored off the Mekong River and other major waterways.[1]

As the need grew to run patrols closer inshore and into the shallow rivers and canals, to deny the enemy their free use, another operation, called Game Warden, began in December 1965 as Task Force 116. Again, the navy had no suitable boats for the task, so it turned once more to a commercially available fiberglass hull, this one thirty-two feet in length. Military contractors added a naval superstructure with two sheets of armor plating along the sides of the afterdeck and the cockpit. The navy thus quickly came up with a thirty-knot craft that drew only nine to eighteen inches of water. It was propelled by Jacuzzi-designed water jets instead of propellers and powered by two 220-hp diesels—just what was needed for the shallow inland waterways of the Delta.[2] These Mark One and Mark Two river patrol boats, called PBRs, brought brown water naval operations into the Delta in 1966.[3]

During Game Warden the navy quickly realized the need for air support. While aircraft carriers were occasionally stationed on "Dixie Station," a location at sea off the coast of South Vietnam, their fast-moving jets with limited loiter capability were not effective for accurate close air support in this environment. Something else was needed.

When gas turbine–powered helicopters replaced the older generation of piston engine choppers, their introduction into Vietnam in the mid-1960s would revolutionize the way Americans conducted warfare. Their increased speed, range, reliability, payload, and firepower gave U.S. ground forces a flexibility and maneuverability that forever altered battle tactics. Along with heavy lift helicopters, like the CH-47 Chinook, which carried arms, ammunition, supplies, and fuel, the UH-1 Iroquois would become the workhorse of the army. In different configurations the "Huey," as it was known, could evacuate wounded as a "medevac" or "dustoff" (a slang term); fire on enemy positions as an attack helicopter or "gunship"; or carry troops into combat as a "slick" (which lacked the gunship's armament). Having no attack helicopters, the navy initially borrowed UH-1B helicopters from the army, which then trained the navy crews, until the navy could develop its own attack helicopter capability. In June 1967 the navy commissioned Helicopter Attack (Light) Squadron Three (HAL-3), nicknamed "Seawolves," to operate in detachments throughout the Delta.[4]

In order to seize the initiative and take the fight to the enemy, the army and navy formed a joint operation in July 1966 called Mobile Riverine Force. By January 1971 it had begun operations in the Mekong River Delta and the adjacent Rung Sat Special Zone. The Marine Corps, however, was unavailable for use in the Delta. The marines had been fully committed to operations along the northern border of South Vietnam, in an area designated as I Corps. They would have been better suited than the army for the mission because of the marines' amphibious warfare capabilities and kinship with the navy.[5] The terrain, climate, and enemy in the Delta resisted the type of conventional warfare the army was prepared to fight. The Delta was a maze of waterways, swamps, mud, jungle, and rice paddies. The lack of roads, the frequent monsoon rains, and the soft, wet soil prevented conventional troop and armament movements by wheeled vehicles. The hot, humid, tropical climate adversely affected man and machine, easily fatiguing troops and reducing the operational capability of helicopters and fixed-wing aircraft. The dense population and intensive agriculture restricted the ability to mass large forces. And, of course, the very nature of guerilla warfare limited the army's effectiveness.

To deal with these circumstances American forces developed an approach that was both new and old. By employing the same tactics that were used in the Seminole and Civil Wars, they deployed, by boat, highly mobile army units throughout inland waterways. The navy's contribution, Task Force 117, began with a large fleet of LST hulls converted to barracks and repair vessels, shallow draft mechanized landing ships (LCMs) converted into "Tango boats," and supporting PBRs.[6] But the navy's role never amounted to more than "a sort of transportation and escort service for the Army's 9th Division," which was engaged in search and destroy tactics, as Adm. Elmo R. Zumwalt Jr., chief of naval operations, later described it.[7] Many in positions of leadership felt the navy could be used more suitably.

In September 1968 just prior to assuming command of the naval forces in Vietnam (ComNavForV), Admiral Zumwalt met with Capt. Robert Salzer (who later became a vice admiral), the commander of Task Force 117. Salzer told Zumwalt that the "search and destroy" mission was losing its effectiveness, and recommended a more aggressive role for the thirty-eight-thousand-man navy force in-country. Zumwalt knew that Market Time provided an effective water and air barrier against infiltration by sea, and Game Warden, with reasonable effectiveness, denied the enemy unrestricted access to the major rivers. But the enemy still commanded uninhibited use of the small waterways.

Zumwalt often sent his staff unorthodox proposals headed with the large capital letters "ZWI": Zumwalt's Wild Idea.[8] His staff at NavForV knew that Cambodia had become a major enemy supply area and that only an aggressive campaign on the small waterways could impose a barrier between this supply area and the enemy units in the Delta. What began as a ZWI became a new strategy in November 1968 named "Sea Lords," the acronym for South-East Asia Lake, Oceans, River, and Delta Strategy. It aimed to close off the water routes from Cambodia.[9] Captain Salzer became "First Sea Lord" —the commander of Task Force 194, serving until December 1968.

The navy would take the initiative by conducting operations in three areas. First, naval forces created a barrier along the major canals in the upper Delta, stretching the entire length of the Cambodian border, from the Gulf of Thailand to the area just west of Saigon known as the "Parrot's Beak" (so-called because of its shape). Second, to seize control of the U-Minh Forest in the southwest part of the Delta, and third, to win back the Nam Can area of the Ca Mau Peninsula, the navy aggressively dispatched forces into areas where little allied presence existed. The commander of naval forces in Vietnam made many Game Warden and Market Time craft available to the new operation. As the Mobile Riverine

Force became "Vietnamized," and operations drew to a close in June 1969, the navy also transferred some of these assets to Sea Lords.

Brown Water Sailors' Need for Air Support

The river patrol boat was the descendant of the World War II PT boat, at least in spirit, if not in design. Workhorses of the brown water navy, by late 1968, 250 PBRs patrolled the waterways of the Delta and Rung Sat. A twin .50-caliber machine gun sat in an open turret up forward on a PBR. An M-60 machine gun or MK-18 grenade launcher could be fired from both sides from mounts amidships. A single .50 was mounted in the stern on which another MK-18 could be carried piggyback. In addition the crew carried small arms such as M-16s and 12-gauge shotguns. A PBR had a crew of four: a boat captain (a chief or a first- or second-class petty officer), an engineman, a gunner's mate, and a seaman. Throughout the war sailors of all rates, from cooks to clerks, boatswain's mates to boilermen, volunteered for duty on PBRs. Patrolling in pairs, the boats covered each other during operations. A junior officer (warrant to lieutenant) became a tactical or patrol officer when riding in one of the formation's boats.

It was supposed to be a routine patrol. At 1400 patrol boats 109 and 110 left the LST that served as their base on the Bassac and entered the Rach Soi canal on the downriver side of Long Xuyen for a thirty-five-mile transit to Rach Soi. Mineman 1st Class Cecil H. Martin, the patrol officer in the lead boat, soon found that he was having trouble communicating on the FM radio, so he instructed Signalman 1st Class Donald P. "Mac" Mcclemons, boat captain of the cover boat, to relay everything to him. The patrol was supposed to meet two other boats coming out from Rach Soi to pass them their mail and pick up cacks (codes) and supplies. The two PBRs, 109 and 110, would never meet them.

Eventually Martin figured they were not in the right canal and decided to continue motoring to Rach Soi. Along the way he finally contacted his CO and found out the other boats were at Rach Gia, not Rach Soi.

Engineman 3d Class Keith L. Erntson, a maintenance man, was a fifth crewman onboard 110; a maintenance man was also an extra crewmember onboard 109; in addition, one of its crewmen was a brand-new seaman. Martin briefed both crews that they would go on to Rach Soi and pull in to the Monitor, a boat that was used as a Naval Operations Center (NOC) to refuel and check the engines. It was dusk and Martin had a feeling things were not right. He told the crews to get into full gear and instructed them that if they saw any sign of the enemy along the banks of the canal to let him know. The patrol was only about three miles toward Rach Soi, at a point where the canal turns about 120 degrees. That's where Martin had thought they might meet trouble.

Martin ordered the cover boat to stay in sight at all times because it was almost dark. The cover boat was right on 110's fantail when they approached the corner. As the lead boat cleared the bend, Martin looked back at the cover boat that was about halfway through the turn just as two rockets lit up the enveloping darkness, slamming into 109.

"Hang a one-eighty and go back," Martin yelled. The coxswain, Engineman 2d Class Hartwell White, the extra maintenance man added to the crew, swung the wheel over. Jacuzzi nozzles rotated, sending jets of water that reversed the course of the 14,600-pound vessel within the length of the boat. These same nozzles then stopped 110 dead in the water in three boat lengths alongside 109.

Martin worked the FM radios, calling for assistance. It seemed that everybody in the world could talk to him except the people he needed to talk to—the NOC and other boats in Rach Gia, only six miles away. He raised the *Eagleton*, the LST, and finally had to call for silence on the net to get it cleared. By that time PBR 110 had returned to the other boat which was then in flames.

Martin knew the crew of 109 were in serious trouble. He transmitted in the blind his estimation of what was going on and reported that 109 was not returning fire and that they needed a medevac. Eventually Martin reached his CO. The other boats were scrambled and on their way. Martin knew that no air support was close enough to do him any good.

PBR 109 had taken two rocket hits. One knocked the radar antenna off and damaged the twin fifties. The other one came through the thin armor plating on the starboard side, went through the radar and out through the other side, taking off the port side radio antenna. That was the one that did most of the damage to the crew.

A PBR's fiberglass hull provided a weird sort of protection. A rocket would often go straight through it without exploding the rocket's armor-piercing warhead (leaving holes in the hull that could be repaired easily), but the armor plating was another matter. A thousand pounds of light-weight ceramic armor surrounded the pilothouse and gun positions. The projectile that hit these areas turned the armor plating into a whirlwind of fragments, wounding every crewman.

Veering out of control, PBR 109 ran aground at the "T" in the canal directly in front of one of the three enemy firing positions. The enemy concentrated a hail of automatic weapons and small arms fire from across the canal and from both sides of it on the flaming boat. Into this maelstrom Cecil Martin and his crew headed at full speed.

Approaching the ambush site, Martin quickly looked around, then directed his crew's counter fire. He placed his boat between the stricken 109 and the blazing enemy batteries and took command of the rescue efforts. Despite being wounded, Gunner's Mate Striker Jackie Touchstone, forward gunner on 109, stood on the bow of the burning boat firing an M-16, yelling at Martin, "Marty, Marty, I hear movement out there."

"Grease the motherfuckers." Martin waved for Touchstone to go back to the twin fifties. "Get your ass back into the guntub."

"The gun's disabled!"

When Martin realized the twin .50 was out of commission, he directed White, Gunner's Mate Seaman Vernon Bryce Lucas, Seaman William O'Donnell, and Engineman 2d Class Harry Jones on his boat to fire on the enemy positions but warned them not to hit 109. Martin figured that the rockets had disabled 109's engine, so he got a line on the stricken craft and tried to pull her off the side of the man-made canal. But the bank's shelf held the crippled boat fast. He had to get the crew off, Martin realized. He did not know that Mac had hit the kill switch when the boat crashed into the canal bank or that the engine could have been restarted. But in the confusion of battle, while directing fire and coordinating the rescue, Martin had no time to second-guess.

As he and his crew carried wounded onto his boat, Martin heard someone calling on the FM trying to get information from him. The male voice was Vietnamese and spoke broken English. But he did not have things right, Martin thought. He decided it was no one he wanted to talk to. When the last of the wounded made it to safety, Martin boarded 109 again to make sure nothing was left behind. Just then, the enemy fire intensified.

Martin grabbed the after .50 and emptied it into the enemy. He then jumped onto the lead boat. "Let's get outta here."

Mac, Touchstone, Erntson, Engineman 2d Class Michael J. Eckhardt, and Seaman James W. Drennan had all sustained wounds, but were now safely aboard PBR 110. As they backed out, three rockets came screaming at them, hitting close astern. The after gunner struggled with his weapon, but then fired at the positions from which the flashes had erupted. PBR 110 then sped down the canal to what Cecil Martin thought was safety until he realized—they were sinking!

The rockets that had hit the boat had loosened fittings around the pumps, and the boat was taking on water faster than the men could get rid of it. Martin opened the engine cover and inserted a hose into a pump and the bilge to suck the water out, enabling the boat to make it up the canal to an airstrip where the wounded were then medevacked.[10]

Martin and his PBR sailors had found themselves too far from air support. For more than eighteen months HAL-3 Seawolf helicopters and their courageous aircrews had provided essential air support to the riverine patrol forces. But there were not enough Seawolf detachments in the Delta, nor enough helicopters. If there were only two helos at a detachment, when one would go down, no Helicopter Fire Team (HFT) was available. And with the limited ordnance that the Huey could carry, and its limited range, something more was needed.

Admiral Zumwalt's staff at NavForV realized the need to greatly increase air support for Sea Lords, as the following memo regarding Game Warden aircraft requirements indicates. This was but one in a long series of correspondence between ComNavForV, the staff at AirPac (Naval Air Force, Pacific), and the chief of naval operations.

> Because of the paucity of air support assets for PBRs, their operations have largely been confined to the major rivers with an occasional incursion into the canals off the rivers. Because of the vulnerability of the boats to ambush in the canals, where the maneuverability and speed of the boats cannot be exploited for self defense, it has been considered prudent not to expose them to that danger without a HFT airborne in direct support. Thus, because of our inability to long sustain such airborne support, the number and depth of such canal incursions has been severely limited. As a result, the enemy has moved his tax collectors back from the rivers into the feeder canals and has realigned his waterway lines of communication to avoid the major rivers as much as possible. [Author's note: The following sentence was hand written into the typed memo, sent three weeks before Martin's PBR canal incursion, for which he was awarded the Navy Cross.] Recent increased emphasis on canal incursions has highlighted the need for additional on-scene support. SEAL team operations have been similarly inhibited.[11]

ComNavForV decided in late 1968 to augment the helicopters of HAL-3 with a fixed-wing attack squadron stationed in the Delta. The navy commissioned Light Attack Squadron Four, VAL-4, on 3 January 1969 at NAS North Island, San Diego, to perform this mission. The squadron's pilots would fly the OV-10A Bronco, and call themselves "Black Ponies."

Petty Officer Cecil H. Martin later would see Light Attack Squadron Four in action. "I was amazed at the firepower of the Black Ponies. We sure could have used it that day near Rach Soi."[12]

3

Making It Up as You Go Along

If an individual wants anything bad enough, life usually brings it,
but in an unexpected form.

—Lancelot Law Whyte, *The Next Development in Man*

Adm. Elmo R. Zumwalt Jr. greatly influenced the development
of the navy's role in Vietnam as commander of naval forces and
later as chief of naval operations. He once remarked that "conducting riverine [brown water] warfare requires ingenuity and
improvisation. There is no body of accepted doctrine on the
subject; the Naval Academy does not offer courses in it; indeed,
there is little empirical experience from previous wars to draw
upon. You have to make up riverine warfare as you go along."[1]
For the Vietnam-era navy, and the Black Ponies, making up the
airpower component of riverine warfare as they went along,
meant improvising an aircraft and using ingenuity to develop
the tactics that would get the job done.

> When I got out there [Vietnam], having come from the Pen-
> tagon and being close to Paul Nitze, who was deputy secretary
> of defense at the time, I said to the staff, "If Mr. Humphrey
> wins the race—the race was on by then—we've got a year to
> get out. If Mr. Nixon wins, we've got three. So we've got to
> plan for a year and if Mr. Nixon is elected we can stretch it to
> three." When I reported to General [Creighton] Abrams he said
> to me in very blunt terms, that he was totally dissatisfied with
> the navy's operation in-country. That they were not involved,

that they were not helping him in the Delta. That's when I started looking for ways in which to optimize our operations and came up with Sea Lords.

Then General Abrams was called back in October by President Johnson. He was ordered to come to Washington unbeknownst to anybody. And he carried that out faithfully because after it was over [CNO, Admiral] Tom Moorer had his exec call me when I made a report, to ask if I was telling the truth. The President said to Abe after getting his report, "I want you to get back out there and muster every Vietnamese with a penis and get them in uniform. I want out." [Author's note: According to Admiral Zumwalt's flag lieutenant, Lt. Howard J. Kerr, General Abrams later met in Saigon with Admiral Zumwalt and the other component commanders who were supposed to show him what their plans were for turning the war over to the Vietnamese. After the air force presentation, Abrams yelled, "Bull shit, bull shit, bull shit!"[2]] And he chewed the air force out for their five or six year plan. The chief of staff said, "He's in a bad mood. Do you want to go forward?" And I said, "Yep, we do," because I thought I had the plan he would like. Our plan did call for turning over all the fighting in a year.

When I reported the briefing that Abrams had approved my plan, which of course had me "bassakwards" with OpNav [Naval Operations] because I hadn't cleared it with OpNav yet, that's when Tom Moorer said, "I don't believe that the President talked to General Abrams. Get Zumwalt on the phone and ask him." Once he understood that that was from the President to Abrams, he then put out the word on his staff to give us total cooperation. It was under that rubric that I then began clamoring for the fixed-wing aircraft to get the job done in the Delta."[3]

Adm. Elmo R. Zumwalt Jr., USN (Ret.)

The Aircraft

When Admiral Zumwalt and his planners decided the brown water navy needed a fixed-wing attack squadron for close air support, they indeed found few resources to draw upon. Certainly nothing in the navy's inventory of aircraft could fill the role. What relevant experience the navy had dated back to World War II and the zenith of the era of propeller-driven combat aircraft, like the F4U "Corsair." Interestingly, late in World War II, and during the Korean War, the U.S Navy and the Marine Corps equipped the Corsair with 5-inch rockets for use in close air support. These were the same rockets that were in part responsible for the fires and explosions on the USS *Forrestal* in 1967, when one of them was accidentally fired from an F-4 on the aft end of the flight deck, hitting an A-4.[4] One hundred thirty-four lives were lost, twenty-one aircraft were destroyed, forty-three others were damaged, and the aircraft carrier sustained seventy-two million dollars in damage.[5] After a Zuni caused another fire in the *Coral Sea* in 1968, Zunis were then removed from all aircraft carriers. Since no one else had the use of them, the Black Ponies got their hands on all the Zuni rockets the navy possessed. They would use them very effectively.

North American Rockwell built the OV-10 in response to the Defense Department's request for an aircraft for counterinsurgency operations. A 1962 Marine Corps study originally identified the need, and the marines became the first to take delivery of the Bronco in 1968, followed by the air force shortly thereafter. While the air force and marines used the aircraft for forward air control, observation, and naval gunfire support, the navy deployed it as an attack aircraft. Other aircraft had been considered for the role, including the Platypus Porter, one of the mainstays of the CIA's Air America.[6]   *Pilatus*

The OV-10, with its distinctive twin boom and forty-foot wingspan, looked somewhat like the World War II P-38 Lightning. Three quarters the size of the P-38, yet with half the horsepower, the Bronco also had three quarters of the Lightning's performance, when the Bronco wasn't carrying a load. Operating at the weights the Black Ponies did, however, their OV-10s were able to get over two hundred knots only when the nose was pointed at the ground. If an aircraft is to operate at low altitude over hostile jungles, it needs to be maneuverable, and strong enough to withstand the G forces encountered when the pilot yanks and banks the plane to evade enemy ground fire. Rockwell designers stressed the Bronco to 7-G forces (less with a full load of ordnance) for pulling off target and evading antiaircraft fire, a force that might pull the wings off a less sturdily built plane.

The fuselage began with a small nose that immediately flared into a large bulbous canopy, which curved around the pilots in a way that afforded excellent visibility of the ground. The aircraft came to an abrupt Manx tail-like end behind the tandem seats with a small cargo bay that could carry three parachutists. A shoulder-mounted wing with squared-off tips afforded high lift for maneuverability at low speeds.

Attached to the Bronco's wings were racks for missiles or rockets. Below the fuselage, like dorsal fins, two sponsons protruded, which housed four M-60 7.62-mm (.30-caliber) machine guns and provided the hard points from which more weapons pods were slung. These pods contained .30-cal. Gatling guns, 20-mm cannon, or rockets. Occasionally, Black Ponies would also drop CBU-55 fuel-air-explosive, parachute-retarded bombs.

Black Pony Broncos usually carried four pods of rockets, or, if carrying a 20-mm gun pod on the centerline, it carried three. The Vung Tau detachment usually did not use the MK4 20-mm pod but did have a limited number of SUU-11 minigun pods. The squadron employed two types of rockets ("forward firing ordnance"), the 5-inch Zuni, and the 2.75-inch FFAR ("folding fin aerial rocket"). The usual weapons load consisted of three pods of four Zuni rockets, and one pod of nineteen 2.75-inch rockets underneath, and two Zunis on each wing. The Zuni was a supersonic unguided rocket, designed to be fired at ground targets (although it had been used to shoot down a MiG over North Vietnam). The Zuni was fifteen feet long, five inches in diameter, carried a high explosive warhead, and packed an impressive wallop.[7]

The OV-10A Bronco had simple systems—mechanical flight controls instead of hydraulics, for example—just what was needed in a guerilla war, where an arrow shot from a bow at a helicopter was known to have brought down its prey. When the arrow penetrated the bird's hydraulic arteries, it bled itself out of control.

Besides being underpowered, the main criticism the Bronco's pilots would level at it was that it did not have air conditioning. In fact, the OV-10 had an inadequate ventilation system, an amazing oversight considering the climates in which it was likely to be used.

The Bronco was not a pretty bird, but it did have a functional charm that grew on its pilots and maintainers. At first painted green to blend in with the terrain, the Broncos were repainted in 1971 a gull-gray white when someone realized that the main threat came from the ground and eyes pointed upward. The number of bullet holes, in fact, did diminish after that.

Why was a propeller-driven aircraft chosen for this mission? Ironically, the phasing-out of prop combat aircraft coincided with the realization, reluctant though it may have been for many military planners, that the U.S. needed prop aircraft to fight a counterinsurgency war. In a study done for the Pentagon in 1970, BDM Corporation reported that fewer than 10 percent of all combat sorties flown by fixed-wing aircraft in South Vietnam were direct close air support missions—a dramatic reduction when the missions were compared to the role played by tactical air in Korea and World War II. The report offered several reasons as explanation. Fifty-four percent of the ground combat engagements reported were either over very quickly or were too small; the ground units thus did not request air support. Army units were five times more likely to call in artillery or helicopter gunships than tactical air. And army field commanders were of course more likely to call on their own aviation units, with whom they were familiar and who could respond in minutes instead of hours, rather than fixed-wing air force or navy aircraft.[8]

To these reasons one could add that, just as we were not prepared for this war in other respects, our airpower was inadequate in types of aircraft, tactics, and training. Wars are won on the ground by the foot soldier. In order for airpower to effectively support the soldier in close combat, it must be quickly available, its capabilities matched to the job at hand, and its tactics integrated with the ground unit's tactics as much as possible. For the most part, the inventory of jets developed since World War II, which were available for close air support, proved to be poorly suited for the role. They were too fast, had too little loiter capability, were not accurate enough in their weapons delivery in close combat, or did not carry enough of the right weapons. In the beginning of the war, the whole system of command and control, of effectively employing the tactical airpower, suffered some fundamental flaws.

The realities of this guerilla war forced us to adapt older, seemingly obsolescent aircraft to new missions. The U.S. converted old cargo planes into effective gunships, for example. Some of these aircraft dated back to before the Second World War. They oftentimes were older than the pilots who flew them: the AC-47 (from the "Gooney Bird"), AC-119 (from the "Flying Boxcar"), and the newer AC-130 (from the "Hercules"). The navy even used old propeller-driven seaplanes and patrol aircraft in ways never thought of before Vietnam.

The Black Ponies were to fill the huge gap between army helicopter support and jet tactical air by adapting a propeller-driven plane to the close air support needs of a guerrilla war.

The Men

When the detailers in charge of assignments for aviators at the Bureau of Naval Personnel got the word that a new squadron would be forming, they had to throw the book out the window. What kind of pilots would they send to an attack squadron that was land-, not carrier-based, and flew a twin-engine turbo prop, not a jet or single-engine prop? What kind of pilots would want to fly an aircraft that was not in the navy's inventory, but was borrowed, one that probably would never be used by the navy again? What kind of pilots do you send to fly a one-of-a-kind mission in the middle of jungle, far from the traditional navy? And what kind of pilots would want an assignment that would take them away from the warfare specialty and community they were a part of, and put them at a disadvantage later when competing with their contemporaries for promotions and selection for command? Turns out, it was not a hard sell.

In the transition to an all-jet navy occurring at this time, air wings and squadrons of the venerable piston-engine A-1 Skyraider, the last of the propeller-driven attack planes, faced decommissioning. The "Spad," as it was affectionately known, or "Able Dog," was carrier-based, and some Spad pilots would transition to A-4s and other carrier jet aircraft. But many Spad pilots contemplated dead ends in their careers. Unable to compete for promotions and commands within their warfare specialty, many Spad pilots would become station pilots, or flight instructors, or be sent to non-flying billets such as recruiters, or meteorologists. The same fate awaited pilots of the S-2, a twin-engine prop that was used in the antisubmarine warfare, electronic surveillance, and carrier onboard delivery communities, that was also being phased out.

When the word about a fixed-wing Game Warden squadron forming up reached VA-176, an East Coast Spad squadron that was slated to transition to the A-6A Intruder, Cdr. Gil Winans followed its development with more than a casual interest (VA-25 on the West Coast and VA-176 were the last two A-1 squadrons). There were limited career opportunities for Spad drivers. Having flown A-1s for fifteen years, Gil realized that this might be the only shot he had at commanding an operational squadron. When the Spad squadron folded, Winans had been sent to the naval air station (NAS) at Oceania as XO of the TA-4 instrument squadron, VA-43. His CO at VA-176, Cdr. Jack French, was slated to become VAL-4's first commanding officer and had been given orders to a staff at NAS Jacksonville in the interim. But tired of waiting, he took orders to be an air boss on an aircraft carrier. It was during this time that the OV-10 was selected as the aircraft VAL-4 would employ.

When the CO's slot opened up, Gil Winans seized the opportunity and got the orders for himself. He flew to Washington, D.C., to meet with the commanders' detailer in BuPers and officers at OpNav and NavAir (Naval Air). They discussed the formation of the new squadron, the men who would be selected, the aircraft they would fly, and the mission. When he asked his detailer if he had been command selected, a formal procedure done in a committee in a prescribed fashion, the detailer huddled with his boss, Capt. Bob Rasmussen, and informed Gil that he was now "selected." Commander Winans was then asked what kind of executive officer he wanted. "Don't give me someone from the War College or anyone else who hasn't been in a cockpit for a while. Give me someone with a lot of operational experience." They asked him what kind of pilots he wanted and he answered, "Only attack pilots."

Winans soon received good news and bad news. While not being able to select his own XO, Commander Winans did get veto power. When the detailers presented him with Cdr. Marty Schuman's name, Winans smiled. "You couldn't have picked a better man," he said. Winans had known Schuman since they were ensigns. But the bad news was the bureau planned to send him only a handful of attack pilots, one of them an A-4 pilot who had gone Cat II (couldn't fly at night, losing his carrier qualification) because of his eyesight, and a few Spad pilots. All the rest were S-2 pilots, mostly from VS and VAW squadrons being decommissioned or nuggets getting their wings who were slated for those squadrons. Winans was disappointed, but could do nothing about it. He decided to make the best of it.

When Commander Winans checked into VS-41 in October 1968 he had to have felt out of place. The S-2 Replacement Air Group (RAG), VS-41, had been selected to host the OV-10 RAG only when NAS Miramar and NAS Lemoore had not expressed any interest in bringing prop planes back to their "Master Jet Bases." The S-2 was a lumbering twin-engine Grumman-built piston-engine plane used for antisubmarine and early warning missions. The joke among attack pilots was that "stoof" (S-2) pilots considered 30 degrees angle of bank to be an unusual attitude—or at least acrobatics. And formation flying? Forget it. Commander Winans even had one of the S-2 pilots come to him complaining that the OV-10 RAG syllabus was in violation of the Naval Air Training and Operating Procedures Standardization Program (NATOPS, the "bible" for naval aviators). "And why is that?" Winans asked. "Because it includes night formation flying." Winans laughed. "There may not be any formation flying at night in the VS community, but there sure as hell will be in Vietnam!"[9]

Winans's fears would soon be allayed when the first group of pilots arrived at the weapons detachment in Yuma. While it was difficult to get "stoof" pilots to dive 45 degrees at the ground, they quickly adapted, and Winans was soon satisfied with the performance of this disparate group of pilots. They had potential, he thought. The attack pilots took the "stoof" pilots under their wings and began the process of turning them into "attack pukes." One of those attack pilots was Pete Russell.

Lt. Pete Russell loved flying prop planes like the Spad and did not want to fly jets, even though his older brother Ken (then a lieutenant commander) was flying A-4s. Pete had graduated from Columbia in 1962 and followed in his brother's footsteps, becoming a naval aviator in 1963. Despite having high flight grades, Pete could not get orders to Spads and flew the E-2 in an airborne early warning squadron. His brother helped get him eventually into the A-1 community, and Pete joined VA-176 at Jacksonville, where he deployed with the attack squadron in the *Intrepid* for its 1966 WestPac (Western Pacific) cruise.[10]

Let me tell you about Pete Russell of VA-176. . . . Daylight rendezvous, five miles ahead of *Intrepid*, five-hundred-foot left-hand turns. I slid across as number two and Lead [the lead aircraft] and I look back at number three, which turned out to be Pete . . . lots of smoke! As he crossed, the smoke was joined by lots of flames! Lead kissed me off and followed Pete back towards *Intrepid*. There were numerous radio transmissions between Pete and Lead and Air Boss. It all boiled down to the old carrier lie, "Ready Deck in five minutes," which was made no fewer than four times over the next twenty minutes. Lead reported that Pete had lost at least two jugs from the four o'clock position of the engine and the fuel fire was still limited to the engine area. Pete reported the plane wouldn't last for another five minutes and he was bailing out! He chucked his oxygen mask and his favorite kneeboard over the side, unstrapped, and was trying to stand up in the seat when he noticed a yellow lanyard hanging loose from his seat pack! "Ah, damn! That can't be packed right, the chute isn't going to work!" So he sits back down, plugs in communications and calls for a ready deck. He finally got a clear deck call, dirtied up in a descending left hand turn, called the ball (high fast and overshooting), and then started to strap in. The LSO gave him an "OK—little not enough engine, 2 wire." One more Spad that lived long enough to transfer to the Air Force because the Navy never installed extraction seats![11]

Dick Davis, SpadNet

Pete Russell had found his element. He was flying combat in a propeller-driven "Able Dog" and having the time of his life. Pete and then–Lt. Cdr. Gil Winans became good friends at VA-176 and often flew together. They would even fly over the Mekong Delta when their carrier was on Dixie Station, flying over the same territory the Black Ponies would later roam. For six months in 1966 Pete Russell's brother Ken flew A-4s with VA-12 off the *Franklin D. Roosevelt* while Pete flew off the *Intrepid*. They used to talk to each other over North Vietnam while they both flew Rescue Combat Air Patrol (ResCap) missions.

On one flight over the North (9 October 1966) Ken listened on his radio as Pete and three other A-1 pilots covered a helicopter trying to pick up a downed pilot just as four MiG-17s jumped them. "I saw them com-

ing down off the perch," Ken recalls Pete as having described the
encounter, "I did a hammerhead stall, headed back toward them, turned
on all fourteen armament switches, squeezed, pushed, and pulled everything on the stick, fired all my guns, all my rockets, and dropped two
bombs." Pete got partial credit for helping Lt. (jg) William T. "Lurch"
Patton splash the MiG, one of two shot down by Spads during the war.

Pete reluctantly transitioned to A-4s after Spads but yearned to get
back into props. He and Gil Winans kept in touch after they both moved
on after VA-176, and when they both learned about VAL-4, they both
sought orders to the new squadron. Gil and Pete would become the only
combat-experienced pilots in the first group of Black Ponies.

When he ran into Cdr. Marty Schuman at the Cecil Field "O"Club one
day, Pete Russell's brother Ken mentioned he was interested in the XO's
job with VAL-4. Schuman had heard about a new squadron being formed
to provide close air support for Game Warden, but it was all speculation,
and he wasn't interested, since they planned to fly the small Porter "tail
dragger." Ken told Schuman that VAL-4 was definitely being formed and
would be flying OV-10s. Schuman listened for a moment and said, "Excuse me a minute." He got up and walked out. Schuman came back about
ten minutes later. "I've got the job," he said. Russell's jaw dropped. Schuman's phone call to his detailer had proved fortuitous.

Marty Schuman had been bouncing around between the Spad community and test and evaluation and, like his friend Gil Winans, he too figured his future was limited, if he wanted command of an operational
squadron. As soon as he heard about VAL-4 he knew he had to become
a part of it.

Even though Ken Russell got aced out, there were no hard feelings. He
was happy for his brother Pete and shared in his enthusiasm, even though
he did not become a part of his brother's new squadron. Ken would go
on to command an A-6 squadron, but not before his brother and Marty
would fly one of VAL-4s new OV-10s to Jacksonville a few months later.
In the first flight the two brothers ever made together, Pete and Ken enthu-
siastically drilled holes in the Florida sky one sunny afternoon while
Marty, with a nervous smile, looked up from the ground.[12]

The two brothers would never fly together again.

Twenty-two fleet-experienced pilots signed on with the new squadron,
almost all of them looking to jump-start a career, or to get one back on
track, or to prove something. It was not unusual for a pilot to be sent to
VAL-4 to make something of himself. Some of the original pilots and their
eventual replacements had black marks in their backgrounds, ranging

from bad fitness reports and being passed over for promotion, to discipline problems and crashing airplanes. When the original plans for filling the rear cockpits with enlisted observers were changed to filling them with nonpilot flight officers—then changed again to put pilots in the back seat—twelve more aviators were needed. The navy then decided to send first-tour pilots directly out of flight school to VAL-4. All of them came from the prop (not jet) pipeline and had no tactical training, not even the most basic.

This group of thirty-four pilots—part of the "plankowners" (the term used for the original contingent of a newly formed unit)—and their subsequent replacements may have been "misfits," as one detailer described them, but that in no way reflected on what they would go on to accomplish. While they may not have "fit" into a normal career mold, these aviators would go on to create a new, original mold, one that would set them apart as unique in naval aviation history.

Three A-1 Skyraider pilots, Lts. Art Savard, Pete Russell, and Robert Stoddert, and one S-2 pilot, Lt. Cdr. Fred Hering, reported to Camp Pendleton in late 1968 where the marines at HML-267 transitioned them to the Bronco and they attended forward air controller school. They returned to VS-41 at NAS North Island, San Diego on 21 October, where they trained the first RAG instructors, Lt. Cdrs. Steve Chappell, Fred "Fritz" Lynch, and Dean Davis.

Joining the first four pilots and Cdrs. Gil Winans and Marty Schuman after they reported in during October were Lt. Cdrs. Len "ZZ" Zagortz, Don Florko, Ron Ballard, Al Schauer, and John Butterfield. Other second tour aviators included Lts. Jerry Goodman, Jerry Wheeler, W. J. "Flash" Leebern (who later was killed in an OV-10 training accident at NAS North Island), Charlie Sapp, and Gary Rezeau. Lts. (jg) Aubrey Martin, Barry Fry, Dan Conrad, Mick Brennan, Bill Robertson, and Denny Bennett rounded out the second tour pilots.

The twelve first-tour pilots reporting from the training command were Lts. (jg) J. W. Brewster, Bob Campbell, Peter Dunn, Dave Edwards, Dan Sheehan, Roy Sikkink, Mike Kersey, Jeff Johnson, Richard Pratt, Mike Quinlan, Glen Ewing, and Jim Chadwick. Warrant Officer 1st Class Donald "Gunner" Mason and Lt. Cdr. William Bartlett, both nonaviators, joined the squadron as maintenance department officers.[13]

First-tour pilots sought out VAL-4 for the same reasons their more experienced counterparts did. They wanted a chance to prove themselves, to get their careers on track, and get into jets. Most of the newly winged aviators had wanted to fly jets but had been denied the opportunity

because of "the breaks of naval air" (substitute "the roll of the dice").
Quite often a student naval aviator would not be allowed to go to jet
training only because the week-by-week quota would not allow it,
whereas everyone the following week would get jets if they wanted them.
Once a prop aviator was winged, it was virtually impossible to transition
to jets. Now that the A-1 Skyraiders were gone, VAL-4 represented a last
chance in the minds of some. It was a chance for adventure, combat, and
if they proved themselves worthy, the reasoning went, maybe they could
transition to tactical jets. Some young aviators would go to great lengths
to get orders to VAL-4.

> Another JG [junior grade] and I got verbal orders to VAL-4 just prior to
> receiving our wings, but his orders were changed at the last minute. Kit
> Lavell offered me his 1967 Corvette and a couple thousand dollars cash to
> swap orders. I declined [but two years of effort would eventually get him
> orders to the Black Ponies].[14]
>
> Graham Forsyth, Black Pony

Many officers more senior and experienced than these newly winged
aviators did not share their vision of VAL-4 as being "career enhancing."

> When I got my wings, I brought my mom down from Kansas City. She's
> sitting out there in the audience with all these proud parents. The admiral
> is pinning the wings on all these people and he's saying, "Well Mr. Jones
> you're going to such and such. The CO there, I knew him. We were class-
> mates at Annapolis," and then he comes to me. "Well Mr. Scholl, congrat-
> ulations. You're going to VAL-4, huh?" I said, "Yes sir." He said, "That's
> Vietnam, isn't it?" I said, "Yes sir." He looked at me and said softly, "Okay."
> Scared my mom to death.[15]
>
> Bob Scholl, Black Pony

Most of the first-tour pilots—referred to as "nuggets" —arrived just
before the squadron was to leave for Vietnam. While the second-tour
pilots got checked out in the OV-10 and went on a weapons detachment
at Yuma, no plans existed for the nuggets other than to go to Vietnam and
sit in the back seat of the airplane as observers. There were some excep-
tions, however. When Bob "Soup" Campbell earned his wings of gold
he got orders to VC-30 but swapped them for VAL-4 orders. Bob was a
1967 Academy graduate, along with Black Pony nuggets Dick Pratt and
Mike Quinlan. Campbell checked into the RAG at North Island during
the week that the pilots were on a weapons deployment to Marine Corps
Air Station Yuma, Arizona. A chief petty officer went over the OV-10

checklist with him and informed him that a pilot, Lt. Jerry Goodman, was returning from Yuma to go on emergency leave. Campbell's first OV-10 flight was a solo to Yuma, through which he had just driven, so he just used his Texaco map and followed I-8. He inadvertently feathered the props on shutdown and owed four or five bucks for "switchology" mistakes, but he had soloed—even before he had checked into the squadron.[16]

Other nuggets got front-seat familiarization flights and some got to fire some weapons on the weapons detachment, but for the most part, the nuggets were paired up with second-tour aviators to be their regular back seat guys.

Two months after commissioning ceremonies at North Island on 3 January 1969, these thirty-six officers and 110 enlisted men arrived at Binh Thuy (pronounced "bin-too-e"), Republic of Vietnam, for a short, intensive in-country training period. The North American tech rep described the arrival in his report:

> Squadron personnel and the four civilian representatives departed from Naval Air Station, North Island shortly after midnight on Monday, March 24, 1969, and arrived in Saigon on Monday afternoon, local time. After a five-hour delay, the personnel were airlifted into Binh Thuy by USAF C-130 aircraft. The airlifted cargo (by three C-133 aircraft) arrived on Tuesday and Wednesday, and the remainder of the week was spent unpacking and setting up office spaces and living quarters.
>
> Squadron personnel attended a number of presentations concerning indoctrination to the area and First Sea Lord and Task Force 116 operations. Admiral Zumwalt, Commander Naval Forces Vietnam, appeared here on Thursday to personally welcome the squadron under his command. He and other commanders have expressed the need for air strike power greater than the limited helos.
>
> Everyone here seems to be in favor of the OV-10A application in Game Warden operations—especially the PBR crews. This area is literally infested with VC units and the PBRs and helos encounter numerous engagements around the clock. Air attacks less than three miles away frequently can be observed from the base at night. However, the Navy claims to have seriously crimped the enemy re-supply operations and believe that traffic across the Cambodian border can be denied entirely as the waterways are completely closed off. The OV-10A is expected to play an important role in achieving this objective.[17]
>
> John Stevens, North American Aviation Tech Rep Report

When then–Vice Admiral Zumwalt visited Binh Thuy on Thursday 27 March, his reception by the troops differed significantly from visits by other brass and dignitaries. Zumwalt was a sailor's admiral, a pilot's admiral. Dashing, popular, young—at forty-seven, the navy's youngest vice admiral—Zumwalt was viewed by the troops as accessible, friendly, and interested in their problems. Most visits by admirals prompted a degree of nervousness and dread. Not so with Zumwalt's. The men of VAL-4 were eager to see this charismatic man whose reputation of listening to sailors' concerns preceded him. Wearing combat greens, Zumwalt would visit not once, but many times—he would even fly with the Black Ponies—and he contrasted sharply with others who followed. A few weeks later the air-conditioned limousine of the secretary of the navy descended upon Binh Thuy (from where, few people knew). It drove across the pierced steel planking—*clackety, clackety, clack*— while the Hon. John Chafee looked through the tinted, rolled-up windows at an ordnance display neatly arrayed for him in front of an OV-10 in the hangar, and without stop, motored on.

Zumwalt would give a pep talk, needed neither by the troops nor him, for he and they already shared an enthusiastic and optimistic view of what they could together accomplish. These were his men. He worked hard to bring them here, where he was convinced they would make a difference. They would contribute to Game Warden's mission of denying the enemy unrestricted access to the waterways of the Delta and help save the lives of his brown water sailors with their close air support.

After three weeks of training and a number of flights on which Black Pony pilots practiced delivering ordnance on free-fire zones, on 19 April, the squadron was declared fully operational and began around-the-clock combat operations.

Still, few people even knew that the squadron existed, let alone where it was located, what its mission was, and what it flew. In addition to learning the lay of the land, developing tactics for close air support, and building the facilities to get this job done, the Black Ponies needed to get the word out to allied units in the Delta.

We were on a patrol shortly after we got in-country. We were on their radio frequency when boats got ambushed. And I heard the guy on the boat say, "Scramble the Seawolves, we're being hit." And here we were almost ready to roll in. Apparently the word hadn't got out that we were there with heavier stuff. We got back to the det and I called a meeting [Author's note: Don Florko became the second officer in charge (O-in-C) at Vung Tau]. We put our heads together. Even though we officially are here and the messages are out, how can we get the word out that we *are* here and we *can* do things? What came of it is cross-pollination. We would go out on boats or with our friends, understand what they do, and trade—they'd want a quid—they would go fly with us so they could understand what we do.[18]

Don Florko, Black Pony

This group of "misfits," eager to prove itself, with borrowed aircraft and *McHale's Navy* ingenuity, wasted no time in demonstrating that they were the new guns in Dodge City.

Only six months before in October 1968, the commander of fleet air in the Western Pacific (ComFAirWestPac) had expressed his objections about VAL-4 using a borrowed aircraft, citing problems with supporting the UH-1Bs that HAL-3 Seawolves had borrowed from the army (he preferred letting the Marine Corps provide a squadron of aircraft).

He added, "I fear that one lone small Navy OV-10 squadron remotely located in the Delta would soon find itself at the aftermost milking station whenever parts support became difficult."[19]

4

The Aftermost Milking Station

Posterity weaves no garlands for imitators.

—Friedrich von Schiller

Light Attack Squadron Four's mission was to provide air support for the river patrol forces in the Mekong Delta and the adjacent Rung Sat Special Zone, including support for SEAL operations and Vietnamese armed forces. The squadron was divided into two operating detachments, Det (Detachment) Bravo, operating out of the army airfield at Vung Tau and Det Alpha at Binh Thuy. Staging out of An Thoi on Phu Quoc Island had also been considered, but rejected.[1] Det Bravo at Vung Tau supported operations in the northern and eastern portions of the Delta. These included operations along the Vam Co Tay and the Vam Co Dong Rivers—Operation Giant Slingshot—and the vital Long Tau Shipping Channel, transiting forty-five miles of the Rung Sat Special Zone, from the South China Sea to Saigon. The Rung Sat was a strategic area surrounding the Long Tau River, which connects Saigon to the South China Sea. The shipping channel into Saigon ran mazelike along this river, which made numerous tight turns, often doubling back on itself, as it snaked through the mangrove marshlands. The military created the Rung Sat Special Zone to patrol this area which, because of the terrain, was particularly vulnerable to enemy mining. River patrol boats (PBRs) escorted boat convoys while Seawolf helicopters from the detachment at Nha Be provided air cover, with occasional support from the Black Ponies on boat cover missions that often lasted three to four hours.

Vung Tau, the old French resort city of Cape Saint Jacques, is nestled on the tip of an eleven-mile-long projection into the South China Sea, which extends southwest and partially encloses Ganh Rai Bay. The Saigon River empties into this bay, located on the northeastern Mekong Delta, south of Saigon. Its wide sandy beaches face azure waters and give Vung Tau the image of being the "Vietnamese Riviera." It was used throughout the war as an in-country rest and relaxation (R and R) facility. The town with its fishing fleet and outdoor restaurants is colorful and relaxing. Thousands of well-to-do Vietnamese and American servicemen flocked there to jump into the surf or relax on the beaches, Bai Truoc (Front Beach) being the most popular. A hike at sunset to the giant statue of Jesus atop Nui Noh Mountain provided a fabulous view.

The U.S. Army airfield at Vung Tau was home to Army OV-1 Mohawks, Cobra gunships, and medevac helicopters, air force C-130s, C-123s, C-7s, CH-54s, CH-47s, O-1 Bird Dogs, Royal Australian Air Force UH-1s, and the navy's HAL-3 Seawolves. Its Runway 18/36 was 4,561 feet long and 60 feet wide and Runway 12/30 was 2,000 feet long.[2]

If one had to fight a war, staging out of Vung Tau was the place to be. No wonder that when VAL-4 Det Bravo moved into HAL-3's facilities, the vacating Seawolves were not very happy.

When we got over there they had these North American Aviation pocket cards that had the picture of the clipped wing OV-10 and the specs on the back. I think that's all the briefing ComFAirWestPac had. They said we had all of our yellow gear pre-positioned and that we'd be all set up. When we got to Vung Tau the tugs didn't have any transmissions in them. They had been stripped; HAL-3 had ripped all of the air conditioning ducting out of the BOQ. There were hard feelings between HAL-3 and VAL-4 initially. We had guys actually who were told to get off target, that it was not our tactical situation and we were not to be any part of it. I only heard of it secondhand. I never had any experience of it myself.[3]

Charlie Sapp, Black Pony

Vung Tau was fairly secure. I remember going to a change of command for a major general who was in charge of a Vung Tau area sub-command and he was bragging about sixty thousand troops under arms, and I thought to myself, there are only fourteen of us trading bullets with the enemy every day. . . . Vung Tau was an R and R center, not only for U.S. in-country, but for the VC. You would be on the beach and the guy on the next blanket might have been a VC.[4]

Don Florko, Black Pony

The officers at Vung Tau lived in a BOQ a half mile off base. A cross between an old French villa and cheap motel, their quarters consisted of individual rooms connected to a hallway and common area with a small kitchen, officers' mess, and a bar. A former Vietnamese Army enlisted man was paid to provide security and Co Hai and her daughters tended the bar and maintained the place. A navy cook and steward prepared breakfast and dinner.

The BOQ attracted a lot of visitors. SEALs and brown water sailors with whom Black Ponies worked would stop by to enjoy the amenities of Vung Tau and visit with the pilots. Black Ponies had a reputation for hospitality throughout the Delta. One of the attractions was being able to stay in the BOQ because four pilots always would be standing scramble duty and were willing to share their rooms. One of the most popular belonged to the junior officer (JO) who had a poster-sized photo of his beautiful girlfriend adorned in not much more than a flight helmet.

Conditions at the main detachment in Binh Thuy were more austere. U.S. contractors built Vietnamese Air Force Base Binh Thuy under the Military Assistance Program on a swamp adjacent to the Bassac River. Premier Ky dedicated it in June 1966. Initially, the Vietnamese Air Force (VNAF) and the U.S. Air Force jointly used the base, but by 1971 VAL-4 was the only American unit flying from the field.

While the Black Ponies were to find it adequate to their task, much of the airfield construction was substandard or in acknowledged deviation from safety criteria, as they would apply to an airfield built in the U.S., or anywhere else outside a war zone. Conventional wisdom cited many reasons for this: the nature of the terrain, the money, and the war. The single Runway, 6/24, was 100 feet wide and 6,000 feet long, with 500-foot overruns. In violation of safety standards, the runway centerline was only 360 feet from the edge of the single, parallel 50-foot-wide taxiway, which connected to the runway with two crosswind taxiways. Two base ammo sheds served as the ordnance storage area and were located immediately north of the eastern end of Runway 6. Positioned as they were, 500 feet north of the runway's overrun centerline, "they presented [according to regulations] a clear violation of quantity-distance safety criteria" — in other words, a lot of explosives too close to the runway.[5]

The asphalt east parking apron adjacent to the control tower was the home of the two VNAF A-37 Dragonfly squadrons, the 520th and the 526th of the 74th Tactical Wing, and the O-1 Bird Dog and U-17 spotter planes of the 116th and 122d. The west parking apron was constructed of pierced steel planking (PSP). On the western end of this apron, VNAF Huey helicopters of the 211th and 217th helo squadrons sat between low protective walls, adjacent to the revetments that surrounded VAL-4's OV-10s.

Black Pony officers and enlisted men lived at Navy Binh Thuy, a small boat base a mile and a half south of the Vietnamese Air Force base. The road that led to Can Tho (pronounced "can-*toe*") three miles farther south divided the Navy Binh Thuy complex. On the eastern side of the road lay the Naval Support Facility, the brown water navy boat base, adjacent to the Bassac.

Black Ponies lived at the Tactical Air Support Facility, on the western side of the road, along with the main detachment of Seawolves. Adjacent to hootches—enlisted and officer's quarters—were the squadron's administrative spaces, chow hall, and dispensary. VAL-4 pilots occasionally landed Broncos on 03/21, the short (two-thousand-foot) runway, dubbed "the short strip," used by helos, and taxied them to a hangar next to the administration building for intermediate maintenance.

The Mission

In the beginning, Black Ponies flew four types of missions: armed patrols, overhead air cover, quick reaction scrambles, and naval gunfire/artillery spotting.[6] While on patrol, normally about three hundred nautical miles, a two-aircraft light attack Fire Team would conduct visual reconnaissance and check for targets of opportunity with the various Naval Operations Centers (NOCs) on the patrol route. For air cover operations, an external fuel tank was added on the centerline, allowing the Black Pony Fire Team four to five hours of on-station coverage over the patrol boats transiting the waterways of the Delta. Each detachment also maintained a twenty-four-hour, seven-day-a-week scramble alert crew of two aircraft and four pilots. The scramble crews launched when friendly forces required immediate assistance and could have "wheels in the wells" within six to ten minutes of a call. Scramble radius extended ninety nautical miles to the southernmost tip of the Ca Mau Peninsula.

A Typical Patrol

Scheduled patrols, sometimes called random patrols, or armed reconnaissance (recce), were planned as two-hour flights. During the brief, the

Fire Team Leader would cover all the items necessary for the flight: the route, the weather, the units the Fire Team might be expected to support, the ordinance load, restricted areas, artillery (arty) advisories, free-fire zones, authentication signals, codes, and emergencies. Once airborne the flight would contact an air force ground control intercept (GCI) site for flight following and arty clearance. The copilot would then begin checking in with the various NOCs for targets.

The initial plan was to have the nuggets fly only in the back seats, where the copilot would be responsible for navigation, communication, and help with target acquisition. After several weeks in-country some of the second-tour pilots began giving the nuggets a chance to check out in the front seat, but it wasn't for a few months that there was a consistent and official effort to qualify them as wingmen.

Black Ponies navigated using a 1:250,000 chart of the Delta, on which 1 inch was equal to 250,000 inches on the ground. This large map was subdivided into areas covered by sixty-five 1:50,000 military tactical charts, which each pilot carried in a bag. These "one-to-fifties" would be used on target where pinpoint accuracy was vital. Target information was given using the military grid system: XS 915,205, or VQ 790,710, for example.

The Black Ponies would obtain clearances, check the positions of the nearest friendlies, and identify the target, just as any forward air controller (FAC) in Vietnam would. Sometimes Black Ponies worked with air force FACs or army visual reconnaissance (VR) spotters, but less than 5 percent of VAL-4s missions were controlled by another FAC.

The VAL-4 OV-10 was the only tactical strike aircraft used in Vietnam that was authorized to place an air strike without a FAC. The Seventh Air Force ran the air war in Vietnam and was not about to let a fixed-wing tactical aircraft work without a FAC. Navy planners had found a loophole in the rules of engagement and the OV-10 was introduced into the Delta as another Game Warden aircraft like the HAL-3 helicopter gunships. As long as it was using only forward firing ordnance (rockets, machine guns, and cannon), the navy thought the air force wouldn't catch on and would rubber-stamp the waiver. The Marine Corps (who reluctantly loaned the OV-10s to the navy) had a vested interest in seeing that waiver go through because, if the VAL-4 Broncos were considered tactical aircraft, they would be counted against the marines' total, thus reducing the number of tactical jets the marines were authorized.[7]

We started out trying to do that [operate under a waiver] and the air force found out about it. I knew George Brown, who was commander of the

Seventh Air Force at the time. His deputy was Davey Jones. Both of them were future chairmen. I went over and explained the special nature of our brown water navy fighting and the fact that we just couldn't go through channels. And they considered it a small enough operation that they were willing to violate their own policy and let us do it.[8]

Adm. Elmo R. Zumwalt, USN (Ret.)

When Black Ponies flew on combat operations, initially the normal patrol altitude was fifteen hundred to two thousand feet. This was later increased to reduce the risk of battle damage. However, quite often, the weather—and the need to remain below it—dictated the en route altitude for patrols.

The wingman would fly in stepped-up combat spread, five hundred feet above and one thousand to two thousand feet abeam and slightly aft (abaft) of the leader, which gave the wingman the flexibility to maneuver while keeping the leader and the terrain below in sight. After working a target, the two OV-10s would join up and inspect each other for possible battle damage, then return to base (RTB).

On target the Fire Team Leader would determine the roll-in heading, the pull-off heading, the tactics, and the ordnance to be used.[9] Initially, squadron standard operating procedures (SOP) considered eight to ten runs typical for a target, but SOP soon changed.

No matter how much flight time a pilot may have, the first time in the front seat on a combat mission is a real eye-opener. The following experience occurred later in VAL-4's history, but much of it probably applied to every Black Pony pilot on his first front-seat flight in-country.

> I flew my first front seat hop with Lt. John Smalling, a familiarization flight that also served as my NATOPS check ride. Everyone around the squadron knew John by the nickname "Wimpy," after the hamburger-devouring character in the *Popeye* cartoon. Usually the front seat "fam" flight included some formation flying, a few practice roll-ins over a simulated target in a secure area, and if lucky, an intelligence target to shoot at with live ordnance for the first time, then landing practice back at Binh Thuy.
>
> During the preflight things looked different to me, perhaps because I knew that I would be flying front seat and firing the weapons for the first time over there. I carefully checked the fuses on the Zuni rockets in the LAU-10 pods and set the switch on the LAU-63 to "ripple." This nineteen-shot pod of 2.75-inch rockets was not much use when fired singly because dispersion of the rockets made it inaccurate. But all at once, in a ripple firing, it was an effective weapon. I noticed how powder burns blackened the

sponsons and the sides of the fuselage in front of the machine guns. The smell of the cordite made my heart race.

While starting the aircraft, we got a scramble call on the radio. John could have asked me to shut down the engines and switch seats, but instead allowed me to fly the scramble mission to An Xuyen Province as my front seat checkout. He was one of the coolest heads in the squadron, completely unflappable. John had been a RAG instructor back in San Diego, along with Lt. Cdr. Steve Chappell. Both were then sent to Vietnam, and each had more hours in the OV-10 than anyone flying the aircraft.

Waiting in the arming area at the end of the runway for the ordnance-men to arm our weapons, my legs quivered from holding the brakes tightly. To signal us that they finished their task, the ordies displayed all the pins they removed to arm the ordnance. I counted them, and gave them a "thumbs up." Once airborne, I didn't have time for doubts.

Fortunately for the guys in trouble on the ground, this mission was rel-atively straightforward. Still, flying the aircraft from the front seat for the first time in Vietnam, and getting a hot scramble mission to do it on, gave me an adrenaline rush. From the front seat, everything seemed new: the sounds, the feel of the controls, the sight of the machine gun tracers and rockets leaving the aircraft, but most of all, the view of the ground—from the unobstructed shot through the windscreen. It loomed up fast when I pointed the nose at the earth.

Dive-bombing as a skill is perhaps no more difficult than many other combat maneuvers. But, psychologically, it goes against every pilot's instincts. I would be hurtling toward the ground, the airspeed quickly building up. Falling forward, my weight pulled against my shoulder har-ness, the only thing holding me back. The rapid change in altitude made my ears pop, sometimes painfully. Everything changed so fast. In the rush to juggle all the variables in my mind, I had to aim, shoot, and most importantly, pull out at the right moment. Over the years, since men began angrily pointing their noses at the ground with airplanes, many have died because of "target fixation," that mesmerization that happens all too easily in this strange environment. Dive-bombing is a violent exercise, and is followed by an even more violent pullout, sus-taining more than 4 G's.

If I was firing rockets, ideally I circled the target at an altitude of forty-five hundred feet; twenty-five hundred feet above the altitude I planned to release my ordnance. That's for a 30-degree dive angle. The steeper the dive the more accurate the delivery because the closer to vertical, the more you can reduce the "six to twelve o'clock error," or the likelihood of hav-ing ordnance land short or long of the target. But, because of the weather and aircraft performance, I could rarely get up to the six thousand feet that was required for a 45-degree dive.

For a 30-degree dive, I was taught back in the States to circle the target in a 30-degree angle of bank, which would put the aircraft on an imaginary 30-degree cone pointing at the target. Theoretically, all I had to do was lift the nose up about 30 degrees, roll a 120-degree angle of bank, then pull and roll the wings back level and the aircraft would be in a 30-degree dive on the cone. At the release altitude, the target should be in the center of the gunsight. With no wind, the gunsight set at thirty-three mils, the correct power setting, starting off with a 160 knots, releasing at 240, and pulling 1 G, I might see this. But theory and practice rarely coincided. I learned by practice to become a human computer, adjusting altitudes for release, and making constant aircraft corrections to compensate for all the other changing variables. Rolling in on target became instinctive, and at times, even distinctive. Some pilots would use a gentle wingover, some a violent "octoflugeron."

When I didn't have the luxury of flying around the target, I would head directly for it, and at just the right moment I would perform a "roll ahead." Lifting the nose high, I would roll the plane inverted, look "up" at the target, pull the nose up to the appropriate number of mils on the gunsight below the target, and roll the aircraft right side up again, established in the dive.

Sitting in the front seat of the Bronco was like sitting on a barstool (so I quickly adapted to it). Since the windscreen curved around my side, I could look to the left or right almost straight down. The only thing between me and the enemy was Plexiglas, and below that, aluminum skin so thin I could poke a pencil through it. The center panel above the glare shield was glass that the manufacturer called "bullet resistant," whatever the hell that means. We all knew it did not mean *bullet proof.*

Once over the target, I took a long time recognizing all the elements: the landmarks others described very patiently for my benefit, the smoke grenades the friendlies popped to mark their positions, and the relative directions to the enemy—all meticulously explained. Even when I was sure I had the picture, I wasn't 100 percent sure. Hell, I wasn't even convinced of the color of the smoke grenade the friendlies popped—and they told me it was purple. Even though John concurred with my description of what I saw as the target, a clump of trees not unlike all the others in the area, I still wasn't sure. I couldn't keep the perspiration that flowed from under my helmet out of my eyes. Damn, it was hot. My eyes burned, my mouth felt like gun cotton.

"I'm in," the lead radioed.

"Got the target?" John asked me over the ICS [intercom].

"Affirmative." I hadn't taken my eyes off the clump of trees. I rolled the aircraft up, over, and into a dive. As the pipper slowly worked its way up to the target, doubt interceded.

"Forget something?" John asked, as I pulled the aircraft out of the dive.

In my concern not to take my eyes off the clump of trees, I had forgotten to flip on the Master Armament Switch. Even if I had been sure of the target, I couldn't have done anything about it anyway.

"Lead's in," I heard on the radio as I orbited high, trying to reacquire the target and get my act together. By the time the flight leader pulled off target, I was so far out of position I could tell he knew it and wanted to roll right back in for another run.

"Go ahead and make another run, we'll be right behind you," John radioed to the lead.

Instead of firing rockets on the next run, I marked what I thought were the enemy positions with machine gun tracers in my dive—and was I ever relieved when they fired back.

"Y'all took some ground fire on that last pass, Pony," the advisor on the ground radioed, with the sound of gunfire in the background.

"I'll get 'em . . . we're in," the lead radioed. "Last pass," he added.

Damn . . . and I hadn't even fired a rocket.

"That's okay, there's always another day," John said, knowingly. "It's always better to be sure," he added, to console me.

"Well, I sure as hell have the target now . . . at least what's left of it," I said, as I saw the lead's rockets pulverize the clump of trees. I watched the aircraft as it went jinking off target.

"Should I dump-X?" I asked, wondering if I should get rid of everything on what I figured would be my last pass. While we weren't the lead, John was the FTL [Fire Team Leader] for the flight. He quickly assessed the situation, and with no ground fire having been reported on the last run, asked the lead to orbit high, while I made three rocket attacks before going home with half my ordnance. Despite everything looking good in my gun sight, the first couple of rockets fell a little short of the target before I realized that I was too slow because I hadn't trimmed for dive airspeed. It was so easy to screw up on target where everyone was watching you, some with a vital interest. Fortunately, in the scheme of things, these were minor, and I remarked to myself that nothing in the RAG adequately prepared one for the real thing. I could not have known at this early stage of things, just how true this really was.

Kit Lavell, Black Pony

Lt. (jg) Mike Quinlan's heart nearly stopped when he heard the call on the guard frequency, "Mayday! Mayday! Seawolf 305. My wingman's shot down and I'm losing oil pressure!"

Quinlan was in the back seat of Lt. Cdr. Len "ZZ" Zagortz's lead Bronco on 28 April and they were in the middle of a diving attack. Apparently Zagortz was not monitoring the guard, so Quinlan tried to get his attention on the intercom—not an easy task in the midst of a rocket run. After a couple more ICS interruptions, Zagortz shot back, "Will you shut the fuck up."

The JOs knew Zagortz to be one of the coolest heads in the squadron, possessed with a quick wit, keen sense of humor, and infectious laugh. Right now, though, the guy in front had his hands full. Quinlan knew he had to be forceful and to the point.

"There's a Seawolf down. We've got to go help."

"Where is it?"

"Pick up a heading of northeast and I'll tell you where to go."

Quinlan heard the Seawolf pilot scream that he was going down, just before his transmission was silenced. The pilot of an Army O-1 Bird Dog spotter plane called out the coordinates over the radio. Lt. Aubrey Martin in the wing Bronco joined on the lead, and they left the target they had been working for a much more important priority. Lt. (jg) Jim Brewster, in the back seat of the wing bird, checked his map too, and he and Quinlan decided the downed Seawolf was only minutes away, but just on the other side of the Cambodian border. The border they were forbidden to cross.

At that moment lines on a map did not matter. Quick thinking did. Quinlan spotted the wreckage of the first helo that had gone down, and it looked as if it had blown up in the air. He did not know that three of its crew had died and one was gravely wounded. Seawolf 305 had auto rotated into a controlled crash near the wreckage. Its crew quickly had dismounted the .30-caliber weapons and set up a defensive perimeter. Aircraft Jet Engine Mechanic 1st Class Lloyd T. Williams, one of the door gunners, in the face of withering automatic weapons fire then rushed to the wreckage of Seawolf 320 and pulled the wounded gunner back to the defensive perimeter

The Black Ponies arrived overhead and got a quick sitrep (situation report) from the Bird Dog pilot. They began firing Zuni rockets at the tree line from which most of the automatic weapons fire was coming and took quite a bit of antiaircraft fire in return. A UH-1D from the 175th Assault Helicopter Company, the "Bushwhackers," out of Vinh Long, also had heard the Mayday and sped to the scene. Hueys from the 229th Assault Helicopter Battalion and other army gunships arrived also, and after several attempts were aborted because of intense ground fire, the UH-1D managed to pick up the survivors. But just as the Huey was pulling away, and the Black Ponies were watching from overhead, low on fuel, the pilot who had just been picked up—was shot through the heart and killed.[10]

We had just started flying in Vietnam and we were wet behind the ears . . . but not after that. . . . It was the first time we worked together with the Seawolves like that. . . . We had been treated funny when we arrived . . . the Seawolves had been there for a couple of years and we were the new kids on the block.

They didn't get the bodies out for another year. It was Cambodia and we weren't supposed to be there. If anything came down, it didn't trickle down to me. I was a lightweight, just a JG. It was the toughest mission I was on the entire time I was over there. The ground fire was unbelievable. It was all over the place. A couple of army guys couldn't get in; there was so much ground fire.[11]

Mike Quinlan, Black Pony

5

Wake-Up Call

I understand no men except those to whom I am bound.

—Antoine de Saint Exupéry, *Flight to Arras*

Even after a few weeks of combat operations, VAL-4 pilots found that many surface units and controllers still were surprised to find that the Black Ponies were fixed-wing aircraft that carried a heavier punch than the Seawolf helicopters they were accustomed to working with. Many of the nuggets, therefore, began going out on PBR operations and patrols with SEALs as a way to get the word out and to drum up business. Lt. (jg) Gary "Zoo" Rezeau found himself scheduled for a two-week stint with the PBRs.

> When I rode up the Vam Co Dong River in an army slick to do my "exchange" tour as a PBR driver for awhile, I wondered how I would be received as a "guest" boat officer. I figured I would not be allowed to do much more than stay out of the way. But they told me I had gotten at Mare Island about the same training that the officers on the PBRs had received. I was not only welcomed when I arrived in Tuy Hoa, but I was given a section of PBRs and put in the scheduled rotation for normal ops. I was told that since I was a Pony, the boat drivers had no reservations about using me like one of the regular guys.[1]
>
> Gary Rezeau, Black Pony

Lt. Cdr. John Butterfield was not one to let the JOs show him up. He too went out on a patrol after visiting Advanced Tactical Support Base (ATSB) Go Dau Ha. Butterfield eventually would become the O-in-C at Vung Tau, and believed in leading by example. One of the patrol officers, Chief Mineman Robert W. Wilson, took Lieutenant Commander Butterfield on his Mark One PBR on a patrol along the Vam Co Dong. Butterfield could not believe Wilson could give eight-digit coordinates until he heard the patrol officer radio them and he could actually see it. What Butterfield and the other Black Ponies learned would be brought back and assimilated into the operations and tactics the squadron would use so many times in providing close air support for PBRs under attack. Chief Wilson later would fly in the back seat of a Black Pony OV-10. This "cross-pollination" made for a more effective ground-air team and undoubtedly saved lives, as Wilson would later attest to when Black Ponies covered him during the Cambodian invasion.[2] Soon the word spread that Black Pony OV-10s carrying three thousand pounds of ordnance could be overhead in minutes to help riverine patrol forces who had come into contact with the enemy and needed some big stuff.

The Parrot's Beak area of Cambodia thrusts into the Delta barely thirty miles from Saigon and was known to be an area of logistic support for North Vietnamese Army (NVA) and Vietcong forces in III and IV Corps. Enemy supply lines ran from this area in Cambodia down the Vam Co Tay and the Vam Co Dong Rivers which come together in an area fifteen miles south of Saigon that was known as the "confluence" and resembled a slingshot. The rockets and mortars that rained down on Saigon and the mines that blew up ships on the channel leading to the city came down from North Vietnam along these supply lines. Admiral Zumwalt had dubbed the latest of the Delta barrier operations Giant Slingshot when it was launched in November 1968 to interdict these supply lines.

When the brown water navy realized the need to deploy and support units to specific areas along the inland waterways for extended periods of time, it developed the advanced tactical support bases. Three or more thirty-by-ninety-foot ammi-pontoon (giant pontoon) barges were connected together and towed to a specific location where they would be moored. The barges connected to an acre or so of high ground to form a base. An ATSB supported a tactical operations center (TOC), berthing and messing facilities, a magazine, a communications van, machinery rooms, generators, and a helicopter landing pad. Advanced tactical support bases were established along the Vam Co Tay and the Vam Co Dong

Rivers to support Operation Giant Slingshot, and later at the mouth of the Song On Doc on the Ca Mau peninsula to support Operation Breezy Cove (a ten-PBR-boat base built on five ammi-pontoons on the Ong Doc River).[3]

Late in the evening PBRs 19 and 72 from River Division 591 were assigned to patrol the Vam Co Dong south of Ben Luc. I was patrol officer in command. At our briefing prior to going out on patrol, we were informed by intelligence that a number of NVA regulars and Vietcong were planning to cross the river in small squads heading towards Saigon. We were to be aware and on the watch for them.

About three klicks down the river from our base camp, we nosed our boats into the bank at a spot where the cover was thin, to search for activity. None was spotted so we backed out and slowly moved down the river about another klick and eased in alongside the bank with both PBRs. Our lead boat tied up to the nipa palm extending out over the water from the river bank and our cover boat pulled in about fifty yards behind us and tied up to the nipa palm also.

Both crews used their machetes to cut several large pieces of the nipa palm and draped it over the boats to provide us with a little camouflage so we would not be too noticeable to anyone on the river. After making both boats secure, the exact coordinates of our location were determined, coded up, and called into our Tactical Operations Center so they would hopefully keep friendly fire off of us. We could not see much of anything on the banks because of the density of the foliage we were tied up to. But we had an excellent view of the river in both directions. An hour or so passed and darkness was less than an hour away.

Two River Assault Group (RAG) boats passed us going up stream and did not see us. But out of courtesy, I picked up the radio mic and said, "You are passing us to your port." Everyone on the river monitoring that frequency would look to their port side and if they saw boats, they would know who sent the message without revealing their position.

Suddenly, and without warning, two low-flying OV-10A Bronco aircraft approached our position coming from upstream about two hundred feet off the deck from the direction of Ben Luc. When they were about a hundred yards or so from us, they opened fire with rapid fire 20-mm cannons and rockets at a position about five hundred yards down the river from us on the same bank. As the Black Ponies passed over our position with guns blazing, hot empty brass was falling on our boats, in the water around us, and in the nipa palm to our starboard. "Get us out of here!" was my command to both boat captains. I wasn't sure the pilots knew we were there so I wanted to make us visible as quickly as possible.

The aircraft circled around and put in a second strike in the same position. After both boats had cast off the limbs of nipa palm and were safely out in the river, I contacted our TOC at Ben Luc. "This is 'Shapeless Two Zero,' is there something we should know about a strike that was just put in down the river from us?"

Their response was, "Approximately fifteen to twenty armed personnel were detected advancing on your position and Black Pony was in the neighborhood, over."

"Roger that and tell them thanks," I answered.

My boat captain, Gunner's Mate (Guns) 2d Class Castro said, "Chief, that was close and they scared the hell out of me when that brass started falling on us. But I'm sure glad those guys are on our side."

"Yeah, me too. Looks like they pulled us out of a bad fight and maybe saved our butts too," was my response to him. The Black Ponies had helped Mitch Wells's patrol out of a tight spot up river from Ben Luc a couple days earlier. They were a welcome sight in the sky by all of us PBR personnel who rode the fiberglass boats on the rivers.[4]

Jimmy R. Bryant, PBR sailor

Vietnamese Air Force Binh Thuy received a mortar attack shortly after midnight on Sunday, 11 May 1969. This was the first attack since the arrival of VAL-4. The OV-10 revetments proved to be vulnerable because two or three aircraft were parked in each one and ordnance was stored in each corner of the revetments. Storage space was severely lacking. Squadron personnel were rearming at the time and had no bunker to retire to. Three rounds bracketed the Bronco revetments, the closest being fifty feet, but no damage was done to the aircraft. The next morning work got under way to make massive improvements to all the squadron's facilities. The Seabees had done an excellent job of building support structures where only months before nothing had existed. But Black Ponies, finding themselves at the "aftermost milking station," needed to take matters into their own hands.

The two combat-experienced pilots in the squadron, Commander Winans and Lieutenant Russell, worked with the other second-tour aviators, sharing their knowledge of flying close air support in Spads. The nuggets, especially, looked up to Pete Russell, who was very approachable, and eager to help out in any way he could. He became an excellent mentor.

The skipper and Pete Russell developed the squadron's tactical doctrine, along with Al Schauer, who had flown A-4 tactical jets, and the other Spad drivers, Marty Schuman, Art Savard, and Robert Stoddert.[5] They talked extensively to the HAL-3 helo pilots and blended what the Seawolves had told the Black Ponies with fixed-wing tactics. Most of it the Ponies made up as they went along, however, flying combat missions in the first few weeks after arriving in-country. But there were an awful lot of unknowns.

Pete Russell knew that the Black Ponies were performing what might prove to be the last "seat-of-the-pants" close air support in the history of aerial warfare. That was what had attracted him to the mission and the squadron. Since this was the era before widespread use of "smart weapons," experienced attack pilots like Winans and Russell knew that the Bronco's accuracy depended entirely on the skills and marksmanship of the pilot. The Zuni and other forward-firing rockets VAL-4 employed lacked the "smarts" to guide themselves to the target. The Black Pony pilot therefore had to maneuver the aircraft to the precise spot in the sky, where, at the right airspeed, dive angle, and G force, he could shoot the rocket at the target and expect to hit it. If he was not at that precise spot, or if any of the other variables were off, the rocket could miss the target completely, even though the pilot had his gunsight's "bull's-eye" centered on the target. When one or more factors were off, the pilot would compensate by adjusting other factors. Hurtling toward the ground at almost three hundred miles per hour, usually in bad weather or at night, often times dodging antiaircraft fire, always aware of the close proximity to friendly troops, the pilot constantly would be making decisions that computers make today. For the Bronco also lacked the smarts—computers and other gadgets—to help the pilot get to that precise spot in the sky. Instead, the Black Pony pilot used airmanship, visual cues, training, experience, and seat-of-the-pants instinct.

Through the efforts of Winans and Russell and all the seasoned aviators, the Black Ponies were building a repository of knowledge and skills that would set the example for the squadron in the months to come. Confidence was building and the nuggets were itching to get into the front seat.

The Routine at Vung Tau

Every third day you were part of a four-man alert crew . . . then usually three or four two-plane patrols, most of the time with a marine observer in the morning or afternoon, where someone would fly him around the Rung Sat. Then there would be a morning first light two-plane that would go up the Vam Co Tay and Vam Co Dong. We'd launch another patrol at dusk while we set up the nighttime alert planes.

At the end of our little ramp we had a bunker that had our schedules and ops briefing area and four racks built in the back corner. The fifth guy was the SDO [squadron duty officer]. The airplanes were usually parked in the first two revetments past the hangar. On the airfield was a Seabee-built bunker, forty by sixty feet maybe, partitioned off into a big space, an ops space, and a bunk space . . . an office, a map on the wall. . . . Lt. Cdrs. "ZZ" Zagortz, Don Florko, and John Butterfield rotated as the first three O-in-Cs.

I had maybe thirty hours in the airplane when I got there. I flew mostly back seat until the new guys started coming. By the middle of the summer they said we've got new guys coming in that had been through a RAG, so we'd better train these ones that we brought with us. They ran a ten-flight syllabus or so during the day, and you'd go out as a number three on a section or just by yourself and go shoot.

But for the first few months, I spent three or four weeks out with PBRs, PCFs, and SEALs, drumming up business. So when I came back to the squadron I had spots on my map that nobody else had on their maps. I had call signs and I knew whom I was talking to.

I got into a firefight while with the SEALs. Both ends of their position fired. Some place in the "Plain of Reeds" (an area in the upper Delta adjacent to Cambodia). I was with Lt. (jg) David "Blackjack" Nicholas (who later was killed by friendly fire while on a patrol). We had met these guys when we all were going through training in Coronado.

For recreation we had an aluminum outboard with a 40-hp motor on the back. We used to ski around the dredge spoils in the Saigon shipping channel up the Rung Sat. We used the "spoil" islands [made of the dirt dredged from the river bottom] as a drop off spot because with the 40 hp you could only carry one guy in the boat while pulling a skier. We'd take four or five guys out, park two or three of them on a dredge spoil island. I saw sea snakes one time when I was skiing and made a strong commitment not to fall down. They tend to form into a large ball, a Medusa's Head kind of thing.

The Seabees had built a three-holer with a screen porch. Carrier sailors and nuggets crapped in it for about a week. No one knew what to do with it when it started stinking up the place. ZZ Zagortz said, "You're the shitter control officer. Solve this problem." I went to the army who gave me regs on the proper way to run a latrine like that. I had scratched my head trying to figure out how to get rid of three sawed-off fifty-five-gallon drums full of shit. Mix it in a four-to-one ratio of feces to JP [jet] fuel, the instructions said. Well, we certainly had enough JP5 around there. The initial clean out was a "fire-in-the-hole" kind of event—twenty-five-gallon drums half full; poured in ten gallons of JP; stirred with a long stick; and lit it. It burned for several days. We got three more cans and rotated. At sundown each day we would burn them out for the next day. The newest detachment person, regardless of rank, would be responsible for that. I was glad to pass this assignment down the line. An E-7 [chief petty officer] who was the last of his group to report in, was really pissed, to mix the metaphor.

At the BOQ we had a CS1 [commissaryman 1st class] and an SD1 [steward 1st class] and a cook and a[nother] steward, who ran breakfast and dinner. Lunch was C-rats. I was the bar officer, and collected all the ration cards and went to the Class Six (army package) store and bought two bottles each of clear and dark spirits and a case of beer per person per month. From the Aussies I would get the warm weather beer, instead of the PBR (Pabst Blue Ribbon) that had sat out in the sun. We traded flight jackets and air conditioners to have access to this stockpile of beer, then a monthly trade of booze.[6]

Bob Campbell, Black Pony

The Routine at Binh Thuy

Breakfast at the chow hall was a social occasion. For Black Ponies it was a chance to meet officers from the other commands, learn the latest scuttlebutt, and catch up on the latest goings-on in the squadron. The previous night's bunker crew would bring news from Vung Tau, the "other side," or about combat operations, and pilots would share the latest lessons learned over a breakfast of reconstituted eggs, stale toast, powdered milk—and the ubiquitous "bug" juice. Anywhere pilots went in the navy, they couldn't seem to get away from this fluid of unknown color and indescribable flavor. Actually the chow at the mess was usually better than that. Most mornings officers would get some meat—bacon or something resembling sausage. Provisions sometimes ran low—or they couldn't catch whatever they were chasing that morning, some joker claimed. Funny how some guys never thought about the food, while others did and would eat virtually nothing but C-rations. Some stayed away from the "mystery meat," but otherwise few had complaints.

After breakfast some pilots caught a ride over to the other side in the duty pickup truck, which regularly ran back and forth the mile and a half between the two bases a half hour before each scheduled flight. Whenever a pilot was not scheduled to fly and his collateral duty was in the maintenance department, he went to the airfield in order to do paperwork and perform his other chores. Once every three weeks a pilot stood the duty in the bunker. Every pilot who was a junior officer served as squadron duty officer for a twenty-four-hour period, during which he was responsible for running air operations from the bunker. The SDO handled the radios and communications with ground and air units, and assigned aircraft and crews to missions, in accordance with the flight schedule.

Most pilots who worked in the maintenance department at the airfield would try to finish their paperwork as quickly as possible, thus freeing themselves up to talk to the enlisted men, load rockets, or hang around the bunker most of the day. This would become their routine whenever possible. They often would sit around the bunker listening to the briefs and debriefs, especially if they were new in-country. They talked to the other pilots and learned through osmosis all the little details of combat flying. And they played acey-deucey to break up the routine. After Commander Burton built the handball court in the back hangar in 1971, the Black Ponies used it around the clock.

Two squadrons, HAL-3 and VAL-4, shared a Quonset hut next to the helo pad at Navy Binh Thuy where the Black Pony Operations Department and the Administration Department had offices. The sign on the door for the "office" that housed the public affairs officer (PAO), the awards officer, and the recreation officer—what was called the JO Lounge—proclaimed, "Heroes are not born. They are made. Right here." And underneath it, another hand-scrawled sign, "If the night is dark enough and the weather is bad enough, we can write it up."

Some Black Pony pilots really enjoyed night flying and would come to prefer night combat missions, which other pilots would say was cause to ground them for insanity. During the day, the sun's differential heating of dissimilar ground features—light and dark vegetation, water—caused thermal convection and turbulence. The air was smooth and calm at night, as long as there were no storms. And if there were, as the night progressed, the thunderstorm activity usually died down. Darkness produced a strange, mixed sense of security and heightened awareness. The body orients itself primarily with vision, and less with the inner ear, and nerve endings—the so-called seat-of-the-pants sensation. At night, when there are fewer visual cues, the body seems to be more alert to other sensations and sounds. Pilots were more aware of engine noises at night, for example. It was as if they operated at a higher level of consciousness. A pilot could see tracers at night, where they might not be visible in the daytime. And while a pilot would rather see what's coming at him, the visual effect at night was often surrealistic, which could result in the mixed signals of danger and beauty. The difficulties of navigating in darkness and weather also counterbalanced the pleasures of night flying.

For one of the new replacement pilots, or "newbie," his first front-seat night combat hop was a different story.

Usually it cooled off after dark, but it didn't seem so that night. The sortie was supposed to be an uneventful random patrol. First we flew through some "arty," or friendly artillery, which we would normally avoid by calling for "arty advisories" on the Fox Mike radio. That night, for some reason, the ARVN sandbagged us as we tried to transit an area that was on the top of someone's list for H and I—harassment and interdiction—or, how to win friends and influence Victor Charlie with high-explosive howitzer shells. The only problem was that the top of the arc of these howitzers' trajectory coincided with our flight level.

Then we had trouble lighting up the target. The ROE required illuminating nighttime targets. That meant dropping a paraflare. At night Black Ponies carried a pod of MK 24/45 paraflares in place of one of the rocket pods. These were white phosphorous flares that burned with two million candlepower at over 22,000 degrees Fahrenheit. They hung suspended for three minutes beneath a parachute after being ejected out the back of the pod beneath the aircraft from an altitude of twenty-five hundred to three thousand feet. The lead aircraft had electrical problems and couldn't launch any paraflares. After I launched the first paraflare, the lead flew into it and promptly extinguished it, fortunately with no serious consequences. After a couple of duds, we had one flare with which to work the target.

I had a couple of minutes to orient myself and pick out the target from among the eerie shadows waving back and forth against the gray-green circular area of ground that the rapidly descending flare lit up. My first roll-in began just as that flare hit the ground. For a naval aviator, the only thing worse than pointing his nose at the ground in the black of night in the Mekong Delta might be pushing over on the approach to an aircraft carrier for a night landing. What a crazy way to make a living!

My Bronco was screaming toward the ground as the last bit of light illuminated the target, a clump of trees at the intersection of two squigglies that intelligence reports identified as concealing an enemy weapons cache. I pickled a salvo of Zuni rockets, including one from my right-wing station, whose blinding flash enveloped the cockpit. The intensity of the light surprised me, and I pulled out of the dive temporarily blinded. I quickly regained vision, eased the G forces, and banked the aircraft to swing around for another attack. This was not a hot target, so I made several runs for the practice of it. My rockets set fires on the ground that served as references for the attack. We couldn't tell what damage we had inflicted, and would have to wait for a sweep of the area by ground forces the next day to provide BDA or bomb damage assessment.

Black Pony "Newbie"

On 25 May 1969 two U.S. Navy PBRs from River Section/Division 513 engaged the VC in a firefight along Cai Lon River, a body of water the Black Ponies called the "All American Canal," after the canal in Imperial Valley, California, where they had trained in low-level navigation. The patrol boat was about twenty miles southeast of Rach Gia, deep into the U-Minh Forest, when it was hit and the crew radioed for assistance. A Black Pony Light Attack Fire Team led by Lt. Pete Russell quickly responded. The commanding officer, Cdr. Gil Winans, was flying Russell's wing that day. The skipper had encouraged JOs to lead flights, and he and Pete had flown many combat missions together, both in VAL-4 and with VA-176. Lt. (jg) Roy Sikkink in Winans's back seat and Russell's copilot, Lt. (jg) Jeffery Johnson, established radio communication with the crew of the boats under fire.

Boatswain's Mate 1st Class Gerald D. Cole, boat captain of PBR 117, was surprised to hear and see the Black Ponies overhead. He had thought the Seawolves had been scrambled, and had never heard of the Black Ponies before their arrival on scene. He was also surprised at how quickly the aircraft showed up after the radio call, especially since the boats were so far down the river from Rach Gia.[7]

After the Ponies had fired all their rockets at the enemy positions, the boat crew directed the flight to a tree line from which they were still taking fire. With only their internal M-60 machine guns left, the OV-10s

Gil Winans looked over his shoulder to watch Pete Russell in his dive. Winans sensed something was wrong—Black Pony 107 was too low. "Pull out, pull out!" Winans frantically radioed as he saw the olive green Bronco merge with its shadow on the dark green jungle below. *drawing by Dan Witcoff*

began strafing the tree line at very low altitude, for the M-60s were not an effective weapon unless the aircraft were close to the enemy.

Russell and his copilot Jeff Johnson, flying in Black Pony 107, watched the skipper's Bronco roll in on the enemy positions, then took an interval as they circled the target. One element of Black Pony close air support doctrine that Winans and Russell had helped write concerned mutual support when working a target. The close interval that Russell took on Winan's aircraft allowed him to be in a dive as the skipper pulled off target. A Bronco would be most vulnerable when pulling off target, so the pilot begins firing the M-60 machine guns almost as soon as he is established in his dive. This keeps the enemy heads down, at least the ones near the intended target, and protects the aircraft that is pulling out. Strafing runs present an even greater challenge because the planes need to fly a tight pattern.

Gil Winans looked over his shoulder to watch Pete Russell in his dive. Winans sensed something was wrong—107 was too low. "Pull out, pull out!" Winans frantically radioed as he saw the olive green Bronco merge with its shadow on the dark green jungle below.[8]

In the middle of Russell's diving attack a single 7.62-mm caliber round smashed through the right side of 107's canopy, striking Pete in the head.

> I was leaning over in the back seat, looking over the front ejection seat, which comes up kind of high. If you want to watch what's going on from the back seat, you have to lean over and look around the side. All of a sudden a single bullet came through the Plexiglas . . . and these . . . pieces . . . came back and hit me in the face. And I sort of slumped over to the left . . . just a reaction to that stuff hitting me in the face . . . and we were in a fairly steep dive . . . I kind of sat back up and made a quick intercom call to Pete . . . and I didn't get any answer.
>
> And then, the control stick was there between my legs and I put my hand on it and moved it around and he wasn't on it any more. And, at that point, we were fairly low and fairly steep and the only thing I really remember is I just yanked back on that stick and we pulled out at approximately thirty-five feet above the canal. . . . All I saw was water. I mean, that was at the bottom . . . all I saw was water.
>
> I pulled out and climbing out, I called Winans and I told him that Pete had been hit . . . and that I was headed back home. . . . I headed back to Binh Thuy and he called and said, "I'm coming with you." And he and Roy followed and eventually caught up with me. I had the engines at full bore all the way home and they joined up on my wing and finally caught up with me. We went on home.

After we landed I was concerned about all the arming switches up in the front that were still hot. . . . All these people rushed out to the airplane after I landed, and I was thinking about all that ordnance possibly going off or something. But at that point, I was shut down and got Pete out, and they had a helicopter waiting to take him to the hospital, but . . . whoever the doctor at the scene was . . . he determined that it was too late for him. He got hit in the cheek, right below his right eye. A single bullet killed him . . . I was kind of in shock . . . I walked around the base. They kind of lost me. I was just . . . in a daze. I went out and walked around the base in my flight suit. Finally after about an hour, everyone was looking for me. They said, "You need to go over and see the flight surgeon."

The guys on one of the boats later came to Binh Thuy. . . . They said they thought we were going right into the canal . . . straight into the canal, nose down. I mean, it wasn't a shallow dive. It was pretty straight.

Pete was a second-tour pilot, had survived one trip into Vietnam, and helped shoot down a MiG.

For the Black Ponies, it was a wake-up call . . . I think everybody now realized this was serious business. . . .[9]

Jeffery Johnson, Black Pony

6

Paying the Price

It is in your act that you exist, not in your body. Your act is yourself, and there is no other you.

—Antoine de Saint-Exupéry, *Flight to Arras*

Jeff Johnson was back in another aircraft in a couple of days flying combat missions. Pete's death had a profound effect on him,
but he kept his feelings in check. The tempo of combat operations steadily increased over the next several weeks, which
helped to take everyone's mind off the tragedy, and allowed the
Black Ponies to handle the loss without undermining their effectiveness. The fact that they lost their most experienced combat
veteran could have shaken their confidence, but most pilots tried
to rationalize it as chance occurrence, a one-in-a-million random event. A "Golden BB," as some pilots were wont to call it.
The XO, Commander Schuman, helped the younger pilots keep
focused on the job at hand.

> I remember I was an ensign in my first squadron, on a
> Caribbean cruise, and we had an S-2 that went down and all
> four guys were lost. By the time the helo came around to get
> them, they were gone. It shook me up because I had never been
> exposed to that—the sudden death of four guys. I remember a
> senior lieutenant who said, "Marty, what you've got to do is
> throw up, get that out of your system, then keep on charging."
> I think I may have gotten some of our guys together and men-
> tioned that story to them. We just kept on going. It didn't have

that big of an effect on us. It was heartbreaking to see Pete leave us but we kept on going. . . . The guys still wanted to fly all the time, and have fun after flying.

After Pete Russell's death, we emphasized pulling out, and once you saw one thousand feet, get out of there. Small arms were our biggest danger. We emphasized rolling in, pickling and getting out of there. . . and evasive maneuvers after the run.[1]

Marty Schuman, Black Pony

It really shook those of us who were young and invincible when Pete Russell got killed. It really brought home the reality of it all. Of all people that I would have expected, a guy who conforms to the rules of engagement, does things by the book as humanly possible; he was the last. . . . So when he got killed with one round playing by the rules. . . .[2]

Charlie Sapp, Black Pony

Mike Quinlan had been Jeff Johnson's classmate at the Naval Academy. As the squadron's legal officer Quinlan drew the chore of inventorying Pete Russell's personal effects and shipping them back to his family in a cruise box. As fate would have it, thieves would break into the cruise box, probably in Saigon, and steal the dead man's belongings.

Cdr. Ken Russell had been flying the C-1 on and off the *Roosevelt* at that time. He happened to have just landed on shore for a remain over night (RON) when he spotted a black sedan waiting for him. A feeling of dread washed over him. "Is he dead or just hurt?" The casualty assistance officer replied, "I don't know. We've got to take you over to AirLant [Naval Air Force, Atlantic] headquarters." That's when he got the word about his brother. Ken then had to fly the plane back to the ship. The CO of the *Roosevelt* graciously let him have use of the C-1. Ken flew up to see his folks, then flew on a transport to Saigon and brought Pete back. He then flew to Navy Brunswick where the captain of the base arranged full military honors for a Memorial Day burial.[3]

Memorial Day services back at North Island in San Diego took on an even more personal meaning, as the OV-10 RAG instructors paused in their preparations for welcoming aboard the first group of replacement pilots slated to go to Vietnam.

With an average onboard count of four airplanes and five instructors, the OV-10 RAG trained ninety-seven replacement pilots and 422 maintenance personnel before it closed up shop in February 1972. Replacement pilots received twenty-five hours of ground training and seventy-five hours in the air during the sixteen-week syllabus. The first week was devoted to learning aircraft systems before starting the ten-week flight syllabus, which culminated with a three-week weapons detachment at Marine Corps Air Station Yuma, Arizona. Replacement pilots then returned to North Island for one week of tactics. During this time they participated in a simulated close air support mission at Camp Pendelton. Finally, before leaving for Vietnam, each replacement pilot underwent three weeks of survival, evasion, resistance, and escape training, and (usually) a PBR orientation.

How to Become (one fifth of) an Ace before Leaving the States

By the time I went through the RAG, all our instructor pilots had spent a tour in-country. All the IPs agreed that our weapons detachment in Yuma, Arizona, could only introduce us to the rudiments of combat. Actually the highlight of simulated combat on the weapons "det" was one of our OV-10s intercepting a Cessna and almost shooting it down—on purpose—with the FAA's permission.

A number of us had been sitting around the swimming pool at the Yuma Marine Corps Air Station O'Club trying to cool off in the 115-degree heat. We had just returned from training flights and were sipping cold beers, listening to Simon and Garfunkel's "Bridge Over Troubled Water," when an urgent call came in for a crew to get back to the airfield ASAP. On the other side of the field, at the civilian airport that shared the runway, a newly licensed pilot tried to start his Cessna 150 himself by getting out and manually spinning the prop. He got it started all right, but wasn't quick enough on his feet to catch the plane as it headed down the taxiway at full throttle. The tower controllers frantically called out on the radio to the aircraft asking what its intentions were. The plane showed them by leaping into the air and heading for blue sky. When everyone realized it was pilotless, thus posing a hazard to the city, a marine helicopter gave chase. But as the Cessna climbed to altitude in a slow circle over the city, the helo had to abandon the pursuit after about an hour. That's when the OV-10s came to the rescue. The only sober crew was the lucky crew, so Lt. Cdr. Jay Schoenfeld launched in a fully armed Bronco.

Over the next hour pilots and controllers discussed various schemes, including shooting down the luckless Cessna. Just when Jay thought he was one fifth of the way to becoming an ace without having to leave the States, the Cessna ran out of gas, banked into a turn in the opposite direction, and headed out over the desert, where it spiraled down to the ground. It almost made a perfect landing, but at the last moment its wing tip clipped a sand dune, and at two hours and thirty-six minutes after its grand takeoff, it ignominiously cartwheeled into the record books as the longest unmanned Cessna 150 flight in history. Reporters interviewed Jay, and the caper made the Yuma and base papers. The next day ground crews painted the black silhouette of a Cessna on the side of Jay's aircraft.

Kit Lavell, Black Pony

Daily increasing cloud formations in the Delta signaled the onslaught of the monsoon season, which had been delayed that year, according to the wisdom passed on by old-timers (anybody who had been in-country more than the guy on the receiving end of such wisdom). Dust had been a big problem since the squadron arrived in April, some of it indigenous, but a lot of it provided by the RMK-BRJ consortium that operated a rock crusher about two-hundred yards from the Binh Thuy hangar. All the aircraft were coated with a thin patina of gray dust that had been turning into sickly-looking mud as the afternoon showers began increasing.

The tempo of flight operations had been steadily building at Binh Thuy, in part, according to observers, because Binh Thuy Black Ponies "live, eat, sleep, drink and complain on the same small base with the CTF-116 Game Warden operations personnel. [And] their cajoling for more patrols is apt to produce more response."[4] Binh Thuy pilots had also been soliciting targets from air force FACs and ground units, who were eagerly providing them. The ROE required Black Ponies to work first for navy units, but "Red Rose" (CTF-116 OpCon), the radar flight-following operations control for the Mekong Delta, had been granting clearance for Ponies, especially when friendlies were entrapped by the enemy.

Post-strike bomb damage assessments had begun piling up and the numbers of structures, bunkers, and enemy that VAL-4 destroyed began exceeding that of any attack aircraft in Vietnam.[5] Damage to Bronco aircraft also began increasing. A .51-caliber round recently had struck a 20-mm gun pod, fortunately not blowing up the ammunition.

On Thursday 5 June Admiral Zumwalt presided over CTF-116's change of command in the shade of VAL-4's hangar, when Capt. J. R. Faulk relieved Capt. Arthur W. Price Jr. That same night a mortar attack somehow missed all the Bronco aircraft and destroyed the chow hall, but the enlisted Black Ponies classified the mess hall casualty as a negligible loss.

On the night of 8 June a Fire Team led by Lt. Cdr. "ZZ" Zagortz scrambled from the Vung Tau detachment to provide air cover for a SEAL platoon surrounded by the enemy. The Black Ponies flew to a point on the Vam Co Dong River where the SEAL team was pinned down and could not reach the extraction point on the riverbank. Nor could the boats reach the pickup area.

Although the ceiling was down to five hundred feet when the flight arrived over the target (preventing the use of flares), the outline of the river bank, guarded use of a strobe light, and whispered radio transmissions from the SEALs provided enough ground reference to commence the attack. The SEALs did not want to reveal their position to the enemy and the strobe light provided only an initial reference since it could only be seen from directly above as the aircraft passed over.

Lt. Cdr. Zagortz limited the initial attacks to the SUU-11 mini-gun pod and M-60 sponson guns (the aircraft were not equipped with the MK4 20-mm pod) because of the low ceiling. Later, when the ceiling lifted to fifteen hundred feet, Zagortz employed the Zuni rockets. Fifteen hundred feet is normally the minimum pullout altitude for Zuni delivery in order to avoid the fragmentation pattern of the weapon. In this case Zagortz had to roll in at fifteen hundred feet, track, fire, and pull out as quickly as possible.

The Black Ponies blasted an extraction route to the river, with the SEALs moving along behind until they finally were able to reach the boats and extract from the area with no casualties.

The SEALs did not know the extent of enemy casualties, since they detected only one dead enemy on their way out in the darkness. But a few days later the Black Ponies received a personal "attaboy" message from ComNavForV. The message cited evidence obtained from captured enemy documents that the enemy had lost the highest number of casualties inflicted by any previous air strike, and commended the Black Pony flight for its precise fire under adverse conditions.[6]

In the armada of the brown water navy, if PBRs were the destroyers, then Swift boats would be the cruisers. Despite being fifty feet in length, they were able to maneuver quite well on inland waterways. In the Sea Lords campaign, when Swift boat operations moved from offshore to inshore, they would work more frequently and closer with Black Ponies. Ensign Dave Wallace, O-in-C of PCF-32, had been based out of Cat Lo in late 1969 and early 1970 and found himself deep in the middle of the Mekong Delta.

The Swift boats were changing at this time, from Market Time to Sea Lords and moving operations into all the rivers. I only did one coastal patrol during this entire time. As Sea Lords progressed more and more we were setting up our own ops. We'd check in with the various provinces and let them know we were in their area, and how many boats. So you'd set up an op. At that point we'd call our control, if we could get them. It was

Sepia, out of Vung Tau, the coastal surveillance center. You'd tell them if you wanted Black Ponies overhead or on standby. I was primarily on a [boat on the] Bassac River and anytime we were on the main river we had Black Ponies overhead or on call. That was SOP. The one time we didn't we just so happened to get into a lot of shit.

We almost took it for granted that Black Ponies would always be around. There were so many times we worked with them. On an average four-day patrol we'd run operations off the river at least once a day and they were always there. We didn't work as much with Seawolves because they didn't have the on-station time. We did use them once in a while but you had to be fairly close to their barge. And I don't mean any disrespect, because I hold those guys in incredibly high regard. But they just didn't have the station time.

When the Swift boats went in—we were different than the PBRs—we'd go in with anywhere from a two- to a six-boat raid. A Swift boat could take a hit or two, even though we were all aluminum, whereas a PBR would take a hit and it would go under. Swifts also carried a hell of a lot of ammunition. It wasn't unusual for us to carry twenty thousand rounds of .50-cal. Plus we had a much higher shooting angle. When a PBR went into a canal they were most likely shooting "up." And all they could do was run. They had to run unless they happened to catch Chuck [the VC] in the open. I'm not knocking PBRs. Those guys had brass balls as far as I'm concerned. The Swift boats could shoot "down," so we could get Chuck to keep his head down a little bit better than they could. So we would stay in a kill zone or around it longer than they could, so we needed something with more station time. That's where the Black Ponies were just beautiful.[7]

Dave Wallace, Swift boat sailor

Wallace, one of the few ensigns to command a Swift boat, had worked with Black Ponies before, but on a Bassac River op one day, he would get his first introduction to the 5-inch Zuni rocket, something he had not seen or heard of before.

I was OTC (officer in tactical command) of the raid, with three boats, in an area where we were constantly twisting back and forth on each other. So you had to be careful if you drew fire because these canals would twist so radically you could literally shoot back at your third boat. . . . We had some Ruff-Puffs [soldiers of the Vietnamese regional force] on the beach that we had put in, and they were to push the bad guys toward us. And of course when they all fled towards the "stealthy" Swift boats chugging out there with their supercharged twelve cylinder diesels—we were going to shoot them all. As luck would have it, the bad guys got between the Ruff-Puffs and the boats and started shooting. And the Ruff-Puffs panicked and started shooting right into the boats at which time we called in the Black Ponies. We had expected the 2.75-inch rockets that kind of went, *bang, bang.*

All of a sudden, *kawoompf, kawoompf.*

I'm going, "What the shit is going on? What are you shooting?"

"Five-inch Zunis. How do you like that?"

We knew a lot of the pilots. We spent a lot of time with the guys on the beach. So they were laughing. They thought that was hysterical. We thought they were dropping 500-pound bombs. They were shooting a hundred yards away from us. They were incredibly accurate. Saved our bacon. All hostilities stopped in about forty-five seconds. That was the end of that.[8]

Dave Wallace, Swift boat sailor

A Swift boat, PCF-37, was making thirty-two knots headed upriver and its O-in-C, Lt. (jg) Bill Lannom, enjoyed watching the lush green foliage hurtle by. The steady hum of the Detroit marine diesels and the rushing sound of the brown water being parted by the aluminum hull gave way to an unusual sound. Lannom looked around. "I was roaring back from a patrol flat out and I heard this noise. I looked aft out of the after window of the pilothouse and there was an OV-10 upside down a couple hundred feet off the river, roaring past going upriver."[9]

Lannom smiled and wondered if the OV-10 pilot was someone he knew, for he too had worked the Black Ponies on many occasions, and had spent time with them on the beach.

Black Ponies bailed us out big time on 3 July 1969 in a canal between the Ham Luong and Co Chien Rivers. The mission was to take targets of opportunity under fire, continuing on, to turn northwest at the "T" where that canal met another. After we turned northwest we got hit, from the starboard side by a homemade Claymore (rods of steel scored with a chisel and laid into the explosive so they'd shear at the score point, as discovered by looking at the shrapnel later). Then they opened up with machine gun fire.

Two Black Ponies were assigned as cover for us and were standing off, supposedly undetected by Charlie. Well, Charlie must have not known they were about, because immediately after the first explosion, I heard a Pony crackle on the radio, "Which side?"

I screamed, "Starboard, starboard, star . . . "

Boom!

They had a rocket in now. On the right bank of the canal. Close, but just right. I don't know how they did it. God they were fast. We hooked a "U" on the canal, checked our wounds and damage and resumed battle stations. We had a five-man crew and we had a couple of army guys hanging out. Four of the five guys plus me took hits. I had to medevac one of them. Mine was the least serious.

At the first hit I looked aft and my aft gunner was bleeding profusely from his mouth. I just thought, oh my God. You had to know Engineman 2d Class Wells. I could tell he was extremely pissed, looking at him. He was firing that .50-caliber so I knew he couldn't be hurt too badly. He had taken a piece of shrapnel in his upper lip. Stuck out the front and out the back. You know how a facial wound will bleed, then stop. It looked terrible, but it wasn't that bad. When it was all said and done, he pulled it out with a pair of pliers.

After we cleared that kill zone, throttles up, and were mopping up and licking our wounds, a mile or two up the canal, that's when the two B-40s came at us from the left side. We had slowed down. My experience was, and I'd been there about five months by then, that once you got it, it was over. Then they got us on the left side.

Both rockets hit the water and erupted more shrapnel. They didn't do much damage to the boat, but that's what got Boatswain's Mate 3d Class Schmidt again. He took another hit that really laid him down. That's when he really started bleeding badly and when the morphine came out of the kit. We throttled up after that one, and started calling for a medevac. We told the Black Ponies and the lead boat and the drag boat, "I'm not slowing down. You can get out of my way but I'm hauling ass out of here."

The Ponies responded with covering machine gun fire down both sides of the canal as we picked up speed, haulin' ass out of there. Those Ponies put down a barrage of fire, flying through .50-cal. fire and ricochets, disregarding their own safety.

We evaced my man and made it back to Cat Lo. Maintenance counted over 120 holes, but had them patched and us back underway in two days.

Our next patrol was to the Bassac where we drove up to Binh Thuy for fuel. I went to the O'Club and asked the Vietnamese bartender, "Are there any Black Pony pilots in here?"

He said, "Yeah, those guys over there."

I went over, and sure enough, the two who bailed us out were sitting right there. Needless to say, being naval aviators, they had a few drinks with me. We then sauntered down to the pier to look at my boat, PCF-37. The Black Ponies decided I was nuts for doing what we did. I pointed out to them— flying through .50-cal. fire and ricochets was as nuts as anyone could get.

They saved my bacon that day. Thanks to all the Black Ponies and the ones who pulled Charlie off our backs like that.[10]

Bill Lannom, Swift boat sailor

On 25 May Lt. Wayne Cowie Clarke had been transiting the Long Xuyen to Rach Gia Canal from the Bassac on a heavily armored 75-ton Monitor, the "battleship" of the Mobile Riverine Forces. Lieutenant Clarke had recently completed a tour as CO of River Division 511 and for a number of reasons, one of which was he had a degree in physics, he had volunteered for a "Duffle Bag" sensor unit. Duffle Bag sensors were the highly classified first-generation acoustic, seismic, and magnetic sensors that originated on the ill-fated "McNamara Line," a wall that the then–secretary of state was attempting to have built in the demilitarized zone. Clarke would much rather have gone with 511 on Giant Slingshot. Instead he ended up with the Duffle Bag detachment at Ba Xoai, a Special Forces camp (A-421, known as A Team) at Chi Lang, on the Cambodian border near Chau Doc.

On this particular day he was headed for an outpost on an intersection of the Vin Te Canal on the Cambodian border. Duffle Bag sensors had been sown along the border for the first time just a few weeks before. Lieutenant Clarke was on the first leg of the journey to sow more sensors and had just left the Bassac River. He was monitoring the sector frequency and the Game Warden tactical push for that area on two AN/VRC 46 radios, listening to the Black Ponies as they were making a strike. They were somewhere between Vi Tan and Rach Gia, he thought. Clarke was carefully listening to the radios, for the Black Ponies were new at the time, and he was comparing it to radio traffic he had heard of Seawolves. He was trying to figure out how he would coordinate a Black Pony strike, if, or when, the time ever came. The Broncos were rolling in and Lieutenant Clarke heard them saying they were taking fire—.51-caliber fire, he thought—but he was not sure. He then heard a new voice come up on the radio, one that had not been talking tactically. A voice saying that a Black Pony had been shot in the head. He will always remember those fateful words. Clarke didn't hear anything more on the radio when the Black Ponies switched to UHF tactical. When he got to Rach Gia he heard the rest of the story about Lt. Pete Russell. Less than a month later, Lieutenant Clarke himself would call in the Black Ponies, and two of the pilots he had heard on the radio that day would put in an air strike for him.

On the Cambodian side of the border, across from the Special Forces camp out of which Lieutenant Clarke and his Duffle Bag team operated, the North Vietnamese trained troops and assembled them, along with their supplies. As soon as they were trained—almost to North Vietnamese regular standards—these troops slipped across the border and moved down into the Delta, where they would attack outposts, ambush patrol boats, and fire antiaircraft weapons at Black Ponies and other allied aircraft. Lieutenant Clarke's job was to detect the enemy's movement as it was occurring so artillery and air strikes could destroy them before they could slip away.

Lieutenant Clarke's men were all volunteers, veterans of at least six months with the riverine patrol forces. In addition to sowing sensors, they also laid remotely controlled mine fields, even though none of them had received specialized explosives ordnance disposal (EOD) training. Clarke's men would sow these sensors along trails, canal banks, rivers, outposts, and enemy infiltration routes, where they were connected via line-of-sight radio communications to operators who would listen for coded tones. The receivers were called "portatales," about the size of a PRC 77 radio. Operators would lay them on their side and stack them, with each portatale tuned to one frequency. When the operator picked up a tone code on the portatale, a number would come up on the display that indicated which particular sensor it was. If it were an acoustic or magnetic sensor the operator could hear what was coming in on the headphones. He would then correlate this information with pins on a wall chart in the command bunker in the Special Forces camp.

On the night of 19 July we had some very good Duffle Bag activations and we knew what we had. I had been beginning to receive good intelligence from the Special Forces people—they previously had been withholding intelligence from us because of a "need-to-know" basis. They had been running an illegal agent over the Cambodian border. There was a building on a hill at Ba Xoai, at the Special Forces camp built around a little hill. There was a town on one side of the hill and a Buddhist monastery right up against the back of the camp. On that hill was a bunker—fourteen by fourteen feet—made of concrete, two floors. The upstairs room was off limits to everybody. It had a lot of army communications equipment accessed by a little wooden ladder. A Cambodian by the name of Mike came and went. He was somebody special, and spoke a number of languages well. This was at a time when we were forbidden to cross the border.

I had a bunch of sensors along trails going to the border. When I fired a sensor I had to go through a routine. The camp commander had tactical release authority for strikes and he gave his releases based upon the positions of the units in ambush each night. Each unit had to specifically tell Forty-fourth Tactical Zone where their position was. I had received a sensor activation and with six digits coordinate accuracy could pinpoint the sensor position on a map or reference it with a stream or landmark, taking bearings on the mountains, for example. I fired at the activations using "155"—eighteen rounds of 155, a mixture of fuse quick, fuse super quick, and white phosphorus. About ten minutes later, Sergeant Price came to me and said, "Lieutenant, did you just shoot here?" I said, "I sure did, Sergeant. I had clearance, good activations, and shot." He had a clandestine crossing going on, apparently so clandestine that no one knew about it and apparently it killed and wounded some of his [Cambodian] people.

On a similar type of activation the night of 19 July we had a Firefly [army fire team with a helo that kicked flares out] mission going. We had artillery on the line. We had Seawolves on the way in, and we put the artillery on hold. Message traffic at the time will say it was special forces intelligence, but it was really Duffle Bag sensor activation that initiated this. Then the Black Ponies arrived overhead.[11]

Wayne Cowie Clarke, River Division 511 and Duffle Bag unit CO

Jeff Johnson and Roy Sikkink roomed next door to each other at the BOQ and were good friends. They had flown together many times and had together experienced the death of another friend, Pete Russell, in combat. Nothing needed to be said between them about the dangers of flying combat missions in the Delta. They understood the risks.

Roy Sikkink had grown up in Tulsa, Oklahoma. He had been an outstanding scholar, a high school and college wrestler in the 115- and 123-pound classes. He attended the University of Oklahoma in the Navy ROTC program. His father had been a B-29 pilot in World War II, and Roy and his brother Paul loved to fly in the converted B-26 that their father Dean flew for a Tulsa corporation. Roy's lifelong ambition was to be a navy pilot, and after he earned his engineering degree, his goal was to eventually become an astronaut.

Roy was an out-going, adventure-loving young man who enjoyed the outdoors, especially the mountains. Just prior to entering flight school Roy and a friend were mountain climbing when a rope broke and Roy fell fifty feet, sustaining severe injuries that partially paralyzed his left leg. He overcame the paralysis, not completely, but enough to pass his flight physical. It took a year of determined effort and therapy, during which time the navy sent him to graduate school.[12]

Less than eight weeks after Jeff Johnson flew Pete Russell's lifeless body back home in Black Pony OV-10 No. 107, he was scheduled for a night combat mission, but could not go. Johnson had come down with the intestinal flu and his friend, Roy Sikkink, volunteered to take his hop.

Lieutenant (junior grade) Sikkink copiloted in Lt. Aubrey Martin's back seat on 19 July as they flew wing on Cdr. Gil Winan's Bronco on an armed recce to the "Three Sisters," an area just below the Cambodian border named for some small mountains, six miles southwest of Chau Doc. The mountains near the border jutted up from the surrounding landscape, the only protrusions in the otherwise monotonously flat alluvial Delta. En route Lieutenant (junior grade) Sikkink took an urgent call on the FM radio and the Black Pony patrol was then diverted to Lieutenant Clarke's Duffle Bag target that was being worked by Seawolves.

During Martin and Sikkink's rocket run, at about twenty-five hundred feet of altitude, Commander Winans and four Seawolf helo pilots observed heavy automatic weapons fire directed at the wing aircraft. Martin's and Sikkink's Bronco went into a shallow dive until it impacted an 870-foot mountain at 2105 hours, exploding in a fireball. Since no radio transmissions had been heard and the aircraft made no erratic movements, all the witnesses concluded that the antiaircraft fire had incapacitated both pilots.

In the night sky above, a quarter of a million miles away, a naval aviator and engineer who had dreamed of being an astronaut entered the moon's orbit in preparation for becoming the first man to walk on the moon.

Far below, in a war-torn speck of land on an otherwise peaceful-looking globe, the nature of the steep terrain and proximity to the enemy where Roy Sikkink's and Aubrey Martin's dreams died prevented an immediate ground sweep. The wreckage had been strewn over a large area on both sides of a sheer mountain peak, and little of the remains could be recovered. A CIDG (Civilian Irregular Defense Group—the official name for the people being led by the U.S. Special Forces) had searched the mountain—and found the enemy too.[13]

He Just Came Home

The night Roy Sikkink and Aubrey Martin were lost—that was my flight. Roy took my flight on that night. Not many people know it. Of course, Roy knew it, and Aubrey. . . .

I was sick that day and I had intestinal flu. I was supposed to go out and fly with Aubrey that night. Roy said he'd take that flight for me . . . and I'll regret that all my life. . . .

I finished my tour in Vietnam and I came home and I knew Roy was from Tulsa. An interesting thing happened, one of those mysteries in life. I got hired by and was flying for Delta in 1978, which was about eight or nine years after I left Vietnam. I laid over in Tulsa on a flight, and I had never before contacted Roy's parents or relatives. And Roy was one of my best friends over there. . . . He had the room right next to me in the BOQ, and he and I were buddies, and that's why he took the flight, because he knew I was sick. I had remarked, "Gee and I've got to go flying tonight," and he said, "Oh I'll go do it for you."

While I was in Tulsa in 1978 or '79, I looked in the phone book, and Sikkink with two Ks is a very unusual name, and there were only about two or three in the phone book. So, I just dialed one of them, and sure enough, it was one of his relatives, and they referred me to his mother, Reba, who was the next one down in the phone book. I told her who I was and that I was good friends with him and was real sorry that I hadn't gotten in touch with her sooner, that I just wanted to let her know . . . that I thought a lot of him.

She said, "Well, you know, we just buried Roy—we just had a service for him not very long ago." And I said, "What?" And she said, "Yes, we just got his remains. . . . He just came home."[14]

Jeffery Johnson, Black Pony

7

Establishing a Reputation

The enduring emotion of war, when everything else has faded, is
comradeship.

—William Broyles Jr.

The first group of replacement pilots was in the middle of
weapons training at Yuma, Arizona, when word of the deaths
of Aubrey Martin and Roy Sikkink arrived via message traffic. Cdr. Verle Klein, slated to be the new XO before fleeting
up to become CO, led a group of JO replacements that included one A-4 attack pilot, Lt. Gerry Mahoney. Two other
second-tour aviators, Lts. Bill Robb and Dean Davis, joined
the squadron later. The rest of the pilots in the class were
nuggets from the training command: Lts. (jg) Pete Ford, Vernon
Rosenberger, Charlie Fail, Mike Wolfe, T. Y. Baker, Mark
Byars, Joel Sandberg, and Larry Hone.

Larry Hone had gone to high school in Tulsa with Roy
Sikkink, so the news really brought things close to home.

When Pete Russell was killed with a single round, it could be
rationalized somewhat as a "Golden BB," a fluke of tragic
sorts, but a random event nonetheless. No one thought something like that could happen again, or happen to them. What
were the odds? But with Roy and Aubrey, they were shot
down. That was very real. When I got over there, and when I
flew in the "Three Sisters" area, I saw what kind of a flak trap

that place was. One day I would learn firsthand, when I saw the NVA setting up triangulated antiaircraft sites. And they would bag another Black Pony.[1]

Larry Hone, Black Pony

John Butterfield is the kind of man who if you saw him in a room full of people but did not speak to him, afterwards you would have guessed his height at about five foot six. But if you had talked to him, you would have sworn later that he was well over six feet tall. Marathon runner-thin, wiry, with a shock of light hair and a ready smile, Butterfield could talk anybody out of anything. And at some time in his life, he probably did. He possessed more energy than he could contain, and one couldn't be around him for very long without feeling as if you had to go out and sprint a mile or drop down and do a hundred push-ups. His enthusiasm was contagious. He never drove when he could walk and never walked when he could run. In the mid-1970s Butterfield was a Farsi-speaking naval attaché in Teheran and ran to work every morning, always using a different route. He got to know the city like the back of his hand. It would serve him well. After the shah fell and Ayatollah Khomeini and his cohorts held fifty-four Americans hostage in 1979, the "Rogue Warrior" himself (later the first CO of the counterterrorist SEAL Team Six), Richard Marcinko, hand-picked Butterfield for the Delta Force unit sent on the abortive hostage rescue mission. U.S. Navy Captain Butterfield's job was to drive a truck loaded with Delta troopers into the heart of Teheran.[2]

The monsoon rains swept through Vung Tau during the late afternoon of 17 August and didn't let up when darkness fell. Lt. Cdrs. Don Florko and John Butterfield imagined that it would be a peaceful, although wet night, and they would not be flying. Two hours after midnight the Naval Operations Center in the Advanced Tactical Support Base at Ben Keo received an urgent call on the radio. A Vietnamese Army (ARVN) Airborne base camp on the upper Vam Co Dong River, ten miles southwest of Tay Ninh City, was under attack by a battalion-size NVA force. The North Vietnam Army regulars unleashed a barrage of rockets, mortars, automatic weapons, and small arms fire at the base, from the north, west, and southwest.

United States Navy PBRs sped up the river in order to flank the enemy and the NOC requested Seawolves for air support on the inland side of the base camp. At 0255 when Seawolves and other light helo fire teams reported they were unable to operate because of the low overcast, intense thunder and lightning, and torrential rains, the NOC requested Black

Ponies through the Ben Luc Tactical Operations Center; TOC Ben Luc, forwarded the request to Vung Tau and the Black Ponies immediately scrambled, despite the heavy rains.

United States Air Force "Red Marker" FAC pilot 1st Lt. Bruce Freeman circled beneath the overcast in the driving rains, where the visibility was less than a half mile. He was not expecting to see any other aircraft arrive, let alone fixed-wing Broncos. He wasted no time in putting them to work. Freeman had been helplessly watching the NVA attack an outpost just one hundred meters north of the base. Elements of the 2d Battalion, 3d Brigade were fighting with the enemy less than fifty meters away. Seven of the twelve men in the outpost had been wounded.

The forward air controller quickly coordinated an airborne defense with the ground elements, the PBRs and the Black Ponies. Florko and Butterfield made repeated attacks on the enemy positions using rockets and, when they had to work very close to the friendlies, their mini-guns. Lieutenant Commander Florko in Black Pony 112 then dropped flares at low altitude to help the troops on the ground. Despite the severe weather and antiaircraft fire, the Ponies were credited with driving back the attackers and saving the base camp from being overrun. Troops sweeping the perimeter at first light found the ground littered with enemy bodies.[3]

The Black Ponies were lucky to have some experienced lieutenant commanders whose leadership kept both detachments on an even keel during these turbulent times. These O-4s were slightly older than those field grade officers in the navy today because it took longer to make rank in those days. Some very steady guys, like Zagortz, Florko, Hering, and Butterfield helped fashion and mold this new squadron, and with the cut of their jibs, provided the example that subsequent lieutenant commanders would follow, if they were to be successful.

Cdr. Verle Klein and the first group of replacement pilots could not have arrived in Vietnam at a better time. The loss of three Black Pony pilots in combat, and the inability to replace them until now, was as much of a limit as the availability of aircraft on the squadron's mission. Just to maintain the daily scramble crews and squadron duty officer, each detachment needed five pilots. That meant the remaining pilots had to fly three or four patrols at each detachment. Besides the normal operational commitments, both detachments devoted a few flights a day for Fire Team Leader training. The first replacement group would be arriving with nuggets who had gone through an entire RAG syllabus, including a weapons detachment. A rush was on to make sure that as many first-tour plankowner pilots as possible could be FTL qualified before the new guys arrived.

As Gil Winans's CO tour was coming to an end, he knew he would be turning over the squadron to capable hands. Marty Schuman was a good friend and proved to be an excellent XO. If Gil had a complaint it was that Marty managed to fly more hours than he did. But that was Marty. He always seemed to be everywhere. Gregarious, back-slapping, and with a keen sense of humor, he could get anyone to do anything. Just what was needed in an XO. With his New York accent, when he put his arm on your shoulder, Gil Winans used to say, you thought Marty was sizing you up for a suit he wanted to sell you. And you always bought it.

In a change of command ceremony on 6 September, Marty Schuman relieved Gil Winans. By the end of the next month, just six months after arriving in-country, this single squadron killed more enemy troops and destroyed more enemy structures and waterborne craft than the rest of the Seventh Fleet squadrons combined.[4] But that success came with a heavy price.

When Gil Winans and Pete Russell flew with VA-176, that squadron came back from its combat cruise with only one casualty. But when he is asked what his memories of VAL-4 were, Gil Winans replies that his overriding feeling was one of dissatisfaction and sadness. Winans had figured that as commanding officer of VAL-4, with his VA-176 combat cruise experience and his best effort, he could bring everybody back. That was his goal. It may have been an unrealistic one, but it was his to set and his to strive for. To have lost someone so close to him as Pete Russell, then to have lost two more pilots, deeply affected Gil Winans. By any yardstick Gil's accomplishments were extraordinary. He assembled and molded, in just a few months, one of the most effective air units in the Vietnam War. He was proud to have put together the squadron, made up as it was of men of disparate backgrounds and no combat experience, but he still felt dissatisfied. And he doesn't know what he could have done differently.[5]

When word spread about the effectiveness of the Black Ponies, it was not just among the riverine warriors for whom the Ponies worked. Captured enemy documents revealed that the Black Ponies caused increasing fear and concern among the Vietcong and NVA soldiers. They even came up with a distinctive name for OV-10, which because of its unusual twin-boom tail, must have resembled a holding pen that local farmers used. What other reason could there be for giving the Bronco the not-very-romantic name of "the pigsty airplane"? What the Black Pony pilots did with the pigsty airplane elicited an even more distinctive response.

> We had been informed that captured enemy documents had revealed that the VC/NVA had "Wanted, Dead or Alive" posters on many of the Black Pony pilots, mentioning them by name. We were "worth" killing to the tune of at least 650,000 piasters. Even at the MACV rate of exchange (about 115 to the dollar) that wasn't chump change. Word spread through the squadron after a Seawolf helicopter had been shot down that the enemy had skinned the pilots and put their bodies back into the helo as a message. There was no doubt—they feared Seawolves and Black Ponies.[6]
> Gary Rezeau, Black Pony

The Black Ponies and Special Warfare (SpecWar) Support

The Black Ponies worked very closely with the navy's SEALs, elite naval commandos tasked with gathering intelligence and operating behind enemy lines to capture, abduct, ambush, raid, and generally create havoc. By providing close air support, often during a critical SEAL extraction, the tremendous firepower that the OV-10 could bring to bear on the enemy saved the life of many a SEAL.

Seawolf UH-1B and UH-1L helicopters and Black Pony fixed-wing OV-10s provided close air support for SEALs throughout the Delta. In addition to gunship support, Seawolves provided armed transport for SEALs. When army helos could or would not extract SEALs after combat operations, Seawolves would often jettison ordnance and equipment and rush in under fire to pull SEALs out to safety. SEALs also knew that, if they were in dire straits and needed the "heavy stuff," they could call in the Black Ponies. Because of their speed, quick reaction time, and frequent random patrols, the Black Ponies could be on target in minutes. With the 5-inch Zuni rockets, cannon, and other ordnance, Black Ponies could bring a devastating array of firepower to bear on the enemy. And their time on-station would prove on numerous occasions to make the difference between a safe extraction and none at all. Many SEAL after-action reports, known as "barndance cards," praise the Seawolves and Black Ponies for their courage and effectiveness.[7]

As the brown water navy evolved in Vietnam, so did the role of the SEALs. Originally formed as a counterinsurgency force, the navy SEAL history, while growing out of the World War II frogman experience, began with Vietnam. In order to counter the new global threat of "wars of national liberation," newly elected President John F. Kennedy issued an executive order for each branch of the military to form a counterguerrilla force. The army's Special Forces became known as the Green Berets and the air force's unit as the Air Commandos. The navy's Special Warfare (SpecWar) commandos became known as SEALs (an acronym standing for SEa, Air, and Land) after the marine mammal that is equally at home on the land and at sea.[8]

Recruited from underwater demolition training (UDT), navy frogmen were trained in U.S. Army, Navy, Air Force, and Marine Corps schools to fight on land or sea, and to infiltrate by air, if necessary. On 8 January 1962 the navy commissioned SEAL Team One at Coronado, California, and SEAL Team Two at Little Creek, Virginia. Each team consisted of ten officers and fifty enlisted men. Eventually the teams would grow to twenty-three officers and 115 men in the platoons.[9]

By March 1962 the navy had sent a SEAL mobile training team (MTT) to advise and train South Vietnamese military units. The navy initially deployed the SEALs in and around Da Nang, where they trained the South Vietnamese in combat diving, counterinsurgency tactics, and demolitions. As the American buildup began, the navy brought the SEALs into the Rung Sat Special Zone with the mission to disrupt enemy operations in this vital shipping channel. The navy also positioned SEALs in the Mekong Delta to augment riverine operations.

As America's direct involvement in the war increased, the SEAL mission changed from "advising" to direct action. In January 1964, Capt. Phillip H. Bucklew, a legendary World War II navy frogman, took over a U.S. survey team tasked with studying the extent of communist insurgency in the Mekong Delta. The survey team, which included a member of SEAL Team One, and was highly experienced in unconventional warfare, issued a report that recommended deploying SEALs in active combat roles.[10]

In 1966 SEALs began operating in "direct action platoons," operating under Detachment Golf and organized as twelve- to fourteen-man platoons, or six- to seven-man squads. Each SEAL would serve a six-month tour of duty in-country, and usually the entire platoon would rotate back to the States together.

The SEAL Team One platoons were known by letter designations and, in order to avoid confusion, SEAL Team Two's platoons were given numerical designations.

Detachment Alpha consisted of all SEAL Team Two direct action platoons.

As SEALs from both teams became veterans of one or more combat tours, they might be assigned to Det Bravo, to advise provincial reconnaissance units (PRUs). Others found assignments to Det Sierra, where they would train the South Vietnamese Navy's *Lien Doc Nguoi Nhia,* or "soldiers who fight under the sea." The LDNN, as they were known, were the South Vietnamese Navy's version of SEALs.[11] Still other SEAL combat veterans would be assigned to Det Echo and the Military Assistance Command, Vietnam, Studies and Observations Group (USMACV-SOG). Known as SOG, it was a cover for top-secret covert operations that included direct action and reconnaissance into North Vietnam, Cambodia, and Laos.[12] The Black Ponies would work with all SEAL detachments at one time or another.

SEALs were trained to kill at short range using unconventional tactics. They soon proved to be the most effective counterguerilla operatives in the Vietnam War. It did not take long for the SEALs to make an impression on the enemy. Using the communist guerillas' own tactics, and wearing camouflaged uniforms and face paint, these elite commandos began to be called "the men with green faces" by the enemy.

Between 1965 and 1972 forty-six SEALs were killed in Vietnam. SEALS never numbered more than 150 men in-country at any one time, yet their small numbers accounted for a disproportionately large number of enemy casualties. Between fifty (confirmed) and two hundred (probable) enemy were killed for every SEAL loss.[13]

Thy Neighbor's Keeper

I was standing my first scramble duty, assigned as the back seat pilot in the lead aircraft of a two-plane Fire Team. At the urgent clamor of the field phone, the front seat pilot, Lt. Charles Sapp, leaped for his gear, and I was only a startled second behind.

Our wingman, Lt. (jg) Jim Brewster, nearly tripped over himself jumping out of the scramble crew bunk, while his copilot, Dan Sheehan, was already headed for the flight line where his torso harness, survival vest, and helmet were prepositioned in the plane. Short, round, and graced with a drooping black mustache, Dan looked and acted every bit the part of the "Frito Bandito," a popular television commercial character. And "Frito" played his role to the hilt. He never ran when he could walk, never walked when he could ride. Thus, his all-out sprint to the revetments alerted and alarmed the line crews even before the klaxon sounded.

As taught during my recent indoctrination, I copied the coordinates, frequency, and call sign of the unit in trouble, while Lt. (jg) Mike Wolfe, the duty officer, plotted the target area on the wall-to-wall map of the IV Corps Tactical zone, which depicted the southern part of South Vietnam.

"It plots out the 210 radial at about forty-five miles," Mike hollered as I rushed out the door.

Charlie had the port engine turning as I climbed into the rear cockpit of our Bronco. When Charlie turned up the starboard engine, I filled him in on what had come over the field phone. "Steer 210 for forty-five miles. A SEAL platoon is surrounded, and the helos can't get in for the extraction. On-scene commander is Seawolf Two Two."

"Scramble One?" he asked, referring to the highest priority.

"Affirmative. They're in deep shit."

Charlie maneuvered the little plane out of the four-foot-thick steel and concrete revetment, with Jim and Frito falling in right behind.

"Binh Thuy tower, this is Black Pony Six—taxi two for Scramble One."

In an emergency, the American observer took control in the tower of the airfield we shared with the Vietnamese Air Force. His familiar tone was assurance that we had priority.

"Roger Pony Six. Taxi to the arming area, and you're cleared for take-off. There's a Caribou on downwind, but he'll hold off until you clear the runway."

As we braked in the arming area, the practiced arming crew swarmed over the aircraft, pulling the safety pins and attaching the electrical harnesses for the rockets, and arming the machine guns. At the same time, I completed my re-plot of the target. As the copilot of the lead aircraft, I was responsible for the navigation and air-to-ground communication.

"Pony One Zero, this is Six. The target is on the east bank of a squiggly located 210 at forty-five miles. Look at chart 51: Coordinates Victor Sierra 910,550."

Jim and Frito located the small stream where the SEALs were under fire. "Pony One Zero has the target."

Taking the runway in a controlled turn, Charlie added power and accelerated into the takeoff roll. Jim worked his throttle to hold perfect position just aft, and the number two aircraft launched in formation. Passing the end of the runway, my eyes—as they always did—fell on the hull of a cargo plane which had been shot down by VC fire prior to my arrival. I suspected the commodore left it there to give us young Turks pause for thought.

Under a full load in the tropical heat and humidity, the little aircraft struggled for altitude. Passing three thousand feet, I began trying to make radio contact. "Seawolf Two Two, this is Black Pony Six enroute with a two-plane Fire Team."

The reply was immediate. "Roger, Pony One Six. This is Seawolf Twenty-two. We've got a SEAL team on the western side of the stream running north and south. There are two tree lines, and the SEALs are on the western one. I repeat—western tree line. The bad guys are in the eastern tree line closest to the stream. The SEAL's call sign is "Maddog" and he's up this push. Seawolf Two Two is circling west of the target at four thousand feet."

"Roger Seawolf. We're about ten minutes out. Break—Maddog, this is Pony Six. The cavalry is on the way!"

"Roger Pony Six. Hurry up—the natives are restless."

Despite his quivering voice, the SEAL radio operator maintained the laconic radio discipline expected of such a crack unit. In the background of his radio transmission, and like the chains of small firecrackers set off on the Fourth of July, small arms fire sounded an angry, insistent counterpoint to his reply.

Once over the target area, I called for identification, and Maddog popped a smoke grenade. "Roger Maddog, Pony Six has green smoke."

"Pony Six, we're within ten yards of that smoke, and the bad guys are in the tree line to our east. We're marking the target with tracer."

The stream of fiery red tracers seemed to be a misplaced thread in the idyllic, lush fabric of green jungle. They pointed clearly to a thick line of trees bordering the stream. The canopy prevented us from seeing the enemy hidden below.

Charlie stood the plane on its wing, let the nose fall through, and rolled out on a line of attack that took us from south to north up the tree line. At four thousand feet he used the machine guns to walk fire into the center of the target area, and at thirty-six hundred feet he pickled off a Zuni. Even in daylight, the flash of the ignited rocket motor was startling.

"Pony Six is off, left." As Charlie yanked the stick, I strained against the G forces to look back at the impact point. "Maddog, was that on target?"

"Hell yes! Pour it on!"

Jim rolled in at an angle to our line of attack. "Pony Ten is in and I've got you in sight, lead."

We made several runs, mixing our ordnance. Sometimes guns, sometimes rockets, and sometimes both. The thick growth seemed at first to quietly absorb everything we threw, and its beauty remained undisturbed. But gradually a cloud of smoke and dust began to form over the center of the tree line. With over half our ordnance expended, we paused in the attack and circled overhead, watching closely as the helicopters tried again for the extraction.

Impulsively, Charlie came up on the radio. "Is there a SEAL down there from Miguel Avenue in Coronado?"

After a short delay, a new voice drifted up. "Charlie, you son of a bitch, what took you so long to get here?"

Charlie replied, "Betty told me I had to look after you, so here I am. Are we having fun yet?"

Lieutenant Charles "Sandy" Prouty, call sign Maddog and leader of a SEAL platoon that had stumbled into a company of Vietcong returning to the war after rest and recreation in the jungles of the Ca Mau peninsula, replied with laughter. There were no firecrackers in the background.

As the helicopters approached the landing zone, we rolled in again to suppress any remaining fire. We continued the runs until the helos had lifted off with the SEALs onboard and had cleared the target area. Pulling out of the last run, the radio came to life again. The soft thudding of straining rotors could be heard in the background as Sandy shouted, "Charlie, you want me to kiss your ass now, or later?"

On Miguel Avenue in Coronado, California, Marsha Sapp and Betty Prouty watched the kids, wondering why civilians were not as caught up in the war as they, and cried together. In the beautiful but deceptively dangerous jungles of South Vietnam, Charlie flew close air support for his next door neighbor, Sandy.[14]

T. Y. Baker, Black Pony

Black Pony Wranglers

One secret behind the success of the Black Ponies was the incredible effort of the enlisted men who maintained the Broncos. Nowadays we would call them "maintainers." Back then they were known as "the men," or sometimes, the "wranglers." Young and hardworking, many stayed beyond their one-year tour and extended for an additional six months or a year. They lived and worked in conditions that would seem primitive and dangerous to most people.

The squadron started out undermanned and would never really catch up. And because of the tempo of combat operations, some specialties, like ordnancemen, were always critically short. Virtually every enlisted man, regardless of rating, loaded rockets and ammunition while they were Black Ponies. Their long hours of backbreaking work in heat, humidity, and monsoon rains and accompanied by occasional rocket, mortar, and sapper attacks had little in terms of daily rewards. But one would be hard pressed to find a Black Pony officer who did not say, thirty years later, that these were the finest men they have ever served with in their navy careers.

I started out as a nineteen-year-old airman in January 1970 and left as a hydraulicsman 2d class in July 1971. When I first got there I couldn't believe how hot and dusty it was. I hated it in the middle of the dry season. And the stench from the low-grade gasoline that the Vietnamese vehicles used and the diesel fuel from all the deuce-and-a-half trucks with the high sulfur content that permeated the air.

I was supposed to be a plane captain but the line chief said, "No, forget it. Your job is to load Zunis." I got proficient at the LAU-10, the LAU-69, and the LAU-68. I learned to arm the planes . . . the only thing I didn't do was load the M-60s. Chief Langlois always left that to an

AO [aviation ordnanceman]. I did an awful lot of ordnance work before I started working my rate as a hydraulicsman.

I started working in my rate after the squadron got a few more ordnancemen. But even still, in VAL-4, when things got very hot and heavy, everybody was called out of the shops to go load Zunis. . . .

On a typical day we woke up at about 0530, depending on whether you were on the night or day crew. We worked twelve on and twelve off. We cleaned up, went to the chow hall for breakfast, and then there were two trucks to get you over to VNAF Binh Thuy. I was always on the first truck that left about 0645, so I could get the "pass down" from the night crew, what needed to be done, what needed to be loaded, and so on. I remember the ordnance chief, Chester Langlois. He was your typical, robust navy chief. He always got on that truck like he just rolled out of the rack with a cup of coffee in his hand. As soon as a third of that cup was consumed he was talking. For a lot of us new guys, the younger ones, he mentored us. We took a lot of our orders and directions from him. He was the one who taught us how to build up and load Zunis. He was very knowledgeable. We'd get there to the line and start taking rockets out of the boxes, put the warheads on, then stockpile semi-assembled rockets—then pull the cart up to the plane and load them. In the first few months I did that for twelve hours. Assemble, haul, load, stage, stockpile—all day long.

Lunch was terrible at the airfield chow hall . . . that air force chow was the pits. I'd usually forgo lunch or had C-rats. Then back to the same routine. When a scramble happened everybody would turn to—pulling chocks, starting the planes, arming them, refueling them, rearming them. Never a dull moment. There were some down times, but always something to do, a buddy to chat with, a story to tell, or a story to listen to. The day went by amazingly fast. So fast that by the time dinnertime ran around, after the 1900 shift change, and we got trucked back to Binh Thuy, we got the last meal that the chow hall served. And it was always good, especially after a day like that and the chow at the airfield. . . .

In the barracks at night, you'd shower and relax. You'd either listen to music from all the stereo systems, big fancy reel-to-reel decks, or drink beer and talk to your buddies. Or try to find some time to scribble a letter home, usually after you collected your mail. Then it was to bed very early—and it was 0530 again.

As I advanced in rank I did more maintenance work like drop checking the landing gear, replacing the strut actuator, and repairing bullet holes. I spent a little bit of time with the check crew back at Navy Binh Thuy, not that much, but working with guys to repair stress cracks that started appearing on the Broncos. The skins were starting to crack at the rivet lines from the G forces. I had a bit of a mechanical background. I did a lot of work on nose wheel actuators. That was very problematic on the Bronco. The rest of the hydraulics and flight control systems were okay. The other real big job associated with keeping this bird flying was repairing bullet holes. I got to do my share of that as well, putting on the patches and so on.

I had just made second class, nearing the end of my tour. One of the planes took a hit from .51 caliber round in a wing spar where the spar and fuselage connect, and it was a real tricky mending job. I was assigned to the North American Rockwell tech rep, working with him for several days. He guided me and I did most of the work as we developed the strategy to repair this wing spar. And we did it. I walked off that job with a real sense of accomplishment. I did a variety of jobs that made the experience interesting.

We worked seven days on and one off. I would sometimes go into Ben Xe Moi or Can Tho, or go to the PX. . . . I'd run shotgun on the stake-bed truck running rocket boxes to the orphanage. I enjoyed spending an afternoon playing with the kids out there. It was a great diversion.[15]

John Edwin Skwara, Black Pony

Looking for a POW

After the new replacement pilots arrived they were divided between Vung Tau and Binh Thuy, and they settled in very quickly. When then-Lt. (jg) Charlie Fail moved into the villa at Vung Tau that served as the BOQ he found himself living next door to Lt. Cdr. John "Jack" Graf, a naval intelligence officer who occasionally flew with the Black Ponies. Jack Graf was a bright, interesting man who attracted many colorful characters as visitors to the villa, many of them beautiful, well-connected Vietnamese women from Saigon government and social circles. Stories circulated about his spy background and there was an aura of *Terry and the Pirates* surrounding the comings and goings of Jack and his entourage.

Lieutenant Commander Graf worked with the Joint Personnel Recovery Center (JPRC), a unit that analyzed intelligence and organized clandestine raids to recover POWs. Graf had a special interest in finding and rescuing American POWs he knew to be held in camps in the Mekong Delta. He had been working on intelligence reports about two crewmembers of an army OV-1 Mohawk attached to the 73d Army Surveillance Aircraft Company out of Vung Tau that had been shot down on the coast of Vinh Binh Province on 9 June 1965.[16] He suspected that they were being held captive in a camp nearby, so he planned a reconnaissance flight over the area in preparation for a SEAL insertion. On 15 November Lieutenant Commander Graf flew in the right seat of an army OV-1 Mohawk piloted by 1st Lt. Robert White, call sign "Up Tight," from the same 73d that the POWs had been attached to. They circled the area, looking for signs of the camp.

A short time later, a U.S. Navy patrol boat observed White and Graf successfully eject from their burning aircraft. Black Ponies were scrambled and extensive air and ground searches failed to find the two men. They had been shot down at virtually the exact coordinates at which the other Mohawk had gone down.[17] Two years later, Black Pony pilot Bubba Segars and Ed Smith, the naval intelligence officer in his back seat, were shot down at the same place.[18] Not long before the flight with Bubba, Smith had read an intelligence document that had been captured thirteen months after Graf's and White's capture. It contained the enemy's interrogation report of Lt. Cdr. Jack Graf.[19]

In the months after Graf was shot down, several SEAL ops had been planned to look for him. Lt. (jg) T. Y. Baker attended a briefing by a SEAL officer prior to launching on a flight to support them on one of these planned ops.

> "Five SEALs will be going into a camp guarded by fifty hard core NVA," the SEAL informed us. Nobody said anything. So I raised my hand and said, "Wait a minute, I want to be sure I understand this. There's five SEALs and fifty bad guys."
>
> He said, "Yeah, we figure the odds are about right."
>
> So I shut the hell up. . . .
>
> Unfortunately, when they got there, nobody was home . . . so we didn't shoot for them.[20]
>
> T. Y. Baker, Black Pony

8

Changing Direction

Death is not the greatest loss in life. The greatest loss is what dies inside us while we live.

—Norman Cousins

The Seventh Air Force complained again that Black Ponies were too effective, and they had been showing up air force tactical air (TacAir). Actually, Ponies had been showing up before the air force could get to the target and, by the time they did arrive, the job had been done and the Ponies had gone home, leaving the forward air controllers who called in TacAir embarrassed. What had been happening is that ground forces in the Delta who came into contact with the enemy and were in critical situations had by then come to know the quick responsiveness, the tremendous firepower, and the accuracy of the Black Ponies. So they had been calling the NOCs in the area requesting Ponies be scrambled. Occasionally both TacAir and Ponies had been called. The latest complaint had been made at the IV Corps combined command level after one such incident where the Black Ponies arrived overhead fifteen minutes after they were requested. The air force O-2 FAC merely orbited the scene and observed the air strike because (since the last complaint) they were no longer permitted to direct navy air strikes. When the air force jets arrived one hour later, the Broncos had long since departed and the ground troops had moved from the area.[1]

Over the last few months 75 percent of the combat missions flown from Binh Thuy had been in support of U.S. Army or Vietnamese forces and 25 percent of Vung Tau's missions had supported forces other than the U.S. or Vietnamese Navy. This meant that only half of VAL-4's missions were in support of navy units, the squadron's primary mission.

Monsoon rains had been diminishing as the year was coming to an end, causing many of the smaller streams and canals to dry up, which had the unusual effect of increasing the density of enemy boat activity, especially along the Cambodian border. The result—more troops in contact, more outposts being attacked, more patrol boat ambushes, and more scrambles.

The alert crew scrambled four times during the night of 10–11 December, hot refueling and rearming to return to the Vam Co Tay River where two PBRs and two ASPBs (assault support and patrol boats) were helping an outpost that had been attacked by enemy forces, killing two and wounding four. Just as a U.S. Army Special Forces advisor radioed that the outpost was being overrun, Lt. (jg) Charlie Fail in Black Pony 105 led an attack that suppressed the assault and allowed the ASPBs to reach the outpost.[2]

Squadron aircraft were being flown an average of 110 hours a month, much beyond what had been projected, which taxed resources to the max. Each month, confirmed results from air strikes exceeded that of any tactical air unit in Vietnam.[3] The twelve new pilots were becoming seasoned and members of the original contingent were counting the days in double digits as they were now "short timers." A new replacement class of ten began arriving in November: three lieutenant commanders, Bill Dobbs, John Westerman, and Jimmy Hanks; and six junior officers, Devin Burke, Graham Forsyth, Larry Laughon, Jim Montgomery, Butch Underkoffler, and Jim Bohanna.

Settling in at Vung Tau

One of the mechs got thrown into the army brig at Vung Tau. I fished him out. The army colonel who commanded the base had crawled under a jeep in front of the chow hall [trying to figure out if it was his]. Unfortunately it had been the colonel's spare jeep, which Butch Underkoffler and I had stolen "fair and square" from the GCI site, a gun control radar they were using as precision approach radar. We used to roll jeeps into the revetment and repaint them. So we had this "regular navy jeep." It had parts that the SEALs up at Cat Lo had given us. We had been driving the thing for months. The navy had given us no vehicles. Every vehicle that we had came out of a junkyard or it was stolen. Or it was traded for. *Cumshaw* is the word for it.

So I went over to the brig and told them that it wasn't this kid's problem, he had only been driving it, and I would look into it. Of course I'm a big wheel lieutenant, for all of about a month. [But] Lt. Cdr. Bill Dobbs, who turned into a flight-time hog, but a really good guy, was brand-new over there. He said, "Hell, we're going to have to court-martial the guy for stealing that jeep."

I said, "Whoa, whoa, just a minute, you don't understand. He didn't steal the jeep." And he said, "Who did?" So I had to fess up. "Well, shit, I did." He goes, "Well, we'll have to court-martial you." So I said, "I think we better talk about this, Sir. Can we kinda like go outside here and . . . let me tell you how this works?"

I explained where everything came from over there. He was the new guy on the block. "See that car you're driving, the O-in-C car? Who do you think that belongs to? There's a certain LST still looking for that."

That wasn't as bad as Larry Hone and [me] trying to move a padlocked jeep, and a guy walks up and said, "What are you doing?" We said, "We forgot the key to our jeep." He said, "Well, that's my jeep." We said, "Oh? We're really sorry."

An enlisted kid named Zinn was the best cumshaw guy at Vung Tau. Underkoffler was a pretty good thief. Butterfield was excellent. He actually went through channels sometimes. He had such a gift of gab, and he was so intelligent that he'd convince them that they really ought to be giving it to us. Sometimes things he traded really didn't exist. He was an operator. We always wanted to play basketball but didn't have any place to play. So the army engineers who ran the sand and gravel quarry drove right by our back gate—we cumshawed for some Scotch . . . a couple truckloads of sand and gravel and some concrete, and we built a wash rack for the airplanes that just happened to be the size of a basketball court. It had baskets at each end. We had some engineers come by and supervise. We actually flew one down.

And Hone and Soup and a couple guys had a less-than-legal transport company going with a couple of army transport pilots.[4]

Gerry Mahoney, Black Pony

"Appropriated" vehicles were driven down from Long Binh. If it were after dark, Black Ponies would fly air cover, because the road was closed at night. Soup Campbell's friend from high school, Walt Collins, an air force C-7 pilot, would take one to three vehicles after repaint and fly them to Binh Thuy, trading for bottles of booze. Other vehicles, usually real Jeeps, went back to Vung Tau. The SEALs ran a chop shop near Long Binh. All this was possible because the roads were closed between Vung Tau and Binh Thuy and no one suspected missing vehicles could materialize in one place that had disappeared from another.[5]

I was the maintenance officer up there at Vung Tau by default. Zinn, the airman storekeeper, I'd fly him around and turn him loose. Give him a couple of chits and he'd come back with a whole airplane load of crap. He was an artist. If you needed something, he'd find it.

Bill Robb had a brother who was a recon marine on the teams that went into the North to pick up pilots. We'd go down to the Grand Hotel, the R and R place downtown, and there's a few navy pilots, a few air force, and a thousand army guys. We'd have a few drinks and about then Bill Robb says, "Our marine can whip anybody in the house." Of course there's only one marine in the house and that poor guy's crawling under the table, saying, "Holy shit! Thanks a lot, brother."[6]

Gerry Mahoney, Black Pony

The Vung Tau detachment had been flying daily patrols over the Saigon River since mid-May when a number of ships had been attacked, and one sunk, as they plied the waters of the Long Tau Shipping Channel to Saigon and back. The armed Light Attack Fire Teams carried external fuel tanks for extended range, and the pilots found the missions boring and uncomfortable. Three to five hours sitting on a hard ejection seat was bad enough, but the enemy rarely fired on the ships when the Ponies were overhead. Ponies complained that the mission was a waste of assets, since other smaller, lighter armed aircraft could be used just as effectively. But their complaints fell on deaf ears since this was indeed a navy mission. A compromise was reached and on Monday 28 July the Black Ponies began flying single-ship air cover patrols with a marine air observer in the rear cockpit. A single Bronco would be loaded with M-60s only, thus freeing up three pilots and another plane, which would help with operational commitments after the loss of Martin and Sikkink and their aircraft. Sending out a single aircraft would have its own dangers, however, as the Black Ponies would soon learn.

On 20 December Lt. (jg) Joel Sandberg and his rear seat observer, a marine captain named Carl Long, launched from Vung Tau on a late-afternoon single-ship mission over the Rung Sat. While working with Moon River Naval Operations Center they descended to low altitude to check out a suspicious looking sampan, eight nautical miles northwest of Vung Tau. The NOC then lost radio contact with the Black Pony OV-10. Fifty minutes later a helicopter spotted the burning wreckage of the Bronco. Hovering overhead, the helo pilots reported at 1730 that the forward half of the burning OV-10 was buried in mud and debris and the canopies could not be seen to determine if the pilots had ejected. Extensive search and rescue efforts found no pilots or signs of them.

Since darkness was fast approaching, Vietnamese Marines were called in to secure the area with a perimeter around the wreckage until recovery teams could reach the area, accessible only by boat or helicopter. Recovery forces, including many Black Pony officers and enlisted men, reached the site the next morning by helicopter. When they dropped into the tidal swamp the men sunk waist deep into the mud. With each high tide, the recovery team had to be extracted.[7]

Lt. Gerry Mahoney and Lt. (jg) Charlie Fail were the first two officers on the scene. They searched for signs of an ejection but determined that no one had. Mahoney saw what appeared to be a row of .30 caliber bullet holes in one of the tail booms, which indicated the Bronco probably was shot down. The wreckage was too far down in the mud, and the tides made it impossible to dig, so the efforts had to be abandoned until conditions improved.

A few weeks later recovery crews returned with boats, pumps, digging equipment, and shoring material. Army recovery experts accompanied the Black Ponies and Vietnamese Rangers. An H-47 "Superhook" helicopter tried to pull the Bronco out but the cable snapped. The plane was too stuck in the mud. Everyone knew the pilot's and the observer's bodies were down there, in the mud. Everyone knew how important it was to recover them. The mud, the tide, the weather, sickly fumes from jet fuel, all conspired to defeat the best efforts of the recovery team. When it became apparent that recovery would be virtually impossible, the pressure built. No one wanted to give up. And in the back of everyone's mind was the knowledge that families and loved ones might forever be condemned to that doubt that would always exist about those classified as missing in action. Through nausea and fatigue, injuries and tears, the men raced against the clock and the elements.[8]

You were in mud and jet fuel up to your waist . . . digging and working the shoring material, plywood and stuff. We brought in pumps to pump out the mud . . . but to no avail. A boatswain's mate we called "Boats" had stuck a probe into the mud. . . . He found something that wasn't hard but it wasn't soft either. . . . There was something there, so we concentrated our efforts on that area. After a while we had some escaping smells . . . that came up out of the ground, so we knew we were in the right area. The Vietnamese Rangers passed around eucalyptus oil for us to rub under our noses . . . they were quite a bit smarter on these matters than we were. It ended up being a bucket brigade of helmets just scooping out mud as we got deeper and deeper. . . .

Finally we got down to the top of the seat . . . and as the ejection seat mechanic, an AME3 [aviation structural mechanic (safety equipment)

3d class] my position was at the bottom of the hole. I found the pilot's helmet first. Eventually we got down to just below the neck. . . . We couldn't get any farther with the mud coming in and the fuselage of the aircraft in the way. . . . So they decided . . . the army recovery guys . . . that they needed the head for positive I.D . . . so I had to cut it off. . . . We passed it up to someone who put it in a body bag. The helmet had his name on it.[9]

Bob Peetz, Black Pony

9

Farewell to the Plankowners

What I felt was the shock, then instantly the relief. Shock, relief.
Fear, the intermediate step, was missing. And during the second
that followed the shock I did not live in the expectancy of death in
the second to come, but in the conviction of resurrection born to
the second just past. I lived in a sort of slipstream of joy, in the
wake of my jubilation.

—Antoine de Saint-Exupéry, *Flight to Arras*

For the enlisted men and officers of VAL-4, their first Christmas in Vietnam was difficult enough, and with the losses they had endured, the pain of family separation would be even more acute. The shared experiences of life in a strange and remote place, of hard work and travail, of combat and death, would also draw the Black Ponies closer together. Beyond the normal working relationships, beyond even the friendships that naturally develop, the bonds between the men who worked, played, and fought together nurtured and strengthened and grew in adversity. The younger enlisted men, many of whom had never been away from home before, found leadership, guidance, and wisdom from their noncom mentors, just as the experienced officers had taken the JOs under their wings. This was at a time when discipline and drug problems and racial discord abounded in the military, especially in Vietnam. Even the relationships between the officers and the enlisted Black Ponies became stronger and more unique than in most other military organizations. The way in which officers and men worked together every day—and during the extraordinary recovery efforts of one of their own lost in combat—characterized the uniqueness of the Black Ponies. Pilots and plane captains talked at length about missions. Officers helped ordies (ordnance men) build up and haul and load Zuni rockets. Enlisted men and officers pitched in together and built schoolrooms out of rocket boxes for local school children. And PO Bob Peetz sought out Lt. Gerry Mahoney to talk out the horror and pain of what he had to do for the benefit of a squadron mate's family. The Black Ponies had become an unusually tight-knit unit.

A few of the original contingent of pilots looked forward to rotating back home in December. Not being able to contain their exuberance, Charlie Sapp and Jerry Wheeler stood on desks in the Ops department, which had been decorated with a scrawny tree, and sang, "I'll be Home For Christmas." The rest would postpone Christmas celebrations for a few weeks. For them and all the other Black Ponies, Christmas in Vietnam would be a surreal experience. In the monthly *Family Gram* (dated 30 January 1970) sent to families in the States, Black Ponies reported:

> Our first Christmas season in Vietnam is one we'll never forget. Christmas isn't Christmas without gifts, so with money from Special Services several hundred children's gifts were purchased and distributed. In Binh Thuy, Christmas day was spent visiting three orphanages, and the pleasure the kids took in the gifts was the highlight of our holiday. In Vung Tau, the men took the spirit of Christmas into the Rung Sat Special Zone to the village people there. The villagers returned the favor by presenting the detachment with a small black puppy now called, appropriately, Rung Sat. The individual parties held at Vung Tau and Binh Thuy were enjoyable, but nothing could replace the pleasure of being with small children at Christmas.
>
> A Black Pony PAO[1]

The third group of replacement pilots reported aboard in January: Lt. Codrs. John Thomas and Jim Hardie; Lts. Ray Bunton, Jim Falls, John McColly; and Lts. (jg) Ray Kellett, Mike Monagan, Ross Hanover, and Tom Bailey. Warrant Officer 1st Class John Meadows and Lt. Richard "Dick" Murkland joined the ranks of the Maintenance Department.

The original contingent of pilots was about to rotate back to the States and the first replacement plots were becoming veterans themselves, one mark of which was the degree of irreverence they sometimes displayed toward the "old timers." The JGs did not like flying with one particular pilot whose name could have been Dilbert and whose airmanship they considered questionable. So the JGs created the "DUDS count," which stood for "days until Dilbert separates." The JGs put a number up on the board in the bunker, and when they briefed a flight, they would say, "The DUDS count is. . ." Everybody knew what it was except for Dilbert. Even when a flight checked in with Red Rose, the flight following service, after takeoff, Red Rose would confirm the DUDS count. It was only in the last week before he was due to rotate out that Dilbert figured out what it was.[2]

Mike Monagan's dad was a California politician. He knew he was not going to stay in the navy and sometimes acted like it. When Lt. Cdr. Jim Becker chewed him out one day, Monagan said, "Excuse me a second, Mr. Becker. Hold that thought while I go out in the hall and see if I can find somebody who gives a shit," and walked out. Monagan said it so smoothly, with an almost diplomatic flair, that Becker just had to smile.[3] The junior officers were pretty irreverent, but not openly insubordinate. They didn't need to be. They could always find a way—usually colorful— to deal with incompetence, indolence, or anything else that rubbed them collectively the wrong way. Usually it was done in the guise of having great fun, often when the offender was in his cups, or otherwise most vulnerable, such as at a gathering in his honor. "Hail and farewell" parties provided appropriate and regular venues, but any impromptu gathering of two or more JOs would work just as well. You didn't want to be a Black Pony if you didn't have thick skin.

The Seventh Air Force changed its policy again and decided to allow USAF FACs in IV Corp, 22d TASS (Tactical Air Support Squadron), to work with Black Ponies. They had to first call in TacAir and could not "scramble" Ponies, but they could divert Black Ponies that may have been on an airborne patrol. The result was that Ponies arrived long before TacAir aircraft, as usual, but it proved beneficial to those on the ground because the Ponies otherwise might not have been called in. At a meeting where the new rules of engagement were discussed, only one air force pilot had been in-country long enough to have worked with the Black Ponies before the ban was lifted. When asked for his comments about working with VAL-4, his reply brought smiles to the navy representatives at the meeting. He said working with the Black Ponies had been great except for one frustrating thing. The Bronco outturns the Cessna O-2 and flies a tighter attack pattern than the O-2 can maintain, he volunteered, forcing the FAC to move his pattern off to the side of the target in order to keep both aircraft in sight all the time.[4]

On Wednesday 21 January Cdr. Marty Schuman flew a strike mission with Admiral Zumwalt in his back seat and Brigadier General Roberts, the TacAir commander, Seventh Air Force, in Cdr. Verle Klein's rear cockpit. The general had wanted to compare the capabilities of the OV-10 and the A-37B aircraft to perform the navy mission. While that was the stated purpose of the flight, it also went a long way to improve the relations with the Seventh Air Force.

When the flight was over, instead of flying back to Binh Thuy, arrangements had been made to land at the short Marston matting strip near Chi Lang, where a helicopter would pick up Admiral Zumwalt. Commander Klein orbited overhead with General Roberts while Commander Schuman made a steep approach to the short strip.

> Marty Schuman had gone out and done his best dive-bombing run. On the way back he said, "Admiral, you're going to be astonished at what a short run these things make on landing." We landed and I heard a god-awful screech and I thought that's a strange sound to be heard under braking. Turned out, I guess he was trying to show off a little bit too much and he came down quite vertically and broke his landing gear. He was mortified. Any landing you can walk away from was fine with me.[5]
>
> Adm. Elmo R. Zumwalt Jr., USN (Ret.)

The aircraft emerged from a cloud of dust on its nose, looking not so much as a busted Bronco as a genuflecting one. The admiral quickly departed, leaving Marty pondering what to call this caper, when Lt. Cdr. Bill Bartlett, Black Pony maintenance officer, pulled out his .38 and promptly shot the offending nose wheel, proclaiming, "Battle damage, skipper."[6]

Nineteen seventy brought even more changes to operations in the Delta. The navy deactivated Task Force 194 in June 1970 and transferred the Sea Lords operations still under U.S command to Task Force 116. The rest of the operations they transferred to the Vietnamese, as part of the "ACTOV" program. Admiral Zumwalt coined the acronym, which stood for Accelerated Turnover to Vietnam, hoping to give the program a sense of action and purpose. The press would dub it, and the public would know it as, part of the "Vietnamization" program.[7]

The Black Ponies found themselves flying fewer boat cover missions when the Vietnamese Navy went out on fewer operations. But single aircraft recon missions over the Rung Sat continued. In a change of command ceremony, Cdr. Verle Klein relieved Marty Schuman as skipper on 5 March. Farewells were offered to departing plankowners, who in turn hailed the new XO, Cdr. Len Rausch, and new replacement pilots. The fourth group of RPs arrived in what would be an almost routine influx of fresh pilots every three months or so. The newest group included Lt. Cdr. Jere Barton, Lt. Tom McCracken, and Lts. (jg) Ed Madden, Ed Sullivan, Ron Beeley, Tim Sikorski, and Randy Wyatt. A significant milestone had been passed. The original contingent of pilots was gone.

Marty Schuman, who as XO and CO had been with the squadron since its inception, left an indelible mark on the Black Ponies. Like his predecessor, Schuman guided the squadron through some tough times. Schuman's aggressive, hard-charging style and outgoing, gregarious, fun-loving manner would remain behind as his legacy. As Mike Quinlan remarked, "Marty Schuman came back with more bullet holes than anybody. He was by far the most aggressive pilot I ever flew with. He came back with absolutely no fuel and no weapons left. That's the way he flew. He even flew through his own Zuni shrapnel." Schuman's reputation was international. When Ponies scrambled to assist PBRs that had been attacked along the Cambodian border, Commander Schuman didn't let lines on the map interfere with helping out the brown water sailors. ComNavForV chief of staff, Capt. (later Vice Adm.) Emmett Tidd, who had been in Marty's back seat, recalled the mission

> that resulted in the Cambodian government's umpteenth warning message to the USA State Department about this "border violation." . . . The next morning when our Ops briefer back at ComNavForV's headquarters in Saigon read to Admiral Zumwalt the report of Cambodia's protest, I had to acknowledge that I, his Chief of Staff, had participated in and blessed (Schuman's) "border violation." Admiral Z had one question, "Did Marty blast the sons of bitches?" When I answered, "Yes, sir! Totally!" His first reply was a big grin, and then he said, "Tell him that's damned good work! Next item."[8]
>
> Vice Adm. Emmett H. Tidd, USN (Ret.)

Gil Winans's and Marty Schuman's leadership had established the Black Pony reputation in the Delta. If you were in trouble and you needed fast, accurate, substantial close air support; you called the Black Ponies. The challenge now was to continue living up to that reputation.

The JO Jeep

In the spring of 1970 a particularly difficult challenge faced the junior officers—transportation. The skipper had a handsome gray pickup truck, and he was often benevolent when others needed its use. But a basic problem had to be overcome—you had to ask him to use it. We were young and he was old, excuse me, older, and it was too much like asking your father to use the family car. The JOs needed basic transportation for many purposes, including to visit the several army exchanges in the area, to drive to the club at the Vietnamese Air Force Base for some significant social event such as a terrible band from the Philippines, complete with female singer, or even to occasionally motor into Can Tho for any or no reason.

Everywhere you looked there were people driving jeeps. They were everywhere. Officers drove them, enlisted drove them, and even U.S. civilians. The burning questions became, "Where were they getting them and was there an endless supply of them and how do I get my hands on one?" This became the topic of numerous discussions among JOs. Occasionally lieutenant commanders like John Westerman or Jim Hardie were heard to say they wished they had some wheels. Even they hated to ask the skipper to borrow his truck.

In talking to some of our U.S. Army friends, we JOs learned that although jeeps were pretty tightly controlled, they did have vulnerability— they did not have a keyed ignition. It required considerable "Yankee ingenuity" to lock them up. This often took the form of a chain looped through the steering wheel and down through the brake pedal with a very solid lock holding it in place. Or the added feature of welding a piece of chain to the steering column, which could be padlocked to a spoke on the steering wheel. Sort of a 1970 version of "The Club."

It's a law of physics that for every action there is an equal and opposite reaction. If it takes ingenuity to lock them up, you know there is a JO out there who will try all the harder to unlock them. This became the driving force in the mind of more than one Black Pony JO as a means to solve the transportation issue.

Our first foray into the "used car market" in Vietnam came one night when an especially shiny, new army jeep was parked of all places, right outside our admin building, across the ramp from our Black Pony hangar. We call this an "opportunity." Lts. (jg) Larry Hone and Charlie Fail stealthily moved this jeep into the hangar. Now, do not think it was an easy task. This particular low mileage, only-driven-on-weekends-in-the-war model had the obligatory chain through the wheel and the brake pedal, which necessitated considerable, very slow, very deliberate movements, back and forth, to move the prize across the road and ramp. The good news for the JOs was that the mission was accomplished. The bad news was that, while some of the finest metalsmiths in all of Southeast Asia masked off the jeep in preparation for a duty navy paint job, the army's crack MPs stumbled upon the bodywork party and promptly spoiled it. Luckily, the MPs were in a reasonably good mood and no one was hauled off. They did have one very angry U.S. Army captain in tow, who demanded that courts martial, lynchings, and even more drastic actions be taken. We were back at square one. Bummer! No wheels.

By this time in my short navy career I had been taught some of the finer points of cumshaw and could trade one USN flight suit for two army flight suits when the market was exactly the opposite. I made some inquiries among some of my contacts in the trading business as to the "price of a jeep—assuming one could buy one." I was told they were not for sale and that a loaner was out of the question. Insurance was very difficult to come by and there was always the possibility of theft. No one knows for sure but a rumor floated about. It seemed that an air force master sergeant in III Corps needed help getting OV-10 parts from an unresponsive air force supply system, and that he possessed the name of an army CWO3 who might know where one might be able to "check out" a jeep.

In the world of MPC [military payment certificates], bad food, and a third world trading economy, one had to determine the bartering value of a jeep. Depending on whom you asked, the price was as high as a helo or as low as a lambro and as difficult to determine as the value of a truck or a fixed-wing airplane. There did to seem to be one universal need among all round eyes in Vietnam, however. Air conditioning.

There was no Sears nearby, so you had to bring them with you from the States or hope that someone before you did. Checking around I found they were all spoken for, being used in very logical places that benefited a lot of people. Thus, they were declared off limits to those whose thought process deviated to wondering where one does get an air conditioner without enraging a lot of people and then getting it into the hands of someone who was willing to trade for something of significant value for it.

Our close allies in the war, the VNAF, had a building near our duty office and bunkroom at the flight line that housed only their flight gear. It was a handsome building with no windows and a single door. Sticking prominently out of a carefully cut hole in the side of the building was a very large, 220-volt air conditioner. It was obvious this was a very sturdy, finely tuned unit as it ran twenty-four hours a day and the moisture from the heavy, damp air of South Vietnam ran out of its condenser pan like a cool stream. This was one great air conditioner with a very lowly role in the war—that of keeping VNAF flight gear cool and dry. Each time you walked by this handsome work of Western World technology, it cried out to be given an opportunity to better serve in this strange war.

Whoever designed this fortress of flight-gear storage had made one significant error in architectural design—the one and only door opened out, not in. To many of you who are scratching your heads on this, I won't go into the fine art of framing and doorjambs but suffice it to say that any JG with a good pocketknife like mine could open this door in a heartbeat.

Meanwhile back at the car lot, this enterprising CWO3 [army chief warrant officer 3d class] had made the offer—a very low mileage jeep in excellent condition for unlimited use in return for a big 220 V, 10,000 BTU or better air conditioner. Putting a deal like this together might seem simple but there is more than meets the eye. Assume you had a nice big 220-V air conditioner. You needed to store it someplace, preferably a place where no one who might be looking for a 220-V air conditioner that happened to be missing might stumble upon it, thinking it was theirs. Then you had the transportation issue, which is at the heart of all this, to get the A/C from point A to point B. In this case, from Binh Thuy in IV Corps to an isolated army base on the Parrot's Beak in III Corps. Even if the skipper loaned us the truck for the afternoon, this would not work. Then you had to get your low-mileage jeep back over 150 miles of contested countryside.

As the line division officer I had the good fortune to know a petty officer 3d class by the name of Donald Reithknecht who was every bit as enterprising as I. The only difference was that he was also bold and reckless.

One particularly dark night I convinced two other JGs, who shall remain nameless—but whose initials spelled T. Y. Baker and Mike Wolfe— to help me rescue the air conditioner from its VNAF confines and relocate it to the connex box I had obtained for "emergencies" (like storing pallets of C-rations and berthing for SEALs visiting from the bush). Using my shroud-cutter knife blade as the master key it originally was designed for, I opened the door to the flight-gear building. We found no electrical plug, just three wires going into the wall. Short on time and tools, we opted for the "quick release" method, and gave it a big yank. This procedure worked, but the sparks sure did fly. It was time to haul ass. Yes, we had borrowed the skipper's jeep to make the move. We threw a large tarp over the cargo and I drove, with the others sitting in the back as we always did when riding with the skipper.

The next morning I struck a deal on the phone to exchange one low-mileage jeep, complete with spotless records, for one big air conditioner. The only logistical issue was that the deal was FOB the warrant officer's base in III Corps, 150 miles away. Here is where the skills of Petty Officer Reithknecht were brought to bear.

A large crate was constructed to hold the cargo, courtesy of the fine personnel at NSA supply. Our admin officer, Lieutenant Commander Hardie, cut a set of permissive travel orders for Petty Officer Reithknecht, and drew up a manifest to accompany the cargo from Binh Thuy to III Corps. One fine navy morning Reithknecht and his cargo got onto a C-123 headed for Saigon. He was now on his own with the valuable cargo and an M-16 checked out from the armory.

Two days later Reithknecht called back to Binh Thuy reporting that he was at his destination, the trade had been made, and now he was looking for a way to get the jeep back to Binh Thuy.

Three days passed and no luck. Reithknecht asked about the road to Saigon and was told that stretches of it changed hands daily. You just never knew who owned it. Being young and reckless, Reichnect befriended a NCO in the intel team and got the word one day that the road seemed to be open all the way to Saigon. Reithknecht obtained three flak jackets and a piece of armor from a Huey, threw in his M-16 and headed for Saigon. Fortunately it proved to be a leisurely ride through the countryside.

Once in Saigon Reithknecht made his way to the big airbase at Tan Son Nhut. Fate seemed to be smiling on him as he boarded a C-123 with his jeep. No flights had been scheduled for Binh Thuy, but one was headed for Vung Tau. After arriving in Vung Tau, he got directions to the enlisted barracks where he showered, had a meal, downed a few beers, made some new friends, then hit the rack.

Several hours later Reithknecht's new friends awakened him with the news that MPs were swarming all over his jeep parked outside. The MPs asked where the driver could be found but no one seemed to know. They tried to move it, but couldn't, given the fact that Reithknecht was an old hand at this jeep stuff and had put enough chains through the steering wheel and pedals that bolt cutters and torches would be required. When the MPs went for reinforcements Reithknecht and his friends quickly relocated the jeep to the airfield where a friendly army enlisted man helped them store it on an H-46 parked on the ramp.

Meanwhile the MPs returned to the barracks with a captain who possessed clear evidence that this jeep had been stolen from this very base! Now it was gone again. They were mad. Especially since none of the navy troops seemed to know who had driven it there nor where it went.

The MPs managed to find the trail to the flight line but too late. The army enlisted guys never told them that they had slipped the jeep onto a C-123 to Binh Thuy only minutes before. A week after the caper began, a smiling, proud petty officer delivered his cargo to an appreciative JG. Even Commander Kline was on hand as the newest addition to the squadron's rolling stock arrived at the base.[9]

Larry Hone, Black Pony

No one ever accused the Vietcong or North Vietnamese Army of being fair-weather soldiers. In fact, the enemy very astutely picked bad weather and moonless nights to attack their foe just as they used all the other elements of nature and terrain to neutralize the firepower and technological advantage that the allies possessed. Nor did the enemy recognize holidays, Vietnamese or American. Or if they did, they recognized them as opportunities. Black Ponies therefore flew most of their significant combat missions in bad weather or at night or at times when others might not expect the enemy to hit.

> We were up near Chau Doc on Easter Sunday morning at that [Chi Lang] base where Marty Schuman made his famous landing. . . . There had been a squadron stand down. The enemy overran the base and we flew back there several times. We were the late night scramble. All hell broke loose. On the first flight they hit the fuel storage and there was a C-7 that was parked near the POL section. After we finished our first load we came back—and since I wasn't wing qualified, I flew the back seat of Commander Rausch with Jere Barton flying wing—and I radioed, "Isn't anybody going to move that damned airplane away from that fire?" And this guy says, "Do you think we're crazy? You'd have to go out and start that son of a bitch." And then it finally blew up . . .
>
> As we came into the area there was a "Puff the Magic Dragon" [nickname for AC-47 gunship] that was shooting down from the sky at a .51 cal and they were shooting up at him. The tracers of three of his guns looked like they were going down the barrel of a .51 cal. It looked like a pissing contest of these tracers going down and tracers going up. When we checked in with him, he said, "Pony, can you do something about him? We're not having a phase on him and he's just leaving all kinds of holes in us."
>
> The XO, Commander Rausch, rolled in and put some Zunis on him and shut him down. Later on, they were hitting the one corner of the outpost and the enemy was swarming the corner and I could just see the bodies piling up, and I'm thinking Good God, how do you motivate somebody to go run into .50-caliber machine guns? After about the sixth wave and you haven't made it to the perimeter yet, how do get those guys to do those things?[10]
>
> Tim Sikorski, Black Pony

The overnight bunker crew got scrambled at 0836 on Wednesday, 1 April 1970. An army Bird Dog O-1 spotter plane had been watching the enemy set up .51-caliber weapons sites in a valley near Tri Ton in an area called the Seven Mountains near the Cambodian border. It was twelve miles south of "Black Pony Mountain" where Lt. Aubrey Martin and Lt. (jg) Roy Sikkink had been shot down and killed nine months earlier. A Vietnamese Army unit and its American advisors were taking heavy automatic weapons fire.

Lt. Cdr. John Westerman ran for aircraft number 115 while his copilot Lt. (jg) Pete Ford copied the coordinates, WR 995,495, the frequencies, and the call signs of the troops on the ground and the spotter aircraft. Lt. (jg) Ross Hanover jumped into the wing aircraft, 114, as his copilot, Lt. (jg) Larry Hone, plotted the bearing and distance to the target.

Nine minutes later the flight had wheels in the wells, headed for the target. Within moments Pete Ford established communications with Pepsi Kettle Oscar on the ground and "Swamp Fox 39," the Bird Dog pilot, who relayed a quick sitrep. The guys on the ground were pinned down in a valley by heavy automatic weapons fire from three sides.

En route to the target area the flight found itself above a broken cloud layer that became almost solid as it approached the mountains, the tops of which stuck out of the clouds like islands in a sea of foam. The target was beneath the overcast, in a valley between the mountains whose peaks projected about two thousand feet above the otherwise flat expanse of the Mekong Delta. The weather was so bad that no air assets could reach the beleaguered troops. Westerman knew that it would be difficult to find the target, much less prosecute it.

Spotting a hole in the clouds, Westerman spiraled down in the lead aircraft while Ross Hanover orbited above. When 115 got below the clouds Westerman found tight quarters for the Ponies to work in. The bases of the clouds appeared to be between one thousand and fifteen hundred feet, and fog enshrouded the mountains. The valley was too narrow to maneuver in.

"Okay One One Four, you can spiral down. I will be out of the way, at four hundred feet, orbiting to the east. You won't run into me or run into the mountains."

Hanover acknowledged the lead and descended through the opening. He spotted the other Bronco and joined in loose spread formation while they flew a visual reconnaissance. They quickly identified the friendlies. They then spotted four trenches in the rice paddies. Swamp Fox 39 confirmed that these were the trenches in which he had seen VC setting up .51-caliber machine gun sites. The O-1 had been orbiting out of the way, but called in hot and headed toward the enemy positions and put a smoke in the general area. He then relayed a bearing and distance from the smoke to where he knew the enemy was.

Westerman circled the flight around the mountain at low altitude while they assessed the situation. The troops on the ground were becoming desperate. Westerman knew everything about this target was wrong. Working it would violate every instinct an attack pilot possessed. The OV-10s were low, very low, and slow. They had to make their attacks from one. direction only, east to west. The enemy would know their altitude precisely, because of the cloud bases. . . . Static on the radio interrupted his moment of reflection. It sounded as if the troops on the ground would be overrun at any moment.

"Let's go get 'em."

Westerman charged his guns and selected the 2.75-inch rockets.

"Roger that." Hanover took an interval on the lead aircraft and set up his weapons too.

Black Pony 115's canopy scraped the clouds as Westerman struggled for all the altitude he could grab. He began firing the M-60 machine guns in a shallow dive and watched as the tracers arced their way down toward the enemy trenches. He pickled a pod of rockets and pulled off as Hanover, rolling in right behind him, began his attack.

The Broncos continued around in a racetrack-like pattern, unable to get enough space between the mountains, nor altitude above them, to vary their attacks. On 115's third pass Pete Ford saw one of the .51-cal sites open up on them from their left side. It appeared to him as if a bright white light were "chattering." Westerman salvoed a pod of Zuni rockets at the site. Larry Hone, in the rear cockpit of the wing aircraft, saw Westerman's Zunis strike their mark, just as 114 settled into its firing run. But as Hanover and Hone covered Westerman's pull off, another anti-aircraft site began firing at them.

"You're taking fire from the south, at your nine o'clock," Ford radioed.

Westerman yanked 115 around to silence the guns. He saw the stream of tracers angling its way toward him, as big as basketballs, he thought. Westerman's upper lip began to twitch, not out of fear, but anger. He selected the SUU-11 pod and squeezed off five hundred rounds of 7.62 mm into the gun site, during which he heard a series of *ping, ping, ping* sounds and felt the Bronco shudder.

"I'm hit, but I'm continuing the run. I can see exactly where they are coming from."

Westerman then banked the aircraft away from the target, just as a secondary explosion erupted. He checked his gauges and the outside of the plane. He and Ford saw fluid, perhaps fuel, venting from an overboard drain on the port nacelle. Everything else appeared normal and their attention quickly returned to the wing aircraft as 114 headed toward still another .51-cal site that spewed a stream of tracers at it.

Hone craned his head to see around the pilot's ejection seat just as Hanover squeezed off Zuni rockets that blasted into yet another antiaircraft site, this one in the open area in the valley. Hone saw the Zunis explode and two people and the antiaircraft weapon blow up into the air just before 114 banked away from the explosion.

Westerman reversed direction and radioed his wingman that he was going after another .51-cal site blazing away at them from a tree line. Before 115 could even shoot, Hanover and Hone saw the lead Bronco burst into flames. Hanover unleashed his last rockets at the antiaircraft site and pulled his Bronco around to rendezvous on Westerman, whose plane trailed flames and smoke.

"You guys are on fire! I recommend immediate ejection!" Larry Hone radioed to 115.

Pete Ford heard the radio transmission and thought, "Hold on a minute. Let's talk about this!"

As both aircraft headed eastward, out of the valley, and away from the enemy, Ford felt an explosion, then looked out at the prop being feathered.

"A large section of your port engine just blew off!" Ford heard over the radio. He felt a *pop, pop, pop* behind him and turned to see smoke coming from the circuit breaker panel behind his seat. He looked out at the port wing, now engulfed in flames.

Westerman did not want to eject near the valley and struggled to keep the plane under control, hoping to nurse it away from the target, if not back to Binh Thuy. As they cleared the mountains, he spotted a large open field and headed for it.

"Hold the stick while I tighten my harness," Westerman told Ford on the ICS. "Looks like we're going to have to jump out of this thing. Head for that field."

Ford took the controls, noticing how sluggish they were. He radioed Paddy Control that they were about to eject.

"I've got it," Westerman told Ford. "Whenever you're set, eject yourself. I'll be right behind you."

The plane passed through eight hundred feet. Westerman tried to keep it level but the Bronco wanted to buck, dive, and turn. The airspeed bled to 110 knots. He had run out of trim and kept the rudder depressed as far as it would go. He thought to himself that he was going to lose that foot on ejection when it smashed into the instrument panel.

A second explosion engulfed the left wing.

"Get out! Get out! Get out!" The pilots in the wing aircraft radioed. Ford looked at the flames curling over the wing. It was time to go.

"No, you eject us both."

At 1015, barely an hour and a quarter after takeoff, Westerman and Ford were bucked from their Bronco.

The ejection seats worked as advertised, but Ford's parachute malfunctioned and he landed hard, spraining his ankle. Westerman landed about thirty meters away from Ford, and the aircraft crashed about two hundred meters away. Swamp Fox 39's Bird Dog and Black Pony 114 made low passes over the two pilots who waved to them that they were okay. Westerman pulled out his survival radio and established communications with the aircraft just as Ford spotted a dozen men in black pajamas about a klick away, moving toward them. The pilots crawled behind their seat pans and pulled out their .38 snub-nosed revolvers. Here they were, out in the open, in the middle of a large, dried out rice paddy, with only an aluminum seat pan and an air-weight pistol for protection.

Hanover and Hone in Black Pony 114 made a low pass over the advancing men and saw that they wore black pajamas and carried weapons, but could not determine if they were friendly. The two pilots discussed the possibility of landing their Bronco in the rice paddy and rescuing their buddies. While the ground looked hard enough, they decided it had too many berms and trenches to make a safe landing. They were also low on fuel. Hone frantically dialed frequencies looking for help and found a Chinook helicopter on a mail run coming down from the north. Before the helicopter arrived, Westerman and Ford determined the advancing Vietnamese were friendly regional forces from an outpost nearby who had seen the OV-10 go down. The downed pilots radioed the orbiting OV-10 about the identity of the regional forces who set up a protective cordon around the Black Ponies until the Chinook helicopter arrived to pick up the pilots.[11]

The euphoria surrounding Westerman and Ford, returning relatively unscathed, swept through the squadron. From the dispensary where they were taken, to the Black Pony revetments at the airfield from where they had been scrambled only hours before, their story spread. The first navy pilots to successfully eject from an OV-10, Westerman and Ford cheated the enemy gunners and death. The euphoria soon gave way, however, and Black Ponies got back to business, the first order being to check out all the egress and survival equipment. Lieutenant (junior grade) Ford's parachute had malfunctioned, and even though he survived, the parachute riggers, ejection seat mechanics, and survival equipment experts would double check all the OV-10s.

10

SEALs and Ponies

But you can't just leave it like this! Come back here and I'll help. Time's cheap.

—William Dale Jennings, *The Ronin*

The number of navy personnel in Vietnam peaked at thirty-eight thousand in 1969, and for the most part, all of them volunteered to be there. Many officers who graduated from the Naval Academy at Annapolis during the war years served with the brown water navy and it was inevitable that many friends came into contact with each other in Vietnam.

Boat School Buddies

Naval Academy classmates have a unique bond that is rooted in the interminable frustration and degradation of Plebe year. Three more years of training and education only serve to make the ties more binding. A good many of us that arrived in Vietnam after flight training had been together through some very demanding circumstances for over five years. Nineteen seventy saw a number of my 1968 classmates arriving in-country to serve with either the Black Ponies or the Seawolves, where we would be providing support to others of our classmates who would be serving on the riverine force river patrol boats or as SEALs. We knew each other and we cared for each other; and we also were very competitive with each other.

Sixty-eighters in VAL-4 included Randy Wyatt, Ed "Mad Dog" Madden, Ray Kellett, Jim Cullen, and myself. The sixty-eighters in HAL-3 included Richard "Buzz" Buzzel, Mike Lagow, Jack "Duck" Ludwig, Kevin Delaney, Richard "Krulo" Krulis, and Larry Poh. [All were lieutenants (junior grade) when they arrived in-country, except for Cullen, who was a lieutenant when he reported to VAL-4 in 1971.] Most of us were good friends as well as classmates, and we felt we could take on the world. The competition between the pilots in the two squadrons was always evident, but our bottom line remained with the troops on the ground and in the riverboats.

A few of us had been friends for a long time. Buzz, Mike Lagow, and I were ex-enlisted. Mike married Buzz's sister, Martha, and many of the others of us had been in each other's weddings since graduation. We were very close, and we had already lost a number of classmates here in Vietnam through late 1970.

In December 1970 we lost Buzz.

He had taken a Huey back from his detachment to the Seawolves base at Binh Thuy for some maintenance. Anxious to get back to his Det, he kept pushing to get the helo "up" as quickly as possible. Finally on a late Friday afternoon, he was able to get airborne and on his way back to the Det. Earlier in the day, however, word had been passed back to the detachment that Buzz's aircraft would be down for a while more, so do not expect it back soon. They had not counted on Buzz's power of persuasion. On the way back Buzz's helo took some heavy ground fire and was immediately shot down and crashed into a dense swampy area. Because of the miscommunication, the Det was not expecting him back, and apparently the squadron headquarters never notified the Det that Buzz and his crew were airborne on their way back. It was not until Sunday after investigating numerous reports of an unidentified downed helo that it was determined Buzz and his crew were dead.

Dick Krulis was the pilot in command of the helo that went to confirm the situation and recover the bodies. "Krulo" came into my BOQ room back in Binh Thuy that afternoon and told me. I will never forget the look and the feel as he came through that door. Buzz and I had been friends since 1963, shared numerous adventures and misadventures, and grew up only two cities apart in Massachusetts. As bad as it was for him telling me, I think Krulo also had to tell Mike Lagow, Buzz's brother-in-law. As I remember there was even a problem getting Mike home to escort the remains. It took the intercession of Martha's godfather, Sen. Ed Muskie, to get the situation resolved and Mike on his way home with Buzz.[1]

Ed Sullivan, Black Pony

No one needed to tell Lt. Cdr. Jim Hardie the weather was bad that night. His last tour of duty was as a meteorologist in the Philippine Islands. He had been one of those Spad pilots who found himself out of a cockpit trying to get back into one. The navy had sent him to postgraduate school in Monterey and made a weather guesser out of him. On this night he was looking at the monsoon rains and guessing only whether or not his flight would be scrambled.

Hardie had flown three carrier cruises, including one with VA-145 on 4–5 August 1964 when the destroyers *Maddox* and *Turner Joy* came under apparent hostile action. President Johnson's premature television announcement that he was ordering retaliatory air strikes forewarned the North Vietnamese. They put up heavy antiaircraft fire over Loc Chao boat base and shot down Hardie's wingman, Lt. (jg) Richard C. Sather. He was killed and VA-145 A-4 pilot Lt. (jg) Everett Alvarez became the war's first POW. Hardie's A-1 was hit in the fuel tank and the hydraulics. He watched Sather's plane explode. "I got pissed," he recalled later, "and went back in. I pickled three nineteen-shot pods on the boats." He made it safely back to the *Constellation*.[2]

Lieutenant Commander Hardie and his wingman, Lt. (jg) Ross Hanover, did get scrambled at 0230 in the middle of the night on 8 April out to the U-Minh Forest, where an NVA battalion had attacked an outpost and were about to overrun it.

> The Seawolves had been scrambled out of Rach Gia. They were running out of ammo and needed heavier support. We went in and made contact and the Seawolves were still there. The base was on the western side of the canal, butted up against it. There weren't any patrol boats in the area. We took over from Seawolves. We could see the mortar and machine-gun flashes. . . . They put tracers out in the direction of the enemy and then we saw the flashes. Ross took off after the mortars to the south, and I took out after the ones to the west. After a couple of runs we silenced the mortars. Then they moved us around. They were getting heavy fire from all around. It was a "John Wayne" type of thing. They said they were pulling in to the inner blockhouse, which they did. They said, "Fire on the outer perimeter." We fired on the fence line and just inside . . . the VC were coming in then and we did stop them.[3]
>
> Jim Hardie, Black Pony

SEALs and Ponies at Dung Island

As a SEAL Team One platoon commander, Lt. Tom Boyhan had established the most impressive combat record of any SEAL platoon ever deployed to Vietnam up to that time.[4] Chief Gunner's Mate Barry Enoch, its leading petty officer, was one of the reasons for Charlie Platoon's success.

On 9 April 1970 Barry Enoch, along with platoon member Lou DiCroce and a SEAL Team Two member named MaCarthy, joined Ron Rogers and his LDNN (Vietnamese SEALs) platoon on an operation near Dung Island, at the mouth of the Bassac River. Dung Island was actually a group of several islands in the middle of the river. The target was a VCI camp on the eastern side of one of the smaller islands, Ong Cha. A four-foot-high dike surrounded the island, which except for a few small canals was completely covered by nipa palm. The VC no doubt felt secure.

The SEALs planned the op for the middle of the night at high tide, with the element of surprise on their side. Inserting on the southern end of the island at 0435 hours, Enoch, Rogers, and the other SEALs waded ashore from the light SEAL support craft (LSSC) in the darkness under the clear but moonless sky. Once inside the nipa palm forest it was so dark that the patrol moved very slowly through the swamp. When the water level reached neck-deep the SEALs had to help the shorter Vietnamese.

Daybreak found the patrol emerging into a dense but dryer tree-covered area when Thai, an LDNN ahead of Enoch, stopped.

"Why are we stopping?" Enoch asked.

"Tich is climbing a tree."

Enoch had known Tich since 1968 and had worked closely with the LDNN. He respected Tich's courage and boldness in combat. And the two men became close friends. Apparently Thai had heard a chicken, and Tich climbed a tree to see where it was so he could capture it.

The patrol then moved ahead to a four-foot dike and took cover. Across the dike lay a small clearing with a hootch from which smoke drifted. A sleeping VC guard sat with a weapon in his lap, and the SEALs saw two other weapons propped against a nearby tree. As the SEALs and LDNNs climbed across the dike, the VC guard awoke but was quickly dispatched with a round to the chest.

The LDNNs rushed into the hootch, and Enoch moved to its side where he spotted six armed men emerge from the back door. Enoch fired an automatic burst from his Stoner carbine, dropping two VC. Switching to semi-automatic, Enoch shot two more VC. After one of them got to his feet, Tich touched Enoch on the shoulder. "You go to hootch and I get them!"

Enoch ran to the front door as Thai emerged, saying, *"Bib Cambo."*

Inside, Enoch spotted a large Cambodian in a khaki uniform with NVA sandals lying in a pool of blood. DiCroce searched the hootch and found documents. Enoch left the hootch to search for Rogers in order to bring him the radio.

A firefight erupted in an adjacent tree line when two LDNNs fired their M-60s at VC trying to surround them in the nipa palm. Enoch was hit and thrown to the ground. He got up and ran to a tree line where he found protection in empty VC fighting holes. Rogers emerged through the trees carrying Tich over his shoulders. Tich had been killed by a single VC round.

When Enoch got on the radio to scramble helo gunships he found his PRC 77 had taken a hit in the antenna and two in the battery pack. Not only had it saved his life when it absorbed the enemy fire aimed at his back, the radio still worked! He was told army gunships—call sign "Vipers" —were on their way. (Vipers were the U.S. Army's 235th Aviation Company, an aerial weapons company out of Can Tho and Soc Trang.) He then radioed the PCFs—call sign "Bureau" —for mortar support, but they were too far away to do any good.

Rogers asked Enoch to move Tich's body back to the hootch while he led the platoon back. Enoch carried Tich's body on his back all the way back to the hootch as the LDNNs followed and provided covering fire.

Enoch then pulled out a signaling device from a plastic bag—a large "T" made of magenta silk. When stretched out, the two-foot-wide letter measured five feet across and ten feet tall. Enoch told himself that it didn't take a genius to realize they were surrounded and outnumbered. There was no doubt they would take even more casualties if they tried to break out.

The SEALs called for slicks to extract them and were told the helos were on their way. Lieutenant Boyhan and Charlie Platoon were aboard a PCF rushing to help.

Viper gunships arrived and engaged the VC while the SEALs prepared for extraction by the slicks. Then all of a sudden Enoch heard a Viper pilot radio that they were low on fuel and had to return to base. Enemy fire soon picked up on all sides of the surrounded SEALs.

Enoch called for an ammo check. Most of the platoon was down to two magazines. DiCroce in the hootch had more ammo so Enoch had him give the LDNNs three hundred rounds from his Stoner (a belt-fed 5.5-mm light machine gun).

The VC increased automatic weapons fire on the SEAL positions. Just then Enoch heard the unmistakable whine of the OV-10 turboprop engines over the roar of enemy fire and grabbed the radio. "Black Pony, this is Threadbare. Can you help us?"

"Threadbare, this is Black Pony One Zero Four. We're overhead."

Lt. Gerry "Doc" Mahoney's flight of Black Ponies had been scrambled from Vung Tau. Mahoney had Lt. (jg) Ed Sullivan on his wing. "Sully" had been in-country only a month and Lt. Jim Montgomery could have bumped him to the back seat when they got scrambled. But "Monty" allowed the newbie to take the front seat. Mahoney asked the SEALs to pop a smoke, and it became apparent that the good guys and the bad guys were on top of each other. Mahoney had no problem identifying the bad guys. They were firing from different positions, including a tree line between the SEALs, who were in and around a hootch, and a clear area upriver where they were planning to extract. They basically had the SEALs surrounded. Enoch gave the Black Pony instructions about the "T," using the word "starboard" to let them know they were navy. That was not necessary. Mahoney knew he was there to help SEALs because the operations officer at Task Force 116 informed him so when the flight had been scrambled from Vung Tau. For a Black Pony, there was no more important mission than helping a SEAL. None.

Mahoney and Sullivan made a number of rocket attacks with Enoch adjusting their fire after each run. It was slow going and they were running out of ammunition and getting low on fuel. They decided to intersperse "dummy" attacks with firing runs in order to keep the enemy heads down and buy some time, a pretty risky venture since the enemy had plenty of antiaircraft fire to send in their direction. The Ponies had realized they would need more help and Mahoney had radioed Red Rose, but he could not get a definitive response about sending help.

"Damn, they want to do the paperwork first and the paperwork isn't going to cure the problem."

Then Mahoney called the duty officer at Binh Thuy directly who immediately scrambled another flight of Black Ponies. They were only a few minutes away.

Just then two army slicks came flying down the river. Enoch was on the radios talking to the slicks, whose call sign was "Warrior" (336th Aviation Company, an airmobile light unit out of Soc Trang). The Warrior lead pilot advised Enoch that they couldn't go in because of "the lack of air support." They said the fixed-wing aircraft couldn't provide close enough support for them to work in tight.

"I couldn't believe what I was hearing but there wasn't any choice but to let them pass," Enoch later recalled. "When Lieutenant Boyhan heard the transmission from his perch on the PCF he was ready to come in after us with 'guns blazing.' I radioed back to him, 'Negative! Negative!' You just had to be there, I guess. Any direction they would have come from would have found them taking VC fire. To return fire would have meant shooting at us too."

Lieutenant Mahoney also couldn't believe what he was hearing. He told the lead helo pilot that he would cover the extraction and that another flight of Ponies would be on station in a few moments. He would have all the cover he would need. The Warrior lead pilot then said, "We don't have enough fuel."

His wingman, a warrant officer, disagreed with his flight leader. "We've got plenty of fuel."

"There isn't a place to put down," the lead added.

"There's plenty of room to get both choppers in there at the same time," the wingman responded. "And if not, I'll go in."

While they argued, Mahoney was getting furious. The lead obviously had cold feet, and nothing his wingman could say was going to get him to go in there and pick up those SEALs.

Mahoney exploded, "You've got a choice. You can either go in there and get those guys out and take your chances, or *I'll shoot you down!*" Mahoney was mad enough to do it, but it was an empty threat for he had no more ammunition.

"Oh no you won't," Warrior radioed back as he flew back up the river, never to be seen again.

Moments later the next Black Pony Fire Team arrived, and Mahoney gave them a quick sitrep before departing, dangerously low on fuel. The second flight was one of the first Black Pony Fire Teams comprised of all junior grade lieutenants. Larry Hone, recently qualified as FTL, led the flight, with T. Y. Baker in the back seat of 102. Mike Wolfe flew wing, with Ray Kellett in the rear cockpit. Hone wasted no time in going to work.

Enoch explained where the VC were and asked the Ponies to fire fifty meters from his position.

"Confirm fifty meters," Hone asked over the FM radio.

The VC automatic weapons fire intensified.

"You better make that twenty!"

The Black Ponies made their first pass firing just machine guns. Hone wanted to make sure of the enemy positions before firing rockets with high explosive warheads.

Enoch watched as the OV-10s passed over the treetops with guns roaring. On the Black Ponies' second run, the VC swung their heavy machine guns skyward and blasted away. Hone saw the muzzle flashes and tracers whizzing by his canopy, but pressed the attack. To positively identify the enemy locations, Hone fired 2.75-inch rockets from low altitude. He didn't trust the dispersion pattern that 2.75-inch rockets produced when delivered at normal release altitude, so he went in again at treetop level.

Enoch confirmed that the rockets were on target and advised the Black Ponies that they were hunkered down and to let loose with the big stuff. Hone and Wolfe then fired 5-inch Zuni rockets from low altitude in the face of intense antiaircraft fire. The VC kept up the fight and when the Black Ponies spotted some VC running for a hootch in a tree line, Hone asked Enoch for permission to fire on it.

"Blow it away!" Enoch radioed.

The lead Bronco launched a Zuni at the fleeing Vietcong. Enoch heard the supersonic crack followed by a tremendous explosion just above and behind him. Shrapnel, leaves, bits of a palm tree, and coconuts rained down all over. Enoch radioed the Black Ponies to find out what had happened. Hone apologized for hitting the top of a palm tree. Enoch watched as the next Zunis from Wolfe's Bronco smashed into the hootch, blowing it to bits.

"Quite an air show!" Enoch remarked.

The LDNNs continued laying down a base of fire in all directions and the Black Ponies made run after run. Antiaircraft fire would shift from position to position and the Black Ponies would adjust their run-ins.

The Black Ponies attacked the VC again to cover a courageous Army medevac crew who rushed in for the dead and wounded. Enoch saw the VC's green tracers chasing the helo's tail rotor as it cleared the treetops.

Larry Hone and his wingman Mike Wolfe were running low on fuel and ordnance but refused to leave before all of the SEALs had been extracted. Hone also elected to mix live with dummy runs to fool the VC. That bought enough time to extract Enoch and the other SEALs and LDNNs, and to bring Lieutenant Boyhan closer to a rendezvous.

At Enoch's direction, Hone and Wolfe blasted a path with Zuni rockets through the weakest side of the VC encirclement, leveling the nipa palm eastward toward the water. Rogers led the LDNNs out to the river while Enoch covered them from the rear, all the while directing the Black Ponies. When his radio started to malfunction, Enoch turned over control of the Ponies to Lieutenant Boyhan. Under probing fire, the SEALs and LDNNs moved quickly through the water and boarded the LSSC.

Boyhan's PCF and the LSSC had been taking fire from VC positions on the Dung Island side of the canal. The Black Ponies began working both sides of the canal and provided cover as Enoch and the rest of the patrol got clear of the islands and out into the middle of the Bassac River.

In his after-action report, Lieutenant Boyhan wrote on his barndance card, under the REMARKS section, "Black Pony placed extremely effective close air support as close as 20 meters to friendly position." And in the

SEALs and Ponies   111

RECOMMENDATIONS/LESSONS LEARNED section, "Don't expect much from Army slick pilots as far as balls are concerned."[5]

The SEALs had counted eighteen VC dead. They had captured weapons, grenades, and documents. Later intelligence discovered that the VC had brought carpenters to Dung Island to build forty coffins for their comrades.

Barry Enoch accompanied the body of his friend Tich up the river to Can Tho. Enoch had attended Tich's wedding and knew his family, so he and Ron Rogers helped make funeral arrangements and accompanied the body to Saigon, where they spent time with Tich's family, friends, and comrades.

Enoch also paid a visit to the Black Ponies.[6]

A Black Pony

A night or two after the Dung Island op the O-in-C of the SEALs in Binh Thuy paid us a visit. We were in the club watching a movie, and he came in and tapped us on the shoulder, and said, "Were you on the Dung Island thing?" and I said "Yeah," and he said, "I guess we better meet you outside."

We knew that, when we put our first rockets in, one of them had hit the top of a palm tree and blown a whole bunch of coconuts and stuff out of it. One of the coconuts had come down and hit one of the Vietnamese and knocked him cold. And they thought we were actually shooting on them. So I walked outside not knowing what to expect. That's when I met Petty Officer Enoch. It was really, really good to see him . . . very emotional.[7]

Larry Hone, Black Pony

A SEAL

Throughout 1970 and 1971, the Ponies flew numerous sorties in support of the SEALs, working almost exclusively in the ground attack role. Many a SEAL owes the lives of his teammates—as well as his own—to the crews of these little fixed-wing olive drab airplanes. I know this to be true because I am one of those SEALs. Today we reflect back on times when we were faced with overwhelming odds, fondly remembering the OV-10s as our "Green Angels" when it was truly too close to call. Let me tell you how they looked from down where I was in the brown water, mud, nipa palm, and green tracers of the VC. . . .

It should be said that the Black Ponies were the winged guardians with a like spirit of the Navy SEALs. Together we had a grim determination to do the job we'd trained for . . . a job we did very, very well.[8]

Barry Enoch, SEAL

The Black Ponies would often work very closely with army helicopter pilots, especially in the coming months. Never again would they run into a situation like at Dung Island and the slick pilot from the 336th with cold feet. More characteristic was Capt. John Leandro who worked with the Black Ponies as a Darkhorse pilot on his second tour in Vietnam. Leandro served his first tour with the 336th where he too was called on to extract some SEALs. The result was more like the working relationship the navy had developed with the army in the Delta.

An Army Pilot

We had what we called "vampire scramble," night standby, and we were told we had SEALs in contact down in the U-Minh, and we were going to land on Sea Float [a mobile ammi-pontoon base moored in the middle of the Cua Lon River near Old Nam Can] and extract them. A light ship, call sign "Lucky Strike," was going to drop flares, and Seawolves were going to cover us. So Randy Olsen, my wingman, and I took off and flew down there. We landed on Sea Float. I was flying with "Ski" from the 1st CAV. We got this briefing from a lieutenant commander. He was telling us, "The SEALs are in contact here. What you've got to do is low level up the river and there's this sandbar. You gotta land there. There's supposed to be seventeen of them, and this is the way it's going to be done, okay?" And then he said, "If you guys pull this off the navy's never gonna forget you."

And we're walking out and Ski says, "Hey 'Twenty-six' [my call sign] did he say *if*?"

I'll never forget it as long as I live. I said, "Yeah, the sonofabitch said *if*." I'll never forget it.

We orbited over the water. Randy went in first. He low leveled up the river. They kicked out two flares. He landed on the damn sandbar. They threw their seven guys in. We had about a thirty-second break. I was right behind him. He's lifting off. They throw off two flares and the damn parachutes don't open. It was like somebody put a light bulb into my eyes. I absolutely lost my night vision. I was on short final and I couldn't see nothin'. Ski was in Randy's aircraft. I had this guy named John Miller, who was a first lieutenant, flying as my copilot. And I said I'm going to turn on the landing lights. He said, "Oh man. Don't turn on the landing lights."

I said, "I can't see. I *gotta* turn on the landing lights." So I turned on the damned landing lights so I could pick up the sandbar. We landed on the sandbar. I chopped down some trees with my rotor blade. We got them all out. Well, we got all but the prisoners. They elected not to come.[9]

John Leandro, army Darkhorse pilot

11

Consolidation

Present fears
Are less than horrible imaginings.
—William Shakespeare, *Macbeth*

As part of the 29 April 1970 joint U.S. and Vietnamese invasion of Cambodia, a majority of the Vietnamese Mobile Riverine Forces were committed to convoy supplies up the Mekong River to help prop up a disintegrating government in Phnom Penh. On 8 May a one-hundred-boat South Vietnamese flotilla sailed up the Mekong into Cambodia to repatriate an estimated eighty-two thousand Vietnamese who had fled across the border to escape the war, and who now faced the dangers of a country in turmoil. Besides the humanitarian aspect of the mission, another objective was to clear the Communist troops from the upper Mekong. Thirty-two hundred South Vietnamese sailors and marines with thirty U.S. riverine patrol boats and advisors accompanied the flotilla. Seawolves and Black Ponies provided air support for the entire operation. Radarman First Class Warren K. "Tommy" Thomson, an advisor on the 54 boat, recalled:

> We took twenty-two boats across and came back with eleven. I took two B-40 rockets in the side of my PBR and it blew the nozzles off. And if it had not been for the Black Ponies diving down on each bank I know as I'm sitting here right now, I would not have gotten out of Cambodia.[1]
>
> Tommy Thomson, PBR sailor

Chief Petty Officer Robert Wilson, who as a chief mineman had taken Black Pony Lt. Cdr. John Butterfield on a patrol several months before and was now with RPG-56, called in the Black Ponies when his boats were attacked by the NVA on the way back downriver.

> We all got dusted off. We lost almost every boat we went up in. Every advisor got wounded. The Black Ponies were the only ones we could contact because our command boat where our skipper was (the senior advisor) couldn't contact anyone. The Black Ponies relayed messages for us.[2]
>
> Robert Wilson, PBR sailor

The political controversy generated in the United States by the Cambodian incursion quickly overshadowed whatever military and humanitarian successes may have resulted, and by 28 June allied forces withdrew across the border. Enemy infiltration through the Parrot's Beak would continue throughout 1970 and more and more North Vietnamese regulars joined Vietcong battalions to attack outposts and riverine forces.

On one of the all too frequent "yellow alerts," a line of Black Ponies stood before the sinks in the Binh Thuy BOQ head showing their usual concern, brushing their teeth before bagging some Zs. Lt. (jg) Graham Forsyth, who had been visiting from the Vung Tau det, peered up to see a guy appear, Major Burns-like, in full battle gear, including an M-14. He stood there, in oversized tin hat, eyebrows arched, puffing from exhaustion, quizzically peering at the sleepy Black Ponies with toothbrushes sticking out of their mouths.

"Don't you guys know we're under a yellow alert?"

The Ponies went back to brushing.

The guy then rushed down the line breaking each bare light bulb with the butt of his rifle before disappearing out the other door and into the night. The worst part of the ordeal for Forsyth was picking broken glass out of his bare feet before hitting the rack.

Someone sent the CO a directive mandating that Black Ponies take these yellow alerts more seriously. That must have satisfied the by-the-book types until several alerts later a senior officer decided to check the head and found a Black Pony JO and a beautiful young Vietnamese woman playing rub-a-dub-dub in the shower while the sirens wailed.[3]

More replacement pilots joined the ranks of the junior officers in VAL-4: Lts. (jg) Frank "Pete" Walther, Mick McCullom, Charlie Moore, Don Hawkins, Bob Scholl, Ed Bastarache, Jerry Beever, Bruce Turner, John

Aunchman, and Al Meszaros. Plans for moving the Vung Tau detachment to Binh Thuy resulted in building improvements at Navy Binh Thuy and the airbase to accommodate the additional men and aircraft. With the additional pilots moving into the BOQ, what little recreational facilities existed soon became strained. A lot of men liked to play basketball but the same guys seemed to hog the small court. Because of their flying schedules Black Ponies got very little use of it. Friction between officers of the various commands at Navy Binh Thuy increased until the Black Ponies took the initiative. Tom McCracken, "a lieutenant who was allowed to be a JG," according to Lt. (jg) Larry Hone, knew how athletics could bring people together. McCracken had been plowed back as a flight instructor in Pensacola for one year to play with the Goshawks, the semi-pro football team the navy put together that was quarterbacked by Lt. Roger Staubach. McCracken was looking for an outlet and he had an idea.

> We used to play basketball and the same guys played all the time. The Seabees, HAL-3, VAL-4, FASU, nobody got along. . . . Sullivan, Bastarache, Meszaros and I got together with the Seabees and built the volleyball court. It turned the whole thing into one fraternity."[4]
>
> Tom McCracken, Black Pony

Morale improved so much that for the first time since Binh Thuy was built the officers intermingled and socialized, on and off the volleyball court. After dark, many officers would walk across the road together to the boat base and join each other at the "O"Club for drinks and the movie that was projected on the giant cloth screen hung outdoors behind the club.

The Purple-Shafted Dingleberry Award

The CO of HAL-3 was a Captain, and thus senior to the VAL-4 CO. As a senior, important-type person, he did not sleep in the BOQ. Rather, he had his own trailer. Unfortunately, his trailer was close to the volleyball court, which at that time was the only form of recreation available to the junior officers. In fact, the volleyball court was active on a daily basis, as JOs and the occasional venturesome senior officer battled. The Captain did not like the volleyball hitting his trailer, and one day he arbitrarily, and without discussion, removed the volleyball net. In my position as Awards Officer, I wrote up an award for the Captain called the Purple-Shafted Dingleberry Cluster, and submitted it in the middle of a stack of legitimate awards. My hope was that the XO, Commander Klein, would rubber-stamp the award and send it up the line. However, he not only read the award, he liked it enough to forward it to the Commodore, who was the senior Navy guy in Binh Thuy. Later, at an all officers banquet, the Commodore presented the HAL-3 Captain with a medal made by VAL-4 machinists, and read the award aloud. The Captain could do nothing but take it. However, we did not get back our volleyball court.[5]

T. Y. Baker, Black Pony

Lts. (jg) Ross Hanover and Pete Ford got scrambled in the middle of the night on 8 June to an outpost under attack. The FM radio in Hanover's aircraft went "down" so he passed the lead to Ford. Even though his radios worked he had difficulty establishing and maintaining communications with the ARVN in the outpost. The enemy had actually made it into the outpost and finally the American advisor directed the Black Ponies to shoot along the perimeter where the VC were entrenched. They saved the outpost from being overrun and a few days later the army advisor told the Black Ponies that their strafing runs had set off Claymore mines that killed more VC than their rockets had. Even more interesting, the advisor told Pete Ford that the ARVN had run out of ammunition because of the partial lunar eclipse that had happened earlier in the week. Apparently the soldiers had fired all their ammunition at the "dragon that was swallowing the moon."[6]

Pete Ford looked like a young Jackie Gleason with a Don Ameche mustache and a deep, infectious laugh. He was the special services officer at Binh Thuy. That was the collateral duty that was known as "welfare and morale" officer during World War II and it was generally given to a junior officer who was into sports and knew how to scrounge a lot of athletic equipment or had a knack for cumshaw. Ford could get an OV-10 once a month to use for this purpose and he would fly up to Vung Tau and pick up Charlie Fail, his counterpart at Det Bravo, and together they would head up to Nha Be in a Jeep to get supplies. On one of these monthly runs Ford became attached to a motley brown pup of unknown parentage whose fate he knew would be limited on the streets of Vung Tau. He named the dog "Arnie," after the pig on the *Green Acres* TV show. (The name was also lent to the trophy given regularly to the Black Pony pilot who flew the most hours as the "Arnold Award" for flight hog of the month.)

Since he had flown solo to Vung Tau, Pete would have to transport Arnie back to Binh Thuy in the front cockpit. He put the pup in the map case and, as luck would have it, on the flight back from Vung Tau Ford ran across another Black Pony flight on a scramble. It was a hot target with troops in contact and Ford's help was needed, and by necessity, so was Arnie's. They joined up to form a three-plane, five-pilot, one-dog

Black Pony show. There was Arnie, pulling 4 Gs in the map case, earning points for her first air medal. (Obviously not inspected closely enough before being named, Arnie would later bear a litter of identical motley looking puppies.)[7]

Cdr. Len Rausch, the new XO, came to Vung Tau one day to inspect the facilities. In one of the open hangars he noticed a small monkey on the rafters and he walked over to get a closer look at him. Lt. (jg) Tim Sikorski who was standing nearby looked nervous.

"Well, who's this?"

"Commander Zee . . . " Sikorski started to say.

The XO probably heard, "Commander, see. . . " and extended his arm, pointing up at the monkey, as if to say, Yeah I see that monkey.

"Commander, I don't think you want to . . . "

"What a cute little monkey."

"Aw, shit." Sikorski muttered under his breath as Commander Zee leaped for the commander wearing the hat.

"Don't do that," a sailor nearby offered. But it was too late, as the monkey ran down the outstretched arm, latched onto the XO's head, and started humping his ear.

The XO's hat and the monkey hit the floor about the same time as Sikorski disappeared around the corner.

Commander Rausch's run-in with Commander Zee was only the latest in a long line of unpleasant encounters with this most obnoxious creature. No one liked Commander Zee except for the enlisted man who supposedly took care of him. Actually the monkey took whatever he wanted and made up his own rules as he went along, causing him to fit in very well with the Black Ponies in the minds of some. That is, until he got on the wrong side of somebody who got fed up with the simian's foul habits. The word was that a primate supposedly higher up on the ladder of intelligence gave Commander Zee a hand grenade and locked him in a connex box where a few hours later the monkey's curiosity did him in.[8]

Lucky and Unlucky Shots

In a business where accuracy was a life-and-death matter, Black Ponies took pride in their marksmanship. But no matter how good he thought he was, a pilot knew that on some days he could not hit a bullet with the side of a barn. And the flip side was—on some days—he could not miss. Ask John Aunchman how one could miss a mountain, miss it completely with a Zuni rocket. But Bruce Turner witnessed Aunchman fire a point-detonating fused Zuni, then as Turner and Aunchman looked back after pulling off, the rocket exploded in a rice paddy—on the other side of the mountain. They knew he could not have missed the mountain. It had to have gone through it.[9]

Turner himself would get a lucky shot working in the mountains up near the Cambodian border.

> I was flying wing and Tom McCracken was lead. He rolled in . . . he shot one or two Zunis. The guy on the ground said it was close, about twenty or thirty meters left or right. McCracken came back on the radio and said, "Roger, my wingman will get it." And I thought, Gee thanks. I rolled in and . . . pickled a Zuni or two . . . and the guy on the ground went nuts. He said, "You got 'em! They had a light back in that cave. It went right into that cave and put the light out!" He really wet his pants. It really made us look good but it was just blind luck.[10]
>
> Bruce Turner, Black Pony

It can work the other way too. Lt. Max Britton, who was known as a good shot, cavalierly told an O-1 "Shotgun" pilot controlling him on a flight, who wanted the Black Ponies to destroy a hootch in the middle of a large open field, "The hootch will disappear." But after a dozen passes, the hootch remained unscathed. Sometimes, more than luck had a hand in some shots, as Tim Sikorski found out.

> On my first front seat hop, southeast of Binh Thuy, Charlie Fail was in my back seat. A Friday afternoon flight and a Chinook was picking up a Huey. They called us and asked us to orbit while they pulled the Huey out. The bad guys started lobbing mortar rounds over at the Chinook. The pilot is getting real excited. He can't get unhooked and he's got a man down. He refuses to leave. . . . He's screaming at us to get some firepower in on this mortar crew. The XO, Commander Rausch, rolls in and hits something but it's nowhere near the thing. They're telling me that it's the bunker behind the hootches on the squiggly and stuff. And my back seat's yelling, "Roll in. Roll in!" And as I roll in the first thing that goes through my mind is, What the hell is a squiggly? Hootches? I look out my window and I can see a village way off to my right. Well, I can see those were hootches. I look in front of me and all I can see is green grass. What the hell are they talking about? If the bunker is past the hootch and I can't find the hootch and if I don't know what the squiggly is, what the shit! I don't have the foggiest clue of what I'm supposed to be shooting at. My back seat says, "Fire, fire!" So I reach over and I go well, I'm not going to shoot a Zuni because I don't know what hell I'm shooting at. I don't know what the hell I'm doing. I still don't know what a squiggly is. So I reach over and I select

a 2.75 and I punch one time, which fires two rockets. I look out and these two rockets go straight out from the airplane about a hundred yards. Then they turn about 40 degrees. And I go, What the shit is that? And I look down and I've got my leg all the way down to the floor, and I'm so far out of trim I can't believe it. I relax my leg. The nose swings around, kind of points to where the rockets are going. . . . In my mind I'm still thinking, What the hell is a squiggly? Where's the hootch? And I know the rockets are going to hit the ground. They're not going to hit the Huey or the Chinook. And my backseat is screaming at me the whole time. The Chinook driver is screaming. About that time I said, Well, it's about time to get the hell out of here. I've shot two rockets. I pulled back and as I'm doing my pull out, they're going, "Fantastic shooting! The rockets went right into the window of the bunker and you took out the mortar crew!"

And I thought to myself . . . I didn't have anything to do with it. All I did was punch out two rockets. They got moved and they got sent downstream somewhere by somebody else's hand, but it certainly wasn't *mine*. The Chinook pilot kept saying, "What fantastic shooting." I'm thinking, This is probably not the time to ask him what a squiggly is. . . .

In my mind I'm saying, Well, I guess today there was going to be a Chinook crew that was going to live and there was going to be a mortar crew that wasn't, and I didn't have anything to do with either one of those choices.[11]

Tim Sikorski, Black Pony

Not all lucky/unlucky shots by Black Ponies were fired from a Bronco, as Lt. (jg) Vernon "Rosie" Rosenberger and Lt. Larry Laughon demonstrated.

We were up there in the bunker at Vung Tau. The bunker was about thirty feet square and had a little sleeping room off to the side. All sandbagged, built out of big timbers, so you couldn't hear anything going on outside. Soup Campbell was at the little duty desk, fiddling around. There was a big post that held the center up and Cdr. Verle Klein had a chair leaning back against it, reading a magazine. I was over in the corner. Mark Byars was in back sleeping and Rosie was at the desk. Rosie decides it's time to clean his beautiful Browning 9 mm. A navy .38 wasn't good enough for Rosie. So Rosie, who knows absolutely nothing about weapons, hauls this thing out, pulls the clip out of it, gets some rags, a rod, and some oil. He's just polishing away and running this thing up and down the barrel and everything.

When he got started Klein said, "What a good idea." So I pull my trusty five-shot chief's special out and Klein pulled out his standard navy .38 and dropped all the rounds on the desk and *clink, clink, clink,* and we put them back together and back in our pockets and went to leaning back again.

While I'm reading a *Life* magazine, Soupy Campbell takes an M79A grease gun and rips it apart on the duty desk. Byars is sleeping. We had horse traded for green asphalt tile squares that we put over the concrete floor and a little curtain between this room and the bunkroom. So Rosie is holding his 9 mm up, "Boy, this thing is beautiful." He's sighting down it and—fortunately he had aimed it at the floor and right into that little bunkroom—and he pulls the trigger. *Pow!* He torches off this little 9 mm and I came off that chair and just levitated, and so had Klein. And then back into the chair I go and so does Klein.

Nobody has said a word.

And this thing has ripped up the tile in the bunkroom and the next thing we hear is, "Huh, huh, huh." And here comes Byars stumbling out. Byars just knows the place has been grenaded. And he just knows there's going to be blood and guts because there's no noise. They're all dead.

And Rosie hasn't said a thing. He's totally shocked. The only thing that was said was by Klein, who casually turned around and said, "Jesus Christ Rosie."

He never said another word. . . . After we flew our hop and came back, Soupy Campbell had written the whole thing up in the duty log, with a creative little ditty to the tune of "Don't take your guns to town, son."

Larry Laughon later tried to imitate Rosie by inadvertently firing a .45 in the Binh Thuy admin building. A metal building with metal desks and file cabinets. The logs and records yeoman is sitting at his desk and this .45 round is going *boing, boing, boing* around the place and winds up on his desk. A little bit warm, but there it is.

He picks it up and gives it back to Laughon. "Did you lose something, Sir?"[12]

Gerry Mahoney, Black Pony

Lt. Cdrs. Jere Barton and Jimmy Hanks were good friends. Hanks had gone through the RAG with Commander Rausch and his group of replacement pilots but suffered a broken eardrum in SERE (survival, evasion, resistance, and escape) training. Hanks had been a simulated POW struck by a simulated captor in a simulated North Vietnamese compound with a simulated blow that landed squarely on an all-too-real ear. He caught up to his shipmates just after Christmas.

Some of the JOs knew Hanks from their days as flight students. Jimmie got his wings in 1958 and had flown P-2Vs and S-2s before getting out of the navy and starting a construction business in Pensacola. With the buildup for the Vietnam War and the need for flight instructors, Hanks was called up from the reserves to instruct at VT-1, the primary squadron where all future naval aviators start out. He earned a reputation of being a patient, easy-going mentor among a group of otherwise impatient, screaming flight instructors. Techno-thriller author Steven

Coonts credits Hanks with saving his chances of becoming a naval aviator when, as a young student, Coonts was having problems before soloing. On a journey he describes in *The Cannibal Queen: A Flight Into the Heart of America,* Coonts mentions flying to Pensacola to look for Jimmy Hanks.[13] When Hanks volunteered for VAL-4, he liked to say that it was the only thing that he ever got in the navy that he had wanted.

Black Pony JOs also got to know Hanks when he put his construction background to work in Binh Thuy and built a bridge to nowhere just in front of the BOQ. Everyone was scratching his head while watching Hanks build across the dusty ditch a wooden span that soon got dubbed "The Jimmy Hanks Memorial Bridge." What had been a joke in the dry season became a much-welcomed public improvement after the monsoons arrived. Jere Barton and Jimmy Hanks would get a lot of laughs out of how the JOs came to appreciate the hands-on approach of their new maintenance officer.[14]

"You know how you get premonitions? I felt like we were going to get hit. I slipped on my gloves, tightened down my seat belt and my helmet and on the last run that's when we got hit," Jimmy Hanks would later recall.

They had scrambled to an area only twenty-five miles northeast of Binh Thuy. Early afternoon, the weather was not bad, the target was. Vietnamese Army troops in contact and their American advisors just off a river fifteen miles north of Cai Be in Dinh Tuong Province were involved in some very heavy fighting. A full, heavily equipped company had the ARVN pinned down and were pounding them with 82-mm mortar and automatic weapons fire.

Lt. Cdr. Jere Barton had been making rocket attacks on the enemy from the same run-in direction, restricted by the position of the friendly troops. He had set up for a strafing run with his Mk 4 gun pod when the 20-mm gun jammed. That is when Lt. Cdr. Jimmy Hanks in his back seat had the premonition.

Wingman Lt. (jg) Larry Hone and his copilot Lt. (jg) Eddie Madden watched Barton's Bronco buffet and burst into flames as three .51 caliber sites opened up on it.

Lt. Cdr. Jimmy Hanks looked to his left as the engine erupted in flames. Barton said something over the ICS that Hanks couldn't understand and attempted to feather the port engine. Hanks tried to talk to Barton but he did not respond. Hanks thought the pilot might have been talking on the FM radio. The flames were spreading and the plane was descending and

Hanks sensed that no one was on the controls. The plane started to yaw violently and roll over onto its back. Hanks grabbed the stick with both hands and mashed down on the rudder with all his strength.

Hanks knew that Barton was wounded, how bad he didn't know, but he was not going to initiate an ejection that might risk further injury to the pilot. He would rather crash-land the Bronco.

"I've got the airplane. If you don't eject us, I'm going to fly this damn thing into the ground!" Hanks yelled over the ICS.

The plane leveled out momentarily and headed away from the target.

"Get out! Get out!" Larry Hone radioed as he saw the flames engulf the wing of the Bronco.

Hanks then thought he heard Barton's voice, "Is it still on fire?"

Passing through four hundred feet Jimmy Hanks had the rudder pedal so fully depressed that his leg was all the way under the instrument panel and he was struggling with the control stick and the words still crackled in his headset when suddenly he was hurtled through the canopy. Barton had initiated the ejection.

> I remember that it was so fast that the G force from the seat made me black out and when I came to I was looking down and I said, There's the trees, oh my God that's grass! Blam! And I was on the ground just like that. Jere was about twenty-five yards from me. . . . The enemy soldiers were about three hundred meters away. You could see them coming out of the bushes. . . . Larry then rolled in on them. He didn't have much ordnance left. He'd go *bap, bap, bap, bap*. . . . They would go down when he did and I'd get up and run like a son of a bitch. . . . At first, I got Jere out of his chute. He was incoherent.[15]
>
> Jimmy Hanks, Black Pony

Hanks struggled to get Barton onto his feet but he couldn't. Hanks was badly injured himself. His ankle was broken where it had hit the instrument panel on ejection, his vertebrae were fractured, and he was starting to lose consciousness. A Cobra gunship settled into a hover between the two parachutes, sending up a cloud of dust. Flames from its minigun snaked out toward the advancing enemy soldiers as it hovered there. An army slick swooped down from the sky and landed downwind from the parachutes. A crewman jumped out, ran to Hanks, grabbed him and hustled him into the helicopter. Hanks slid onto the floor of the Huey, barely conscious, and before the crewman could run back to get Jere Barton, Hanks and the Black Ponies above watched the most horrifying thing they would ever see in their lives.[16]

We are watching from overhead. A slick comes in and lands . . . one of the command and control slicks that's got some light colonel out of Saigon who has come down here to get his flight time. . . . You've got this other slick that landed in such a way that, let's say that he was at the foot end of the body on the ground, with the parachute being up by the head. This slick landed down by the feet, so if there were any downdraft, it would be blowing it away from how he was lying on the ground. He's sitting on the ground. The crewmen had gotten out to get Jere. This other slick comes in, for no reason. There's *no* reason to. He's not a gunship. Just comes screaming in. Down hot. Just pulling collective like crazy. His downdraft inflates the parachute on the ground, causing it to rotate, pulling it up into the rotor of the other slick on the ground . . . and Jere is taken right into the tail boom and the tail rotor. . . . That helicopter just jumped. You could see it bend the entire tail boom . . . and see the ground right behind it. . . . We knew immediately what had happened.[17]

Larry Hone, Black Pony

12

Bucking Broncos

Fire is the test of gold; adversity, of strong men.
—Seneca

As the U.S. Army wound down operations in the Delta and began phasing out the army air field, VAL-4 decided to shut down Det Bravo and consolidate all assets at Binh Thuy on 21 July 1970. The move made sense from an operational standpoint. Pilots and enlisted men from Binh Thuy had been rotated through the Vung Tau detachment as much as possible as a way to let them enjoy the amenities of the area. Rest and relaxation facilities would still be available, but the squadron would no longer have a regular presence at Vung Tau.

> There were about four officers and a bunch of enlisted guys who stayed at Vung Tau after the planes departed who moved what was left. They had an LST that they were going to put everything on. A lot of the enlisted troops had their Vietnamese women. When it came to moving day all of a sudden here were all these Vietnamese women with their chickens and chairs. They thought there would be room for them and they would go get on the ship. It looked like the *Queen Mary* leaving. Our enlisted troops had told them they could go along. Needless to say they couldn't. . . . It looked like something out of World War II. A hundred Vietnamese women with kids, parents, stuff on their backs, suitcases, and they thought they

were going to ride the LST to Binh Thuy. And of course the enlisted guys are trying to hide because they don't want to run into them.[1]

Tom McCracken, Black Pony

By September 1970 the ACTOV program was well under way and virtually all U.S. brown water naval assets had been turned over to the Vietnamese. While most Vietnamese Navy units had American advisors, the boats went out on fewer and fewer patrols. And control of coastal waters and rivers began to pass once again into the hands of the Vietcong and NVA. By mid year VAL-4 was being used mainly as an airborne quick reaction force.

Butch Underkoffler and I went to the Philippines, ostensibly for survival training. While there, we found a monkeypod carving of a man with his head up his ass. We brought it back to the squadron and created the "Head Up and Locked Award." This award was given to the officer who made a big screw up, and it was his to keep until someone screwed up worse. The award was voted upon by a committee of junior officers who met in secret, and likely in a drunken stupor. The first recipient was, I believe, John McColly, who received the award for thinking one night over Cambodia that his wingman was a MiG. The award was retired by Commander Klein when he took it back to the States. I am told it remained on his bar until he attained the rank of admiral, at which time his wife felt that a wooden statue of a man with his head up his ass was not appropriate for an admiral's bar.[2]

T. Y. Baker, Black Pony

Commander Len Rausch assumed command of the Black Ponies on 3 September, relieving Verle Klein. Under Klein's leadership VAL-4 had consolidated assets at Binh Thuy, established a Fire Team Leader training program that allowed junior officers to quickly gain front seat combat experience and leadership responsibilities, and guided the squadron through changing missions. By the end of the year, 94 percent of VAL-4's missions would be in support of ARVN units as the Black Ponies became primarily a quick reaction force, or hired guns.

The new XO, Cdr. Jim Burton, was joined by replacement pilots Lt. Cdrs. Bob White, Ken Williams, Tom Langston, Jim Becker, Fred "Fritz" Lynch; Lts. John Smalling, Bob Hurley, Howard "Hotch" Hotchkiss; and Lts. (jg) Lynn Henish, Mike Lamberto, and Sam Chipps. Also joining the squadron were Lt. Gaylon Hall and CWO Sam Fleming in the Maintenance Department and a flight surgeon, Lt. Larry Getz.

Lynn Henish showed up at Binh Thuy wearing fatigues with the name "Fisher" on them. The first stop for new arrivals after getting off the plane at Tan Son Nhut was the Annapolis BOQ in Saigon. Henish had met a guy named Fisher who was on his way back to the States and acquired his fatigues. Commander Rausch called the new replacement pilot Fisher so much that the name would stick.

On 16 August Lt. Cdr. Jim Hardie and his wingman Lt. John McColly scrambled to assist a U.S. and Vietnamese Navy unit in contact with a large force of Vietcong near Rach Gia. Hampered by low clouds, the Ponies were forced to make all of their runs beneath a five-hundred-foot cloud base.

> It started out with troops on the ground sowing [Duffle Bag] sensors, and the Seawolves went in to extract them. On the extraction, they came under fire. It was *crachin* monsoon weather and we had to stay low, about three hundred feet, following the "blues" [canals, rivers] to get there. The helicopters were running out of ammo. There were PBRs on the blue to the north. They were taking fire. I was lead and John McColly was my wing. We made one run then split up because we were basically in the clouds and had to 180 out and talk to each other to keep out of each other's zone of fire. We'd pop out of the broken clouds at five hundred to eight hundred feet, adjust and shoot, then pull back up in, then come back around. We'd call in and off. We were talking to Rach Gia. They could hear the enemy (through the sensors) and could hear us. They said at one particular time, "Hey, you got them. We can hear them. You're hurting them." So we concentrated on that area.[3]
>
> Jim Hardie, Black Pony

In the early morning hours of 13 September Black Ponies were scrambled to assist a SEAL Team One platoon that had been attacked by a forty-man Vietcong force. Lt. (jg) Don Hawkins, with Lt. Tom McCracken as his copilot, led the flight to the location where three army and Seawolf helicopters had been hit trying to cover the SEALs. With wingman Lt. (jg) Tom Bailey and his copilot Lt. (jg) Charlie Moore, Hawkins had to maneuver the flight beneath a low, broken cloud layer to attack the automatic weapons sites on three sides of the SEALs' position. Working as close as 150 meters to the SEALs, and firing their rockets at low altitude in the face of heavy antiaircraft fire, the Black Ponies silenced the enemy guns nearest the extraction point. The SEALs were able to withdraw as the Ponies covered their successful extraction.[4]

Lt. (jg) Ed Bastarache had been in-country not much more than a month and was flying his first front seat hop on a hot, muggy, late afternoon of

29 September. Lt. (jg) Pete Ford in the back seat of 105, the lead aircraft, managed to find an "intel" target that would provide some needed target practice for Ed. As they were heading toward Tuyen Nhon up near the Parrot's Beak the Black Ponies received an airborne scramble. A mail boat had just been ambushed on the Vam Co Tay River.[5]

Two PBRs from River Division 594 had been preparing to set up a "night 'bush" in conjunction with a Duffle Bag operation on the industrial canal out of Tuyen Nhon near the old French Foreign Legion outpost that served as a tollbooth. Boat captains Davies and Jones, both first class boatswain's mates, got the word over the radio that the mail skimmer had been attacked. The PBRs rushed down the river to the ambush point to begin firing runs while radioing for air support.[6]

Black Pony 105 and his wingman Lt. Cdr. John Westerman in 111 arrived overhead at about the same time. Lt. Cdr. Fred "Fritz" Lynch, in the rear cockpit of 111, had been in Vietnam only a month also, having come from a tour of duty as an OV-10 RAG instructor at North Island.

The gunner on one of the PBRs, Rob Mott, a seaman, watched Black Pony 105 fire a Zuni rocket at the enemy position and saw the Ponies taking fire from an RPD, a .30-caliber automatic weapon. He then spotted what looked like a flare ignite underneath the Bronco.[7]

Pete Ford and Ed Bastarache heard and felt antiaircraft fire hit the underside of the OV-10 and then saw the flames shooting out from underneath.

"We're hit and on fire!"

Ed pulled out of the dive, leveled off, and trimmed the plane. Westerman aborted his run-in and started to rendezvous when Fritz in the back seat of 111 yelled over the radio to 105, "Your Zuni pod is on fire!"

Bastarache selected the switches to electrically jettison the rocket pods but nothing happened. He then pulled the manual ejection handle. Still nothing.

The LAU-10 Zuni pod on sponson station number 2 was cockeyed, probably hit by the antiaircraft fire, and the rocket motor on one of the two remaining Zunis had ignited. Flames from the Zuni were cooking the underside of the plane and the entire rocket launcher pod. Ford and Bastarache could see the floorboards glowing red.

"Get out, get out! Get out!" Lynch yelled over the radio.

"Pete, do you want to eject yourself? Then I'll go out. Or do you want me to take us both out?"

"Take us both out," Ford replied.

Just as Bastarache pulled the ejection handle he heard Pete Ford's lament, "God, why me *twice?*"

Ford's seat rocketed through the canopy and in the seven-tenths-of-a-second delay before Ed's seat fired he said to himself, "Fuck, my seat's not working!" Then he went out.[8]

Pete Ford's second ejection from a Bronco was not as smooth as his first trip up the rails in the LW-3B seat—that time six months earlier when his parachute had malfunctioned.

> I remember a lot of fire. I left my mic plugged in. As we went out, the mic raked across and ripped open the corner of my mouth and went up across the edge of my nose and then went up and hit me in the eye and damn near tore my eyelid off. Coming down in my chute I'm bleeding like crazy and I couldn't see, there was so much blood in my face. . . . I didn't know what happened. I didn't know if I got shot on the way out or what. I thought I lost my right eye. We had gone out at about three thousand feet, and I kept pressing my glove against my right eye to stop the bleeding and looking out of my left eye, trying to get the lay of the land. Then I realized we were coming right down in the target area.[9]
>
> Pete Ford, Black Pony

Westerman and Lynch watched the pilots jettison the Bronco and immediately called Mayday on guard. An Aussie voice quickly responded then joined them on the tactical frequency. He was about fifteen minutes out and headed their way. Seawolf 46 also responded that he was inbound to their position.

Ed Bastarache's feet had hit the instrument panel pretty hard on the way out, but fortunately his steel-toed boots saved his feet from serious injury. His hands tingled, burned by the rocket blast, and when he came to his senses in the risers beneath the billowing canopy floating eerily, almost soundlessly toward the ground, a sharp *crack, crack, crack* shattered the silence.

> We were taking ground fire in the parachutes. . . . I was dangling from the parachute, and the map bag . . . the maps were falling all over the sky. . . . I could hear them shooting at me. They say you can steer those chutes but that's bullshit. . . . I'm trying to get on the right side of the canal and trying to steer the chute but it's going where it wants to go. The reason why Pete went down so fast was that his seat never separated, so he had an extra two or three hundred pounds hanging on him. As a result, he just hit the ground a lot faster than I did.
>
> Pete is already on the ground, and I'm still floating up here. He's not moving so I figure he got hit, so I'm a little concerned about his situation. Quite a while later, it seemed like—I'm sure it wasn't that much longer— I hit the ground. . . .

I got up and started running towards Pete because I thought he might have been hit and was down. Then I heard some shots and dove into a canal. So I was lying in the water with my nose sticking out, my gun in one hand and my radio in the other. I looked up and I saw this plane fly by and I saw that it didn't have a canopy or people in it. And I'm thinking, That's weird. I'm probably looking at it from a weird angle because I'm tucked back into the weeds.[10]

Ed Bastarache, Black Pony

The bucking Bronco, having thrown its riders, had no intention of coming down to earth anytime soon and appeared to be lazily circling the area. Westerman even got close to it as he was calling Black Pony base to scramble another fire team. Lynch and Westerman heard from the approaching rescue helicopter that Bastarache had checked in on his survival radio, but no one had not seen or heard Ford.

At that moment Pete Ford had his hands full.
Again I had an ejection seat malfunction. This was the rainy season . . . and I came down in a canal. I started drowning and I couldn't figure out why. Then as I was trying to analyze what was going on I realized I was in the ejection seat. I didn't get man/seat separation. So I reached down and undid the lap belt and that freed me from the seat. Then I was able to get my head back above water again. . . . Because of my preoccupation with my eye, coming down I never realized I was in the seat.

I pulled in the chute and stuffed it in the seat and sunk it all in the water so there wasn't any sign of me. I wasn't anywhere near Ed and didn't have any idea where he was. So I swam up this canal and saw a field of elephant grass and behind it even taller plants. I backed in and smoothed over the grass and got back in there as far as I could. I sat back in there and I'm up to my neck in water and mud . . . so I know nobody could come up behind me without me being aware of it. And out in front of me I have a good field of vision for about a hundred meters. . . .

I sat back there with my snub-nosed .38 with the star shells in it and my PRC-90 radio talking to John overhead. I could hear Ed talking on the radio too, although I didn't have a clue where he was. [11]

Pete Ford, Black Pony

Westerman and Lynch had a good idea where Ford and Bastarache were, now that they were in radio contact. The PBR sailors, meanwhile, had put together a "scratch squad" (a group of guys who had not moved their boats out yet, sailors who would be used as infantry) at the ATSB and loaded them on a slick for pickup. "India" 19, the Australian Royal Air Force slick, and Seawolf 46 arrived in the area about the same time and quickly spotted Bastarache. With the Seawolf gunship covering the rescue, the Aussie crew picked up the front seat pilot and then started looking for the copilot. But Pete Ford was still worried about the bad guys.

> The Aussies wanted me to pop a smoke. I didn't want to do that. I didn't want to give my position away. . . . I had already survived now. I wasn't about to give away my position. I used the same procedures for calling in a helo that I learned at J-West [jungle survival school, Western Pacific]. He finally spotted me. He set down in the clear area in front of me. When I tried to get up, I couldn't even move. They mud was sucking me down. The door gunner, a big guy, unstrapped and basically threw me into that helicopter.[12]
>
> Pete Ford, Black Pony

As soon as the two Black Ponies were safely aboard the helo, Westerman joined up on the pilotless Bronco.

> I decided I was going to go shoot the damned thing down. We pulled up behind it and went *brrrrrrt,* about six or eight bullets came out. I kind of considered coming up next to it and pushing it up on a wing or whatever, but it was bouncy, there was a lot of turbulence. . . . The last time I saw it, it was heading towards Saigon, and it disappeared into a cloud. I called Saigon and said, "You have an unmanned airplane heading your way." It must have turned around again. It was my one shot in life to shoot down an airplane, but I didn't have any damn bullets left.[13]

The Australian helicopter headed north towards Saigon and Black Pony 111, low on fuel, headed back to Binh Thuy. Ford's face was caked with mud and blood but he felt lucky to be alive. He had ejected from a Bronco twice, and both times, the escape system had malfunctioned. But he was alive to tell about it.

> They called the navy and told them they were taking us up to Long Binh. The navy said no, they would send a Seawolf to get us . . . They took us off the helo . . . and brought out all this Victorian Bitter beer and by the time the helo showed up Ed and I were feeling no pain. Not only that, they put cans of beer in every pocket we had in our flight suits. I could hardly walk. I had a case of beer in my flight suit.
>   Then the helos went all the way back to Binh Thuy. Then the flight surgeon said we needed to go to Long Binh. By the time I got medevacked to the hospital I had on only pajamas, no ID, no shoes, no uniform, no nothing. . . . The doctor was concerned with repairing the tear duct in my eye. He sewed it up . . . and I had a patch on it. The ward at Long Binh was terrible. All facial injuries . . . all ground troops. . . . They were concerned about

these guys giving up the will to live. . . . I was just trying to sleep. . . . They moved me into an ambulatory ward. I went to see a supply sergeant and talked him out of a pair of fatigues and some boots. I got this uniform . . . no insignia, no ID, no orders, nothing . . . and without my doctor knowing, hitched a ride on an army "six-by" [truck] over to Tan Son Nhut and then over to Navy COFAT, an air transport facility. I knew the chief that worked there in the mailroom and he got me on a mail plane back to Binh Thuy. When I showed up down there the flight surgeon went nuts and called back up to Long Binh. But they let me stay.

I got back in the saddle again in three weeks. One week to recover, then R and R. I said I couldn't decide whether I wanted to go to Hong Kong or Bangkok. The skipper said, "Well, I'll tell you what, I'll give you tickets to both."[14]

Pete Ford, Black Pony

13

Father Mac, the Warrior Priest

All places that the eye of heaven visits
Are to a wise man ports and happy havens.
—William Shakespeare, *King Richard II*

Father Ed McMahon, who had been a Catholic missionary in a war-torn Congo, found himself one day being confused with a mercenary. Missionary or mercenary—his captors did not seem to care. Imprisoned and awaiting execution, Father McMahon took things into his own hands and escaped.

But Father McMahon could not run away from danger, for he was drawn, not by a need to risk his life, but by a mission to serve those men who did choose to—as their profession. Father Mac—as he was known to fighting men—became a navy chaplain and eagerly volunteered for Vietnam.

Lt. Cdr. Joe DeFloria was the officer in charge of Detachment Golf, SEAL Team One at Binh Thuy from September 1970 to April 1971. DeFloria had a number of SEAL platoons in the Mekong Delta under his command.

As the commander of Det Golf, DeFloria was responsible to CTF-116 for special warfare operations. He had served a previous tour as officer in charge of Alpha Platoon in Nha Be. DeFloria was just settling in to his new assignment after two years with the Experimental Diving Unit when he would meet a very unusual man who would become a lifelong friend.

Skivvy Check

I'll never forget Father McMahon . . . he sort of adopted the SEAL team guys. He came aboard as a forty-something-year-old, brand-new navy guy, and he was a Jesuit priest. He was the chaplain, and he loved special warfare; he really wanted to get into combat.

The weekend he arrived in Binh Thuy, we were in the officers' club, and he was there dressed in his brand-new greens. He had his cross on and his lieutenant bars. His hat came down over his head. We were having a couple of beers—SEALs, Black Ponies, and Seawolves.

This little ensign guy who also just reported aboard was in there, reading a book, and we went over to him to do a skivvy check.

We walked up and said, "Hi, Ensign, how ya doing?"

He said, "Oh fine, Sirs."

We said, "Would you be wearing skivvies by any chance?"

Now, nobody wore skivvies back in those days; they were uncomfortable because of the environment we operated in. . . .

We said, "How about getting on your feet, Ensign."

So he stood up, and everybody looked down his pants and said, "Yeah, he's got skivvies on."

All of a sudden about fifteen sets of hands went down there, trying to rip them off.

Father McMahon was at the bar, watching this whole thing, and said, "You guys are the greatest. You guys are the funniest. Damn it . . . my kind of people."

So we said, "Well, how about you, Padre, do you wear skivvies?"

He said, "You wouldn't. I'm a man of the cloth."

Well, we got hold of him and just shredded his skivvies.

I remember going to the hospital with Father McMahon to see [two petty officers] Paul "PK" Barnes, who had lost his leg, and McClaren, the boat-support guy that lost his leg. We walked in, and these two guys were arguing over who has the shortest stump.

Father Mac told all the nurses and doctors, "These are my people."[1]

Joe DeFloria, SEAL

Father Mac began hanging out with his kind of people so much that he soon became one of the boys. Personable, caring, compassionate, he was all of these things and more—he could talk salty like a boatswain's mate, drink with the best of them, tell funny stories better than most of them, and play poker better than any of them. And he would prove his courage on many occasions, for Father Mac had an unusual plan.

Father Mac's Plan of Attack

I flew a lot in the Black Pony CO's back seat (Cdr. Bob Porter). Well, the thing is, I just loved it, and I never got sick, of course, but I loved flying. And, on one combat mission, he grayed out, and I took over the plane—just until he came back to his sensibilities—because I wasn't that good. I could just about keep the plane level, but that's about all. And so I did, and then when he took over, I saw in the mirror that he was okay, we went back into the formation. . . .

I'll tell you why I flew so much with the Black Ponies. There's a thing in the navy about going to chapel. A lot of you men will not come to chapel unless the chaplain is part of their section, brigade, ship, whatever. So, I wasn't getting any of the aviators, and I couldn't figure it out. And then Bob Porter said something to me one day. He said, "These guys aren't going to start going to chapel until you start flying with them."

And I said, "Really?" Because I love to fly, you know. "Do you think I could do that?"

He said, "Sure."

And that's how the whole thing came about. And honest to Pete, to tell you the truth, it worked. It really worked. We had HAL-3 and VAL-4 guys coming to chapel, both Protestant and Catholic, precisely because we were flying with them. And that's the only reason I did it. Some people might think, gee, he was very brave, and he wanted to be with the men and all that. That wasn't it at all. I'm not very brave . . . it was a marketing ploy.

In other words I wanted to get these guys into chapel and pray and get their souls close to God, so that was the whole point of it. But it was really a great, great experience. I loved it because I admire aviators so much. And . . . I felt the naval aviators were the greatest in the world. Now, I flew with the army guys, too. I flew with the Loach pilots. And their fatality rate was pretty high. . . . We lost a heck of a lot of them, and so I flew with them. I really did that to encourage them in their work. But my heart was with the naval aviators.[2]

Father Ed McMahon

Father Mac was drawn to those who he believed most needed him—those on the point of the spear. Rear echelon types could find other spiritual comfort and guidance. "Comfort the afflicted and afflict the comfortable" could have been his motto. When he wasn't performing his more formal priestly duties in Binh Thuy, or helping at the Providence Orphanage at Can Tho, Father Mac would always be with the fighting men, in the field or flying over it.

One day the delivery helicopter out to Hai Yien near Square Bay brought the SEALs a much-appreciated regular visitor. Besides the company, the SEALs looked forward to Father Mac's visits because they knew they would be playing blackjack. Not that they expected to win. At ten cents a chip, the stakes didn't seem high, but Father Mac always cleaned house. The SEALs nevertheless had fun losing to the padre, and knew where the money went—to the Providence Orphanage.

"God knows what you have; that's why I win and you lose."

After a late poker party with Father Mac, a loud *bam!* awakened Harry Constance, a fireman 1st class, in the middle of the night. Other shots followed as Constance picked up his Stoner and ammo belts from the foot of his bed and rushed outside to meet Master Chief Robert Gallagher (an interior communications electrician), the rest of the SEALs, and Father Mac.

The initial shots had come from an elderly Vietnamese civilian whom the one hundred ARVN soldiers in the compound considered *dinkidao* [crazy]. The old man had just wanted to be useful, both Gallagher and Constance believed, and so they had entrusted him with an old carbine and a few rounds of ammo. A good thing, for he stumbled upon the sapper attack and, in effect, sounded the alarm.

Gallagher and Constance quickly organized about twenty ARVN on a berm along a one-hundred-yard stretch of perimeter. No sooner had they positioned themselves than they learned from the old man that three sappers had slipped behind them in the tall grass. The fight then began, with heavy fire opening up from just beyond the perimeter, followed by fire from the three sappers behind the SEALs.

The SEALs tossed grenades over the berm and fired a LAAW (light antiarmor weapon) at the Vietcong outside the perimeter.

"Over the berm!" Constance yelled. They dove over the berm and fired toward the inside of the compound at the sappers. When fire erupted from the VC outside, the SEALs jumped back to the other side, leapfrogging back and forth like that for an hour. When Constance turned for the corpsman to send him to radio for air support, he looked up to see Father Mac.

"Father Mac, what're you doing?"

"I'm out here to help."

Constance quickly dispatched him for more ammo. When he returned, Father Mac toted a box of Stoner ammo and a box of M-16 bullets, each weighing about fifty pounds! He swiftly distributed the bullets.

"Father Mac, throw me down some more Stoner," someone would yell, and Father Mac would run the ammo can over to the guy and feed him the ammo.

"Praise the Lord and pass the ammunition," Father Mac would say, then he would drag out some more and distribute it as the firefight blazed on. He carried M-60s, grenades, ammo, whatever was needed.

The enemy had them so pinned down that Gallagher knew they had to take out the sappers or face being overrun. He invited Constance and two other SEALs to join him and they assaulted the sappers' position.

As he ran along the berm firing his Stoner at them, the VC threw a grenade at Constance. The explosion blew him into the air and twenty-five feet away, rendering him unconscious. The other SEALs tossed grenades at the sappers, blowing them up.

Father Mac helped carry Constance back to the team house in the compound. Constance had suffered burns over his arms and a mouthful of loose teeth, but miraculously, no frag wounds. As he had tumbled through the air, the hot barrel of his Stoner must have repeatedly beaten him about the arms and upper body. Father Mac attended to his wounds and gave him morphine, but Constance insisted on getting his clothes back on and rejoining the fight.

"All right," Father Mac reluctantly agreed, "I'll follow you back out."

As Father Mac helped the dazed and disoriented SEAL back out to the perimeter, a VC climbed out of the canal less than thirty feet from them. Constance fired a burst from his Stoner. "You're dead," he dazedly intoned.

"He's dead, all right," Father Mac proclaimed after examining the VC. He then proceeded to rifle through the enemy's backpack where the chaplain soon found explosives and detonators.

"Praise the Lord! Harry, he was headed to your SEAL team hootch to blow it up, I bet. You and I could have been in there when it blew! Thank God we came out here!"

When morning came, a main force VC battalion of around three hundred men had been repelled decisively by six SEALs, a hundred ARVN, an old man, and Father Mac.

Father Mac raised money for the Providence Orphanage in many ways, but his favorite was taking money from SEALs at the poker table. While they willing obliged the good padre, new sources of revenue needed to be opened up. And with them, more souls would be exposed to Father Mac's ministry.[3]

As the U.S. Navy turned over to the Vietnamese the remaining river and coastal fighting vessels in 1970, it would also transfer many of the bases from which they operated. ComNavForV placed the My Tho, Phu Cuong, Long Binh, Kien An, Chau Doc, Tan Chau, and Ha Tien operating bases under Vietnamese control. During this same period, the Vietnamese Navy took over the six advanced tactical support bases established on the Vam Co Dong and Vam Co Tay Rivers for the Giant Slingshot operation. But the last ATSBs would not be turned over for another year and would be the focus of much enemy activity requiring Black Pony and Seawolf air support.

In June 1969 the U.S. Navy had anchored the mobile pontoon base Sea Float in the middle of the Cua Lon River on the Ca Mau Peninsula, and it encountered heavy Vietcong opposition. The strong river currents and the remoteness of logistic support facilities made Sea Float difficult to maintain but the base denied the enemy a safe haven in this isolated corner of the Delta.[4] A few months after establishing Sea Float the navy set up nearby an advanced support tactical base like those on the Vam Co Tay and Vam Co Dong Rivers for PBR operations. The "Breezy Cove" ATSB supported patrols on the Ong Doc, a river bordering the dense and isolated U-Minh Forest area. Staging from the ATSB at the mouth of the Song Ong Doc, U.S. and Vietnamese PBRs of Operation Breezy Cove repeatedly intercepted and destroyed enemy resupply activities on the Ca Mau Peninsula.[5] Resupply activities in this area would prove crucial to enemy activities throughout the U-Minh Forest. Over the next eighteen months the U-Minh would be the focus of the most intense fighting ever encountered in the Mekong Delta, and the area in which the Black Ponies would fight their last battles.

At 2230 on the night of 20 October a company-sized enemy force attacked the Breezy Cove ATSB and the adjacent village with rockets, mortars, and heavy machine guns from both banks of the Ong Doc. Scores of mortar rounds fell on the ATSB within the first few minutes of the attack. Amid the explosions and chaos engulfing the base, 325 men scurried to their boats. The PBRs returned fire and the Coast Guard cutter *Bering Strait* salvoed 5-inch naval gunfire onto pre-selected targets along the banks of the river. Wounded were evacuated to the USS *Garrett County*, offshore in the Gulf of Thailand.

Three flights of Black Ponies were scrambled. The first, led by Lt. (jg) Don Hawkins, arrived overhead in the midst of the confusion and was unable to establish radio communications. The ammunition storage area then exploded, sending a fireball above the altitude of the OV-10s and lighting up the cockpit like the morning sun. Hawkins's flight had to return to base and refuel. But a second flight of Ponies, led by wingman Lt. (jg) Pete Walther when the leader experienced difficulties, arrived overhead at 0100 and was able to establish communications with CTG 116.2.

Walther and his copilot, Lt. (jg) Ross Hanover, were able to identify the enemy positions, but the pilots in the lead aircraft could not. Walther placed an air strike on the mortar sites, then moved his fire to a troop concentration that was preparing to overrun the base. The Ponies then remained overhead to direct friendly air strikes and fire. Walther's flight was credited with stopping the assault. The ATSB, virtually destroyed, burned all night. Two U.S. sailors had been killed in the attack and twenty-six were wounded. In the adjacent New Song Ong Doc, enemy mortar rounds had killed seven civilians and wounded thirty-three.[6]

On the night of 29 November Lt. Tom McCracken in Black Pony OV-10 number 103 scrambled with Lt. (jg) Charlie Moore in 113 on his wing to assist an outpost just south of Ha Tien under heavy attack. The Light Attack Fire Team placed a strike on enemy 82-mm mortar positions and troop concentrations. Hampered by inoperative flares and a low cloud ceiling, they had to use enemy rocket and mortar flashes as the only visible reference. They silenced all enemy mortar fire in five passes.

> The outpost was getting close to being overrun. The weather was really bad. We would roll in at eight hundred and shoot at four hundred feet. They had given up the perimeter and all they had was the inner circle. At the highest, we were at a thousand feet. We didn't shoot much in the way of Zunis at all. The guys on the ground said we caught the bad guys in the open. It was real hard keeping track of each other. The cloud layer was about fifteen hundred feet but the target was at about six hundred feet above sea level.[7]
>
> Tom McCracken, Black Pony

Forced to work beneath the overcast, the flight had exposed itself to enemy fire and the fragmentation pattern of its own rockets in order to draw enemy fire on itself, thus lessening the fierce attack on the outpost. The Black Ponies then remained on station to provide air cover for two army medevacs.[8]

On 1 December the South Vietnamese launched Tran Hung Dao Seventeen, the largest military operation of Military Region IV. Aimed at the Vietcong and North Vietnamese base camps and sanctuaries in the U-Minh Forest, this would be the largest allied offensive of the war in the Mekong Delta. Light Attack Squadron Four provided constant overhead coverage for convoys transiting the canals as well as close air support for the ground units of the 21st ARVN Division.[9]

The U-Minh had been an enemy sanctuary for twenty years. The audacity of the allied operation elicited a predictable response. Over the coming months, the enemy would probe, test, and attack all the support bases and outposts in and around the U-Minh Forest. Father Ed McMahon was visiting his sailors in the first week of December at one such base.

We'll Help You Out

At the end of the Ho Chi Minh Trail was a small U.S. Navy base at Kien An held by about seventy sailors. Sailors are not trained to hold a land base. Marines and army can do that, but our boys were sitting ducks. I used to go up there because I felt sorry for them.

On the night of 4 December 1970 we got hit by NVA, and they had everything but the bugles and the blue uniforms. And there were seventy of us, and there had to be hundreds of them. But, our kids . . . our sailors got really pissed off because our navy corpsman nearly got decapitated. There was a marine officer that took a bullet right through the heart. A couple of our guys really got badly hurt.

When these suicide troops first got under the tower, we had an old first class petty officer named Pappy. . . . He was from Alabama, a big red-headed, red bearded guy. . . . He went up in this tower and got an M-79 and was shooting at these guys charging us. Well, I got scared for him, and I ran up in the tower after him, and I said, "What can I do to help you?"

And he said, "Father, I don't think you should be shooting that weapon."

And I said, "Listen, they're only atheists, and atheists don't count."

And he said, "Lock and load."

But I didn't shoot at anybody. I took a .50 cal and I put fire out, but it was up in the air. I didn't shoot at anyone. . . . There were about four hundred of them and seventy of us. I was trying to keep my American kids alive, that's all.[10]

Father Ed McMahon

On the night before, just north of the base, a three-boat PBR patrol had spotted mortar flashes and moved in to provide support. Radarman 1st Class Warren K. "Tommy" Thomson, an advisor on the 54 boat, got on the radio and called the base.

I saw the flashes coming out of the mortars and I took them under fire. I was shooting back of the hootch line there where they were. The marine officer who had security for the Seabees while they were building that base called me up and said, "Check fire. There's friendly forces over there." I said, "Negative sir, I can see the mortar flashes." He said, "I said stop shooting." I said, "Aye, aye, sir, I'm clearing the area. My friends don't shoot at me." We got underway and left. They dusted off sixteen Seabees that night. The next night they got hit again and dusted off more Seabees and they dusted off the marine officer as well.[11]

Tommy Thomson, PBR sailor

While Father Mac was helping his guys on the ground, a Black Pony Fire Team that had been scrambled arrived overhead, led by Lt. (jg) Charlie Moore, with Lt. Cdr. Jimmie Hanks on his wing. Lt. Cdrs. Fritz Lynch and Jim Becker were the copilots.

When we got to Kien An we weren't really configured for this type of a night flight. We had taken whatever plane was available. I was the lead aircraft but I had the flares. The other aircraft did not have any. We really needed them when we got there because they told us that the enemy soldiers were coming in over the concertina wire. We had to find them quickly. So on the first pass I went in to punch out a flare and I dropped them. I dropped the pod. So now we've got no flares. We've got nothing. And these guys on the ground are screaming. They are in bad shape. They are hollering and screaming. They are scared shitless. I said, "Dig yourself a hole. Pull the dirt in on top of you. I'll put it on the wire."

So we alternately went down and got them to shoot at us so the other aircraft could see where the tracers were coming from. And that's how we knew where the perimeter of the base was. Because he told us they were coming through the wire. I didn't know where the wire was because I couldn't see it. So I figured the only thing to do was, if we could get them to shoot at us, we could see where the tracers were coming from. And that's how we would know where the perimeter was. I don't know how close I came, but we didn't kill any friendlies. And I put it right on top of them.[12]

Charlie Moore, Black Pony

Lt. (jg) Charlie Moore's flight was credited with stopping the enemy attack and saving the base from being overrun.[13] And Father Mac had time to reflect.

When it was all over, we really won that battle. We know we did because the NVA left their dead there, and the VC leader, and they don't usually do that. . . . So, the bodies started to deteriorate.

I remembered a sign I had once seen the ARVN put on a body of VC killed outside a South Vietnamese fire base: "Born in the North to die in the South."

Later, someone took a skull, a VC skull, and they nailed it to a board, and they used my poem, "Born in the North to die in the South; come to Kien An and we'll help you out." They put that on the sign in the Vietnamese language. And they put red and green running lights in the eyes of the skull. . . . And they nailed this damn thing on the top of the tower.

Now, Admiral Matthews heard about it, and of course, the Buddhists feel that if you're not buried below the ground—you know, here's a skull up on the tower—you won't go to heaven. Well, he called me in, and I didn't know anything about the sign or the skull or anything. Nobody told me anything. I left right after the battle.

Matthews called me in and said, "It's your fault, and as a clergyman, you ought to be ashamed of yourself."

I said, "What the hell are you talking about?"

He said, "Don't give me that, don't act stupid. You know what you did—put that goddamn sign up there in Kien An."

I turned to his adjutant and I said, "Commander, I don't know what the hell he's talking about."

And he said, "Just shut up."

The admiral got so pissed off he flew a helicopter with the adjutant and me up to Kien An. We circled the tower—no sign. Thank God. So, we landed, and the admiral was a little sheepish and said, "Well, Father, I might owe you an apology; I don't see anything."

And with that, one of our navy chiefs, one of the Filipinos, the guy who did my cooking for me, said, "Admiral, come on in the chiefs' club and have a beer."

Admiral Matthews said, "Good idea," and we walked down, and I'll be damned—on the door of the chiefs' club are the sign, the skull, and the two lights. And he just looked at me, and I looked at the ground, and he said, "Well, it can't be seen from the air. Let's go in and have a beer."[14]

Father Ed McMahon

The Mekong Delta was his parish. And Father Mac liked to make house calls. His flock was made up of American fighting men. But more than any other, Father Mac's "kind of people" were SEALs, Black Ponies, and Seawolves. SEAL Det Golf O-in-C Lt. Cdr. Joe DeFloria could attest to that.

Allegiance

It was New Year's Eve of 1970, and Capt. Marty Twite, the skipper of the Seawolf det in Binh Thuy, Commodore Spruit, myself, Father Mac, and a couple of others were in this pickup truck, and we were going over to the air base for New Year's Eve. So, we're all in the truck and we drive up to the gate and the guy stops us. He says, "Who in the hell is in charge here?"

Twite says, "I am. Is there any problem?"

"No, sir." So, we had a few drinks there and we wound up going over to the "crackshack," the nurses' club. So, we get in there, and it's probably

11:30 at night, just before midnight, and we're all having fun and dancing and all that. Twite was half in the bag, as we all were, and somebody came up and said, "Hey, Joe, they're really giving Twite a bad time there at the bar." So, I say, okay, and walk in there, and Twite says, "Joe, that son of a bitch here won't give me a drink."

I said, "What the hell's the problem here?"

The guy says, "Who the hell are you?" And boom, I hit the guy, and all of a sudden the whole place is fighting . . . *wham, bang, bam,* and McMahon is yelling, "Come on you guys!" And then we hear the sirens coming, so we scattered and broke it up.

The next day the base commander says he wants to see Twite, DeFloria, and Spruit. And McMahon says, "I'm goin' with ya."

So, we go over and see the guy, and he says, "You people ought to be ashamed of yourselves. We're over here, having a nice get-together. . . ."

He then called us barbarians or something and McMahon jumped to his feet and said, "What are you talking about? Do you know who these people are? Do you know these guys are up there risking their life every day for you while you're sitting there on your big fat ass?"

And the colonel says, "Well, Father, I don't understand if your allegiance is to your God or to the SEALs."[15]

Joe DeFloria, SEAL

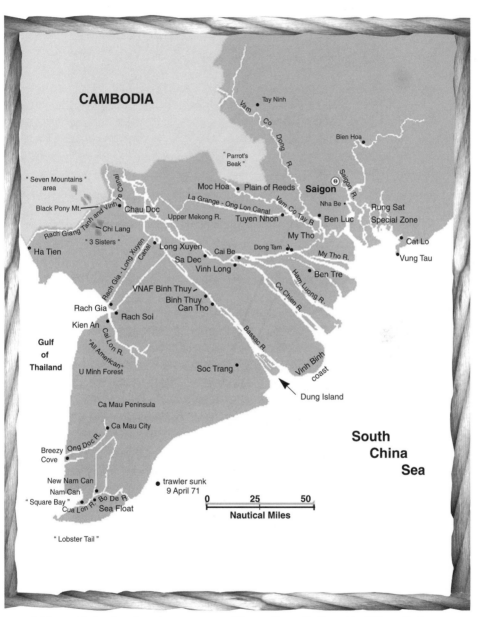

Mekong Delta Landmarks *courtesy of Roger Powell, Graphic Effects Ltd.*

Commanders Winans (CO) and Schuman (XO) cut the commissioning cake
U.S. Navy

Plankowners 3 January 1969. *Left to right,* Goodman, Bennett, Conrad, Martin, Savard, Zagortz, Pratt, Russell, Edwards, Wheeler, Sapp, Rezeau, Campbell, Brennan, Schuman, Dunn, Leeburn, Schauer, Winans, unidentified man behind Winans, Robertson, Stoddert, Hering, Chadwick, Mason, Fry, unidentified man, Florko, Sikkink, Sheehan. (Not in picture, Quinlan, Ballard, Bartlet, Butterfield, Ewing, Johnson, Kersey, Brewster) *courtesy of Ken and Tudy Russell*

OV-10 BUNO 155503 (side number 115) over a PBR *U.S. Navy*

OV-10A Bronco with its ordnance displayed in a Vung Tau revetment *U.S. Navy*

"War is hell." Hawkins on the beach at Vung Tau *courtesy of Don Hawkins*

Ordnancemen break out 5-inch Zuni rockets. *Left to right,* Two unidentified men, Aviation Ordnanceman 3d Class Lefferts, and Aviation Ordnanceman 2d Class Brown) *courtesy of Larry Hone*

Left to right, Schauer, Sheehan, Leebern, Hering, Johnson, Sikkink, Stoddert, Conrad, with Pete Russell in the cockpit; note the pierced steel planking (PSP), also called "Marston matting." *courtesy of Ken and Tudy Russell*

OV-10 BUNO155503 (side number 115) flies over a river. This Vung Tau–based aircraft was shot down over the Rung Sat on 20 December 1969. Capt. Carl Long and Lt. (jg) Joel Sandberg were killed in action. *U.S. Navy*

Cdr. Verle Klein and the JOs. This picture was taken after the JGs ordered caps to imitate commanders' caps, with oak leaves and "scrambled eggs." The caps sported two chrysanthemums for oak leaves and two OV-10s firing lightning bolts for scrambled eggs. The JGs made Klein an honorary *Trung-uy* (Vietnamese O-2 rank, similar to U.S. Navy JG). *Left to right,* Beever, Rosenberger, Wyatt, Moore, Monagan, Hawkins, Walther, Ford, Kellett, Baker, Hone, Klein, Madden, Bailey *courtesy of Charlie Moore*

Two Broncos roll in

On the flight line at NAS North Island after completing RAG training. *Left to right,* Sullivan, McCracken, Sikorski, Hanks, Beeley, Wyatt, Madden, Barton, Rausch *courtesy of Tim Sikorski*

Jere Barton just prior to the scramble on which he was killed in action. *courtesy of Jimmy Hanks*

Jimmy Hanks and the line crew at Binh Thuy *courtesy of Jimmy Hanks*

Completion of RAG training at NAS North Island. *Left to right,* Turner, Lynch, North American Tech Rep Ira Hughes, Smalling, Bastarache, Scholl, Meszaros, unidentified man, Becker, Aunchman, Florko, Goodman *courtesy of Jim Becker*

Briefing in the bunker at Binh Thuy; *left to right,* Bastarache, Henish, Morris, Smalling *courtesy of Jim Becker*

"Dobbs's last flight"; *left to right,* unidentified CTF-116 staff officer, Becker, Hanks, Dobbs, Hardie *courtesy of Jim Becker*

"Officers swimming pool," a swamp next to the revetments at VNAF Binh Thuy *VAL-4 "cruise book"*

AEC Devine at the "enlisted swimming pool" *VAL-4 "cruise book"*

Black Pony enlisted men and officers *U.S. Navy*

Unwinding in the author's BOQ room at Binh Thu after a combat mission. *Left to right,* Lavell, Harroun, and Segars

Bob Porter next to an enemy 12.7-mm antiaircraft gun that was captured during the "Battle for the U-Minh Forest."

Doc Rodgers paddling to work in a rocket canister canoe.

Max Britton reading a letter from home while sitting atop the trailer, his feet on the bomb shelter.

Pete Wylie with a Zuni rocket

Gintzer, *left,* and Parkes in VNAF Binh Thuy bunker at Christmas 1971

Black Pony "wranglers" at Binh Thuy

Two OV-10 Broncos kicking up sand over the Vinh Binh beach.

OV-10 Broncos with CBU-55 FAE bombs

Lavell next to OV-10 BUNO 155472, Gandalf the Gray Wizard. This aircraft is now on display at Carolinas Aviation Museum, Charlotte, North Carolina.

OV-10 Bronco firing a Zuni rocket *U.S. Navy*

The August 1990 presentation of a print by aviation artist and former Blue Angel, Capt. R. L. Rasmussen (Ret.), who is the current executive director of the National Museum of Naval Aviation, where the original painting hangs. In the Pentagon OP-05 Ready Room are, *left to right,* Vice Admiral Dunleavy and Black Ponies Capt. Mick McCullom, Capt. Ray Morris, and Capt. John Butterfield (Ret.) *courtesy of Larry Hone*

Ordnancemen loading 2.75-in rockets *U.S. Navy*

One of the last group photographs of the Black Ponies before they were decommissioned six months later. *Front row, left to right,* Segars, Wylie, Fleming, LoBalbo, Pyle, Arthur, Hal Smith, Lavell, Salmi, Williams (with Arnie the dog), Hurley, Rodgers, Britton. *Back row, left to right,* Pell, Andvick, Bumford, Lamberto, Schoenfeld, Salzman, Smalling, Henish, Porter (with Commander Zinn [Zee's replacement], the monkey on his shoulder), Chappell, Burton, Morris, Hotchkiss, Clarke, Leever, Despain, Hall, (unidentified officer behind Hall), Langston

Father Ed McMahon ("Father Mac") today, as chaplain of the New York Yankees, and with Derek Jeter and Jorge Posada. *Photo by Maria Bastone, courtesy of* Our Sunday Visitor

Westerman, *right,* and Ford before they were shot down. Note the original squadron emblem, before it was changed to a Black Pony. *courtesy of Pete Ford*

14

SEAL Extractions

When shall we three meet again
In thunder, lightning, or in rain?
When the hurlyburly's done,
When the battle's lost and won.

—William Shakespeare, *Macbeth*

On the night of 21 December Lt. Tom McCracken led a Fire Team scrambled to assist a five-man patrol from SEAL Team One's X-ray Platoon that had been ambushed by VC during their insertion sixteen klicks east of Ben Tre. Heavy fire by an estimated fifteen-man enemy force mortally wounded the patrol leader and automatic weapons man. Enemy fire also wounded the radioman and Vietnamese guide. The Black Ponies placed a strike on enemy positions and provided cover for a reinsertion of the SEALs to recover the body of the SEAL killed in the ambush.

Radioman 2d Class Harold Baker, the rear security man, rushed into the river during the initial fire, barely able to swim with his heavy load of equipment, to rescue a fellow SEAL. When he struggled ashore, he was dragging the body of a patrol member with him. Back on the bank Baker began a fierce counter-barrage, keeping the enemy force from overrunning the position. He then administered first aid to his team and helped evacuate them. Electrician's Mate 3d Class James Ritter and Chief Electrician's Mate Frank Bomar, a former PRU advisor with half a dozen SEAL Vietnam tours to his credit—both X-ray SEALs—died in the attack.[1]

Trapped in the Mud at Square Bay

Half of Lt. Dick Moran's SEAL Team Two/Ninth Platoon was split and sent to a small American position in an outpost village close to Square Bay called Hai Yien. The village consisted of a compound—six hundred meters by three hundred meters surrounded by dikes and concertina wire—in the middle of the jungle almost fifteen miles from the coast. About 250 civilians, 150 ARVN, and five enlisted SEALs called it home: MC Bob Gallagher and POs Harry Constance, Dickey Cyrus, Bobby Osborne, and Mike MacDonald.

Gallagher, Constance, and the other men had learned that a high-ranking VC who ran the entire district lived near Cua Song Bay Hap (or Square Bay). The SEALs planned an operation to go get him. On 22 January 1971 they inserted across tidal mud flats in a lower than expected tide. Caked in mud and behind schedule, Gallagher ordered Constance and Osborne to stay behind to provide security at the first hootch they encountered. Gallagher and the others crossed a canal to hit the hootches on the other side.

Osborne stood watch as Constance disassembled his Stoner, which was caked in mud and inoperable. No sooner than he had taken his weapon apart, Constance heard the unmistakable sound of oars slapping against the wooden hull of a sampan. He looked up to see four black pajama-wearing main force VC with AK-47s aimed at Gallagher and the other SEALs crossing the canal. The VC had not yet seen Constance or Osborne, who were now about fifteen feet from them as the VC floated by.

Constance signaled Osborne and they opened fire, Constance with his 9-millimeter pistol and Osborne with his shotgun, killing the first two VC. The second two jumped into the canal. In the excitement of his first combat, Osborne had emptied his shotgun.

"Bobby, we gotta get 'em!" Constance screamed, knowing that the VC would soon emerge from the water firing their AKs. Osborne instinctively threw his 250-pound body into the canal, screaming, "Yaaaaa!" Unarmed, but full of adrenaline and ferocity, Osborne extended his arms, and as the VC popped to the surface, he slammed the two surprised enemy against the sampan.

One of the VC slipped from Osborne's grasp into the water. Osborne strangled the other, while pounding his fist repeatedly into the man's face. As the other VC surfaced again, Constance pumped three shots into him with his pistol before the enemy could fire his AK-47.

Gallagher and the others joined up with Constance and Osborne. Knowing that their shooting probably woke up every VC in the vicinity, the SEALs re-floated the sampan and placed into it the body of the head VC, whom they had identified. They had a difficult, two-hundred-yard trek through the mud to the middle of the bay in what was now broad daylight.

A Vietcong company had followed the SEALs' mud trail to the bank overlooking the bay. There, the enemy set up their automatic weapons. The SEALs were not just sitting ducks; they were mired in the mud.

The VC opened fire, splattering the mud all around the SEALs. Gallagher, MacDonald, and Cyrus had M-16s; the others had only pistols. They valiantly fired back while pushing like mad to get to the open water, but knew they wouldn't make it.

Shells ripped into the sampan as they radioed for helos. Constance remembered that when the SEALs had been sent to Hai Yien, the higher-ups told them not to expect air support. The radio crackled with static, then Constance heard, "This is Seawolf Two Three. We've scrambled to your emergency. We'll be inbound to your location in ten minutes, over."

The SEALs told the Seawolf pilot that in two minutes the battle would be over. They were almost out of ammo and the VC were about to smoke them.

Gallagher had been out in the open, heading toward the sampan as bullets hit all around him. When he joined the other men who had been covering him, Gallagher ordered the men to get as far down into the mud as they could. It had been almost ten minutes since the Seawolf helo had called, but the SEALs could only see an empty, blue sky above, and bullets raining all around them. Just then, the incessant static gave way to that eerie silence that descends upon a radio when someone with a powerful transmitter keys onto your frequency.

"Moosejaw Seven Bravo, this is Pony One One Three," came the deep, resonant voice with the southern drawl from the sky above. "Have you in sight. We're coming inbound hot. Suggest you get down."

Lt. Cdr. Ken Williams led a flight of two Black Ponies, with Lt. Cdr. Fritz Lynch on his wing. In Williams's back seat was Lt. Cdr. Ron Mullins, an intelligence officer who worked with SEALs on the Joint Personnel Recovery Center team.

"Big guns! Big bullets! Big rockets! We might pull out of this after all!" Harry Constance rejoiced to himself. "Where the hell did he come from?" Constance shouted, "There aren't supposed to be any friendlies anywhere near us!"

The Black Ponies had been orbiting overhead, monitoring the radio traffic. And when the shooting started, they looked down and saw the

SEALs trapped in the mud. They watched the muzzle flashes and as soon as Lieutenant Commanders Williams and Lynch identified the enemy positions they rolled in on them.

Constance had run out of bullets, so he lay on his back in the mud, watching. Two tiny specks emerged from the sun streaking straight down. He saw plumes of fire thrust forward as 5-inch Zuni rockets headed for the VC guns on the bank. The sharp *crack* of the rockets breaking the sound barrier preceded the steady *brrrrrt* of the mini-guns. Then, almost instantaneously, the entire tree line and bank erupted into explosions. Constance watched fireworks-like flames burst seventy feet into the sky as the air exploded with the ear-shattering reverberations of the bombardment.

"Yes! We win!" they all shouted as the Black Ponies unleashed their remaining ordinance on the VC and then rendezvoused overhead.

"Moosejaw Seven Bravo, it's been a pleasure," Williams radioed. "We're heading back to Binh Thuy. Have a good day. Out."

As the SEALs were making the last few yards to their SEAL team assault boat (STAB), the Seawolves arrived and worked the target over to take out any remaining VC.[2]

Black Pony pilots sometimes would not know if the SEALs or other units on the ground that they shot for made it out okay until having returned to base. If the target were hot, the pilots would scramble more Ponies even while on target, provided they were within radio range. Sometimes the Fire Team would have to fly within radio range, or the unit on the ground would use a landline. The flight back to base could be agonizing for the pilots, for they knew they could do no more for their comrades on the ground.

Even when Black Ponies knew the men on the ground were safe, every pilot needed to know how well they performed their job of close air support. Feedback was necessary, even vital to building and maintaining the skills to do the job. But it was often difficult to get feedback. Occasionally, bomb damage assessment (BDA) reports would follow a mission by several days if an allied unit swept the area. After-action reports by units on the ground might credit the air units with killed-by-air (KBA) body counts, but not always, and in a war in which these kinds of numbers were always suspect, most pilots did not give them much credence.

After an op, SEAL platoon members would fill out their barndance cards. Like the spotreps that Black Ponies typed out after a mission, these detailed after-action reports made their way to ComNavForV in Saigon and up the chain of command. Occasionally, message traffic back to VAL-4 would summarize the after-action reports and provide an "attaboy" or other pat on the back.

The best feedback, however, came from the mouths of those the Black Ponies supported. Sometimes a SEAL would make it back to the Binh Thuy base and look up a Black Pony pilot who shot for him.

After the Square Bay op, Master Chief Gallagher gave Harry Constance a pair of lieutenant's bars and sent him back to Binh Thuy posing as an officer in order to obtain some much-needed supplies. Constance looked up Pony 113 and found him at the "O"Club. Ken Williams greeted Constance like an old friend. "Sit down, buddy! Have a drink. Tell me, how good did we do?" Constance was eager to tell him.

We relived the battle. One of the things we found was that pilots never knew the extent of damage they caused. They zipped in, dumped their load, and zipped out. They didn't know if they scared off the enemy, shot a water buffalo, or decimated a VC battalion. They loved getting direct feedback.

We sat there for an hour and a half, buying each other drinks, reliving the entire mission. We cleared the table, making marks. *I was here, they were there, you were there. . . .*

"You can go to your aircraft and paint a '30' on the side because just knowing how many muzzle flashes there were and how quiet it was afterwards—I don't think forty or fifty people were hiding. I think they were toast. It could not have been any other way."

We went into it, having a close-knit, combat camaraderie sort of good time. I always saw a unique camaraderie among naval units that was distinctly lacking in army units. Everybody in the navy would turn to and lend a hand for this one unit under fire, but the army guys sometimes wouldn't give a shit.

I was always amazed that anytime we went anywhere and we needed stuff we got it right away. We'd go out to a ship and they'd give us everything they had. I briefed Black Ponies and Seawolves a couple dozen times in Binh Thuy—as in, "This is a special op, and we're going to do preplanned target A, target B, and target C, and we will need preplanned fire, etc." And you'd be sitting around and the pilots would say, "You know what's better is if we could fly around over here and do this. . . ." They were some great planning ops. It was just great that we could get things going like that. . . .

As soon as Ponies would come on station, especially if they came in for a low level pass, we'd stand up, light up cigarettes, wave—the war's over for us, especially if the contact is not close, because you *know* what the other team's doing! They're trying to run for a big hole. . . . When Sea-wolves came in and fired those 2.75s—although devastating—they weren't that loud. They'd break off because they were running low on ammo and the Pony would be on-station, waiting to shoot. We'd know what's com-ing and the Vietcong would be thinking, "We scared away the helicopters." And these OV-10s would come out of the middle of nowhere about Mach two and let 'em have it, *voom, voom, voom!* The Zunis would break the sound barrier, *crack, crack, crack.* Psychologically, it was devastating. The Ponies couldn't be seen or heard right away—like you could hear the heli-copters for five minutes. "Oh . . . but we're going to get hit by helicopters. Oookay. We got plenty of time. . . . " They never heard Ponies. *We* heard them on the radios. We were lucky.[3]

Harry Constance, SEAL

Black Ponies would frequently receive visitors seeking particular pilots to thank for a close air support mission on which they worked together. Sometimes the visitors had even more important things on their minds.

I was ordnance officer at Binh Thuy (around September 1970). This SEAL comes by asking for me by name. He was a really big guy. He said Mike Slattery, whom I knew from flight school, sent him over there. "You've got those thingamajigs that those bullets run through on your airplane." He was referring to the flexible tubing in the sponsons that feed the M-60s.

I said, "Yeah, we do."

And he said, "Well, I would like to get one of those."

I said, "Those things don't break, so we don't have any extra ones. What the hell do you need one of those for?"

He said, "Well, I carry an M-60. And I've got this pack." The guy car-ried one of those large canisters of bullets that were 150 pounds or so. He had it built onto a strap so he could carry it on his back. He was the point man on the SEAL team. He said, "Every now and then I have to go to work. And I've got to throw these bullets out into the grass. And I can shoot until the bullets get caught up to my body. Then I got to stop work-ing. Then I got to throw these bullets back out onto the grass to be able to shoot again. If I had one of these feed mechanisms, I could build it right onto that canister and right onto my gun and I could just keep right on working whenever I needed to."

I go, "Holy shit. Hey Chief, take one of those off that airplane. We can get by without it. This boy really needs one of those. He needs to work."[4]

Tim Sikorski, Black Pony

And on other occasions, visitors to the home of the Black Ponies man-aged to find the person they were looking for.

Late summer of 1970, while standing the duty in the bunker, a young army soldier came in looking for "Black Pony 14." I explained that we did not use personal call signs at that time and would only use the side number of the aircraft that we were flying.[5] So there was no way to know who 14 was without knowing the details of the strike. He said he had worked with a flight the previous week, in the Seven Mountains area, and had gotten pinned down. Two Black Ponies came to his rescue and put in the closest air strike he had ever been involved in. His men were separated and VC were between the two groups. The Black Ponies put in their ordnance one rocket at a time on to the VC position, sometimes within twenty-five feet of him or his men.

I then said that I was the wingman on that flight, [for] which Commander Rausch had lead. We knew the situation and knew how close the friendlies were to the strike area and would only fire one rocket per run. I noticed on his Ranger cap, in the band, were a bunch of rings circling the hat. I asked what the rings were for.

"Those were rings from smokes that I had used when I lost men to friendly fire. Your strike was by far the closest I had ever worked aircraft. None of my men was injured. . . .

"Thanks."[6]

Tim Sikorski, Black Pony

15

Hunter Killers

Rascals, would you live forever?

—Frederick the Great

Radarman 1st Class Warren "Tommy" Thomson had worked
with Black Ponies many times, including during the invasion
of Cambodia when his 54 boat survived with ten others out of
a convoy of twenty-two PBRs, and also the night Kien An was
attacked. He knew Father Mac very well, but had not known
he was at the base that night. Thomson would work with
Black Ponies again on 28 February 1971, when at 0614 in the
morning he and the Vietnamese sailors from RPD whom he
advised had broken ambush with three PBRs south of Rach
Soi on the Cai Be River. Thomson was in 58, the northern
boat, a Mark Two Alpha. They had enemy movement out in
front of them all night long, but they couldn't get in close
enough to take them under fire. They broke ambush just after
dawn and were running up the river. Thomson was up on the
bow sitting on the "rounddown" (rounded edge).

> For some reason I put my flak jacket and helmet on, and I
> never wore a flak jacket and helmet. Toha, the Vietnamese
> boat captain, was driving the boat and he was hugging the
> edge of the river because in a PBR the shallower the water
> the faster you went.

I saw two aiming stakes, and I saw the first recoilless rifle pop. I knew what it was as soon as it happened. We took two 57-mm recoilless rifle rounds in the port fuel tank and the second hit right behind it. It blew us completely aground.

I woke up and the ammunition was cooking off and the engines were running full bore. I jumped into the coxswain's slat and we had two cables that were the fuel cutoffs for the engine. I was so scared when I grabbed them I broke both of them. Of course the diesel was running, and it was so hot it wouldn't shut off anyway.

Everybody was dead except Toha. . . .

When both 57-mm recoilless rifle rounds hit in the fuel tank the explosion blew Toha up into the canopy then back onto the engine covers. The inside of his stomach was all ruptured. I yelled at Toha, "Get a machine gun and jump off!"

We didn't use the Vietnamese radios because they were unreliable. I had a PRC-25 radio and I had it tied down to the engine covers. I took my K-bar knife and cut it loose. I jumped over the side with the radio. Toha had been hurt and he couldn't get back on the boat, so I picked him up and started carrying him south where the other boats were. They couldn't get close to us. A full battalion of NVA was in the way.

It started getting dark. I began calling in air strikes. We recently had lost a Seawolf out of Det Eight that was flying out of the strip at Rach Gia. Since they only had one bird they couldn't send it. But we got a pair of Ponies that had been on patrol.

If it hadn't of been for them I wouldn't have gotten out of there.

I ran south along a dike to join up with the other boats, even though Rach Soi was north of us, when a poor little old fisherman in black pajamas stepped out of his hootch. I dropped the PRC-25, dropped Toha, and pulled out my .38 and fired three shots at him and [the bullets] still hadn't hit the World yet I was shaking so badly. Toha told me he [the old man] was a fisherman so don't sweat it. So we took off running again. That's when we went over to a canal and got underneath a nipa palm.

We hid under the nipa palm all night. . . . I called in strikes over and over. . . .

When the boats picked me up, I put Toha up on the bow. Then the adrenaline just left me and I fell down and started throwing up. I couldn't stand up. That was one of the worst firefights I had the whole time I was over there.

I told them, "Let's pull this damned PBR in the middle of the river. I don't want to leave a monument to Charlie." So we pulled it into the middle of the river. The boat was burnt down below the waterline. It melted all the blowers on the engine. The only thing left on that boat was the block of the two 6053 Detroit Diesel engines.

I had gone into the "chief's quarters," where the radios and radar were. I reached into the KY-8 and pulled my "sandwich" out, and put it into my side pocket, which of course zeroed everything out on the KY-8. Washington was more concerned about the crypto than anything else. They sent the SEAL team that worked with us at Rach Soi and they put twenty pounds of C-4 on this boat lying at the bottom of this river. They widened that river by about three times.

The Ponies were some of the greatest things that ever happened to a PBR sailor.[1]

Tommy Thomson, PBR sailor

New replacement pilots joined the Black Ponies in early 1971: Lt. Max Britton and Lts. (jg) Mike Despain, Joe Keller, Hal Smith, Ray Morris, and the new commanding officer, Cdr. Bob Porter, who assumed command on 3 March from Cdr. Len Rausch. The changes in the Mekong Delta in the year that Cdr. Len Rausch was XO and CO were dramatic. Large areas that had been enemy controlled for decades, areas where farmers and fishermen had been displaced, now showed signs of renewal. Fishing, commerce, and boat activity returned to coastal areas and inland waterways throughout the Delta. Commander Rausch thought that the most dramatic evidence of this change was the difference he noticed over the year while flying at night. Where very few lights could be seen the year before, now one could see lights from villages throughout the Delta.

The Sikorski Debrief

I gave (a rather senior officer) his last failed check ride . . . for Fire Team Leader qualification, a week or two before leaving Vietnam. We went down to the U-Minh. He got the coordinates. I was in his back seat. Another senior officer and Al Meszaros were on the wing. They found the target. My front seat could never find it. We sat there for an hour and a half looking for these coordinates. I'd mark it on the map and pass it up to him. "Well, this is where I'm going to shoot." And I'd say, "No, that isn't it." And he'd say, "Does the wingman have it?" And I'd say, "Yeah."

He just couldn't read a map. He asked for a DME [equipment to measure distance from a fix] but that didn't do any good. Finally, I said, "It's time to go home." And he said, "I can't go home yet because I haven't fired."

"We've been circling the target for an hour and a half. It isn't my problem that you haven't fired."

On the way back he asked the wingman to join up on him. We were at twenty-five hundred feet and he does an aileron roll. Now, we haven't shot one ounce of ordnance. We're in cruise flight with a fully loaded OV-10 and he does a section aileron roll. We scoop out at about five hundred feet with the wingman much lower than we were . . . I don't say a word. . . .

When we get back, I was so damn mad I couldn't believe it. I threw my helmet all the way across the ready room like a bowling ball. He goes, "Did I pass?"

"Not only did you not pass . . . " and I pulled out my .38, "But I should blow your fucking brains out 'cause I'll save more lives if I kill you now."

Then he wanted to leave because he didn't like how the debrief was going. I said, "If you walk out of here I will definitely blow your fucking brains out."

He wanted to bring me up on charges because I threatened a superior officer. All Commander Rausch said was, "Hey, Sikorski said you didn't pass. You didn't pass."

When you're short, you really don't care. . . . When Bob Scholl did my going away party he said, "We're going to have a Sikorski debrief." He walked into the room and threw his helmet across the room, and pulls out his gun and says, "This is how Sikorski debriefs!"[2]

Tim Sikorski, Black Pony

As the Black Pony mission slowly evolved, pilots found themselves working more and more with U.S. Army aviation units in the Delta. Army fixed-wing aircraft were limited in the role they could play and could not fly tactical air support for their own army ground units. The air force controlled the TacAir mission and, except for marines and Black Ponies, flew all U.S. close air support missions requiring more firepower than helicopters alone could provide. In the Delta, after U.S. Air Force units left VNAF Binh Thuy in 1969 and 1970, this meant TacAir would have to fly down from the Saigon area. While Vietnamese Air Force A-37s operated out of Binh Thuy, few Americans—or ARVN for that matter—liked working with them. While the VNAF had some good pilots, as a whole, they were frequently unreliable, inaccurate, and had a reputation of not flying at night, on weekends, or in bad weather.

The army's OV-1 Mohawk could have been used as a weapons platform but was restricted to battlefield surveillance and reconnaissance. The Mohawk was a twin-turboprop Grumman-built aircraft that holds the distinction of being the only fixed-wing aircraft ever built specifically for the U.S. Army since the U.S. Air Force split off from it in 1947. The OV-1 was ideally suited for guerilla-type operations. By employing radar and infrared detection systems, the Mohawk negated one of the VC's major advantages—the use of darkness and weather to cloak his activities. The radar could detect a wide variety of vehicular movement, land or water borne, and the infrared could detect heat emissions, such as cooking fires or boat engines, associated with guerilla activities. These sensors were not dependent upon ambient light, but were equally effective at night—when the guerilla soldier was most active.

Mohawks from the 73d Surveillance Airplane Company out of Vung Tau would team up on night combat missions with Black Ponies as "hunter-killers." The OV-1 would identify targets and the OV-10 would destroy them. The 73d moved from Vung Tau to Long Thanh (North) Army Airfield in February 1970, breaking up what proved to be a promising team.

Later in 1971 a two-aircraft U.S. Marine YOV-10D detachment would work with Black Ponies at Binh Thuy performing the same type of mission. The YOV-10D had an advantage—it sported a 20-mm chin turret. The detachment of Night Observation Gunship System (NOGS) Broncos had a second generation "Pine" forward-looking infrared (FLIR) and a laser designator, the predecessors to today's more sophisticated systems. The NOGS would work at night, often pairing up with a Black Pony Fire Team. "Leatherneck" (the NOGS call sign) and Black Pony aircraft made for quite a team. The NOGS bird could find a single human being hiding beneath triple canopy jungle growth at night. Firing a 20-mm HE round without tracers, the NOGS would "sparkle" a target and the Black Ponies would then fire Zunis at it. On 14 July "Leatherneck 56," 1st Lt. Jim Dearborn, and "Black Pony 27," Lt. (jg) Sam Chipps, stopped a VC mortar attack on Duong Dong, the district capital on Phu Quoc Island, despite an electrical fire in the NOGS aircraft.[3]

Light Attack Squadron Four would go on to work with another "hunter-killer" team. However, this one was all-army, with the Black Ponies backing them up as the TacAir element. In the last year of the squadron's existence, the Black Ponies would work so closely with army aviation units that they effectively became hired guns for them. One of those units was "Darkhorse," C Troop (AIR) 16th Cavalry, whose operations room at Can Tho displayed a sign that read,

And lo, I beheld
A pale rider astride
A dark horse, and the
Rider's name was
Death

Darkhorse had been the air cavalry troop assigned to the "Big Red One," or 1st Division, that in 1970 became an independent troop of the 164th Aviation Group, operating out of Can Tho. The unit was divided into three platoons: lift, gun, and scout. Lift platoon UH-1H Huey slicks carried troops into landing zones (LZs). Gun pilots flew the AH-1G Cobra gunship, known as a "snake." Scout pilots (call sign "Outcast") flew the OH-6A Cayuse Light Observation Helicopter (LOH), know affectionately as the "Loach." The OH-6A was like a sports car—thirty feet long by four and a half feet wide, and weighing 2,160 pounds. The Loach carried a pilot, copilot observer, and a crew chief–door gunner. They would fly just a few feet above the ground looking for the enemy, and in eye-to-eye combat, engage him. In the long history of warfare, military scouts stand out as a special breed. Always out in front of friendly troops, at the point of the spear, the first to make contact, usually outgunned, the scout possessed an extraordinary blend of skills and courage. With the advent of the helicopter, "aeroscouts" became modern-day Kit Carsons and Jim Bowies operating in three dimensions above the battlefield.

A hunter-killer team consisted of a Loach scout and a Cobra gunship. The Loach pilot scouted the area looking for signs of the enemy, hoping to draw fire. The scout crew chief, on the right side behind him in the back, was the door gunner and responsible for throwing grenades out the door. Grenades included smoke of various colors, Willie Pete (white phosphorus), and concussion. Besides his M-60, the crew chief would also have an M-79 grenade launcher, an M-16, a shotgun, and various "toys."

> Some of the Darkhorse pilots would go flying with Black Ponies and we'd fly with them. I got a chance to fly front seat in a Cobra and left seat in a Loach. Before going out on a scout mission we'd help make some of the "toys," as the crew chiefs like Danny Miller would call them. Miller was an E-5 ("Buck" sergeant) who with his pilot Robert Todd was shot down in December 1971 in the U-Minh.[4] Before each mission Miller would make his toys. He would take a C-4 brick, break it in half, and wrap it around a concussion grenade. Then he would take a 2.75-inch rocket out of a Cobra, unscrew the nose cone, pack it full of C-4, put a concussion grade inside the hollow point, pack C-4 around it, and then he would drop that from the Loach. He would also make a "grass cutter" from a concussion grenade by taking thirteen rounds of M-60 and linking them together and sliding them in butt first on the concussion grenade. He'd then take thirteen more rounds, link them together, and then slide them in, bullet to bullet. Then he'd toss that from the door. He'd carry twenty to thirty of these "toys," as well as two to three thousand rounds of M-60.
>
> Kit Lavell, Black Pony

A platoon of Cobra pilots usually numbered eight, with two to an aircraft. There were usually never more that eight Loach pilots in a platoon at any one time. Each had a crew chief assigned to him. The rapid turnover of Loach pilots would often deplete a platoon of experienced pilots. During CWO2 Jim Wood's ten-month Charlie tour, out of twenty-one Loach pilots, nineteen went home dead or wounded.

Jim Wood was the "old man" of the outfit. He was twenty-two years old when most of his compatriots were nineteen or twenty, having just graduated from souped-up Chevies to Loaches. Chief Warrant Officer Two Wood would find himself one spring morning in the U-Minh Forest in one of the strangest situations he would ever experience in Vietnam.

Vietcong and North Vietnamese Army forces had been planning a reversal to the setbacks that ARVN and allied forces had dealt them over the last several months. The 21st ARVN Division had intruded on what had been a virtual enemy stronghold in the U-Minh Forest area of the western delta. Enemy forces would spring a trap, a trap that would set into motion a year-long escalation of fighting that would bring the Black Ponies and Darkhorse close together as a fighting team.

At first light on the morning of 21 March, an air cavalry "package" (AirCavPac) flew from the 31st Regimental Command Post of the 21st Division. The CavPac consisted of four Loaches, four Cobras, three slicks, and a UH-1H command and control ship. CWO2 Jim Wood in his Loach launched first.

> I had been in-country about six or eight months and nothing much bothered me. I was the lead pilot and we were down on the deck and it was just an eerie feeling. There were footprints everywhere. It looked like the Ho Chi Minh Trail. There was stuff everywhere and we couldn't get anybody to shoot at us. They had us recon an area because they wanted to put some infantry in and I told them don't do it, this is a bad area, do not put them in here. Go a couple of miles to the north and east and put them in. They said thanks very much, but we're putting them in here anyway.
>
> We were heading back to refuel, and of the first five copters that were coming in, the first two were shot down. And that day turned into an all day and into the night battle. . . . It turned out to be an NVA heavy weapons detachment.[5]
>
> Jim Wood, army Darkhorse pilot

The slicks had just put in sixty ARVN troops when the supporting helos began receiving withering 12.7-mm antiaircraft fire from three widely spaced sites. In a mater of minutes two Cobras were shot down, one of which burned on impact. All four pilots were wounded, one critically. The commanding officer of the 164th Combat Aviation Group himself picked up the critically wounded pilot. Warrant Officer Wayne Burk, who piloted one of the Cobras that was shot down, recalled:

> I remember it being a real overcast day because of the rice fires. We couldn't stay above the fifteen-hundred-foot small arms envelope. The ARVN had been in contact and were in danger of being overrun, so we went in very low. . . . I remember making two or three runs, then just getting plastered. Hydraulic light, engine fire light, smoke in the cockpit. Tony Flowers may have been our C and C [command and control] that day. He said the ship was on fire with the flames well above the rotor head. We had gone in with scouts initially but we cleared them out of the area because, with the restricted visibility, we couldn't cover them properly. . . .
>
> Buddy Dehoff in the front seat turned off all the electrical power, which stopped the smoke. Then I zeroed out the airspeed over the jungle. . . . They suggested that you back it in . . . go down tail first. Somewhere we had lost all engine power so we didn't have any hydraulic power or electrical and the thing was on fire. We zeroed out the airspeed and finished the auto rotation right above the trees. The last thing was to bring the cyclic back and get the tail into the jungle. I remember falling forever. . . . We hit on the tail and sort of scrunched to the left and then the aircraft came down hard on the right side such that my cockpit canopy door couldn't be opened. I remember rockets coming off. Buddy got out and waited for me to get out. I just sat there and told him I'd had enough. He came back.
>
> Eventually I took off my helmet and the "chicken plate" armor and climbed over the rocket side. . . . I'm not sure how long we were down . . . but eventually we found a couple of scouts the ARVN had sent out for us. Sometime later our own scouts flew in one at a time and each of us climbed up on a skid. . . . They flew us back to where our slicks were. They got us on Hueys and medevacked us back to Binh Thuy.
>
> It was quad fifties that brought us down and there were so many holes in the cockpit—7.62s, a mixture of small arms and quad fifties. I remember in one of the dives not being able to turn because if I did, there were tracers on both sides.[6]
>
> Wayne Burk, army Darkhorse pilot

Burk spent three weeks at Third Surgical Hospital in Binh Thuy with compression fractures. The doctors were going to send him to Japan for therapy, but he got up from his hospital bed and asked them to show him the X-rays. He then refused the treatment. Back at Darkhorse, Burk would fly, get helped out of the Cobra, get therapy, then fly again because Charlie 16th had lost so many people. He would be shot down four times.[7]

During the remainder of the day, the fighting continued and by 1600 all the flyable helicopters in the Mekong Delta were in the area. Low clouds, smoke, and fog prevented TacAir out of Saigon from supporting the helicopters. But a Black Pony flight led by Lt. (jg) Charlie Moore with Lt. Cdr. Jim Becker on his wing found the target below the low clouds and placed a strike on the .51-caliber sites. Early on the morning of 22 March, a Black Pony flight led by Lt. (jg) Don Hawkins in 113 with Lt. Cdr. Fritz Lynch in 107 joined the battle. They were credited with the destruction of a 12.7-mm site and a .61-mm mortar and saving the lives of the ARVN soldiers and their advisor.[8]

> They asked us to put a strike in ten meters away. I said, "You don't understand. This Zuni's got a fifty-foot fireball."
>
> They radioed back, "Go ahead and do it. Either you are going to knock them out or they're going to get us." Fritz and I put the strike in.
>
> When it was all over, they said, "You did super. You never came any closer than seven meters to us."
>
> I felt like saying, "You son of a bitch." And I just laughed.[9]
>
> Don Hawkins, Black Pony

Later in the morning another Loach was shot down. By the second day, of the thirty-seven helos in the air battle, five would be shot down and another five damaged so badly they barely made it back to the nearest staging field. Twenty of the remainder received battle damage.[10] And CWO2 Jim Wood flew another scout mission.

> The next day I went out again for first light VR as the lead scout pilot. One of the eeriest things that I saw in my entire tour was to come across a guy with one leg chained to a wheeled .50-caliber antiaircraft gun. He was dead and he was left behind. They pulled out and were completely gone the next morning. We spent hours looking for them.[11]
>
> Jim Wood

By the third day ARVN forces had advanced to the enemy positions and found two 12.7-mm antiaircraft guns and five burned-out barrels. Total enemy dead amounted to only thirty, and only a few more weapons were captured. Friendly casualties amounted to thirteen killed and thirty-one wounded. And the enemy had shot down or damaged eleven helicopters—more in two days than in the previous three months in the U-Minh.[12] A very expensive "victory." From that day forward two changes would shape the rest of the war in the Mekong Delta. The 21st ARVN Division would build eight more bases for battalion-sized units. These bases would be used to stage aggressive forays into enemy-held territory and would themselves become the targets of sustained and bloody attacks. And the second change would be the increasingly close working relationship the 21st ARVN Division and the 164th Combat Aviation Group would develop with the Black Ponies.

Lt. Howard "Hotch" Hotchkiss was wounded in action on 5 April but flew the aircraft back to base and landed safely. Hotch flew his plane back to the base after a round intruded into his cockpit, shattered the landing gear handle, passed under his left leg, went through the ejection handle between his legs (almost ejecting or "punching" him out) and penetrated his right leg. Although it was painful, Hotch didn't think he was losing too much blood, but he couldn't tell for sure. So, according to SOP, he radioed home that he'd taken a hit. Back at the base, everyone gathered around the radio waiting to hear Hotch when he checked in. This was a really big deal, because the guy in the back of Hotch's aircraft was a marine observer and would be of no use to Hotch (or himself for that matter) if Hotch passed out. The marine was not a pilot and could not have landed the aircraft. Hotch tried to talk the situation over very calmly with the backseat guy, who could only guess at how badly Hotch was hit, since Hotch was feigning "coolness."

Hotch made a straight-in approach and landed on the deck quickly. Every available man rushed to the de-arming area at the end of the runway, where a truck was waiting to get Hotch to the dispensary or to a helo if he needed to be medevacked.

The aircraft came to an abrupt halt, the propellers unwinding in the breeze, and men swarmed over the plane to pull Hotch out. With all the drama leading up to that moment, as in some war movie, one could see the letdown when they pulled Hotch from the plane only to discover that there was not more blood. Sure, everyone was glad Hotch was safe, but shouldn't there have been a little more blood?

Hotch was so . . . well, embarrassed . . . there is no other way to describe how he felt, that he later declined the Purple Heart, despite suffering a real and painful wound. But the XO ordered him to attend the awards ceremony to receive it anyway, because it was "important for the men, and you earned it, even though you shouldn't have been where you were to get hit in the first place."

That may have been a debatable point, but at the time Hotch really didn't want to be at an awards ceremony. And to make it worse, he had come down with the flu. It wasn't the leg wound that made his knees wobbly, as he stood at attention under the scorching sun. Just after the skipper pinned the purple-ribboned portrait of George Washington on his sweat-soaked jungle fatigues, Hotch fainted.

"With the way he made a nose dive onto the PSP, he should have been given another award, or at least a nine-point-oh for style," Lt. (jg) Mike Lamberto, who had been standing nearby, remarked.

In a squadron that created its own rules, that encouraged hanging it all out, flying by the seat of your pants, there was an implicit corollary—don't screw up—or if you do, do it with a sense of style—do it colorfully. None of the Rules or the Corollary were written down—there were no directives, procedures or policies to cover them, no one ever spoke about them. But they were understood.

Hotch was a good guy who was trying to fit in, but who seemed to have a reverse Midas touch. Hotch was like the donkey Eeyore, from the "Winnie-the-Pooh" tales, with a black cloud perpetually over his head. Hotch earned everyone's admiration when he overcame his fear of heights and climbed the huge water tower at the army base at Can Tho on the eve of the annual army/navy football game to paint "Beat Army" for all to see. But then he became the butt of jokes when he jumped into the back of a pickup, tripped and missed, and landed on his chin sprawled behind the truck, just about shattering his jaw. The full beard he grew while his chin healed would become his badge; it also provided a source for light-hearted banter, and eventually, merciless badgering. The CO didn't like beards, although navy regs permitted them, which Hotch pointed out to anybody who asked while he made a point of avoiding the CO.

When Admiral Zumwalt visited the Black Ponies again, he gave a talk to the assembled squadron, outlining, among other things, his plans to fight the rising drug problem in the navy. No one stood up when the admiral invited questions, except for Hotch, who asked when the plan went into effect. Soon, the admiral promised. Not soon enough, replied the lieutenant. Everyone was embarrassed . . . except for the admiral and the lieutenant. Admiral Zumwalt gave his personal commitment to action, and Hotch, knowing the urgency of dealing directly with the problem as a division officer, sat down, satisfied.

But Hotch wasn't the only one. Commander Bob Porter himself managed to alienate many in the squadron within a week of his own arrival in January. So much so that, not long afterward, as a bizarre joke, someone rolled a base-ball painted green into his room in a "simulated fragging." Like many of the pilots, the CO lived on alcohol and adrenaline. He flew hard and partied hard. After a few days of hectic flying, and nights of hard drinking, he would dis-appear from the center of attention for a while. When he emerged, regardless of the flight schedule, he commandeered an aircraft and crew, flew as many missions as he wanted for a few days, then repeated the cycle all over again.

16

The Trawler

But screw your courage to the sticking-place, and we'll not fail.

—William Shakespeare, *Macbeth*

Rear Adm. (later Vice Adm.) S. Robert Salzer became Com-NavForV in April 1971, serving until April 1972. In assessing Sea Lords the former commander of River Assault Force said that "despite SEA LORDS' successes, the sporadic and frequently inadequate nature of ground force participation in the interdiction effort precluded full realization of its potential. . . . Significantly, after Vietnamization of the barriers, ground force participation in these operations virtually ceased."[1] And as it ceased, by mid-1971, for all intents and purposes VAL-4 no longer was performing its original mission.

Market Time forces had detected during the war at least twelve North Vietnamese steel-hulled trawlers trying to infiltrate arms, ammunition, and supplies into South Vietnam. One managed to escape, but the others were destroyed, usually by being run aground and blown up, either by the trawler's crew or by allied naval or aerial gunfire. The third such trawler intercepted and destroyed, on 19 June 1966, yielded 250 tons of captured arms, as well as documents that painted an ominous picture. Some of the Russian, Chinese, and North Korean arms and ammunition had been manufactured less than one month before being captured. Navigator's log, charts, and the engineer's "bell book" revealed the trawler's infiltration route from Haiphong to South Vietnam to be the same route taken by previous infiltrators.[2]

Shortly after Rear Admiral Salzer assumed command of Naval Forces Vietnam, the allies detected renewed enemy attempts at infiltration by sea. According to Salzer, "Infiltration was the first threat that we participated in back in '65 and it became a very pressing consideration in 1971 and 72. . . . First of all, it was unmistakably clear that the North Vietnamese were trying major infiltration by 150- to 200-ton trawlers, loaded with ammunition."[3]

A navy P-3 Orion patrol aircraft spotted a North Vietnamese SL-8 infiltration trawler in the South China Sea, north of Borneo and east of Vietnam, at 1742 local time on Wednesday, 8 April 1971. The P-3 tracked the 168-foot trawler, the largest detected during the war, as it headed south. The P-3, whose call sign was "Back Door 06," handed off covert surveillance to the Coast Guard cutter *Morganthau* at 1845 on 9 April.[4]

Lt. Cdr. Bob White, VAL-4 operations officer, spent many hours over the next three days at CTF-116 operations center across the road at Navy Binh Thuy following the Secret "secured" message traffic concerning the trawler. Lt. (jg) Charlie Moore was the squadron's classified material control officer, but VAL-4 did not have a safe secure enough for Secret material, so the messages had to be read and remain across the road. White briefed the skipper about the efforts to track the trawler. Intelligence sources predicted its course as leading to the Mekong Delta.

Word spread among Black Pony pilots that the trawler might attempt a landfall sometime in the following seventy-two hours. Anticipation and excitement at the possibility of bagging such a trophy was tempered only by the realization, confirmed by intelligence, that the ship possessed radar-guided 37-mm and two twin-mounted 23-mm antiaircraft guns, along with an expected array of .51 caliber, automatic, and small arms weapons. Such devastating firepower could make short work of the lightly armored Bronco if the pilots were not both good and lucky. Over the next few days each Black Pony had ample opportunity to reflect on his skill, and how lucky he just might be.

The *Morganthau* continued tracking the trawler as it approached the Great Natuna Island, just north of Borneo, where it abruptly changed course and headed north toward the Mekong Delta of Vietnam. The Coast Guard cutter *Rush* relieved the *Morganthau* at 1040 on Sunday 11 April and continued shadowing the trawler.

Before retiring for the night Cdr. Bob Porter instructed Lt. Cdr. Bob White to awaken him if it looked as if the trawler would be making a landfall that night. Commander Porter wanted to lead the flight of Black Ponies scrambled to attack the ship.

As operations officer, Bob White approved the flight schedule that Lt. (jg) Lynn Henish, the flight schedules officer, had drafted the day before. By the luck of the draw, the bunker crew Sunday night would be Lt. Bruce Turner and Lts. (jg) Charlie Moore, Ed Bastarache, and Joe Keller. These four pilots did not know if they would be called upon to attack the trawler, but they were prepared.

The scramble aircraft that sat in the revetments carried full loads of Zuni rockets armed with "bunker busting" 48-pound warheads. Each carried a delayed fuse designed to penetrate what the rocket hit before exploding. On the wing stations, the aircraft had four Zunis with proximity fuses that would be ideal for flak suppression.

The squadron duty officer listened while the four pilots briefed. Each pilot was fully aware of the type of antiaircraft guns the flight would likely encounter if they were scrambled to attack the ship.

The army's G2 Air at the Air Intelligence Office in Can Tho, Capt. Ernie Wells, followed the trawler's progress also. He exchanged intelligence information with army Capt. George Walker, the section commander for the two YO3A silent running aircraft based at Vietnamese Air Force Base Binh Thuy. (The YO3A aircraft detachment belonged to the 73d Army Surveillance Aircraft Company at Long Than North.) Walker previously had attended a briefing at which he was asked to have his pilots fly the YO3A along the coastline at night searching for intelligence that might be used to predict where the trawler might offload its cargo.[5]

Warrant Officer Richard Osborne's YO3A lifted off into the darkness from Runway 6 at VNAF Binh Thuy. While the moon was full, it would provide no illumination that night because of the overcast and occasional marauding rain clouds. This would not hamper Osborne, for he and his observer would use starlight (night vision) equipment to ferret out the enemy along the eastern side of the Ca Mau Peninsula, seventy nautical miles south of Binh Thuy. He had a pretty good idea where to look and would be in communication with the Market Time patrol aircraft and ships in the area where the trawler was headed. Osborne's mission was to monitor small boat activity in the canals and waterways emptying into the South China Sea where the VC were expected to transit on the way to pick up the trawler's cargo unloaded just off shore.[6]

2318 H ("hours" local time)

At 2318, the North Vietnamese trawler entered the territorial waters of the Republic of Vietnam. The P-3 reported back to CTF-116 where Lt. Cdr. Bob White listened on the radio and knew the Black Pony bunker crew three miles away at the airbase would be scrambled. He also knew that that the much-anticipated mission would go to four well-qualified pilots. At about 2335, CTF-116 sent by secure radio to the Black Pony duty officer the message the pilots knew was coming. The squadron duty officer hit the scramble horn to alert the plane captains and the ordnance men. The flight crews sprinted from the bunker to man the waiting Broncos and were airborne within six minutes.

Warrant Officer Osborne, orbiting in the YO3A at the mouth of the Cua Ganh Hao, a small river on the Ca Mau Peninsula, knew something was about to happen. He was watching scores of vessels that all seemed to come together at the same time, concentrate, and then start moving down the little estuaries emptying into the Cua Ganh Hao. He remarked to himself that despite coming from several different areas, their movements appeared extremely well organized. They obviously were in communication, and he reported this over the radio.

Over the next few minutes the YO3A monitored the occasional radio exchanges between the *Rush* and the *Morganthau* (the Coast Guard cutters), the navy patrol gunboat USS *Antelope* (PG-86), the P-3, and the Vietnamese Navy PGMs 603, 619, and PB 715. As Warrant Officer Osborne listened to the allied warships while they discussed positioning, the small vessels he had been monitoring stopped and began going back up the estuaries. He reported this on the radio just as the *Rush* ordered the *Antelope* to close and challenge the trawler. When the *Antelope* fired a warning shot across her bow at 2343 the enemy trawler returned fire.

2355 H

Lieutenant Turner led the Light Attack Fire Team to the rendezvous coordinates, arriving at about 2355, where copilot Lt. (jg) Moore established communications with "Cracker Barrel," call sign of the on-scene tactical commander. Since the CO of the Coast Guard cutter *Rush* outranked the CO of the *Morganthau*, the *Rush* was the on-scene tactical commander. The word from Cracker Barrel was to orbit and wait, which the Fire Team did for forty-five minutes.[7]

The allied vessels fired at the trawler in the darkness, maneuvering with the enemy ship as it tried to evade capture. The UHF radio traffic was punctuated with calls as the ships sailed into, and tried to avoid, each other's gun lines.[8] Shallow coastal waters, the black night, clouds and rain, all contributed to the fog of battle. The P-3 was called in to drop paraflares for illumination but had difficulty finding the trawler and illuminated the Coast Guard cutters at first.

0037 H

At about 0037 Warrant Officer Osborne checked in on the UHF frequency. A few minutes later Osborne watched as the ships exchanged gunfire for about forty-five seconds before he heard a frantic call on the UHF.

"Iceland X-ray, Blue Water, this is Cracker Barrel, cease fire! Cease fire!"

From his vantage, Osborne thought the allied ships, running without lights, had surrounded the trawler, and had fired over the enemy vessel at each other.[9]

Osborne in the YO3A, and the Pony pilots in the OV-10s, orbited nearby, listening on the radios. They heard the ships discussing with the P-3 pilot where the trawler might be, and at about 0040, Pony lead aircraft copilot Moore radioed Cracker Barrel that they were still standing by. The *Rush* replied, "We don't think you guys can even find it."[10]

"Give us a chance," Moore asked.

The *Rush* then identified its own position for the Ponies with a "red-eye," using a red light shot straight up (so the enemy vessel could not see it) just as Turner brought the flight directly over the ship. He then turned to the heading that Cracker Barrel gave him and began timing. When he determined the flight had gone the estimated distance to the target, Turner punched out a paraflare, which quickly lit up the sky.

"I got a tally!" Bastarache radioed from 111, the wing aircraft.

"Roger," Turner replied. "Checking for clearance, Cracker Barrel," he quickly added as he set up for a rocket attack.

"Rog, go right on it." Cracker Barrel answered.

"You got a tally, Triple Sticks?"

"That's affirm," Bastarache replied.

"Okay, I'll be going in."

"Roger, I'm in behind you," the wingman replied, just as the trawler opened fire on Turner's aircraft, which had been silhouetted by two million candlepower from the flares it had just ejected behind itself. Bastarache watched as the lead aircraft, drawing intense fire, rolled in on the trawler. He couldn't believe what he saw. "Surely he'll be shot down," he thought. Miraculously, 101 emerged from the muzzle flashes and hail of tracers and zoomed into the sky.

Bastarache selected the Zuni rockets, flipped the Master Arm switch, and as he rolled the aircraft over into a dive, heard the electrical hum of the copilot's seat. Lt. (jg) Joe Keller lowered his seat all the way down, placed the map bag between his legs, and as the nose of the Bronco dropped toward the trawler, Keller began calling out the altitudes over the ICS.

"Three thousand . . . "

The enemy gunners unleashed a barrage of antiaircraft fire at the wing aircraft as it hurtled toward the enemy ship. Bastarache had never seen anything like that before. The sky burst into a phantasmagoria of multi-colored lights. "It's like driving through Las Vegas at a million miles an hour," he thought. Yellow, red, green tracers . . . all looking for him. Tracers that looked the size of basketballs passed over the canopy.

"Twenty-five hundred . . . "

The trawler loomed in the gun sight. Bastarache ignored the tracers and concentrated on the pipper, the dot in the center of the sight's "bull's-eye" as it slowly worked its way toward the muzzle flashes.

"Two thousand."

The pipper rose to the target just as the Bronco reached release altitude and Bastarache pickled four Zuni rockets. He pulled the stick into his lap and sent the aircraft skyward.

0042 H

Thoughts rushed through Turner's mind as he watched Bastarache pull out. It was a funny trick of perception, he thought, but Ed's plane was nowhere near him, yet it looked as if it were almost beside him in the glare of the paraflare. "What am I going to do with all this ordnance? I'm too scared to shoot!" he thought. He was not alone. All four pilots felt the same way. But training, instincts, and adrenaline soon took over.

"I'm off left," Bastarache reported.

"Rog, I got you. I'm still lights out and I'll be in," Turner replied.

0043 H

Bastarache craned his neck to look back at the trawler, trying to see where his rockets went. "Rog . . . can you judge my hits?"

"Roger, you were a little left and a little short," Bastarache heard Turner reply, as Black Pony 101 began its second rocket attack. Bastarache pulled 111 around tightly to keep Turner in sight and to roll back in on another rocket attack before the flickering, dwindling illumination went out. He then saw the sky light up and multi-colored balls of fire envelope the lead Bronco. "How could he not be shot down?" Bastarache thought.

"Heavy fire, heavy fire!" Lieutenant (junior grade) Keller radioed from Bastarache's back seat. "They're firing all kinds of stuff up at you!"

"I'm in," Bastarache reported as he rolled the Bronco over into a dive, aiming to put his Zunis right on top of the muzzle flashes. He salvoed his rockets and smartly pulled the Bronco skyward with the force of 4 Gs as the antiaircraft fire followed him.

"Off, left."

"Roger, let's make this as few as possible. He's got big stuff coming up."

"Roger that," Bastarache replied, as the flares went out and the sky went ink black. "You still got me, Charlie?"

"I've got you in sight," Lt. (jg) Charlie Moore radioed from the back seat of the lead aircraft.

"Why don't you come around and drop another flare?" Bastarache suggested since the lead aircraft was in a better position.

Turner had begun a climb from three thousand to four thousand feet and maneuvered to launch another set of flares. "Roger, flares will be out at four."

Bastarache searched the sky for the lead aircraft, but rain clouds began obscuring his vision. The radios crackled with static before the next transmission.

"Blue Water and Iceland X-ray, Cracker Barrel. Request you close in on the trawler and we'll set up on him again."

Bastarache then watched as the flares ignited. Before he could adjust his vision to find the trawler in the blackness below, he saw the flashes of what looked to be the 37-mm. They were followed by the twin 23-mm antiaircraft guns pouring streams of large yellow tracers into the sky where the flares—and Black Pony 101—seemed to hover motionless. "Put your lights out! He's got a good tally on you and he's firing heavy stuff at you."

0046 H

Turner flipped off the anticollision light—the red rotator—and climbed to five thousand feet. The clouds were making it difficult to keep the trawler and the other aircraft in sight, and the last set of flares quickly extinguished in the rain before the Black Ponies could begin another attack. While Bastarache turned toward the trawler to punch another set of flares, unbeknownst to him, the pilot of the P-3 was trying to avoid getting too close. He obviously did not want to become a target for anti-aircraft fire, or to run into the OV-10s.

"I'd say seven miles," the P-3 radar operator reported on the intercom. The pilot in command replied, "I don't want to get any closer than that."

"Roger."

"Did you hear that . . . are you listening to what's going on?"

"Yes, Sir."

"You see what they've got on that thing that they're shooting at them?" the pilot asked with a rising voice. "They're shooting at them with antiaircraft guns from the trawler."

Bastarache headed for the trawler and punched out more flares over him and immediately heard "Taking Fire!" from Black Pony 101.

"I'm in," Turner radioed as he dove for the trawler.

"Okay, I'll be in behind you."

Turner rolled in from five thousand feet and watched the tracers snaking their way toward him. He remarked to himself that the extra altitude did not seem to help much as the tracers did not burn out until well above the aircraft. The extra altitude did make it harder to track the ship, and of course, kept the aircraft in the dive longer. Copilot Moore had raised his seat to get a better look as Turner salvoed a barrage of Zuni rockets, then pulled out.

0050 H

Bastarache noted the position of the antiaircraft fire streaming up again, reset his switches, double-checked them, and then rolled in as Turner pulled out, but from a different angle. Behind him, copilot Keller raised his seat all the way up. "Hell, I'm never going to see a better show than this," he thought. The tracers continued, but it looked as if the gunners were having a harder time tracking the aircraft. The paraflare was drifting downwind and beginning to burn out, so the planes were more difficult to see. Bastarache selected the VT-fused Zuni rockets on the wing stations and pickled a string of them as he heard Turner call over the radio, "Taking fire!" *Whoosh, whoosh, whoosh, whoosh* echoed in the cockpit as more Zunis sped toward the target, now shimmering in the shadows of the dying paraflare. The Zuni rockets screamed into the trawler and flashed huge balls of molten shrapnel the length of the ship as they burst only feet above the deck.

"Christ Ed! Oh yeah!"

As Bastarache in the wing aircraft pulled out barely fifteen hundred feet above the enemy vessel, the number of tracers arcing up toward it suddenly diminished. The proximity fused Zunis had suppressed some of the heavy guns, probably the 37-mm, or had taken out the gunners who manned them.

Bastarache watched Turner's lead aircraft as it dove, then pulled out. "Off, right."

"Rog, you didn't take any fire that time," Bastarache reported, "but I think we might have got them on the last pass." But when he went lower to punch out more flares, the trawler opened up on him again. "He's alive, he's alive!" Bastarache radioed, "He's still shooting!"

The two Broncos climbed back to altitude.

0052 H

"Zero One, Cracker Barrel. When you've expended your ordnance, request you clear to the west and let me know at the time."

"Zero One, wilco," Turner answered.

Bastarache spotted the trawler again from between the clouds. "He's directly between me and the last set of flares."

"Okay."

"He's maneuvering in circles at this time."

"Okay, I've got you in sight, Ed."

"Okay, can I go in?"

"Go ahead."

"Roger, I'm in at this time." Bastarache rolled in on his fourth rocket attack after having selected the Zunis with the bunker busting warheads.

0053 H

Meanwhile the P-3 pilot was turning the big four-engine patrol craft to avoid getting too close to the action. "Okay, we're steady 090, Radar. Now talk to me!"

"Roger, we'll go out about five miles and begin our orbit again."

"Okay," the P-3 pilot interrupted. "Look out the port window here. There's all kind of stuff going on."

Bastarache's Zuni rockets hit amidships and exploded deep within the bowels of the ship, sending a fireball skyward.

"He's on fire." Turner radioed from overhead.

"He's on fire!" the P-3 pilot yelled into the intercom.

"You got him, Ed! He's on fire," Turner added as he maneuvered to begin another attack.

The voice of the P-3 pilot rose in excitement. "They got him! Yeah, look out the port side there, crew. You want to see what's happening."

0054 H

But before long, more clouds moved into the area, obscuring the trawler from the P-3 and the Black Ponies. Bastarache dropped lower to put out more flares.

"I'm in at this time. . . . He's still alive! He's still putting out fire!" Bastarache radioed as hit the pickle button directly over the smoking ship. "It's hung. No flares left."

"Say your angels."

"I'm at three five. Do you have a tally on him?"

0055 H

Turner did not have the trawler in sight, so Bastarache talked him toward the trawler, where he ejected another set of flares.

"I got a tally on him if you want me in, " Bastarache offered.

"Go."

"Say again please."

"Go ahead," Turner added.

"Roger."

"This is your last run-in."

0056 H

"Roger, last one." Bastarache then rolled in. Approaching release altitude he began pickling his remaining rockets and saw them hit short of the ship. He elected to press it when he realized that he had not readjusted the mil setting on the gun sight after increasing the roll-in altitude. He walked the last rockets up into the stern of the ship where he saw them explode at the waterline.

0058 H

Lt. Bruce Turner made a last rocket attack and then rendezvoused with the wing aircraft. The pilots watched the burning trawler list severely and begin a sharp port turn. As they rendezvoused above it, the ship went around in circles, like a dog chasing its tail. The delayed detonating Zunis had apparently disabled or locked up the rudder. An oil slick of about twenty-five times the size of the ship surrounded it. At 0100 the Ponies returned to base for another set of aircraft. They would not need them.[11]

What happened next is not clear, but at 0145 the trawler exploded and sank at coordinates WQ 478, 883.[12]

17

Battle for the Forest of Darkness

And oftentimes, to win us to our harm,
The instruments of darkness tell us truths,
Win us with honest trifles, to betray's
In deepest consequence.

—William Shakespeare, *Macbeth*

The U-Minh Forest had a reputation grounded in folklore, like the Okefenokee Swamp or the Everglades, going back more than a millennium. For years the enemy effectively owned the U-Minh, and it became the political and military nerve center of the Vietcong organization in the Mekong Delta and the headquarters of the the Communist Party (COSVN) in Military Region Three (which included most of the Mekong Delta). From their U-Minh stronghold, one sixth of South Vietnam's population and its most important food-producing region were within the enemy's grasp. The first phase of the allied U-Minh campaign began in December 1970 with the strategy to establish three major fire support bases for operations of the 21st ARVN Division's three regiments.

The first phase of the U-Minh campaign ended, by government decree, three weeks after the Black Ponies sank the trawler, which had been trying to resupply enemy units in the area. The first of May 1971 might have been an arbitrary date, but proved convenient for political ceremonies when President Thieu visited the Rang Dong firebase, home of the 33d Regiment.[1] The worst fighting in the U-Minh—and the Delta—was yet to come, however. And VAL-4's mission would evolve even more into one of providing close air support to troops in contact with the enemy. Total navy personnel in-country at the beginning of 1971 amounted to only one third of the 1968–1969 peak of thirty-eight thousand. A few months later, when it came time to pull more navy units out of Vietnam, logic was on the side of ComNavForV for deactivating VAL-4. However, because of the turn of events in the Delta in 1971, and unusual changes taking place within the Black Ponies, pressure was being exerted from the field all the way up to Gen. Creighton Abrams, commander of all the U.S. forces in Vietnam, to keep the Black Ponies in the Delta. The way the Black Ponies performed close air support gave the squadron a new lease on life. Light Attack Squadron Four flew close air support as it had been done in Korea and World War II—but had not been done since. Moreover, the Black Ponies worked as effectively with the army as the army's own helicopter attack units.

Replacement pilots Lt. Cdr. Steve Chappell and Lts. George Leever, Roy "Bubba" Segars, Lts. (jg) J. K. Pell, Neil Salmi, Steve Salzman, Mark Pyle, D. K. Sheldon, Ben LoBalbo, and the new flight surgeon, Lt. Steve Rodgers, reported aboard. ComNavForV turned over "Solid Anchor," the last American operation, to the Vietnamese Navy in April 1971, ending U.S. Navy operations in South Vietnam, except for a small number of advisors, HAL-3, and VAL-4—which ceased flying Tran Hung Dao patrols on 21 July.[2]

The Marine Corps YOV-10D detachment was preparing to depart. The Black Ponies had enjoyed working with the Night Observation Gunship System. And the men of the marine detachment had gotten along very well with the Black Ponies, after an initial "misunderstanding." Early on some Black Pony pilots had thought one of the marine officers had taken an immediate dislike to the navy squadron. When he first saw the Black Pony ordnancemen in their cut-offs—shirtless and coverless, with sweatbands, beards, and beads—the officer had tried to mete out marine, or perhaps just military, discipline to them. When the skipper heard about it, he called the officer into his office and promptly gave him hell.

Usually "Afterburner Bob" —as Commander Porter, a fighter pilot who had come from the F-4 Phantom community was known—was more a man of action and less of words. On more than one occasion he was known to fly a mission and say nothing at all. No calls on the radio to the ground, to his back seat, his wingman, or to the tower when he returned. He just fired his ordnance at a pre-briefed target in a "free fire" zone, flew back home at treetop level, and buzzed the tower in a popup fan break. After getting out of the aircraft, he immediately jumped into his Ponymobile and left.

In August new replacement pilots Lt. Cdr. Jay Schoenfeld; Lts. Jim Arthur, Ad Clark, Kit Lavell; and Lts. (jg) Tony Colantoni, Lyle Andvik, Pete Wylie, and Jim Bumford reported aboard in time for the peak fighting in the U-Minh campaign.

The infamous "Forest of Darkness," the U-Minh, is a heavily foliated area along the western, or Gulf of Thailand, coast of the Mekong Delta, which the South Vietnamese government had abandoned to the enemy until December 1970, in part because the terrain made military operations by the government so difficult. A foot or more of water covered the ground at least eight months of the year. Elephant grass grew six to eight feet high among the trees. Numerous winding streams and waterways were connected like a grid with geometric, straight canals that averaged three feet in depth. Stagnant marshlands and occasional savannas interspersed the area. It could have been "the kingdom of perpetual night," to use Shakespeare's phrase.

The first phase of the U-Minh campaign began in December 1970 with the strategy to establish three major fire support bases for operations of the 21st ARVN Division's three regiments: the 31st, the 32d, and the 33d. Each base possessed 105-mm and 155-mm howitzer batteries and depended on helicopters and boat convoys for resupply. The only dry ground came from dikes along the canal or next to individual rice paddies—or what soldiers were able to build up out of the mud. The intrusion of the ARVN into their previously secure forest domain obviously alarmed the Vietcong and NVA, and the audacity of the ARVN to build permanent forts elicited a predictably violent response: the firebases became the targets of a steady stream of assaults. The pattern was usually the same. A rocket or mortar barrage would surprise the base defenders, which the enemy hoped would also demoralize them. Mortars would be launched—82 mm and 120 mm—from as far away as thirty-nine hundred and fifty-seven meters respectively. Vietcong assault troops would then fire lightweight Chinese-made 75-mm recoilless rifles, modified to include a mortar sight, from behind tree lines up to eighteen hundred meters away.

Vietcong and North Vietnamese Army soldiers proved to be very resourceful. They could sneak a devastating array of firepower up to the perimeter of ARVN forward firebases. Enemy soldiers often carried rockets in two sections very close to the outpost, assembled them quickly, and fired them from just about any kind of launcher, including a metal tube, a wooden trough, or even two sticks serving as a resting fork. While they were not very accurate, the light weight and mobility of these weapons more than compensated by enabling them to be carried to within a couple of hundred meters of the fort, accurately aimed, and fired in salvos from the darkness. A direct hit could blow a gaping hole in a wall and destroy a bunker.

After a mortar or rocket barrage, often times the enemy would launch a diversionary attack, and then send in sappers as human bombs. Armed with explosives, the sappers would run up to the accordion wire surrounding the base perimeter, fall on it, and then detonate their charges, opening a hole for their comrades to run through.

Many such assaults took place in the first several months of the U-Minh campaign. Enemy assaults increased in May and July, with the heaviest combat of the campaign occurring during the "September Battle," which would begin on 4 September.

One of the first combat missions the Ponies flew in support of the 21st ARVN Division during this battle was on Labor Day as the XO, Cdr. Jim "Spike" Burton, led a scramble mission to the U-Minh, with Lt. (jg) Mike "Lambro" Lamberto flying wing, with copilot, Lt. Kit Lavell. They flew to the Hieu Le District town near the Rang Dong firebase, the 33d Regiment Command Post in the U-Minh Forest. The NVA 18-B Regiment had engaged the 33d and elements of the 31st, which had been heloed in two days before.[3]

The flight never got above eight hundred feet on the way to the target because of the overcast. If Ponies had to fly below two thousand feet, which was within the range of small arms, they usually flew as low as they could to avoid them. The thought being that if they were flying by the seat of the pants at treetop level, by the time the bad guys heard them, the Ponies would be gone, and the bad guys could not get a shot at them. At least that's how the reasoning went.

The Black Ponies spotted the forward firebase as they emerged from the broken clouds and intermittent showers. The bright morning sun tried to fire its rays at them from between the blackened, billowing cumulonimbus, and shafts of sunlight eventually burst into a rainbow over the target. But the pilots didn't have time to appreciate the gesture. Unable to achieve the vantage that altitude would afford them, they had to make several quick, low passes, literally over the bad guys, in order to assess the situation. That's when the Ponies saw them. Like little toy soldiers scattered on the floor in front of them, they saw a bunch of men scurrying between the trees, running toward a 12.7-mm machine gun set up at the end of the tree line. Apparently the Ponies surprised these guys, who probably thought the weather was too miserable for flying. The Black Ponies tried to climb between the clouds to make a rocket attack, but couldn't keep the ground in sight long enough and had to abort their first run in a dizzying rolling pullout just above the trees.

The Ponies would not have much time before the enemy set up their weapon, a 12.7 mounted on a two-wheeled cart with a long tow bar serving as one leg of a tripod when the weapon was used against ground targets. The enemy soldiers were apparently trying to tip it up into the anti-aircraft position. As soon as they did, it would be firing six hundred rounds of high explosive projectiles per minute at the OV-10s. Black Pony scuttlebutt was that the enemy fashioned crude wire gun sights that when attached to the barrel would provide just the right amount of lead for the OV-10's airspeed to nail it as it pulled off target. If the Bronco was in its sights and within its three-thousand-foot lethal range, it could be history. Spike warned Lambro to take a decent interval on him because he was going to launch Zuni rockets from an almost level run at five hundred feet. The fragmentation pattern from the rockets' explosions would extend outward and upward several hundred feet, so they would have to make a hard break turn, pulling at least 4 Gs, almost as soon as they launched them.

They turned toward the target at five hundred feet with machine guns blazing. No by-the-book mil setting for the gun sight needed on this run. This was all seat-of-the-pants. Spike fired a salvo of Zunis at the spot where the tracers burned out on their arc toward the ground. The rockets went sailing over the treetops. A quick pop on the stick. The arc of another barrage bent down into the trees. A fireball billowed up, and then debris hurtled toward them . . . hard break turn . . . copilot Lavell's helmet slammed into the canopy. Over his shoulder Lavell could see Lambro's rockets sailing over the trees. From the angle he had on his aircraft behind him, with his neck twisted tightly to the side, the blood and adrenalin surging into his brain, the rockets looked like a succession of freeze frames as they left the plane, got bigger, then impacted. It was like the crude self-animation in a small book he had as a kid, *Air Fighters of America* (The Better Little Book) . . . "See 'em MOVE, Just Flip the Pages—as the aircraft flies over and drops its ordnance on the enemy. . . ." But this was no kid's game. They continued their hard turn all the way around to the target with hardly any time to set up. Machine guns popping again—the first set of rockets skipped like rocks in a pond and impacted below the target this time, slamming into the rice paddy just in front of them, blowing mud up over their flight path. All their remaining rockets then left the aircraft like a freight train headed straight for the end of the tree line. And in a spectacular explosion the Pony pilots saw the machine gun and several bodies hurtled above the fireball as they broke hard to avoid them.

Marking Time

One hazy morning after the duty driver had deposited a group of fresh pilots at the bunker, several Black Ponies sat around the acey-deucey board drinking coffee and listening to a flight debrief. Lts. Max "Blue Max" Britton and Roy "Bubba" Segars had just returned from a scramble. They were laughing as everyone else stood around shaking their heads. Apparently, Max and Bubba had discovered that the VC had been listening in on their radio conversation with the good guys, who were in close contact with the enemy. "How did you know?" the squadron duty officer asked, incredulously. Every time Max asked the friendlies to pop a smoke grenade for identification, he said, two smokes of the same color appeared, about 150 meters apart. The good guys kept saying they were popping only one smoke. "So how did you know which smoke was the bad guys'?" the SDO asked, looking to the other pilots in the flight for an explanation. The back seat guys just shrugged their shoulders and shook their heads. Seems that after numerous attempts to identify them, the friendlies popped a green smoke, and the bad guys, apparently out of green, popped a purple. "Did anybody say anything?" the SDO asked. Everybody looked at each other in silence. "Well?" More silence. "Yeah," Bubba chimed in, "I said, 'I'm in on the goofy grape!'" Without hesitation and with confidence, Bubba rolled in and blew the purple smoke away with a barrage of rockets. And took everybody's breath away. Including thirteen bad guys'.[4]

Max and Bubba made quite a team on the ground as well as in the air. When Max reported aboard and went to the armory to pick up a weapon, he asked the armory officer, who at the time was Lt. Hotch Hotchkiss, for one of everything he had. Max became especially fond of a Bell Laboratories M31A1 .45-caliber submachine gun—what he called a "grease gun" because of its hair trigger—which he kept next to his rack when he slept. In the middle of one night he accidentally bumped it, discharging it into the thin plywood ceiling, and apparently into the room above. Max froze in his rack, and when he heard no noise, became convinced he had killed the guy sleeping in the room above. Mustering the courage to check out the situation topside, Max found the guy still asleep. Since the bullet hardly penetrated the plywood, Max thought the weapon's muzzle velocity was too low and promptly canned it.

A few months later Max was celebrating the Fourth of July after participating in an impromptu air show put on by *Afterburner Bob's Flying Circus*. After some beers and armed with two .38s, Max tried to shoot the sky above the BOQ but missed, sending bullets through several rooms. Cdr. Jim Burton, the XO, had to disarm him, and then tell him, "Max, go to your room," a phrase everyone conveniently used on Max from then on.

Jim Burton was the prototypical executive officer. No detail escaped him. And while he handled routine executive functions of the squadron well, he said it wasn't paperwork that interested him, but rather the welfare and morale of the squadron's enlisted men and officers. He enjoyed a reputation as an aggressive pilot. Six years before, as a lieutenant flying A-4s with Attack Squadron 164 off the USS *Oriskany*, Burton was bagged by "triple A" over North Vietnam. He stayed with the out-of-control aircraft until the last possible moment in order to get out over the water, where he ejected and was rescued. No one could remember the particulars of how he earned the nickname "Spike," though someone may have thought that he had betrayed a confidence and stabbed somebody in the back. Like most nicknames mercilessly given by pilots to one another, it may or may not have been grounded entirely in fact. Nicknames often had sticking power in inverse proportion to their truthfulness.

Spike did have a well-deserved reputation, however, as a shrewd businessman. He was known as one of the best cumshaw artists in the navy. Jim Burton would say that cumshaw is the old navy practice, really the art, of trading for, or otherwise using your ingenuity, to get what you want. It could be described as the real art of the deal. Two new replacement pilots quickly learned of Spike's skills firsthand when they decided to room together and "bought" the room belonging to the XO.

As we walked back to the BOQ with the XO, Spike made his sales pitch to us. New pilots usually inherited the rooms of pilots rotating back to the States. Many of the eight-by-eight-foot windowless rooms in the two-story wooden structure had improvements made by previous tenants. In addition to the metal beds and desks, most were filled with remembrances of home—pictures, posters, letters—and many had war trophies, like AK-47s or SKSs, or an occasional B-40 rocket launcher. One had a parachute hanging from the ceiling. Almost all had the obligatory centerfold pinup. A few rooms had stereos, fewer still, books, although almost all had copies of the PACEX [Pacific Exchange] and Navy Exchange catalogues from which just about anything could be ordered at prices much cheaper than stateside. Some rooms were quite elaborately modified, including walls removed to make "suites" shared by more than one officer.

Commander Jim Burton had such a layout. One of the connecting rooms had two bunks stacked one above the other and a built-in wooden desk with bookshelves. The other room could be used as a sitting room and had a bamboo and hardwood bar, complete with refrigerator. The XO strongly encouraged us to make our decision right then, because he would offer it to the other replacement pilots, and he assured us, it was a bargain that would be quickly snatched up. We bought everything, including the air conditioner, refrigerator, and bar. We sure did. We would later learn we could have bought the entire BOQ for what we paid the XO for his old room.

Two Black Pony "Newbies"

In August, a number of pilots would DEROS (date eligible to return from overseas) including Lt. Bob Scholl, who had flown with Commander Burton on one of Burton's first front seat hops, one on which they flew to a free fire zone to give the front seat pilot practice firing live ordnance. They came upon a hootch with a woman outside. Even though it was a "free fire zone," and the Black Ponies had blanket clearance to fire on anyone (who of course had to be enemy), Scholl stopped the pilot from shooting. This was not something Black Ponies did. When they got back on the ground, Burton remarked, "Thanks, I learned something today." From that day on, the two men developed a respect and friendship that would characterize the relationship between the XO and many of the JOs. Commander Burton would take an interest both in the welfare of the junior officers and in their careers. When Scholl received orders for a new assignment after VAL-4, Commander Burton was the first one to seek out the young officer.

Jim Burton had been a high-ranking naval officer at The Hague in the Netherlands, a pretty prestigious job. He heard about my orders. I was to become an intelligence officer at the U.S. Headquarters in the European Command, Stuttgart, Germany. And he said, "Bob, do you realize what you've got here?" And I said, "No, XO, all I know is I'm going to Germany."

He said, "These are really special orders. They're really great. Come to my room tonight. I want to talk to you about them."

So I went down there that night. He said, "Bob, you're going to be dealing with some highly, highly classified material." This was a really great speech. I love the guy for this. "Sources are extremely sensitive. If you divulge any of these secrets, or any of the sources, people could die and it could do irreparable harm to your country. I know a little bit about your background. I know your parents were immigrants. And I know that you've made it on your own to this point. You've done well. You should be proud of yourself." In the background I could hear *da, duh, da, da, da, da* (the Star Spangled Banner) . . . "You've done well. You owe this country. You owe this country a lot. It has made all this possible. You couldn't do this. . . . But people will approach you to buy some of this classified information. They will ask you to sell out your country. Bob, you owe your country everything. Whatever you do, don't sell out your country. . . . But if you do sell—don't sell cheap."

I thought, you know, those are words to live by. And this from a guy who made a fortune over there selling paintings.[5]

Bob Scholl, Black Pony

18

The September Battle

There is history in all men's lives.
—William Shakespeare, *King Henry IV,* Part II

It would be argument for a week, laughter for a month, and a good jest forever.
—William Shakespeare, *King Henry IV,* Part I

Despite its name, the "Second Annual Awards Ceremony" at the "O"Club was a "hail and farewell" party—presented in the form of a roast and usually held monthly when a new replacement group arrived and a group left. This particular party would be the second one at which Doc Rodgers acted as master of ceremony, hence the title. Because of his creative talents, which ranged from stand-up comedy to song writing, and guitar playing to skit writing, these increasingly elaborate affairs earned a reputation that extended from Binh Thuy to Ben Xe Moi.

For a healer, Doc could be merciless—but only with his humor. He practiced the best medicine—a mixture of the healing arts which includes a smidgen of physician, psychiatrist, sage, and father confessor, along with comic relief in full measure. A truly Falstaffian character, he would become the epoxy that held this flying machine together.

At the ceremony Doc recited the following doggerel that he had composed for the occasion:

The Ponies do scramble, both rainy days and nights—
Returning to Binh Thuy in an awful state of fright.

Their hands they are trembling, their skivvies they are wet,
Their faces are pallid, their brows full of sweat.

Bob Porter, our skipper, a man who knows no fright,
A shrewd aviator, who never flies at night.
He terrifies his back seats at altitudes so low—
Will anyone fly with me? Oh no, skipper, no!

Jim Burton has nearly driven us to drink
By flying much lower than any man would think.
Is that a kind of new Loach, no, it's our XO.
Will anyone fly with me? No, XO, no!

The Ponies are made up of men both brave and bold,
But smart enough to want to be around to grow old.
Our bullet holes get numerous, when we fly low and slow—
Please fly as my wingman? Oh no Hotch, oh no!

VAL-4, we salute you, with heads uncapped and bowed—
Those of us who leave here, will always be proud.
We've raised our voices in laughter and in jest—
But are these things truthful? Oh yes, skipper, yes!

For the Black Ponies flying a random patrol to the U-Minh early Sunday morning on 12 September, the little ditty they had heard at the party may have been going through their minds. And they hoped that they were not flying through some kind of magnet for hot VC lead. For on that flight and on numerous others over the next few days, Black Ponies flew some of the most intense close air support missions in the squadron's history. Flying in support of ARVN units and their American advisors (who had been in almost continual contact with the Z-8 and Z-9 Battalions of the NVA 95-A Regiment and VC main forces in An Xuyen, Chuong Thien, and Kien Giang Provinces since 4 September), the Black Ponies found the fight they were looking for. It turned out to be not only a chance to work closely with troops on the ground in a significant operation, but also a demonstration that with their use of aircraft, weapons, and skills, Black Ponies could save lives with close air support in a sustained ground assault.

The new replacement pilots, not yet being wing qualified, had to fly mostly back seat because the scheduled front seat hop they had been scheduled to fly would invariably turn into a scramble.

On the afternoon of 16 September Lt. Bob Hurley led a scramble with Lt. (jg) Ben LoBalbo on his wing to the Bien Nhi firebase in the 32d Regiment area of operations. The night before, under the cover of heavy rain, about fifty sappers had penetrated the northern side of the perimeter and the bunker crew had scrambled to provide air support, helping to drive them off. On that morning, elements of the Z-8 and Z-9 Battalions, NVA 95-A Regiment, had attacked from the south. When the Ponies reached the firebase, the ARVN had driven the enemy away with five armored personnel carriers, and Hurley's flight attacked the enemy's forward positions, just outside the firebase. In one of the most unusual sights to be seen in the Delta, the ARVN loaded tracked vehicles onto LCM-8 boats and took them to the base. They could not move very far when off-loaded, but managed to provide the firepower needed, in what was probably the only effective use of tracked vehicles in the Delta during the rainy season, if not ever.[1]

Lts. (jg) Mike Lamberto and Ray Morris scrambled to a company-sized outpost of the 33d Regiment that almost had been overrun by the NVA. Controlled on target by Darkhorse 6, an army C and C ship, the Black Ponies saved the outpost from the enemy troops that occupied the eastern side of the compound, only thirty meters from the friendlies.[2] Lieutenant Jim Arthur and Lt. (jg) J. K. Pell would save it again the next day.[3]

> Lieutenant (junior grade) Lynn Henish and I flew a mission to provide air cover for boats resupplying the 33d command post, along the Song Cai Lon, the river that ran from the Gulf of Thailand from Rach Soi southeasterly into the U-Minh, which Black Ponies called the "All American." After the boat convoy had safely transited the area, they released us. From our vantage point about thirty-five hundred feet above the boats, I turned on the 8-mm movie camera I had mounted in the cockpit, rolled the aircraft inverted and pulled the nose through into a "split-S" maneuver. The Bronco came screaming out of the sky and leveled off just a few feet above the water, roaring right past the boats and the ecstatic soldiers and sailors waving at us. I pulled the nose up and did a victory roll, knowing the guys in the boats got almost as much fun out of this as we did.
>
> Kit Lavell, Black Pony

Returning from the air cover for the boats, the Fire Team joined a scramble to an area near the 33d forward fire base and worked with an army Air Cavalry Package (AirCavPac), a combined helicopter operation headed by Colonel Franklin, the senior advisor to the 21st ARVN Division. In the air above the target, army Col. Joseph Ross Franklin reigned supreme. He was a charismatic and controversial officer who on 15 March 1971 was unfairly accused of covering up war crimes while serving a previous tour with the 173d Airborne Brigade. His accuser, Lt. Col. Anthony Herbert, the most decorated soldier in the Korean War, repeated his accusations in *Life* magazine in July, as he would in the *New York Times Magazine* on Labor Day, and then on Dick Cavett's TV show the following night. Herbert went on to write a best-selling book, but became the subject of an unflattering *60 Minutes* piece after which he accused CBS of trying to discredit him. He later sued *60 Minutes* and CBS but dropped the suit.

From a vantage above the battlefield, Franklin shouted orders over the radios to units on the ground as well as to the Cobras waiting to "prep" a new LZ for the Huey slicks orbiting the scene, waiting to unload more ARVN troops. He would verify the positions of ground elements, coax reluctant ARVN commanders, direct the Cobra gunships in their attacks on the enemy positions, and bark orders to the advisors on the ground. Franklin knew every call sign, every name, every detail, and ran the show with precision and a unique personal flair. The Ponies orbited high, keeping radio silence. Franklin knew exactly where they were, when to call on them, and eventually gave them specific directions. He was quick in displaying both his pleasure and disappointment to all participants, including the Vietnamese commander who outranked him.

Because of the nature of the terrain, the area was one of intense fighting at very close quarters. On all sides, elevated dikes surrounded large rectangular rice paddies, long ago abandoned by farmers. Banana trees in long, thick lines covered these dikes that farmers had built up out of the mud. High elephant grass grew in between the trees, further concealing bunkers and other fortified positions from which the enemy could pin down advancing soldiers. Rarely did opposing forces engage each other at distances of greater than fifty meters, and soldiers often fought from tree line to tree line, bunker to bunker, hand to hand. Colonel Franklin later described it as similar to the fighting among the hedgerows of Normandy, France, after D-Day in World War II.[4] A dreaded and deadly crossfire frequently peppered the ARVN and their American advisors from two or more sides with withering machine gun fire.

The enemy also used 12.7-mm antiaircraft guns in clusters of three or four, separated by several hundred meters, in interlocking or overlapping fields of fire. They would catch an aircraft coming or going from two or more positions, and evasive action would often take the aircraft over other gun positions. The CavPack pilots did not need to remind the Black Ponies that enemy gunners had damaged or destroyed numerous aircraft and killed or wounded many pilots during the U-Minh campaign. All Black Ponies had a healthy respect for the enemy's capabilities. Watching the Cobras taking fire while they methodically worked the tree lines from low altitude with their miniguns, the Black Ponies had even more respect for their capabilities—and courage.

The Cobras marked the enemy positions for the Ponies with 2.75-inch rockets. The Ponies carried full loads of Zuni rockets armed with "bunker busting" 48-pound warheads with delayed fuses that penetrated the ground before exploding. The lead Pony lined up on a tree line, rolled in from the six-to-twelve o'clock position, and unloaded a long string of Zunis that ripped into the ground, tore the banana trees out at the roots, and busted the bunkers they concealed. The Cav pilots shouted ecstatically over the radios as the four aircraft unleashed more than seventy Zunis within seconds, leaving behind tons of flattened trees, busted bunkers, and hopefully an easier time for the soldiers on the ground to advance to the next position.

As a second–tour aviator and one of the more experienced lieutenants in the squadron, Bubba Segars went out of his way to help the new replacement pilots adapt to combat. Bubba really enjoyed navy life, especially the life of a combat aviator. It was great fun for him, and centered on a dynamic balance of seven elemental forces, six of which were lift, thrust, weight, drag, drinking, and shooting. He once survived a mid-air collision when he ejected from his crippled A-4. This embodied him with a degree of magic or luck, at least in the minds of many pilots to whom such misfortunes were both occupational hazards and the result of forces beyond human control. "Bubba's Misadventure" (when he was shot down and evaded capture) only added to his aura of luck. The skipper relied on Bubba to teach tactics and weapons to the JOs. Bubba was great at explaining the essence of combat flying and all of its details of weaponry, systems and tactics. He practiced well Einstein's dictum, "In explaining things, be as simple as possible, but no simpler." He had also been put "in hack" by the skipper—restricted to his quarters for rowdiness—more times than anyone could remember. He had a reputation for being hard-charging, hard-drinking, and hard-headed. He and Cdr. Bob Porter were very close, despite the fact that on his first front seat hop in-country Bubba dropped all of his ordnance on friendly territory.

> Bubba's first front seat flight was on Commander Porter's wing. As so often happened to the skipper's wingman, he came back with his ordnance still on the plane. Bubba felt pretty bad about the whole thing. When we got back and into the chocks, and he had not shut the engines down yet, I had safed my seat and was about to unstrap when I heard this tremendous crash. I thought, "Oh shit." I stuck my head out the side and all the ordnance was lying on the ground. He had felt so bad about the whole thing that when he went to set the parking brake he pulled the

manual jettison and cleaned off everything. It cost him a couple of cases of beer for the ordnance crew.[5]

Bruce Turner, Black Pony

On one of my first hops in-country I drew the duty of flying air cover for the Miss America USO show, which the rest of the squadron got to attend. As for Bubba, in whose backseat I flew, I didn't ask him, but no doubt, he probably volunteered.

We drilled so many holes in the black sky above the USO show that I began nodding off. Suddenly, the lead aircraft radioed us that troops on the ground had foiled a sapper attack out beyond the perimeter. They needed us to quickly attack the enemy positions. Everything happened so fast. We didn't have to look for the coordinates; they were directly below us. When the friendlies marked their positions with strobe lights, tracers erupted from a nearby tree line.

While the lead aircraft stayed high, Bubba turned out our lights and made a low pass over the tree line from which the shooting came. We were much lower than I was comfortable with, or thought we should be. Leveling off from the shallow dive, Bubba flipped on the external lights. Instantly, I saw green lights converge on both sides of the plane and instinctively thought they were wing lights from two planes crossing our flight path. But was one of them flying backwards? As they rapidly passed over our canopy, followed by others, I realized they were tracers. Bubba stomped right rudder, driving my helmet into the canopy, then dipped the right wing and fired a salvo of Zuni rockets in a blinding flash that lit up the cockpit. Before we pulled off from our dive, these supersonic telephone poles filled with high explosives made their connection. The black abyss below our nose burst into a string of bonfires as the rockets blew up the tree line.

On our next attack, Bubba fired the 20-millimeter cannon in a low-altitude, shallow dive. In a habit picked up from when I was a flight instructor, when I am with someone else who is doing the flying, I always rest my hand on the quadrant behind the throttle to prevent it, or anything else, from inadvertently shutting the bird down before I can walk away from it without making a "silk descent." During the attack I felt the throttle ease back almost to idle. I shoved it forward. I reached to brace myself on the glare shield. Out of my peripheral vision I spotted the throttle slowly inching its way back again. I jammed it forward again. I braced myself on the glare shield once more, watched the airspeed bleed off to about a hundred knots, and stretched to look over the ejection seat. That's when I spotted it. Shit. Bubba was intentionally pulling the throttle back, which slowed us down, further exposing us to antiaircraft fire—just the opposite of what I wanted at that moment. The staccato *thud, thud, thud* of the cannon quit just as Bubba and I both jammed the throttle forward and we pulled off target, out of ammo.

As soon as I jumped out of the aircraft after we pulled into the revetments I angrily ran to catch up to Bubba. "Hey, what were you doing back there? Why were we flying so slow?" From the expression on his face I could have been asking him. "Why do bears biff in the woods?"

Bubba's reply was, "It gives me more time in the saddle to shoot these fuckers."

Kit Lavell, Black Ponies

Bubba would always take a training syllabus hop on which he flew back seat as the Fire Team Leader and turn it into a "shooting hop." Most newbies liked flying with him because of this.

A new replacement pilot flew front seat with Bubba out to the 33d again, the morning of 18 September, on a sortie to destroy more enemy bunkers with delay-fused Zuni rockets. While working the target, Bubba kept dialing and monitoring frequencies, hoping to find something a little more exciting to do than bust bunkers. His efforts paid off when he overheard a scramble crew on their way to an area nearby, and Bubba's flight rushed to join them. When they got to the coordinates, the newbie in Bubba's front seat was still in combat spread formation on the flight leader as they passed over the target, several minutes ahead of the flight which they were to join. Bubba was the FTL of the flight and he was handling the communications with the ground elements as well as directing the flight leader and the wingman—in his front seat—to the target.

"'Durable Episode,' we've got about a dozen guys out in the middle of a rice paddy. Where are the nearest friendlies?" Bubba shouted into the FM transmitter and before getting a reply: "Have you got 'em in sight?" Bubba asked the newbie over the ICS.

Before he could even answer, Bubba ordered the flight leader to make an immediate right turn.

"The nearest friendlies are in the outpost, Black Ponies."

"I got them," the newbie told Bubba, as he watched the specks pass beneath their right wing.

"Understand nearest friendlies are two klicks to the west. We've got the bad guys out in the open, can you give me a clearance?" Bubba radioed on the FM. Then immediately shifting to the UHF, he called to the flight leader, "We're rolling in first, we're at your two o'clock, follow us in." And virtually simultaneously, over the ICS, Bubba said, "Charge your guns."

"They're already charged, Bubba . . . "

"Yeah, right . . . and hold off on the Zunis . . . they won't be much good. . . . " Then on the FM, Bubba shouted, "Got my clearance?"

"They're headed for the trees," the newbie said as he rolled in. He was ready to pull off without firing if they didn't get the clearance in time, but it came before he rolled wings level. Everything was happening so fast, the newbie wasn't even sure he was flying the plane. Bubba had been so frantically giving directions and handling everything, the newbie even thought he could feel Bubba's hands on the controls.

"Kick the rudders back and forth like this," Bubba said, as he yawed the nose from side to side with the rudders just after the newbie established the aircraft in the dive. "Walk the strafe around. . . ."

Everything was a blur. The newbie hadn't reset the deflection on the gun sight, but it wouldn't matter. He would pull the trigger based more on instinct than anything else, and in fact saw only the tree line up ahead to which the NVA were running, not the men themselves. Then he realized that they were below a thousand feet in the 20-degree dive—the trees now looming big in the gun sight. He pressed it a couple more seconds, kicking the rudders gently side to side and then he released the trigger and pulled the stick back into his lap, sending the aircraft skyward. His vision rapidly telescoped down into a small colorless circle surrounded by gray, and as it became merely a small dot, he released the back pressure on the stick, reducing the G forces, allowing the blood to flow into his head again, and restoring his vision.

"Wing-over into another run!" Bubba shouted to him.

He had neither seen nor heard the flight leader roll in behind him, but looking over his shoulder as his senses returned he saw the aircraft about 45 degrees abaft as he pulled off target. The newbie's nose was about 40 degrees above the horizon and the airspeed was rapidly bleeding off. He stomped right rudder, rolled the aircraft almost inverted, pulled the nose down toward the target and rolled wings level. The tree line was about 10 degrees off centerline to the left, so he dipped the wing to make a quick correction, then reached up to the Master Armament Switch. He realized that he had not turned it off when he had pulled off target. He let go a long burst of strafe, then pulled off target, jinking to avoid enemy ground fire, just in case.

"I'm off, left," he grunted into the radio as he pulled 4 Gs coming off target. "Master Arm off," he said to himself.

The two aircraft worked the target in a "wagon wheel," each rolling in from a different compass quadrant. They had no nearby friendlies to worry about being hurt from their exploding rockets and didn't have to

FLYING BLACK PONIES

worry about dropping spent brass from their machine guns on anyone's head. Not that they could see anyone's head. In fact, they saw no one after the first pass, but they knew exactly what trees they were hiding behind. Or what was left of them. They used up all of their bunker-busting Zunis, cursing, on the way back home, their misfortune that they didn't have proximity-fused warheads to use on the relatively exposed enemy troops. As the adrenaline wore off, it began to sink into the new replacement pilot's mind that these were human beings he had so excitedly caught in his gun sight. They were the enemy. But that didn't stop a range of emotions that began welling up inside him.

On a night scramble, an experienced pilot launched a "5-inch flare," firing a high-explosive Zuni rocket, when he meant to fire a flare. Fortunately it injured no one, but the skipper put him in hack for five days, an extraordinary punishment since it was at the beginning of the series of back-to-back scrambles that lasted days, and the Black Ponies needed every available pilot. A sage said that the squadron had two types of pilots: those who made switch mistakes like this, and those who would. A few days later, the skipper committed the same error, in broad daylight, as he fired a Zuni rocket over the horizon, when he meant to drop a CBU bomb. No one was ever punished again for a "switchology" mistake.

At 0300 on 16 September 1971 the enemy launched a widespread offensive across the U-Minh. Elements of all three NVA regiments in the Delta attacked eight of the ten major firebases. Beginning that morning, Black Ponies flew back-to-back, around-the-clock scramble missions until 18 September. The most significant battle in IV Corps during the war, the offensive would last until 21 September.

Scrambled Thoughts—168 Hours of Them

Starting with the blast of the scramble horn, I stagger out of the bunker and into the dim red light of the cockpit shaking sleep from my brain as I try to comprehend numbers—I map coordinates, frequencies, callsigns— when moments before all I had to focus on was the insides of my eyelids as I dreamed of my wife, my daughter, loved ones, playing baseball, going to the movies on Saturday night. But reality has yanked me back—gotta get this damn thing started! number one turning, the backseater jumps in, turning two, power levers back to get the props off the blocks, Petty Officer Fox, the plane captain, pulling the chocks and the bird lurches on out to the arming area, hands up in the air to signal the ordnancemen it is okay to pull the safety pins and arm the rockets as Chief Bostick, Petty

Officer Sullivan, and the other ordies back carefully away from the spinning props the aircraft speeds down the taxiway on the scramble from which we will return all too soon a hot turnaround and sent on our way only to come back for more fuel and ordnance and it's not even daylight yet as Petty Officer Carson joins the others to lift the heavy rocket pods up onto the next set of aircraft awaiting the new bunker crew called to the other side early to relieve exhausted pilots who pour into the truck and Airman Brown drives us back to the BOQ where we will sleep about four hours as all the other available pilots have been subjected to the same cycle and to hell with the three combat missions per day rule. Are we talking about Rules here again? and we fall out of our racks for it is our turn once more the hot sun beats down on our heads while we speed back to the airfield in the back of the pickup truck carrying cockpit instruments, fuel controls and other parts cannibalized from the hangar queen at the short strip which will not be needed as all airworthy birds are flying their tails off and some not so airworthy that metalsmiths and electricians, mechanics, avionics technicians work on under the blistering sun because the hangars are crammed with aircraft, some up on jacks as Petty Officers Dempsey and Lunsford remove an engine that was shot up this morning and it's not even close to lunch time but no one will see the chow hall for days and the supply of C-rats is getting low as are the Zuni rockets and the AOs are joined by pilots to screw on fuses, load ammo belts into sponsons, stuff rockets into pods "How's it going out there skipper?" Chief Meikle asks, "What can I tell the men?" as night falls but the tempo doesn't, the duty officer has long since stopped blowing the scramble horn since every flight now is a scramble, flares fight darkness, shadows fight flares, darkness fights us all, "the outpost is being attacked again, hurry Black Pony" men are dying, a constant shuttle of aircraft to and from the U-Minh and pilots to and from the airfield, fatigue building in man and machine, in and around the hangars lights everywhere as every available wrench, hammer and tool is turned, swung or twisted, Petty Officers Gause and Ray and other metalsmiths patching bullet holes, "read you five by . . . what? . . . read you five square . . ." Petty Officer Elliot repairing but trying to listen to the Fox Mike radio while being blasted by the propwash and roar of the engine Petty Officer Scott is running up nearby, it's almost dawn and no one can think of sleep, food, or anything except the job at hand, fingers smashed, knuckles bruised, muscles pulled as yeomen and hospital corpsmen are pressed into service loading ordnance in a predawn thunderstorm the dust and grime now flow as mud mixes with sweat, oil, jet fuel and hydraulic fluid red yellow purple sunrise steam rising from the PSP along with the temperature and tempers as the day begins anew yet stale with events of yesterday and the day before in one long continuous blur a pilot and a plane captain in a hurried discussion about the mission each reading the fatigue on the other's face not sure if they just said the same thing to each other only hours before "how is it out there, Mr. Lavell?" as an aircraft comes back with no pods having dropped them into the Bassac after losing an engine "gimmeagoddamnbreak . . . more frigin' rocket pods to lift!" sweat oil tears fuel blood "Okay . . . standard brief guys . . . meet you in the arming area" hands up again taxi for takeoff never get above three thousand feet no cool air no time to waste no rest for the wicked no screw ups now no this can't be I was just here wasn't I? or was that yesterday tracers fill the sky "off left" aaarggg "rog, I'm in hot" fly by the seat of our pants "good job Ponies send me some more" hot refuel and rearm and back to the target again men are dying and back again then in the rack to dream it all over again as another day turns into another night and another day dawns and then . . . silence. The radios are eerily silent. The scrambles finally stop. The sun sets. Rest arrives. Darkness.

Kit Lavell, Black Pony

There had been such a shortage of pilots that a number of non-aviators such as Doc Rodgers, Lt. Gaylon Hall from the maintenance department, and intelligence officer Lt. Ed Smith found themselves volunteering to fly in the back seat of the Bronco. After the long, continuous seven-day scramble ended, the Black Ponies flew periodic scrambles and numerous scheduled missions for a few days more in support of the ARVN in the U-Minh. Saigon informed the squadron it had set numerous records for the war during this week for whoever keeps score. But the rewarding thing for most—besides the fact that it was over and they were alive—was the number of lives on the ground saved with Black Pony close air support.

On 23 September U.S. Army Col. J. Ross Franklin sent a letter to the VAL-4 commanding officer which he requested be given to all Black Ponies and incorporated into their military records. Franklin wrote:

Most importantly, by providing close support (sometimes to within 25 meters of assaulting troops) as well as accurate support at night, the Ponies on several occasions permitted ARVN troops to overrun NVA positions before the enemy could withdraw or recover his weapons. As a result, at least five enemy battalions were decimated and over 200 weapons captured. . . .

In over twenty-seven months with U.S. and ARVN combat units (to include service in all four corps areas) I know of no more professional, dedicated, or effective combat aviation unit in any service than the Black Ponies.

Your often uncanny ability to hit the target under any conditions has resulted in your organization being the best known in the Delta. . . . Particularly impressive is your record in working with the ARVN.

Your patience and ability to draw out necessary target information from the ARVN was frequently the key to success on the ground. . . . You should all be proud of the enviable reputation you have with the 21st ARVN Division and the essential role you have played in the U-Minh Campaign.

I have noted that with ARVN commanders at all levels, if they know only two words in English, those words are "Black Pony."[6]

When the scrambles ended on Saturday 18 September, the Black Ponies partied hard that night. In other words, things returned to normal.

Getting Your Birds Straight

I awoke Sunday morning by grabbing my flight boots and sprinting out the door only to have Jim Arthur yell at me to stop. I wasn't even scheduled to fly. When I took myself off autopilot, Jim and I decided to check out the chow hall for the first time in days. I felt as if I were on the "backside of the power curve," that strange regime where actions produce an effect opposite to what is expected, where to slow down you have to add power, and to speed up, you must take power off.

As we were walking back from breakfast with our heads still in something of a fog, the remnants of the good time we had the night before, we passed a guy in a fresh set of fatigues, obviously new in-country. His black collar insignia looked like the "crow" of a 3d class petty officer. The fellow didn't salute us, which was pretty standard fare around there, so I was surprised when Jim turned around to chew him out. Seeing his name tag when we first passed, Jim yelled out, "Barnes, get the hell over here," and as he approached, "Don't you salute officers?"

Jim was an all-navy wrestling champ and looked it, which along with being taken by surprise, was the reason I figured navy Captain Barnes with the "chicken" on his collar sheepishly rendered the two lowly lieutenants the salute they demanded. The moral, I guess, is that if you're flying in a fog, get your birds straight.

Kit Lavell, Black Pony

19

Orphans of the Storm

Truths which remain sealed to the savants are disclosed to the children.

—Joachim de Flore

The Mekong Delta with the rich lushness of its vegetation is a steaming petri dish of an environment that always amazes a Westerner. A pool of stagnant water one day would be a biotic broth the next, a ubiquitous flowering of life, replete with fungus, mildew, mold, and rot. Cuts and sores would never heal. It was impossible to stop things from growing—unless you used Agent Orange.

Before the year ended, the Black Ponies' last XO, Cdr. Ron Pickett, reported aboard, along with replacement pilots Lts. Dave Church, Harry Gintzer, Ed Woods, Jim Cullen, Dale Ware; Lts. (jg) Nick Harroun, Lance Mahew, Pete Black, Steve Josephson; and joining the maintenance department, Lt. Cdr. Bob Pastrie and WO Jeff Widman.

The Black Ponies worked increasingly as "hired guns," flying close air support for army advisors and their ARVN counterparts. Typhoon Hester brought rains even more severe than usual, and along with them, increased enemy activity in the Delta, especially at night.

The stormy or wet season in Vietnam lasts from May through November as the southwest monsoons blow in from the Indian

Ocean. The normal thunderstorm activity increased in mid-September 1971 and seemed to get worse in October, when Typhoon Hester swept through the area. Typhoons usually originate to the east of the Philippines, and this one took its time reaching and eventually passing over Vietnam. The weather made navigating even more difficult. And as always, enemy activity seemed to increase with the bad weather.

Lt. John Smalling led a Fire Team on a Saturday night foray out to the 33d. After the Black Ponies placed an air strike for an American advisor, he asked the Black Ponies to switch frequencies to talk to one of the ARVN commanders outside the firebase. The Ponies did, and began a most unusual conversation.

"You see me, Black Pony?"

Of course they didn't. The overcast sky merged into the earth below in a seamless black void. They had no idea where he was.

"We don't see you yet. Do you see us?"

"I hear you Black Pony. You see me?"

Even if they were directly over him, unless they knew what to look for, the Ponies would not have seen him.

"Negative. Do you have a strobe?"

"Oh yes Black Pony. I have strobe. You see me now?"

"What color is your strobe?"

"My strobe blue, Black Pony."

"Roger. Understand blue strobe. We are looking. Do you see us?"

Very quietly, he brought the Ponies closer to his position by a process of give and take over the radios. He would give them a heading and listen for their engines. The pilots would then take a guess where in the absolute darkness he was. He would then give the Ponies another direction. They had no more flares that worked. They finally found his blue strobe light, in the middle of the downpour. He confirmed his location with tracer fire. Smalling asked how they could help him.

"I no need help, Black Pony."

"Did I hear him OK?" Smalling asked the copilot over the ICS.

"I thought he said he did not need help. Negative help," the copilot replied.

"Negative help? Do you want us to shoot for you, over?" John radioed.

"Negative. You no shoot for me."

"You no want us to shoot VC?"

"No VC."

"We don't understand. Are you sure you don't want us to shoot for you? Why did you call us?"

After a long silence, John was about to key the mike to repeat his question.

"I just want see you, Black Pony. I just want see you."

The pilots couldn't help but feel the desperation and utter loneliness of this man, an orphan out there in the storm. Similar encounters would happen to other pilots several times over the coming months.

After breakfast on Sunday 19 September, Lt. Jason Sloan took a new replacement pilot on his first visit to the Catholic orphanage. They borrowed one of the squadron's "appropriated" trucks and loaded it up with lumber, sacks of cement, sand, and gravel and headed for Can Tho, the town just south of Binh Thuy.

In a torrential rain Sloan steered the deuce and a half around the cyclos (pedicabs) and lambros (tiny motorized covered pickup trucks) gathered in the middle of a muddy intersection that were deciding which was biggest—and hence which had the right-of-way—and turned off the main thoroughfare. As they approached the orphanage gates on the tree-lined street in Can Tho, the rain stopped. The clouds made way for the sun, and warm light greeted them. Sloan jumped out of the truck to open the gate, and then drove into the compound. The orphanage consisted of several well-maintained concrete buildings behind a tall brick and mortar wall.

They parked the truck next to the main building and were greeted by Sister Eugenia, the Mother Superior, as they walked up the stairs to the spacious veranda on which the nuns received visitors. A railing that was painted blue ran around the floor covered with red and white checked linoleum—which the men recognized as remnants from a Black Pony Sears-supplied cumshaw run.

Sister Eugenia, a small, bespectacled woman with a smiling face and large protruding front teeth, white as her nun's habit, spoke passable English. The Black Ponies spoke no Vietnamese, except for a few standard phrases. They sat fidgeting on red vinyl-covered chairs fashioned out of oak barrels, making small talk, while another nun brought them a tray with two bottles of warm Coca-Cola and two glasses, each containing two ice cubes.

A light breeze gently evaporated the perspiration on their faces, flushed from the afternoon drive. Sister Eugenia was obviously very comfortable with Sloan. He was anxious to get to work, and she was extending the courtesies for the benefit of the new visitor. The other pilot sensed Sloan's impatience and asked Sister Eugenia if he could see the rest of the orphanage.

After a quick tour of the main building they walked out to the large courtyard, which was used to dry the clothes and diapers for the 165 children who lived at the orphanage. Beyond the courtyard they saw the playground for the older kids. As soon as they rounded the corner, a boisterous band of children mobbed the two Americans. Dozens of little boys and girls ranging in age from about four to eight grabbed and pulled at them, laughing and yelling, desperately seeking attention. And the Black Ponies, of course, were eager to supply it. Smiling eyes, wide grins, and beckoning arms pulled them into the children's little world. The boys wanted to roughhouse, play tag, and wrestle. The girls wanted to play catch with a playground ball and eventually joined the boys and the men in a game of tag. Most of the children knew a few words of English, and a few spoke the language fluently, like the tiny six-year-old girl who had spent eighteen months in an American hospital for corrective leg surgery. Most of the boys wore shorts and were shirtless, except for a few T-shirts, one with the words "New York World's Fair" emblazoned on the front. Most of the girls seemed to have similar plaid shirts or plaid dresses that looked handmade. While the clothes were worn, all were clean. Some children showed signs of physical ailments—limps, scars, and rashes—but all were energetic, laughing, and obviously enjoying the attention. They could have been mistaken for children on the streets of any major American city. But they were not.

After an hour or so, Sister Eugenia sent Sister Marie Angéle, a young nun-to-be who had not yet taken her final vows, to rescue the Americans. The Vietnamese novitiate had a very special quality. She didn't need to say a word to the children. She smiled, held out her arms, and gathered to her about ten at a time, stroking their heads, embracing them, holding them, and calming them down. She then spoke softly to them in French, a language in which many Vietnamese were fluent. The children then smiled at the American pilots, waved goodbye, and ran around the side of the building, where they occasionally peeked around the corner and giggled.

After the time they spent with the older children, the Black Ponies helped Sister Marie Angéle feed the two dozen or so infants in the nursery. One of the cutest was a little girl who had a heart problem and had been abandoned for the nuns to raise. The good Sister held her very close as she went from baby to baby, checking diapers, refilling bottles, adjusting blankets, all the while softly singing a French lullaby.[1]

Pilots usually drew the overnight scramble duty once every five or six nights (except some senior officers and others). I found myself getting more than my share of it, including quite a lot of other night missions. To those lessons in life learned the hard way, such as—Never eat at a place called Ma's (except when in Pensacola eat at Ma Hopkin's boarding house); never fight a land war in Asia; and never play cards with a man named Doc—I could add:

never piss off the schedules officer in a combat squadron, especially when fighting a land war in Asia. I flew many night flights with others in the same situation—Hotch, as well as Bubba—who would just as soon fly at night. In fact, I had only three day hops in two weeks, and two of them were scrambles . . . with the schedules officer. By midnight or 0100, the scramble crew was usually asleep, and only the duty officer remained awake. Just outside, the enlisted men of "night check" worked in and around the hangars or on aircraft in the revetments. Sometimes I would remain awake late into the morning hours writing in my journal or penning letters. But more often than not I would use the opportunity to read.

I was interrupted by the static on the secure radio, as the duty officer began copying the coordinates, frequencies, and call signs for the scramble. My three compatriots probably thought they were dreaming when the scramble horn went off. Minutes later, we were headed for the U-Minh Forest.

"Did you copy all that, 'Pony 17?'" the lead pilot radioed.

"Affirmative," I replied. We had been orbiting the intersection of the All American canal and some nondescript squiggly where an ARVN company and its American advisors were fighting it out with an NVA unit of unknown size. We had been scrambled to the same place last night. Tonight I flew the wing aircraft on a scheduled patrol and everything looked like it would be a repeat of last night. Except for the .51 cal.

"I'm rolling in north to south. You roll in on a heading of 160, copy?" the flight leader radioed.

"Pony 17, wilco," I replied. That meant I would be pulling off directly over the antiaircraft gun where it would have its best shot at me. This was one of those difficult calls. The good guys were in such close proximity to the enemy that we had to take great care to avoid firing a short round. A "short round" is a rather innocuous-sounding term that refers to any ordnance that falls short of, long of, or misses the target. A short round could easily injure or kill friendlies, if they are close by.

While working a target, many factors affect how close to troops you shoot, such as weather, groundfire, terrain, where the enemy is in relationship to the friendlies, and how that might affect the roll-in direction and pattern you fly. If at all possible you want to avoid a diving attack on the enemy where the friendlies are directly ahead of them, at your "twelve o'clock" position. The most likely error a pilot makes is to shoot either long or short of the target. Likewise, you try to avoid diving directly over the friendlies into the enemy position because a "six o'clock" error might hit the good guys. Another reason to avoid diving directly over the friendly position is to not drop spent brass from your machine guns on their heads. In the scheme of things it's not dangerous like a short round, but they say it's annoying.

"I'm off, right," the lead radioed as he pulled off target, away from the stream of tracers heading toward him.

"Oh shit," I thought. "That means I'm an easy shot for that guy on the ground." I would have preferred to attack from the east or the west, away from the antiaircraft gun, but then the good guys would have been at my six and twelve. I had to think fast.

"I'm at your three o'clock and I'm going lights out. I'm rolling in on a heading of 340," I radioed. The lead didn't acknowledge me. "Damn, what do I do?" "Lead, did you read me?" Still no response. "This'll be my decision. Hell, isn't this what they pay me for?" I roll into my attack with machine guns blazing. I select every Zuni I can and start pickling when I see the tracers head straight for me. A string of rockets light up the sky. "Oh damn." They're falling short, splashing into the canal. Ease back on the stick, relax your grip. I must have been pulling more than 1 G. God, I'm glad the friendlies are off to the right. Pickle again. A series of explosions light up the windscreen as I pull back on the stick and head for the stars. The force of 4 Gs pulls me down into the seat as sweat pours down my face, burning my eyes. "Off, right," I grunt into the radio as I swing the plane around to the left and look for my lead's lights.

"Nice shot, Pony 17."

"Yeah, but what about the ones that landed short," I thought. "What if there had been friendlies there?"

All the way home I kept thinking about how easy it was to make even the slightest mistake.

In the room adjoining our bunkroom, Jim and I set up a bar, and it began to attract a regular crowd. Despite the tension between Bubba and me, still lingering from the USO flight—on which I pushed while he pulled on the throttle—he stopped by one night after everyone had left.

"What's up, Bubba?"

"Nothing . . . just looking for a drink."

"Shouldn't be that hard to find around here, I'm sure there's *beaucoup*. Come on in, you look like you really need one."

After we broke out the bottle of scotch for him and a long silence as he drank what I had poured him, Bubba finally looked up from his glass.

"What's the worst mistake you could make flying over here?" he asked, with an uncharacteristically quiet voice.

"I'm not sure I understand."

"How would you feel if you hurt a friendly with a short round?"

I thought at first that it had happened to him. But I was really taken aback as Bubba recounted how he was unable to console Lt. (jg) Steve Salzman who had cried after learning that he had fired a short round that injured some ARVN soldiers.

Several weeks before, I had heard that a senior officer inadvertently fired a rocket on his roll-in and it hit a Buddhist pagoda. The rocket skidded up the steps and through the door, hitting a monk in the butt, as he bent over praying, but fortunately not hurting him seriously. But this was the first time I heard of someone being seriously injured by us.

Kit Lavell, Black Pony

The Black Ponies had a reputation for accuracy unequalled by any air unit. The squadron's CEP—circular error probable, or average distance from a bull's-eye—was around twenty to thirty feet with Zunis, even less with cannon and only slightly more with 2.75-inch rockets. No computers, just seat-of-the-pants. Pilots determine the "stand off," or minimum distance from friendlies where a pilot would shoot, by adding the CEP to the radius of the fragmentation pattern of the ordnance delivered—the "killing radius" —plus a safety factor. Most Black Ponies worked inside of this distance on those occasions when the enemy was in close contact with the friendlies who were about to be overrun, and the friendlies asked them to do it. They were in a world of hurt, and their hope was they were better dug in than the enemy was. More than one Black Pony had an exchange over the radio like John Westerman did, that began with a SEAL saying, "Shoot the hootch." Westerman replied, "Where are you located?" Then the words, "In the hootch. They're coming in the window. Shoot the goddamn hootch!"

Other air units may have had reputations of accepting short rounds as an inevitable consequence of the business. The Black Ponies never did. And they flew fixed-wing close air support as it had not been done since World War II and Korea. They flew night and day, in some of the worst weather imaginable, yet their air support was closer and more accurate than anything else around was. Many of the ARVN would not call in their own VNAF A-37s or A-1s, but would hold out for Black Ponies.

On several occasions the Black Ponies had been requested in desperation by ARVN commanders to put ordnance virtually on top of their own position. It was to save them from the enemy, and the Ponies (reluctantly informed by American advisors) learned afterward that a friendly was wounded. But the ARVN did not want the Ponies to find out because they understood the pilots' deep concern and did not want to jeopardize their chances of having them help them out of the same jam next time.

The Black Ponies grieved when they learned that a friendly was hurt. For most Black Ponies, if they felt any fear and anxiety, it was caused by concern for helping friendlies out of life-threatening situations and not hurting them while doing it. If Black Ponies lost any sleep, it was over the frustrations and anxiety of helping these people before it was too late, or about fighting the elements on the way to finding them. Rarely did they include concern for being shot at in the process.

A Black Pony rarely talked about deep personal feelings, and never about fear, danger, death, or courage, except in a mocking way, as in: "I pre'near got my ass shot out of the sky by that fifty-one cal. . . . You won't find me going back there [but you know for sure he will]. . . . Hell, my mamma didn't raise no dummy. . . ." And of course, he never actually uses the words *fear, danger, death,* or *courage.*

The enlisted men's barracks were located just behind the officers' quarters and outwardly looked just like them. The inside spaces were larger, however; two or more men bunked in a room. Also unlike the BOQ many of the rooms sported psychedelic posters and black lights, which were all the rage at the time, but also evidence to some that the enlisted men might be using illicit drugs. Any division officer watching the men work under the conditions that prevailed knew the squadron did not have a drug problem. The army base down the road at Can Tho was another matter, where thousands of idle soldiers and cheap, readily available heroin and opium created an environment rife with drug abuse. Black Pony enlisted men had little free time on their hands, the biggest single reason drugs didn't make an inroad into the squadron. A surprise raid arranged by superiors at the staff (and according to the scuttlebutt, by the HAL-3 CO) yielded little in the way of drugs, but uncovered an arsenal of unauthorized weapons that could have armed an ARVN battalion. It didn't take a clairvoyant to read what was on the men's minds.

The officers would also undergo body searches and room searches. Instead of the normal flight schedule, everything was put on hold when the entire squadron stood down. The officers were assembled early one morning and ordered to strip. No one knew what was going on.

> Commander Porter said, "I'll go first." I remember Porter had on red socks. "As of this moment the war is over," he said. Nobody knew what this meant. They even had a guy stationed in the head who had to inspect each toilet before it was flushed. He never lived it down. We called him O-in-C Shitter. Shitter actual.[2]
>
> Bob Scholl, Black Pony

Commander Porter spent a lot of time with the enlisted men. One morning he showed up with a broken hand at Doc's office after a binge in the barracks—a boxer's fracture as Doc described it—sustained, according to the CO, from karate chopping the wall. Doc Rodgers wanted to ground him, but the CO balked, at first suggesting, then ordering Doc to put a cast on his hand, specially formed for gripping the stick, including his index finger and thumb positioned for the trigger and pickle button. Doc reluctantly obliged.

Cdr. Jim "Spike" Burton, the XO, began looking for a new "cumshaw" officer to replace him. Since Spike would be leaving soon, the talent search started in earnest. But more than one person would be needed to fill his shoes. In fact it would take more than a few resourceful people to pull up the slack. Arguably, more than any other unit in modern naval history, this squadron depended on cumshaw for its very existence, as isolated and seemingly forgotten as it was by the real navy. It had very little officially assigned to it, and couldn't just requisition something, despite critically needing it. Some rear echelon mother fucker (REMF) would have asked, not why they wanted it, but "Just who in the hell are you?" They couldn't simply fill out forms, requisition requests, or depend on routine regulations. They had to be resourceful—innovative—they had to cumshaw. Some would even accuse them of stealing—but that would only be by their definition if you were following their rules.

Black Ponies possessed about a dozen-and-a-half vehicles—like the JO Jeep; few were officially assigned to the squadron. Every few months Ponies had to explain where the vehicles came from. Then they had to be even more resourceful—and innovative. In a long line of cumshaw artists, Spike was one of the best the Black Ponies had ever seen. And he inspired others. After all, he also had a tradition to uphold. He could not tarnish the image of Butterfield and Campbell, Baker and Underkoffler, Hone and . . . well, just about every Black Pony at one time or another. Lambro traded trinkets for steaks, and steaks for plywood for the enlisted men's barracks. Max flew air cover for some guys who drove a stolen jeep all the way from Saigon. No one ever asked Max what he would have done if the guys had gotten caught on the road back to Binh Thuy.

The skipper drove a Holden, an Australian version of a Chevy II, assembled by VAL-4 aircraft mechanics and metalsmiths from thousands of bartered, bought, and stolen parts; it was painted black with a red insignia and black pony on the doors. Black Ponies dubbed it the "Ponymobile." They traded an aircraft engine to the air force in exchange for a car engine for the skipper's Ponymobile. Max brought the engine for the car back from Vung Tau in the back of an OV-10 and almost crashed when the loose engine shifted on liftoff. Bubba exchanged an air conditioner for a jeep, which he swapped for a helicopter, which he traded for a U-6 Beaver, an old, radial-engined, tail-dragger plane that he hid at the army helo field. Hoping to use it for recreation, Bubba got caught when squadron fuel reports showed the use of avgas. Can you imagine that? Some REMF knew the OV-10 burned jet fuel. Go figure.

The easiest marks turned out to be the Vietnamese who found themselves at the mouth of the American supply cornucopia, the fruits of which spilled out in abundance. When vehicles broke down, they parked them in compounds, to be replaced by new equipment Uncle Sam was all too quick to pour forth. Black Ponies just swiped the rejects from the junkyard. This applied to a lot of other equipment and supplies too. Spike got a bit too cavalier one day and pilfered a bunch of plywood right from under the nose of a Vietnamese Air Force general, and had to build, overnight, a regulation-size four-wall handball court in one of our hangars to hide the evidence.

Because of the upcoming Vietnamese elections, Black Ponies "stood down" for a couple of days, with no flying except for maintenance test flights. This was a chance to catch up on paperwork, deferred maintenance, and other important matters, so some used the opportunity to help Doc Rodgers prepare for the Third Annual Awards Ceremony that was to be held Friday 8 October. Doc asked a few JOs to help with the skits. He was planning the most elaborate production yet and wanted to impress some new invitees—Red Cross "doughnut dollies" and nurses from the "Third Surge," the Army's surgical battalion at Can Tho.

The two-day stand-down coincided with a monsoon deluge, making everyone stir-crazy. The Jimmy Hanks Memorial Bridge even got washed away. Doc could be seen in the downpour traveling to work from the BOQ, paddling across the flooded volleyball court in a kayak made from an old rocket container. Who could forget the sight of Doc Rodgers frantically paddling to keep the swiftly moving current from carrying him off?

Huge white cowboy hats arrived, "Hoss" hats like the hat the character by that name wore in the TV show, *Bonanza*. Ad Clark, Jim Arthur, and Kit Lavell had ordered them from the States. Wearing the hats was tantamount to insubordination. Spike threatened to put the three pilots in hack, but then promised to forgive them as long as they dyed the hats black. The three Ponies found some old shoe polish and acceded to his request.

20

Hail and Farewell

The air age fans mankind with a sharp choice between Winged
Prose or Winged Death.

—Billy Bishop

After everyone had settled in and was flying high at the
"O"Club Friday night, Doc Rodgers banged on the table with
his forceps and called for silence. The roar of the crowd
increased by about thirty decibels as various projectiles went
flying in his direction. Looking for help, Doc tugged on the
arm of one of the nurses to get her to stand next to him and
run crowd interference. After a few hoots and whistles, the
noise died down to a steady but acceptable roar, and Doc
cleared his throat.

"Honored guests, gentlemen and aviators. We welcome you
this evening to our Third Annual Awards Ceremony. Many people have asked, 'Why are we here tonight?' The answer is simple—because we are not there . . . we are here tonight to honor
those who are there . . . or in any case, not here . . . so there.
Catch 22. An explanation is in order to clarify the special mean-
ings and significance of tonight's proceedings for our guests
from the Red Cross and from our comrades in arms from the
Third *Scourge* . . . who may not be familiar with the peculiari-
ties of Customs. Customarily, VAL-4 is the most peculiar of all.

"Our awards ceremony, instituted in the distant past, is
intended to give the appropriate recognition to those who,

having served their sentence—or rather their tour—in Vietnam, are returning home. Also honored at this time are those persons who, though they remain behind, are in some way outstanding or whose deeds cry out for recognition.

"Many of our awards will give just and fitting honor to some. Others will receive the stigma they have rightfully earned." More hoots and whistles, then a cannonade of rolled up and wetted paper napkins shot over the crowd, the "incoming" no doubt originating from those figuring they'd shoot their "stigma" first.

"We sense the tension mounting, so let us begin."

An appropriately recorded drumroll echoed off the walls.

"The first award is the Turkey of the Year Award given to that man who embodies that quality most fitting for this award—*Mediocrity* in his field.

"The nominees are: Number One, Lt. Cdr. Thomas Langston for his musical efforts on the guitar. Number Two, Uncle Tom Langston for his unquestioned navigational abilities renowned throughout the Delta. Number Three, Mr. Langston for his amazing digital dexterity on the armament panel—exceeded only by his ability on the guitar. Number Four, Lt. Bob Hurley for being Lt. Bob Hurley."

Doc ripped open the envelope.

"The unanimous winner is Uncle Tom Langston for his navigational ability. The first part of this award is one can of U.S. government-issue C-rations turkey loaf. The second part of this award—a cash prize—will be awarded in Vi Thanh. If the recipient can find it.

"The second award is presented through the courtesy of Anheuser Busch. The nominees are: Number One, Lt. Roy 'Bubba' Segars for his commando raids in the wee hours of the morning in search of liquid gold. Number Two, Lt. Cdr. Ken Williams who single-handedly wore out eighteen church keys in one week. Number Three, Lt. Cdr. Bob White, number two of the 'Budweiser Buddies,' for his supporting role in 'I Can Smoke As Much As Ken Williams Can Drink.' Number Four, Lt. George Leever for his performance of 'What Made Milwaukee Famous Made A Loser Out Of Me.'

"This award is presented in absentia to Lt. Cdr. Ken Williams. Receiving the award for him this evening is Lt. George Leever. The award is a case of beer. Unfortunately the recipient drank it before he left. However, we are sure that he is sadder . . . *Bud Weiser!*"

More hoots and Doc ducked as an empty beer can flew over his head.

"The third award is the Steve Chappell Athletic Prowess Award, presented to that officer who has through total neglect of his collateral duties kept himself physically fit, mentally alert, and three weeks behind in his paperwork. The nominees are Number One, Cdr. Bob Porter for his bone crushing karate lesson. Number Two, Cdr. Jim Burton, our XO, for almost single-handedly building the handball court and indisputably, single-handedly, monopolizing it. Number Three, Lt. (jg) J. K. Pell for having more hours in the handball court than in the OV-10.

"The winner—the commanding officer. Incidentally, he won this award broken hands down. The prize is the loan of one Farquhar and Gazinnia cast cutter deftly wielded by. . . ."

The skipper thrust his cast forward, but Doc knew the time had not yet come to remove what proved anyway to be of little impediment to Afterburner Bob's bravado.

"Before we continue with our awards this evening, a little nonsensical—I mean nonmusical interlude, as we have a recitation of *The Saga of the Four Great Birdmen.*

Four JOs then got up and read:

In the beginning there was the Delta and ComNavForV who moved over the brown waters. And there was at that time, vicious beings that crawled through the mud and slime. These were called SEALs. And there in the Delta many strange and powerful denizens which skimmed across the brown waters. These were called PBRs. But ComFAirWestPac was not happy and thus he spake, "Let there be creatures of the air to watch over the Delta." And great Wolves arose from out of the sea, and mighty winged Black Ponies screamed from their perches.

And thus the task force was completed. And ComNavForV gave these winged Ponies dominion over the Delta, over the SEALs of the mud and slime, over the PBRs of the brown waters, and over the Wolves of the sea.

To care for these winged Ponies he brought forth a race of Birdmen, fearless and daring, to guide these great winged beasts. Of these Birdmen we sing.

The junior officers went on to make fun of the four pilots whose tours of duty were now coming to an end—Bob White, Tom Langston, Ken Williams, and Bob Hurley. With artistic flare and verve, the JOs chronicled these poor souls' shortcomings, the proof of which they provided by reading the new orders their navy had given each of these men. Most everyone laughed and clapped. Some sat there stunned, appalled at what a crummy set of orders these men received for placing their lives on the line for a year in that strange war. But they slipped back from reality just in time, however, and raised heavy heads from drink just in time to see Doc stride to the front of the room again amid a cacophony of boos and curses.

"Our fourth award is the Max Britton Memorial Ordnance Award given to that man who has typified the VAL-4 ability to wisely and effectively utilize our ordnance assets. The nominees are Number One, Lt. Hotch Hotchkiss for his timely innovation just several weeks ago of a 5-inch flare. Number Two, Lt. Cdr. Tom Langston, who when he began to note that he was unable to put his rockets on target one night, cleverly put all his flares on target in an attempt to burn the enemy. Number Three, Lt. Gaylon 'Lock and Load' Hall for his continued target practice and his difficult trick shot with the M-16—shooting at the CONEX [shipping container] box with the XO inside.

"The winner—Lt. Gaylon 'Lock and Load'" —Doc paused for a beat as someone loudly snapped shut the top of a Zippo lighter—"Hall for his ill-conceived assassination attempts." The prize, a genuine M-16, was ruined when a round cooked off in the chamber.

"Our last award of the evening is the NATOPS Safety Award. This is presented to that member of the squadron who has done most to make safety a prime concern despite personal considerations and with thought only to the greater welfare of his shipmates.

"The nominees are: Number One, Doc Rodgers, the flight surgeon, who was worried mostly about making lieutenant commander and allowed the skipper to fly with a cast on his right hand. Number Two, Lt. John Smalling, the safety officer, who was also worried mostly about making lieutenant commander and allowed the skipper to fly with a cast on his right hand. Number Three, Cdr. Robert Porter, the skipper, who wasn't worried about anything and flew with a cast on his right hand. It should be noted that the cast was so heavy that it was only with great difficulty that the plane would climb more than fifty feet above the Delta.

"The winner—Lt. Cdr. Tom Langston for his 8-G rolling pullouts, thus overstressing every plane in the squadron. The prize is a map of the Delta showing the location of over seven thousand OV-10 rivets.

"The audience will be pleased. . . ."

"Aw, no we won't," several in the audience cried out in unison.

"The audience will be pleased to know that word has just come in from the Bureau of Personnel that Lieutenant Smalling has been appointed naval air attaché to the People's Republic of Upper Volta.

"*Ensign* Rodgers's next set of orders will take him to the billet as senior medical officer at the Loran Station on Rurutu Island. We wish him best of luck with the cannibalism problem.

"Thus we end this special awards ceremony and thank both our victims and our audience for their indulgence."[1]

"Wait a minute . . . I'd like to say something," Tom Langston shouted, as he stood with his guitar in hand, proudly reacting to the crowd's merciless display of affection for him.

"No rebuttals!" someone shouted. "Look, he's got a weapon!" another yelled. "Quick, disarm him!" a third screamed, as he grabbed Tom's guitar.

In the pandemonium Tom pulled out a sheet of paper and began reciting a poem.

Farewell to Flying

Good-bye to flying and what it means,
Freedom flying through the sky.
Farewell to design of such machines
Each factor tailored so it would fly,
Best way to its own design.
Good-bye to this living and this sight,
That stems in the way our lives align.
Farewell to flying—farewell to flight.

Good-bye to the feeling that I could reach
For sun and clouds and stars in heaven,
That I could feel and that I could teach
The ways of flight and how to leaven
Others to this way of the sky;
And also how a weapon will fight
And also—perhaps—how to die.
Farewell to flying—farewell to flight.

Good-bye to this promise gladly borne
In knowing this oneness of the sky;
In shaping the wind as garment worn
Around plans and controls and thus to fly
In perfect harmony on these wings.
And counter harmony—inward sight
To find that to oneself it brings
A deeper sorrow of farewell to flight.

Good-bye to reaching for the sky,
With thundering jet and wings of gold.
Good-bye to the quiet engine's sigh

As throttled back the clouds enfold
You while the instruments tell
You whether the flight path's left or right
And straight to runway—flying well,
The touchdown easy—farewell to flight.

Good-bye to a duty to my country
Which has primed the actions I might take;
Which fashions objectivity
In the judgments I've had to make.
Good-bye to immediacy of decision,
And decisions which must be right
To preserve and protect our country
In the battles which we fight.

Eighteen years have I labored in the vineyards of the sky.
The wine so sweet that always the measure overflows.
Even when the flight was rough or I've seen some others die
The meaning has been heady.
Defining what life knows,
Of living in freedom reconciled to self and nature's design.
So I am glad to have recognized the measure and inner sight
And thankful for perspective of the way my years align.
*Farewell to this perfect freedom—fare*well to this freedom's flight.

Everyone stood speechless for a moment, then with a few murmurs, they shuffled toward the door, until someone shouted, "Hymn!"

"Hymn . . . hymn . . ." the drone arose from the assembled.

"Hymn . . . hymn . . . Fuck him!"

Everyone then staggered back to the BOQ to hit the rack. White, Williams, Langston, and Hurley would soon be on their way, aboard their freedom's flight home.

Sweat dripped from the newbie's chin as he took careful aim and cursed under his breath that the entire world would see that the Black Pony pilot was afraid of heights. He knew Lieutenant Sloan was looking for signs of weakness. What he wasn't aware of were all the other eyes focused intently on him, wondering if he would misstep, if he would make a mistake. Just when he thought he would make it, everything fell apart and he crashed to the ground.

An explosion of laughter echoed off the orphanage walls as the children rushed to see if he were okay. A mass of tubing and braces and wires pinned him to the ground. If only he could have secured that top bolt as he perched precariously on the top of huge jungle gym he and Sloan had brought to the orphanage. The mass of unassembled parts had been donated from the States. They didn't have any of the plans, but thought they could figure out how to assemble it. They would have done better had they brought some construction engineers from the Seabees.

They took a break and played with the kids. The cute little girl they had held and fed and loved three weeks before had died. Several others replaced her, just as desperate for care and attention. Sloan would spend many hours at the orphanage over the coming weeks. He spent some of the time repairing or building things, but most of the time he played with the children. They would hear or see him drive up and would wait patiently as he did his work until they knew he had finished and could play with them. Actually he never finished, but had to devote some time to work because he knew the children could take up all the time he could spend with them, which would have been fine with him. He never finished the jungle gym in his attempts to assemble it. The older children were so much fun to be with because they took so much joy in receiving a little attention. The nuns felt sorry for him after an hour or so of horsing around because the children just did not want to quit.

Angéle spent almost all of her time with the babies in the nursery. Sloan spent endless hours helping her, bathing the infants, changing diapers and bandages. Anyone who has taken care of his or her own infant—healthy, comfortable, and safe in its own home—can appreciate the heartbreaking task of taking care of dozens of orphaned babies. Many of them were sick or infirm, stuck in the hot, humid, cramped nursery, amid the flies and mosquitoes, with a shortage of medical supplies, diapers and clothing. Sloan would change hundreds of diapers, bathe the infants, wrap them up, and hold them while feeding them. This would free Angéle to give the extra attention the sick babies required. Sloan admired Sister Angéle for her devotion to the children. Sloan found pleasure in helping her, but the hours of difficult, unrecompensed work were also a revelation of his character.

The image of Sister Marie Angéle holding one of the new babies—as Sloan stood admiringly to the side—could have been painted on an icon. The image of Angéle became indelibly impressed in his mind, and Sloan could not help but think she was the most beautiful and serene woman he had ever seen.

On Sunday night 10 October Lieutenants Hotchkiss, Segars, Sloan, and "Crazy Moe" had been scheduled for the last-go. The rains were so bad, however, that they discussed canceling their night random patrol, scheduled for a 2230 takeoff.

The Delta was quiet. The pilots may have been a little apprehensive about the weather, but were nevertheless disappointed when their launch was postponed, as had the bunker crew just prior to their 2100 launch. Just before they were scheduled to man their aircraft, at 2200, the rains let up somewhat, the ceilings raised, and both crews decided to cancel the bunker crew and launch the last-go.

The normal routine for the bunker crew after they returned from their scheduled random patrol began with pre-flighting their next set of aircraft, which would then sit in the revetments with switches thrown, and everything poised, cocked and waiting for a scramble. By the time the pilots finished their preflight, a driver would usually be pulling up to make a much-anticipated delivery—that night's movie. Earlier in the evening, generally at 1900, Black Pony officers had watched the movie in the trailer, adjacent to the BOQ. As small as it was, at least twenty guys could pack themselves into the trailer, which was equipped with a few couches and chairs, an air conditioner, and a refrigerator. A movie was one of the great escapes for Black Ponies. As soon as the men rewound the film, the driver would pick it up and speed it to the airfield, sometimes with "midrats" —midnight rations—or leftovers from that night's meal at the chow hall. Hopefully he also remembered to bring the "skinnyscope" —if the movie turned out to be in CinemaScope. But if he forgot, that never stopped the Black Ponies. By now they were used to a distorted view of the World. The driver would then motor back to Binh Thuy with the pilots from the last-go who did not want to stick around and see the movie. That night, they would just have to miss watching *The Summer of '42* with the bunker crew.

Sloan would get to fly 101, the skipper's bird that night, *The Baron's Mistress,* something he had been looking forward to, since it carried a 20-mm cannon on the centerline that, unlike most of the others, usually worked. Because of their poor design, at least a third of the time these cannons jammed after a burst of only a couple of rounds. Rarely did Ponies get all two hundred rounds out of them. But when they did, the 20-mm was extremely accurate, and the Ponies could could work to within a few meters of friendlies. The ordnancemen on night check asked him to be sure to try this one out, because they had just modified it again for the zillionth time in order to get it to work better. Sloan would be glad to oblige them.

The weather turned ugly again shortly after takeoff. They barely made it to a thousand feet when the wingman noticed that Hotch's lead aircraft began scraping the bottoms of ragged black clouds. He had begun to lose sight of Hotch's aircraft in the darkness, so he opened the throttle and tucked in a little tighter on him. The rain increased and began obscuring the windscreen. The wingman focused on flying tight formation, but noticed out of his peripheral vision, in the dim red glow, the altimeter unwind below a thousand feet. Crazy Moe in the back seat was in a lousy mood and all he did was bitch over the intercom, "This is stupid. . . . This is really stupid." He refused to switch FM frequencies to follow Hotch's back seat as he called around looking for a ballgame.

Hotch's voice crackled over the radio. A provincial forces outpost in Vinh Binh was under attack. Sloan managed to convince Crazy Moe to switch FM frequencies just in time to hear the PF say that the enemy had just mortared their outpost from positions less than a klick away. "They should be almost on top of them," Sloan thought. They were. But it would take almost an hour to find them in the rain. The VC probably had long since melted into the slime and the mud. But if they hadn't, Sloan vowed, he was going to take them out with that big gun.

It seemed to take forever to identify the outpost and get clearances. Sloan kept looking at the fuel gauge. Fortunately, he thought, they were just across the river from Black Pony home base. Then he remembered how long it took them just to find this outpost. He glanced over his shoulder to see what the weather was like back toward home.

Muzzle flashes lit up the ground outside the outpost. There were no friendlies outside the confines of the fort for miles, so these had to be the enemy. Surely they had to have seen the Ponies, as low as they were. Did they think the Ponies couldn't, or wouldn't attack them? Hotch decided to punch out one flare. The wingman took aim on the spot where he saw the muzzle flashes. The bad guys would be sitting ducks. Sloan pushed over into a shallow dive, depressed the pickle button and fired a quick burst of the cannon that shook the aircraft with its staccato discharge as dozens of high-explosive projectiles, each deadly as a grenade, flung toward the ground and—the gun jammed. He quickly pulled off target and switched to rockets. Sloan watched as Hotch rolled in; then Sloan saw the tracers arc up toward the lead aircraft from another location. Before Hotch even pulled off target, Sloan shut off his lights and rolled in on where he saw the tracers. He thought he saw shadows dart out from a clump of trees in the flickering glare of the dying paraflare. The flare hit the ground, sparked, then extinguished just as the pipper on the gun sight reached the clump of trees. He salvoed half his Zuni rockets. The cockpit lit up with the brilliance of a dozen suns and he pulled the stick into his lap and banked the plane away from the explosions. Sloan flipped on his running lights, looked for Hotch where he thought he would be, and set up for another run. Across the target Sloan saw a dozen rockets leave the dark outline of a cloud, and like a bolt of lightning, strike the ground in an incandescent glow. Sloan spotted Hotch as Sloan was pulling up and heading straight toward him.

"I'm at your twelve o'clock," Sloan radioed, "and I'm in." Hotch's plane veered sharply to the wingman's right, and they passed within a few hundred feet of each other as the wing aircraft dove for the last attack. Sloan aimed for where he thought he saw the shadows the last time and "walked" a string of rockets all the way to the tree lines where the enemy had probably taken shelter. He pickled every remaining rocket he had.

The Black Ponies had been so intensely preoccupied with working the target that they didn't notice the weather worsening between them and home. They broke off the attack and struggled to find their way home in the deteriorating weather. Sloan banked the airplane toward Hotch and set up to rendezvous on him. Beyond his aircraft Sloan could see the dark bottoms of the lower cloud layer sloping toward the ground as it moved northwestward toward the base. The low ceilings behind the storm's front would make a visual approach and landing impossible. With this frontal system moving fast, the pilots knew they would have to beat it if they were to make it safely back home. They poured the coals to it and made it back on deck just as the squall line passed over the base.

After the flight, the pilots had to wait for a ride back to the other side, where they didn't arrive until after 0200. "We've got the pound cake, but I couldn't find any peaches," Hotch reported, after rummaging around in some cardboard boxes. "I think DeSpain got to them first."

Whenever Black Ponies got a new shipment of C-rats the driver usually dropped them off at the bunker. Whoever was there got first dibs at finding the gems. Mike "Peaches" DeSpain usually got to them first. Occasionally he left some of his favorite rations to divvy up and since Hotch and Sloan spent more than their share of time in the bunker, they sometimes even got to the cache before he did.

"But I did stick some fruit cocktail in the air conditioner this morning. Here's a John Wayne," Hotch said, as he tossed over the P-38 can opener.

"Well . . . I'll compensate with a little more Jack Daniel's. War's hell, you know," Sloan answered.

In the incandescent glow of the safe little place that quarter inch plywood would cleave from the world of darkness outside, pilots often talked through the night, relaxed in the pleasure of each other's company.

21

Riders on the Storm

I'll note you in my book of memory.
—William Shakespeare, *King Henry VI*

The Black Ponies added several new missions in late 1971. The Ponies would fly single-ship naval gunfire missions along both coasts of the Delta, with a Marine 1st Air/Naval Gunfire Liaison Company (ANGLICO) air observer in the rear seat spotting and directing naval gunfire on inland targets. Preplanned air strikes "fragged" by the Delta Regional Assistance Command in Can Tho tasked Black Ponies to drop CBU-55 FAE fuel-air explosive bombs to clear areas of booby traps, mines, bunkers, and enemy personnel.

Because of all the recent scrambles, Black Ponies had depleted their inventory of Zuni rockets, and the squadron began scheduling more flights with the CBU-55 FAE. It was a free-fall bomb that opened up into a cluster of three one-hundred-pound canisters that were separated and carried to earth by parachutes. The device released a gaseous mixture or vapor cloud of fuel-air explosive a few feet above the ground, then detonated it, causing three large fireballs stretching into a pattern each fifteen meters in diameter and almost three meters high. Three hundred pounds per square inch of over-pressure from the explosion—fifteen times that of conventional bombs—would crush booby traps, mines, or anything else in their path. They looked like miniature atomic bombs.

Light Attack Squadron Four was the first operational unit to use this new weapon, developed the year before at the navy's China Lake facility in the California desert. Initially intended to clear landing zones, the ARVN increasingly requested it to be used to penetrate bunkers, caves, and tunnels. Pilots did not find it an easy weapon to drop accurately because the slightest wind could turn an otherwise accurate delivery into a fiasco after they released the bomb. Most found it impressive to watch, both from the air and on the ground. The ARVN troops even created an elite club from among those who worked with the weapon, its members distinguished by the long, red cloth ribbon and CBU arming safety pin that they wore around their necks.[1]

Commander Burton, the XO, led a flight to Kien Tuong Province near the Parrot's Beak, where the 16th Regiment of the 21st ARVN Division had been in heavy fighting over the last few days. After all the monsoon rains cleared, the weather proved perfect, the winds negligible, and everything went as planned. The Ponies were uncomfortable about how close the friendlies were, having seen how even a slight wind could drift the parachutes many meters away from the line along which the bombs were dropped. They elected to make a "lay down" delivery, straight and level at five hundred feet, 170 knots, after the fire suppression section pulled off target from unleashing about thirty Zunis. According to the army "Shotgun" aerial observer, the suppression section, two OV-10s armed with wall-to-wall proximity fused Zunis, had taken ground fire when they pulled off.

> I was tucked in tight on the XO in close formation and would pickle my bombs when I saw the XO's leave the aircraft. I couldn't help but look below the lead plane at the tree lines and occasional hootches whizzing by, thinking that someone had to have me in their gunsight, and here I was, low, slow, and flying straight and level.
>
> The flight headed straight for the target at low altitude, moments behind the suppression section. It seemed an eternity before I saw the XO's bombs drop, and I pickled mine at virtually the same instant. We made a smooth rolling pull out, climbing back to rendezvous with the rest of the flight, and to the safety that altitude afforded us. The target had been a set of bunkers adjacent to a canal. Only one bomblet missed the target, drifting a few meters toward the canal, exploding spectacularly in the water and sending a mushroom cloud of vapor into the sky and circles of muddy waves down the river.

Black Pony pilots enjoyed CBU flights primarily because we could fly back home "slick," sans the drag of rocket pods, the aircraft free to fling itself through the sky unrestrained by the lineaments of battle, and the pilot's spirit free to follow it. On the way home that day we did a six-plane tail-chase around some towering cumulonimbus clouds—a line of aircraft with only a few feet of nose-to-tail separation between us. I was tail-end Charlie.

Most pilots have remarked that they have never seen more beautiful clouds than in Vietnam. While flying, a pilot senses no speed unless he is close to the ground, where he gets the feel of relative motion. But these clouds were moisture laden and billowing, a pure white, solid looking, even close-up, and flying around them was as if I were flying around incredibly huge snow-covered mountains. The sense of speed and carom as I maneuvered around these clouds could not be duplicated on earth. Imagine downhill skiing at two to three hundred miles per hour. Virtually straight down the side of a mountain, then zooming almost vertically up the next one. The force of four times gravity pulling me down, until sailing off the peak, flipping inverted, weightless, and then going down the other side—upside down. Then underneath the next mountain—up a slope, squeezing between two peaks—too close to the next one. Clipping the top off it—but despite the feeling of a collision at nearly three hundred miles per hour, it is not the looming solid mass that it appears to be. Zooming up, over, and around the clouds, all the while using radius of turn only—cutting the corner—to maintain the interval on the aircraft in front.

On postflight inspection, I found a bullet hole in the nose wheel door. It had been aimed right between my legs.

Kit Lavell, Black Pony

Over the next few weeks, the Z-4 Battalion, NVA 18-B Regiment began linking up with its beleaguered sister battalion, the Z-5, in the northern part of the U-Minh that Black Ponies called "The Hump." Lieutenant Sloan would fly five scrambles to the area in three days in support of the 32d Ranger Battalion, along with Hotch, Lambro, and Jay Schoenfeld. After the last one, the pilots went to the trailer to watch the movie, *Little Big Man*.

That night Sloan had the bunker duty. In the quiet of his room, before going off to the bunker, Sloan recorded a cassette tape he would later send home telling his family that a friend of his, an army helo pilot, was killed the night before.

It was an hour before the first "cookout" in a long while. The XO had cumshawed some rib eye steaks that the Ponies would soon be throwing over the hot coals that filled the large drums sitting between the BOQ buildings. As some pilots lay dozing in the sun, soaking up the rays, recharging their batteries and waiting for the volleyball game, they became aware of someone standing over them.

"You number ten lazy GIs," Co Lang said, hauling half the BOQ's laundry over her frail shoulder as she passed them by.

Sloan visited the orphanage on Friday 15 October to try to finish assembling the jungle gym. No sooner had he begun to work on it than the skies opened up, the rains fell, and a miniature flash flood washed the partially assembled structure through the courtyard and up against the wall where it would sit for several more days to rust. He sat under the roof overhang and gathered up the screws, nuts, and bolts, then dried them off. Sloan then helped Sister Angéle gather up the children, many of them new kids, including a set of twins, and a little baby with a cleft palate. The electricity had gone out, and they lit candles against the darkness brought on by the unusually strong afternoon thunderstorm.

The rain pounded the windscreen in front and seeped through the cracks around the canopy and vents. The OV-10 leaks like a '40 Ford ragtop in a storm. The pilot bent his neck around to look out through the side of the canopy into the darkness, looking for anything familiar, besides the weather, with which by now he was depressingly well acquainted. He had been flying that heading for five minutes, at a thousand feet, with his wingman tucked in tight formation, trying to find his way back to the base.

"We should have seen the Bassac by now," Bubba said from the back seat.

"There it is."

"Okay, now I'll show you the 'Bassac One Approach,'" Bubba said, "Turn north over the river."

Since Black Ponies had no reliable navigation aids, they had to use a makeshift instrument approach, more seat-of-the-pants than precise instrument flying. Standard procedure called for the aircraft to let down over the water near the mouth of the river and fly up the Bassac. That night they followed procedure, as far as it took them, then they improvised. Skimming over the water until they reached the island in the middle of the river adjacent to the airfield, they tried to avoid the clouds, turned to a compass heading, and began timing. After a number of seconds, they looked for the approach end of Runway 24, where, hopefully, they could spot the runway and land. On that night, they barely made it.

In the middle of all the miserable monsoon weather, 21 October dawned with bright, clear blue skies, one of the most beautiful days imaginable in Vietnam. After the last-go returned from flying, the pilots talked through the night under a magnificent procession of stars, one of the most incredible skies they remembered ever having seen. As the night marched on and the humidity increased, rings of vapor swirled around the more prominent leaders of this starry parade.

The bad weather returned and reached a peak on 25 October when Typhoon Hester marauded through the Delta. Hotch, Bubba, Crazy Moe, and Lavell had the bunker duty that night. The rain was so heavy they just knew they wouldn't be flying. After the movie they crawled into the rack and promptly fell asleep.

Something awakened me. I rolled over and squinted at the luminescent hands of my wristwatch. 2300. I could hear the rain, even through the four-foot-thick ceiling and walls. Heavy timbers ran overhead in the two bunkbeds. Drops of water seeped through cracks between the cement mortar and concrete-filled metal rocket pods out of which the walls were constructed, and ran along the timbers, falling on one of the top bunks in which I lay. The song "Riders on the Storm" by the Doors ran through my mind. I climbed over the side of the bunk and quietly jumped to the floor. Opening the door of the bunkroom quickly so as not to allow the bright lights of the ready room to awaken the other three men, I slipped through the opening, pushing the heavy door closed behind me. That's when the scramble horn went off.

"Impossible," I thought. "We can't fly in this." As the rest of the crew jumped out of the bunkroom. I sneaked a look outside. The rain had stopped, but the ground was so saturated that a foot of water covered the PSP as it waited to drain off.

We sloshed our way to the aircraft shaking our heads and inspecting the sky for more signs of a break in the weather. Low scud clouds roamed the airfield. Maybe that's the frontal passage, I thought. I strapped into Bubba's back seat and watched as Hotch started the lead aircraft in the revetment across from us and promptly disappeared in a renewed downpour. A feeling of dread washed over me.

The taxiways were flooded also. I wondered how we could take off if the runway was flooded too. Fortunately—or unfortunately—the runway had no standing water on it, and we lined up for takeoff. As Hotch took to the runway, Bubba looked at the clouds at the point of liftoff and decided to shorten the takeoff interval between aircraft. Formation take-offs were prohibited, and at night, the lead aircraft takes the runway alone, aligned on the centerline. Only when the lead is on the takeoff roll does the wing aircraft take the runway. On this night, Bubba was right behind Hotch, and when Hotch was airborne, sucking up his gear, we were lifting off less than a few hundred feet behind him.

Hotch leveled off to avoid the low clouds at the end of the runway as we joined in formation on him at about five hundred feet. We turned to the initial compass heading that would take us to the outpost in the Cao Lanh District of Kien Phong Province that was being overrun.

Hotch radioed for us to handle the communications with the outpost. Apparently he needed all the help he could get from his back seat to navigate. And as I later learned, Crazy Moe was in another one of his moods and just bitched and complained all the way to the target, which took forever to find. When the TOC told us that the weather in the area was so bad that the helos wouldn't launch, I figured we would probably turn back. But Hotch kept pressing on.

How we found the outpost I'll never understand. It was like crawling on your knees in the dark on a narrow girder one hundred stories up on a skyscraper under construction, looking for a hot rivet in a thunderstorm. Once over the outpost, low clouds and rain greatly restricted visibility and any effort to maneuver for the attack. When we finally were able to begin a rocket attack, we had fuel enough for only two passes. During a run, the guy in the back usually has nothing to do but call out altitudes on the ICS as a help to the pilot. On that night, Bubba and I had done a lot of talking as we looked for the outpost while flying close formation on Hotch through the bad weather. Over the target we would do a lot more.

A normal diving attack was impossible because of the low clouds that we constantly had to jig and jag around and through. I would try to keep an eye on the target and help orient us, as Bubba would try to maneuver the airplane for the attack. To make matters even more interesting, at our altitude, we were well within the range of every rifle and automatic weapon on the ground.

Hotch yelled over the radio as tracers arced up toward us. We looked over our shoulders as we rolled into a steep turn, with the nose low, preparing for the roll-in on the target. We were "pop eye," going in and out of clouds, and I looked down at the attitude gyro just as we rolled past ninety degrees angle of bank. I became disoriented. But I knew we were almost inverted, still in the clouds, and the altimeter was unwinding below two thousand feet. I hesitated . . . first to orient myself, then to see what Bubba was going to do. Having served a tour of duty as a flight instructor, I was accustomed to guys putting me into unusual attitudes . . . but this was different.

"We're upside down, Bubba."

The aircraft's nose fell toward the earth.

"Bubba, keep turning right, keep turning, turn! . . . right rudder . . . now pull the nose up . . . bring her up! Okay, level out. Stop turning. Ease the stick back."

The altimeter bottomed out at nine hundred feet before we started to climb again. We were still in the soup, and we had just made a complete barrel roll with our nose pointed at the ground.

"You okay?" I asked.

"I am now," Bubba replied, "I had vertigo."

The aircraft zoomed out of the cloud. Hotch was at our two o'clock high.

"There's the target," I said, looking over my shoulder again.

"Rog," Bubba said on the intercom. "I'm in now," he called out to Hotch over the radio as we rolled in again—all without missing a beat. When we got back on the ground Bubba and I said nothing to each other, but our relationship changed after that night. The next day Bubba signed my wing qualification papers. I would no longer have to give up a scheduled front seat if we were scrambled.

The next day I flew with Max Britton to Vinh Binh, the mission on which I would earn wing qualification. At first, I couldn't seem to keep the rockets in the same province. Max reassured me that we all have days like that. "Let me tell you about the flight on which I announced to the U.S. Army Shotgun spotter, 'That hootch will disappear.' About a dozen passes later and all my ordnance expended, it remained untouched. Sometimes the harder you try the harder it gets." I took his advice to mean it was a Zen kind of thing.

We too were working for a Shotgun spotter in an O-1 Bird Dog. He was directing our attacks on suspected ammunition caches hidden beneath the heavy foliage along the coast of Vinh Binh Province. Vinh Binh lay just below Vinh Long, the province across the river from us. Its coast was sixty miles from our base. We knew the area to be virtually controlled by the enemy. We had read the intelligence reports identifying this target as an "ammunition factory" and storage area. Intelligence types believed that boats had off-loaded supplies on the beach from trawlers. Max's story took the pressure off me and I put a Zuni right where the Shotgun asked me to and got a big secondary explosion.

After the flight we went to the trailer for a few drinks. Several hours later, on my way to the chow hall, I spotted Max, sitting atop the trailer, his feet dangling against the adjacent bomb shelter, silhouetted against the monsoon sky, reading a letter from home. I thanked him for the advice.

Kit Lavell, Black Pony

Later that night Max and Bubba appropriated the skipper's car and took it to Can Tho where they went drinking with the Darkhorse pilots. They made it all the way back onto the base only to inadvertently back the Ponymobile into a ditch a few hundred yards from where they stole it.

After returning from a night flight some pilots stopped at the admin office to read the message traffic. Max and Bubba were looking for a few good men with strong backs to pull the Ponymobile out of the ditch. As the pilots were sitting at the desk on one end of the dimly lit room being persuaded, they overheard the admin officer at the other end take an urgent phone call from the dispensary. One of our enlisted men had taken his life. He wasn't even twenty years old.

How do you explain such a tragedy? How do you tell someone back home? How do you tighten those ties that bind loved ones separated not just by miles but even more so by loneliness, concern, fear, and even desperation? Separation has always been the silent enemy of navy families. In war, silence gives consent to desperate deeds.

Not many nights later, while sitting at the same desk, the same Black Ponies overheard another tragic call. The wife of one of our pilots had taken her life, in San Diego. The pilot would be rushed back to the States to his two small children, never again to return.

Lord guard and guide the men who fly
Through the great spaces in the sky.
Be with them always in the air
In dark'ning storm or sunlight fair.
Oh hear us when we lift our prayer
For those in peril in the air.

   The aviators' verse from the navy hymn

22

Light Attack Quack

I have aged so much that all that I was is left behind me.

—Antoine de Saint-Exupéry, *Flight to Arras*

"Looks like I get to fly with Lieutenant Toooba again," the pilot told the SDO when he checked the flight schedule to see which bird was assigned to him. Next to his name was that of his back seat pilot who was designated only as "TBA." When he went out to preflight it, there was his "to be announced" co-pilot, already looking it over.

"Hi, Doc. Ready for another Air Medal?"

To hear Doc Rodgers tell it, most of his time was spent treating VD. That's what he liked to say. Surely he did spend a lot of his time at it. But he also volunteered many hours of his day to give much-needed medical treatment to the Vietnamese, especially children. He would treat malaria, stomach worms, dysentery, malnutrition, infections, and wounds suffered by civilians. To get away from things, he did quite a bit of flying in the back seat of our aircraft. He tried to be low-key about it, in part because of the Geneva Convention, he said. With all the back seat time he was accumulating, he became so adept at navigation, handling the radios, and doing all those things expected of a copilot that he became the skipper's usual back seat guy. Of course, no one else really wanted to fly in the skipper's back seat anyway, except for Gaylon

Hall and Father Mac. Doc did so much flying (123 combat missions) that he found himself on some pretty hot flights, and began getting written up for awards, including Air Medals and Navy Commendation Medals, which he eschewed. With all the unit awards the Black Ponies had earned, the Presidential Unit Citation ("PUC"), the Navy Unit Citation ("NUC"), and the Meritorious Unit Citation ("MUC"), Doc was probably the most decorated flight surgeon in the navy.

"Fuck, between the NUC, MUC, and the PUC, I look like a field marshal already," the bird surgeon would proudly proclaim.

"You're so good at alliteration, you ought to be the awards officer," the awards officer offered, "then you could write them up too."

"Hey, we could change our squadron's motto," Doc added, "Not 'Death before dishonor,' but, 'If you feel good about it, write it up!'"

Strapping into the aircraft, Doc, like the pilots, did not wear a G suit. Because of the heat, virtually every pilot flew without G suits, but they had built up a tolerance for the G forces to which they constantly exposed their bodies. They would also use the "grunt and bear it" technique when they pulled off target: forcing air down on the diaphragm by a strenuous grunt, and then a slow exhalation, which had the effect of constricting the flow of blood away from the upper body, thus preventing blackout.

Many pilots lost so much weight over their tour that their torso harnesses became too big. In the event they had to eject, the harness might have caused an injury. The quick-release Koch fittings on the torso harness attached the wearer at the upper body to the parachute assembly, which was part of the ejection seat, and at the lower body to the rigid seat survival kit. The integrated torso harness was like a full body girdle whose purpose was to absorb the opening shock of the parachute by distributing the force throughout the body. It was vital that it fit perfectly. Pilots often went to the paraloft to have Parachute Rigger 1st Class Morgan adjust it for them

Against regulations, some pilots would wear the two-piece army flight suit because they could run around in the heat with just the trousers and a T-shirt until having to go fly, then they could just throw on the top piece and go aviate. In a daily ritual a Black Pony pilot checked to see if he had inadvertently left anything in his pockets other than an ID card, and then ceremoniously put the rest of his gear on. It was as if he were a devout altar boy, layering his body with sacramental garments while removing from his mind extraneous baggage in preparation for an experience not of this earth.

Many pilots carried individualized gear. Lieutenant Lavell wore his version of a flying scarf, a lucky "combat chamois." He had several narrow strips of chamois sewn together, which he would wear around his neck and use to soak up perspiration while on target. He got the idea from Bubba, who called it a "combat sha-*me*."

Pilots were always thinking about what would happen if they were shot down, and as part of the mental drill they all went through almost daily, they frequently inspected and reviewed what was in their survival vests.

The SV-2B survival vest had about five pounds of survival equipment in it, most of it standard items like the AN/PRC-63 or 90 survival radio, MK 79 pencil flare gun, MK 13 Mod O signal flare, signal mirror, sea dye marker, MC-1 switchblade knife, air weight .38-caliber pistol, and medical and general packets. The packets contained things like Band-Aids, soap, aspirin, amphetamines, caffeine, compass, and mosquito nets. Most pilots would also customize their survival vest by including additional items they thought necessary or desirable in a survival situation. Some pilots carried baby bottles with water and extra flares and replaced the air weight .38 with a government-issue .45-caliber automatic pistol.

Just as a salesman prepares the pitch he will make today, the professional tennis player practices his strokes, and the surgeon reviews the latest techniques, combat pilots would mentally prepare themselves daily—for death. Not theirs, they hoped, but the consensus among those who flew in the Delta was that, if they were shot down, they were likely to be killed if caught. And if not, they might not last long in captivity. Unlike in the north—where POWs could be taken to a prison in a city and their lives had political value—in the guerrilla environment of the south, pilots at best were a burden to those who would have to drag them along through the jungle. Intelligence sources and general opinion resigned most Black Ponies to the belief that their best chance of survival if confronted by the enemy on the ground was—kill them first.

Waiting to Launch

I reach out to touch the switches in the cockpit of my OV-10 roasting under the hot afternoon sun. I sense myself attached to the aircraft, which of course I am, but I visualize my heart connected to the bird's hydraulic system and my nervous system tied into the electrical system. In a hazy almost-dream, I try to will the Bronco awake, but can't muster the electrical energy. A tap on the prop from Airman Loera, the plane captain, awakens me as he switches on the external power and points the fire extinguisher at the engine. Consciousness flows from my brain into my hands, and I point to the number one engine, rotate two fingers to signal turn-up, and push the starter toggle switch forward with my left forefinger, completing the connection between my nervous system and the bird's electrical circuitry . . . and awakening it. The START IGN ON *light illuminates as energy flows through all the wires and circuits, spinning the starter, the two-stage centrifugal compressor, the three-stage axial turbine, and the accessory section, a heavy rotating mass of shaped, finned and polished metal surrounded by an annular combustion chamber. As the RPM passes 6 percent, my fingers advance the Condition lever, the speed sensing switch energizes the ignition unit and the igniter plugs in the combuster as fuel bypasses the fuel control unit and is injected directly into the engine. I feel the surge in my own body as the prop begins to spin faster and the RPM increases . . . the shift from Exhaust Gas Temperature to Turbine Inlet Temperature,* START IGN ON *light out, 53 percent RPM, starting fuel is cut off and electrical energy is directed through the Power Management Control System to the fuel control . . . a higher level of consciousness . . . it now breaths on its own, air sucking through the inlet above the prop and into the impeller, compressing and mixing with fuel, the cracked and refined residue of other creatures whose energy ceased to flow eons ago, igniting and expanding now as gases driving the three-stage turbine which transfer this captured chemical energy into mechanical force through a shaft and reduction gears to the eight-and-a-half-foot, three-bladed aluminum propeller whirling clockwise in the stagnant air, wafting unburned hydrocarbons toward my nose . . . as I sit watching the TIT rise to 930-degrees centigrade, the oil pressure reach 65 PSI and the RPM stabilize at 98 percent. I breath the fumes deeply and push the* INST PWR *switch to the* INV NO. 1 *position, sending electrons from my autonomic nervous system flowing into and from the d-c bus through the invertor arrayed as alternating current in three phases to the primary bus, the instrument bus, and on out to the instruments . . . I hear whirring, humming, the clicking of the attitude indicator erecting itself . . . I adjust the RPM and look out to the number two engine as the plane captain runs around to it, and I go through the same procedure to wake up the right half of my body and bring it on line.*

A Black Pony

On this flight, Doc would get a lot of stick time, part of a secret program to teach him how to fly and have him eventually lead an entire flight from the back seat. The Black Ponies would make him a Light Attack Quack!

But this time Doc didn't get a chance to practice landings back at Binh Thuy because his flight joined up with the skipper's on the way home in a four-plane tail chase. Approaching Binh Thuy the skipper called for a four-plane diamond formation, and Doc's plane slid into the slot, about three feet below and behind the lead aircraft.

About a mile from the end of the runway at three thousand feet, the skipper pushed the nose over and aimed for a point about one hundred feet above the bunker which the flight passed approaching red line airspeed of 350 knots in a timber-rattling roar. The CO kissed off the section leader from his left wing, who then snapped his aircraft into a 4-G break turn. Two seconds later Doc's plane broke behind him, with Doc in the back seat easing the throttle slightly to take an interval on the plane in front and easing the nose up to keep the lead on the horizon as they climbed to pattern altitude. All the while Doc pulled a steady 4 Gs, slowing the Bronco down to landing speed. He never rolled wings level, keeping about 60 degrees angle of bank almost until the 90-degree position off the end of the runway. He could shallow his bank a couple of degrees there as they slowed down enough to drop the gear and flaps. The throttles went all the way back to the NTS range, where the props acted like speedbrakes, and as Doc passed over the threshold, the airspeed bled off to optimum angle of attack. He rolled wings level and greased it in, a few hundred feet behind the section leader who was on the opposite side of the runway centerline on his roll out. Much to the delight of the other pilots, Doc's flying skills were steadily building.

Jim Arthur would walk around with the "combat stare," as he called it, one eye bugged out, the other squinting and twitching through an imaginary gun sight, with his right forearm extended as if gripping the stick, his index finger twitching spasmodically in sync with his eye.

"Not that far off," many a pilot would remark.

In the blur of those days, which not so much passed as flew by, the adrenaline highs stuck out in the minds of the Black Ponies, an addictive craving for combat gnawing on one side of the psyche, while the instinct for self-preservation gently tugged at the other.

Waiting in the bunker late one afternoon for the start of an All Pilots Meeting (APM), a group of guys sat around the briefing table playing a game. What had started out as a board game that simulated global conflict had been modified by replacing the board with a map of Vietnam, and when that got too boring (almost immediately), with a large map of the world. Along the way, new rules were added and the game evolved into a sophisticated simulation that stressed knowledge of history, geography, and skills in power politics, diplomacy, alliances, negotiations, and just plain cunning. The games would go on for days, with players moving in and out, as in a floating crap game.

Over the months pilots had fun playing this game, primarily because they got a chance to see a side of the other pilots that they wouldn't have experienced otherwise. Ordinarily if you ask a combat pilot for his opinion about politics or world affairs he will tell you he has none. It needs to be that way, for the most part, for there is usually little luxury for anything else in war. It doesn't mean aviators are uncaring or self-centered or shallow. It doesn't mean they are incapable of sensitive, reflective thought. It doesn't mean they might not hold differing or even unconventional political opinions. It means that when their lives and the lives of those around them are at stake and they have a mission they must carry out, they are preoccupied and single-minded. They are so programmed—to use today's vernacular.

Bubba Segars was with the group of pilots who had just arrived from the other side. He burst into the bunker carrying an armful of maps and charts and broke up the game. As an assistant to the operations officer, Bubba would often conduct the APMs. Today Bubba briefed the pilots that recent intelligence reported NVA units amassing weapons along the coast of Vinh Binh Province, deposited there by trawlers. He pointed out on the map a suspected "ammunition factory" just a few klicks inland.

Bubba also announced, to the accompaniment of groans, that the squadron would be stepping up the VARS missions—visual aerial reconnaissance and surveillance. Nobody liked to fly those boring single-aircraft flights that, they insisted, were nothing more than sight-seeing along the coast with an air intelligence officer or other non-pilot observer in the back seat. Bubba then showed the pilots a chart he concocted that plotted enemy assaults on outposts and other enemy engagements against the phases of the moon. It may have looked funny, but no one laughed. It was the truth. The enemy liked the rain and darkness because it equalized things, especially limiting the use of U.S. airpower. Bubba had gathered the intelligence info for his charts from Smitty (Lt. Edward Smith), the intelligence officer who was officially attached to VAL-4. (At that time he was not technically an intelligence officer but served as one.)

I was not an intel officer at the time. I was an 1110 (line officer). I went to work first for then-Capt. William Crowe (who later became chairman of the Joint Chiefs of Staff), but at that time senior advisor, Tran Hung Dao campaigns, Delta naval forces. When I first met him he asked, "Are you an 1110 or 1630?" I said, "An 1110." He said, "Good. I keep asking for intelligence officers and all they send me are 1630s."

I had no intelligence training before I got there. I gave my first intel brief to Captain Crowe, offering my best guess on what was going to happen in the Mekong Delta. To my utter horror, everybody starting launching strikes all over the Delta based on what I had said. All of a sudden it became very obvious what the consequences of guessing wrong were. I proceeded at that point to think things over again.

The next morning I got up and gave a briefing that would have made DIA [Defense Intelligence Agency] proud. I used every weasel word in the book. When no strikes resulted, I breathed a sigh of relief. I started out the office door, the last one out, and I heard Captain Crowe's [low, slow, staccato] voice behind me, "Edwaaaaard! Come back. Let's talk. Now let's get this straight. Operational responsibilities around here are mine. The guessing responsibilities are yours. I don't care what the intelligence types tell you, it's just all a bunch of guessing. And the only truth is to be the best goldarned guesser going."

Good advice.[1]

Edward Smith, Black Pony

On Friday 29 October, while flying a single-aircraft coastal surveillance mission, Bubba Segars and Lt. Ed "Smitty" Smith were shot down on the coast of Vinh Binh, in the area Bubba had briefed the Black Ponies about only days before. After evading the enemy for thirty-three minutes and being picked up by an army helo in a daring rescue ("Bubba's Misadventure" in chapter 1 of this book), a few people began joking that Bubba would become a "black ace" (the opposite of an ace, who destroys five enemy aircraft), by losing five of our own. Bubba later flew A-4s in Attack Squadron 127 where he ejected from his second Skyhawk jet after an engine failure. He would also have many more close calls over the years. But Bubba proudly points out that he saved many aircraft other pilots might have lost, including a few F-18 Hornets when, many years later, he was an acceptance test pilot for the navy at the McDonnell Douglas factory.[2]

Everyone knew that Bubba was back to normal when a few nights later he took the ammo can that caught the water from his air conditioner and dumped it from the second deck onto a HAL-3 lieutenant commander. Apparently the guy didn't like Bubba's refusal to salute him, or his logic that "junior officers are not required to salute other junior officers, and a lieutenant commander is a junior officer." Bubba later explained, "Me and Admiral Zumwalt have one thing in common: *We've both gone as far as we're going in this navy.*"

As the armory officer, Lt. Jim Arthur got to write off all the squadron's missing personal weapons to Bubba's Misadventure. Reading the reports, you would have thought that Bubba had been running guns.

After Bubba's ordeal on the ground, many pilots increased their running and physical training, despite the heat and humidity. In the years before the physical fitness craze changed attitudes, pilots put physical fitness on the priority list just above getting poked in the eye with a sharp stick. But what would you expect from guys still on the upswing of the immortality curve? Volleyball or handball was okay, and some guys lifted weights (in addition to bar glasses), but anything else for most of them took time away from flying and drinking. The climate, the food, the water, the flying, all conspired to rob pounds from most pilots. Despite drinking as much water as they could, most pilots lost a few pounds each time they flew, between the heat and pulling so many Gs.

After someone gets shot down, most pilots find themselves trying to recall little details from the SERE (survival, evasion, resistance, and escape) training they went through at Warner Springs, in the foothills above San Diego. After not getting any food for a couple of days, they had been dropped in the boonies, given a head start, and then chased by instructors posing as North Vietnamese. The longer they could evade capture, the less time they had to spend in the "prisoner of war" camp, a most unpleasant day-and-a-half experience. The most vivid thing a pilot would remember, besides the "waterboard torture" and the "black box," was a painful thirst. No wonder most Black Ponies stuffed baby bottles of water into the leg pockets of their flight suit.

The month ended as it had begun—with bad weather. In fact, there was little to distinguish one day from another for the Black Ponies. All days were the same. All nights were the same. For the bunker crew standing scramble duty it was just like any other night. But before it was over, each night brought something new, something unexpected.

It was nighttime in the Delta. The sun had set, and when curfew fell, the cyclos, lambros, bikes, cars, and motorcycles abandoned the roads, and the sampans beached along the riverbanks and sides of canals. Stillness, interrupted by the sounds of insects—the buzzing of mosquitoes, so big they should be made to carry paraflares and follow the ROE. The shadowy jungle blurred to black, the rice paddies faded to a grizzly gray, and only the occasional lights from villages penetrated the curtain that fell over the Delta.

Behind that curtain, the Vietcong began to move. Groups of men, women, and even children met in dimly lit hootches, where they planned tactics, then split up. Messengers were dispatched, arms were retrieved from caches, tax collectors were sent forth, assassination teams were unleashed, and small guerrilla units methodically set up ambushes. Squads surreptitiously assembled outside provincial outposts, and larger units joined up with main force regulars, poised to attack forward firebases. The stage was set. The curtain would go up whenever the Viet-cong decided.

Tonight the Black Ponies played lead roles in this elaborate production. The bunker crew flew all over the Delta looking for a ballgame, only to get a call from the Vinh Long Province TOC, just across the river from Binh Thuy, as they were headed home. The weather had been fine west of Binh Thuy, but a squall line was moving across the coast to the east, and they could see the thunderstorms over Vinh Long. Typical of the enemy, as soon as the rains came out, they would raise the curtain on this long-running tragedy.

Although the outpost was less than twenty miles away, they spent the usual half hour trying to find it, eventually having to fly around in the rain below a thousand feet, under the overcast. The Black Ponies didn't have enough altitude to launch flares effectively, and it was dark enough that they needed them. They had precious few seconds to orient themselves, acquire the target, and shoot before the flares hit the ground. The outpost reported that the Ponies were taking fire, but the pilots saw no tracers or muzzle flashes because of the clouds.

Afterward, they flew on a heading of 240 at one thousand feet, as the rain pounded their windscreens, until they passed over the Bassac, descended to five hundred feet and slowed to 130 knots. At the northern tip of the small island in the river just off the end of the runway, they made their turn and landed, just as the squall-line slithered over the airbase.

By the time the two aircraft de-armed and taxied into the revetments, the rains totally engulfed them. The pilots sat in the planes for about ten minutes, then decided to make a run for it when the rain did not let up. They were so wet and tired that they fell into the rack, but could not sleep.

Sometimes an outsider would ask a VAL-4 pilot why Black Ponies would often take as great a risk in pressing a target when no American lives were in jeopardy as when American lives were.

"We've got special procedures for when Americans are in trouble," a Black Pony would explain, referring to what they called a Scramble One, the most urgent call for air support. But despite that, Black Ponies flew all scrambles the same way. And they would have a hard time explaining why. But they really didn't need to.

Every pilot would probably tell you he would not lay his life on the line for a Vietnamese—but he did it every day, every night, willingly, eagerly. To some extent, one could attribute it to professionalism— "I'm just doing my job" —and surely there was always the element of adventure, the lure of flying on the edge, the adrenaline rush. But it could also be attributed to how close Black Ponies felt to the Vietnamese soldiers on the ground. Over the months they got to know many of the ARVN they flew in support of, and developed a great respect for them, especially those of the 21st ARVN Division.

Max Britton had the SDO duty and a hangover, causing him to feel, he said, as if he had been "et by a wolf and shit over a cliff." One of the pilots forgot his code wheel and radioed in to Max to bring it to him. Max told him to come and get it himself. The XO heard the exchange on the radio, stormed into the bunker, relieved Max of the duty and put him in hack again, with what had now become the familiar— "go to your room, Max."

At the Fourth Annual Awards Ceremony on 5 November, Doc and a handful of the JOs sang "Bubba's Ballad" to the tune of "Ghost Riders in the Sky."

A little gomer went strolling one dark and windy day,
Along the coast of Vinh Binh he went along his way,
When all at once a mighty plane in the sky he saw,
A plowing through a ragged skies and down a cloudy draw,
    Yippi ay oh, kay yay, Black Pony in the skies.

The M-60s were a blazing and sending flak of steel,
The Zunis were a cooking off—their hot death he could feel,
A bolt of fear went through him as they thundered through the sky,
For he saw the Ponies coming hard and heard their mournful cry,
    Yippi ay oh, kay yay, Black Ponies kill today.

Bubba's face was gaunt, his eyes blurred, his brow was soaked with sweat,
He tried to mark the gomers' spot, but Ray ain't seen them yet,
He's rolling in with strafe alone—no rockets did he have,
He tried to pull the pony out—the controls had been hit bad,
    Yippi ay oh, kay yay, Black Pony dropping out of the sky.

The AK hit the Pony hard—it screamed a screech of pain,
Somehow Bubba pulled the ring and jettisoned the plane.
Two chutes they did blossom in the twilight skies,
The gomers were so close to them they saw ole Smitty's eyes,
    Yippi ay oh, kay yay, Triple Sticks on the beach.

Bubba lost his little buddy—and hauled ass to the beach,
He only knew that he'd be safe if he was out of reach.
He treaded water frantically, and only showed his nose,
While Smitty calmly stood there—and worked the radios.
 Yippi ay oh, kay yay, rescue on the way.

The time they spent upon the beach must have seemed like years.
Meanwhile back at Pony base their comrades fought their tears,
And every single Pony was thrust into the air,
And rescue it did come—with little time to spare.
 Yippi ay oh, kay yay, "Tailboard" saves the day.

We hope that we have learned today the frailties of men,
We thank God for the chance to see our comrades safe again,
We hope that in the future your altimeter won't lag,
'Cause Doc in the dispensary has a brand-new body bag.
 Yippi ay oh, kay yay, Black Ponies in the skies.

23

Change in the Air

The ghosts I have summoned, I cannot get rid of now.

—Johann Wolfgang von Goethe, *The Sorcerer's Apprentice*

Change was in the air. November began with a new group of replacement pilots reporting aboard. Another group had returned to "the World." After the battle of the U-Minh and all the scrambles of the last few weeks, many Black Ponies developed an increased self-confidence. Bubba's close call gave everyone pause to reflect on his mortality, but tempered no one's boldness, least of all Bubba's. Even the air itself changed abruptly. The thunderstorms became more isolated and sporadic. As the monsoons died, so did the frontal activity, with its layers of rain-laden clouds that made flying and navigation difficult. And, some pilots would swear—there was more lift in the air.

Black Ponies flew fewer of the old types of missions: air cover for SEALs, except for a couple of missions to Dung Island at the mouth of the Bassac, where the SEALs still liked to snatch VC in the middle of the night; and boat cover, except for an occasional convoy. They flew less coastal surveillance and naval gunfire spotting missions. And the Ponies also flew fewer missions for army Shotgun aerial observers, who eventually left Vietnam on 10 November.

But Black Ponies found themselves working more with army AirCavPacs and MiniPaks, which began calling VAL-4 directly. Ponies flew so much with the 164th that many VAL-4 pilots would spend their off-duty hours with them at their "O" Club in Can Tho. And as the frequency of close air support for ARVN units increased, VAL-4 pilots began spending more time visiting the units in their areas of operation (AOs) learning more about their tactics and procedures.

Because of the language barrier, a young lieutenant at ComNavForV staff in Saigon invented a "brevity code" to help pilots and ARVN soldiers communicate. Lt. Francis Houlian had accompanied Admiral Zumwalt on his visit to the Black Ponies several months before, when Hotch collared the CNO seeking help with enlisted-personnel drug problems. Houlian (later a rear admiral who commanded the San Diego Naval Base) had developed the brevity code to help pilots communicate vital information over the radios while on target by using a series of numbers to represent phrases.

Black Pony pilots also furthered communication by visiting the Vietnamese soldiers in their forward firebases where they each learned more about the other's role, tactics, and personalities. Pony pilots and ARVN also managed to assimilate a few of each other's standard phrases. This helped create that bond that comes only from face-to-face contact.

On an early morning mission Black Ponies flew to the Lobster Tail—the Ca Mau Peninsula at the southernmost tip of the Delta. ComNavForV assigned the highly classified destination at the last minute: they "fragged" VAL-4 to provide air cover for a "Bright Light" operation—an attempted POW "extraction." But ground controllers cancelled the mission just as the OV-10s arrived in the area, and as with other similar missions that Black Ponies had flown, this one ended with frustration in an aborted attempt to rescue Americans thought to be held prisoner in the Delta.

Later that evening, Sloan went to the orphanage where he talked to Sister Angéle. Late that night he made a tape, which he sent to his parents. Sloan talked to his mother about "a beautiful starry night" which he wanted "to spend with someone special." On this tape, he told his mother he was "in love with that novitiate at the orphanage." She knew whom he meant.

Large portions of the Mekong Delta bore little allegiance to the Saigon government, and in some areas, even less to the National Liberation Front. Two religious, mystic sects—the Cao Dai and the Hoa Hao—dominated much of this area. The Cao Dai worshiped Lao Tzu, Buddha, Moses, and Christ, as well as Joan of Arc and Victor Hugo. The Vietminh assassinated the founder of the Hoa Hao in 1947, engendering the lasting hostility that made An Giang the only province in the South where the NLF never gained a foothold. Nor did the South Vietnamese government, for that matter.

Flying over the area, it stood out from the other provinces because of its neatly ordered rice paddies, groves, farms, and villages, always a rich green, devoid of the bomb craters and other scars of war seen everywhere else. Black Ponies found it a safe place to take pilots new in-country to practice roll-ins. It was the only area in the Delta that they knew to be really secure.

The bunker crew was surprised, therefore, when they found themselves scrambled to An Giang on a series of scrambles. Black Ponies were needed to support a small Ruff-Puff outpost near the village of Hoa Hao in an area where a perpendicular branch of the river connected the Bassac with another tributary of the Mekong, like the rung of a ladder, at a place Ponies called "the crossover." Regional forces and popular forces were part-time soldiers, and their forts usually contained living quarters for their families inside the compound. This fort had taken a barrage of mortar rounds inside its walls.

On one of the scrambles, a Black Pony pilot discovered that the light in his gun sight reticle (that illuminated the crosshairs) burned out in the middle of a rocket attack. He reached up and switched to the number two filament, but it too went out. He continued the attack and fired his Zuni rockets using the tracers of the machine guns as a reference. After a while, shooting without a gun sight would almost be considered routine. Black Pony pilots would develop so much experience at firing rockets under such differing conditions that they developed a seat-of-the-pants feel for where to fire them. Zunis could be launched at a point where tracers began to burn out, and 2.75-inchers, since they were slower and dropped quicker, had to be fired slightly above the tracers.

On the way back from the An Giang scrambles the Ponies took a circuitous route, flying over the Bassac at low level to just above Long Xuyen, then southwest along the Rach Gia canal toward "Ceremonial Mountain." Along the banks of the canal they could see houses that were built of wood, bamboo, and straw, as well as of bricks and tiles of baked clay dug up from adjacent rice fields. Enormous water jars stood on either side of doorways. Between the ashen-colored thatch roofs, they could see vegetable gardens, and shelters for water buffalo, farm equipment, and grain reserves. Surrounding the dwellings, banana trees, areca palms, guava, and mango trees competed with tall bamboo for sunlight. They flew low enough to see pigs in sties, chickens in coops, and geese waddling around.

They climbed to meet the cumulonimbus clouds billowing above Ceremonial Mountain, which, at 726 feet, was little more than a papule on an otherwise placid and near-perfect landscape. The air was much cooler now. The luminescent whiteness of the clouds radiated a mood-altering glow. The flying Black Ponies chased each other around the clouds until they drove the images of war from their minds.

Among the VAL-4 enlisted men, the men of the Aircraft and AvWeps Divisions worked under some of the most difficult conditions imaginable. The enemy occasionally rocketed or mortared the airfield and there was always the threat of a sapper attack. The tempo of activity was unrelenting and the working conditions abysmal. Heat, humidity, rain, and jungle rot, plus the lack of tools, equipment, and spare parts, only brought out the best in many of them. They meticulously fabricated what they could, and jury-rigged what they had to—just to keep all the birds in the air.

The men had little in the way of diversions, except for the bars in town and the club on base and whatever organized sports they could put together in their off time. At the large army base in Can Tho, a few miles away, thousands of men sat on their hands with very little to do, and drugs posed quite a problem. Although officers caught a few drug abusers, given the environment, VAL-4 was very lucky not to have had a similar problem. Alcohol was quite a different matter, though.

Just keeping everything on an even keel presented a struggle. The more experienced petty officers tried to help many of the younger enlisted men keep a sense of perspective, which was tough, as so many were away from home for the first time in their brief navy careers, thrust into that crazy environment. Unlike the pilots whose daily experiences of danger and excitement infused meaning and texture into their military lives, the men who kept the planes flying had to sublimate frustrations, find rewards in the mundane, and work hard to stay motivated.

Division officers, as pilots whose life depended on the performance of their men, took great interest in the welfare of the enlisted men. Some division officers would often go into the town of Ben Xe Moi, adjacent to Can Tho, and tour the bars, checking on the men. They would travel in groups to thwart the "cowboys," roving gangs of kids who would descend upon lone Americans, slashing the pockets of their fatigues with razors to quickly empty them of their contents. Veterans of these attacks displayed "Ben Xe Moi hash marks" —sewn-up slits on their pockets. In making their rounds, the officers enjoyed a few drinks themselves and would often eat at some of the restaurants, which could be risky. Some even earned a reputation of being liberty hounds.

In his unorthodox style, Cdr. Bob Porter really looked out for the troops. He spent a lot of his nonflying time with them, and he could frequently be found drinking with a number of the men, more so in his quarters now, rather than in the enlisted barracks, after breaking his hand. He was a tough disciplinarian, but fair. Light Attack Squadron Four may have been a rag-tag outfit in some ways, but it was an incredibly effective outfit. And it was in large part because of the enlisted men, the skipper knew.

> When I was aircraft division officer the men painted my name on the side of a Bronco. The pilot whose name graced the side of that bird had rotated back to the States, so it was my turn, and it was the next available aircraft. I had been flying different aircraft a lot, and the men knew how I felt about this Bronco. When it came back from being repainted the gull-gray that all our green Broncos underwent in an attempt to reduce the number of bullet holes originating from those whose eyes were pointing skyward, I got a surprise. My name was on its side. And on the nose the men had painted "Gandalf the Gray Wizard" along with Gandalf's "rune." I had flown (and would continue to fly) 107 on some of my most memorable combat missions. It got many men on the ground—and me—out of some tight spots. This was the aircraft that Jeff Johnson brought Pete Russell home in. Several men in the Aircraft Division had been reading Tolkien's *Lord of the Rings* trilogy, which I had read years before. We would occasionally talk about the books. I had mentioned to them on several occasions that I thought 107 had a magical quality to it, a personality of sorts that comes from wisdom and experience. I always felt safer flying in it. Pony 107 had seen a lot. . . . The men must have thought so too, for they painted "Gandalf" on it.[1]
>
> Kit Lavell, Black Pony

On the night of 18 November Sloan went to a "farewell" dinner at the orphanage. This was an adjunct to their yearly "benefactors'" dinner which combat operations had prevented him from attending. They scheduled a separate dinner for Sloan because he had done so much for them. Sister Marie Angéle was conspicuously absent, having chosen to remain in her room. Sister Eugenia, the Mother Superior, instructed another nun to go and bring Sister Angéle to the dinner. Sloan suggested that this was

Gandalf the Gray Wizard in its revetment *drawing by Dan Witcoff*

not necessary, but Sister Eugenia insisted. Only by asking Sister Eugenia to grant him a favor was Sloan able to successfully implore the Mother Superior to allow Angéle to remain in her room, since that, apparently, was what the young nun wanted.

The next day Sloan sent a tape to his parents telling them he did not know what he would do about Angéle, but his engagement to his fiancée back home was off.

U-Turns Permitted

Five hundred feet on the altimeter. We were within the reach of the demons who could thrust up at any moment and snatch us out of the sky. Within the sounds of silence, intermittent static and crackle spat from the radios. "Hurry, 'Pony One Seven,'" urged the voice from the darkness below.

It was a race for life and death. If we didn't find the 33d Regimental outpost soon, they would all be dead. Even if we got there soon, they might not be alive. At this speed and altitude, in the darkness and rain, the slightest inadvertent movement of the hand would splatter us all over the terrain. It almost seemed as if Death were converging from all quadrants on this one spot.

"What am I doing here?" I thought. "Damn, this is crazy. There are no Americans in the outpost. I don't owe these people anything. Why am I sweating?" I was cold. Trembling, I reached to turn up the cockpit heat. Sweat poured from under my helmet.

"There it is," I said to Bubba on the ICS.

"Delta Bravo, we're overhead," Bubba reported.

"Great. The outpost reports heavy mortar and automatic weapons fire from the west and southwest. The bad guys are reported inside the perimeter. The good guys have abandoned the western section of the outpost. They're in deep serious. The only friendlies in the area are the men in the outpost. They're outside, just east of the eastern wall. You've got clearance, initials Foxtrot Tango. Get 'em, Black Ponies."

"Rog, cleared in," Bubba replied on the FM radio. "Let's make everything count," he said to me on the ICS.

We had lucked upon the outpost in the darkness, passing almost overhead. A small fire inside the perimeter illuminated the inside walls of the triangular-shaped structure enough for us to maintain visual contact with it as I banked the aircraft into a circle around it. We had just flown out of a squall line when we came upon the outpost. The ceiling of broken clouds sat now at two thousand feet, with scattered scud clouds at about one thousand feet, and patches of rain showers roaming throughout the area. I'd seen worse.

The rules of engagement required us to illuminate nighttime targets with parachute flares. Normally we would drop them at about twenty-five hundred feet above the ground, which afforded us about three minutes of tremendous candlepower over the target. But the enemy could see us as well as we could see him. And when we had low ceilings like this, that made us sitting ducks.

"You stay high, I'm going to lay flares on the deck," I called out over the UHF to my wingman.

"Wilco."

I rolled the aircraft into a 120-degree angle of bank turn and let the nose fall below the horizon I could only guess was out there somewhere. I turned out my exterior lights, selected the flare switch and the Master Armament Switch and kept the outpost just to the right of my nose while I headed for the ground on a northerly heading in a shallow dive.

"Is your radar altimeter working?" Bubba asked.

"Affirm. Got it set at one hundred feet."

I eased a little left rudder and aileron and back on the stick slightly as the radar altimeter warning sounded and I leveled off at one hundred feet. I hit the pickle button on the stick, and the flare came out with a thud.

"You're taking fire, Pony One Seven!" my wingman shouted over the radio.

"See anything, Bubba?"

"Negative."

"Pulling off left," I warned Bubba, then I yanked back on the stick, the force of 4 Gs slamming us into the seat and pulling the sweat out from under my helmet, causing it to pour into my eyes. I let the nose come up about 30 degrees and then unloaded the aircraft, dipped my wing to the right, then rolled quickly into a 60-degree angle of bank to the left. I wiped my eyes with the combat chamois draped around my neck. Looking over our shoulders we both spotted the green tracers at the same time, arcing up behind us and to our right.

The flare ignited on the ground in a white phosphorus ball of light. I spotted my wingman's lights at my ten o'clock high and shallowed my angle of bank to rendezvous with him.

"I saw muzzle flashes about two hundred meters north of the flares," my wingman radioed.

"I thought I saw the tracers coming from the tree lines south of the flare," Bubba said.

"Pony One Seven, the outpost says the NVA are launching B-40s from the western perimeter," Bravo Delta reported.

"Can they spot the bad guys in reference to the flare?" Bubba asked Bravo Delta.

"Wait one."

"Let's put more flares down," Bubba said.

"I'm in on another flare run—watch for muzzle flashes."

Two clicks on the mike indicated my wingman's acknowledgment. This time I aimed to lay the flares south of where the first set went, and south of where I thought I saw the muzzle flashes. I made my second pass on the easterly heading.

"Pony One Seven. Outpost says the enemy is one hundred meters north and one hundred meters south of the flare. Repeat. Two locations. First is one hundred meters north, second is one hundred meters south."

Passing one thousand feet in my dive, the rain on the windscreen increased for a few seconds, then let up just as I saw tracers 10 degrees off my nose. The glowing stream of tracers looked like water from a garden hose that was being whipped around slowly to get us. As their turning motion stopped, the red balls that had appeared to be following one another at slow intervals seemed to be bunching up into a single red dot that now became fixed in a position just to the left of the center on my windscreen. My thoughts turned to Pete Russell who had rolled in on a target only to have a round come through the windscreen and hit him in the head. I hoped they didn't have me boresighted.

I kicked left rudder, skidded, and then pulled a 4-G, level right turn, quickly followed by a jink to the left again. I punched another flare out the rear of the aircraft just as we passed over the outpost at one hundred feet.

My wingman yelled, "You're taking fire from the outpost!"

"Holy shit," Bubba said over the ICS, "Stay low, don't pull up!"

Tracers from three directions passed over the canopy. The throttles had been locked full forward since the beginning of the first pass, but I jammed them further into the firewall. I quickly deselected the flares, and made a hard right turn, still only one hundred feet above the jungle below.

Before our energy dissipated, I traded the airspeed for altitude and made a zooming, climbing right turn, looking over my shoulder for the wing aircraft. I spotted his lights directly across the right-hand circle both our aircraft were inscribing over the target.

For the next sixty seconds, Bubba and I reviewed what we had seen and quickly discussed the enemy positions with the wing aircraft. We all concurred that there were three sources of antiaircraft fire: two just 150 meters west of the outpost, and one literally on the other side of its south wall.

Pilots usually have little time for reflection while flying around a target. Sure, you'd be thinking all the time. But most of what you do is almost instinctive, more a learned instinct, coming from hours of practice, drill, mentally flying through every situation the imagination could conjure. But even so, often it requires the kind of thinking a basketball forward does when presented with a surprise move, or that of the quarterback looking for a receiver while being blitzed. You have to make a decision. You're conscious of making it—and painfully aware of its consequences.

"Pony One Seven, the outpost is taking heavy rocket fire!" Bravo Delta screamed.

I could see the muzzle flashes from the two western positions and the explosions along the eastern wall of the outpost where the good guys must be holed up.

"Okay, let's get the two targets to the west," I radioed to my wingman. "I've got the southern one, you've got the northern one. Two passes max. Hold off for now on the guys along the south wall. Don't pull off over them. I'm in from the north." As soon as I said this, I was in my dive with half of the 5-inch Zuni rockets selected to fire with one punch of the pickle button. Again, the rain obscured my vision. I almost aborted the run, but then the windscreen quickly cleared as the pipper on my gun sight slowly inched its way up to the target.

Unlike in practice back in the States where I could fly in a precise pattern, here, I took what I could get: low altitude, shallow dive, dodging clouds, target obscured by rain, turbulence, darkness, antiaircraft fire, whatever. This was the last of the real seat-of-the-pants flying, with no computers, no gadgets, just Kentucky windage. But it wasn't just numbers, coordinates, altitudes, airspeed. If I was off, well—close doesn't count here.

The entire sky around the aircraft lit up as a stream of rockets left the aircraft at supersonic speed.

"I'm off, right," I radioed.

"I'm in," replied my wingman.

"I think you got 'em," my wingman's back seat reported.

I could see the tracers from my wingman's machine guns blazing away, then the flashes of light headed for the ground. Ten virtually simultaneous explosions took out the entire tree line.

"Nice shot!" I yelled over the UHF.

As I was about to roll in again, Bubba said, "Hold back a pod of Zunis, Okay? We might need them."

"Roger that," I replied. Angling the aircraft for the roll in, I could see reason enough, as the wing aircraft drew a stream of antiaircraft fire from the south wall of the outpost on his pullout.

"You're taking fire from your seven o'clock," I radioed.

"Pony One Seven, the outpost reports heavy automatic weapons fire from all along the western wall. Apparently the bad guys own that end of the compound. Can you put anything on top of them?"

"Off, left," my wingman reported.

"Pony One Seven is in," I radioed.

"I'll save a pod for them," I told Bubba, who responded affirmatively to Bravo Delta's request. My wingman rolled in when I was in the chute, and as soon as I pulled off, he pickled his remaining rockets. None of us saw any fire on this pass.

"Hurry, Pony One Seven, these guys are getting real anxious."

"I'm in. You orbit high."

"Wilco," my wingman acknowledged.

I selected the centerline weapons station, my twenty-millimeter cannon. The rules of engagement required us to illuminate the target; they didn't say we had to keep it illuminated. The flares had quickly burned out, but fires within the compound threw enough light on the west wall that I knew I couldn't miss. A very shallow dive afforded a good look and enough time in the saddle to squeeze off a good long burst. The staccato *thud, thud, thud* of the cannon shook the aircraft.

"Pony One Seven, Bravo Delta."

"Go ahead Bravo Delta."

"I've lost contact with the OP."

"We've got one more run and we have to RTB," Bubba said. "Do you want us to put ordnance next to the west building?"

We heard no reply for at least a minute as we climbed back to two thousand feet. A hole opened up in the clouds over the outpost, affording us another five or six hundred feet of altitude. From our new vantage, we could still see occasional muzzle flashes from the NVA positions along the west wall. Besides my four sponson-mounted M-60 machine guns, whose primary usefulness was to keep the enemy's head down when I was in a dive, I had only one pod of four Zuni rockets. Bubba taught me to always hold some rockets back, for when I might really need them, a trick he learned from Bob White.

"Are you Winchester?" I asked my wingman.

"Affirm." He had no ordnance left.

The four remaining Zuni's had VT, or proximity fuses, which detonate about three meters above the ground, spraying shrapnel in an arc about one hundred meters wide, killing anything exposed, including friendlies if they were that close. SOP was to remain at least one hundred meters plus our CEP away from friendlies when firing.

The friendlies here were less than a hundred meters away from the bad guys, but hopefully dug in. Bravo Delta reported that he had just gotten a call from the outpost. The remaining survivors were all together and braced for whatever hell we could rain down on the enemy troops just a few meters away from them. He found it difficult to understand them, Bravo Delta said, because they had to whisper over the landline for fear of giving away their position.

"What are you going to use for a mil setting?" Bubba asked, as a polite reminder that I needed to readjust the gun sight. We discussed mil settings, altitude for release, and roll-in heading. I began sweating again. Bubba asked Bravo Delta to relay to the OP that we had to use VT fuses and for the ARVN soldiers to put whatever they could between the NVA and them.

I fired the remaining Zunis in a line alongside the western wall of the outpost and looked over my shoulder on pullout. None of us saw any ground fire. Bubba radioed that we were returning to base and asked if they wanted us to return after refueling and rearming. Bravo Delta said, "Yes." Bubba told him that we would monitor his frequency all the way back home.

While we still had the weather to contend with on the way home, we all felt looser than on the trip out. Still, the mood was somber. We were hoping that we had done enough. But we were relieved—very relieved, to be going home.

About half way home, the silence was broken. "Pony One Seven . . . Bravo Delta . . . can you return?"

We knew he didn't mean return after refueling and rearming. He meant return—as in *right now*.

"What do you think, Bubba?"

"We've got flares, don't we?"

Bubba was a genius.

"The bad guys might not know the difference," he added.

We made a U-turn and Bubba radioed that we were on our way. We arrived overhead at just about bingo fuel state. Wasting no time, I rolled into a shallow dive with my lights out while my wingman orbited high and

I pressed it to a hundred feet before punching out a flare. Before the enemy could even react, I made a level turn back toward the outpost, eased the nose over and just as the flare lit up the sky, I launched another one on the ground just outside the perimeter. Pulling off target, we spotted more tracers. I orbited high for a couple of minutes, then made another pass, launching our last flares.

Dropping the flares on the ground from low altitude fooled the enemy into thinking we had ordnance, which—we later found out—allowed the defenders to regroup and ward off the attack.

As exhausted as I was when we returned, all I could do was lie in the rack in the darkness of the bunkroom. Had we done enough? Will they call us again in a few minutes, or hours? I remember feeling I really didn't want to go back out there again. But I knew I would. All I could think about was the darkness. How alien it felt. Darkness, desolation. The "kingdom of perpetual darkness." I hated it, and yet, its seductiveness beckoned me in a way that was comforting, almost alluring.

Kit Lavell, Black Pony

24

Trolling

Two o'clock in the morning courage: I mean unprepared courage.

—Napoleon Bonaparte

Black Ponies offered rides in the back seat on combat ops to "special friends." Chief among these were U.S. Navy SEALs and men like Lt. Cdr. Jerry Fogel, an aviator serving a tour of duty as an air ops advisor attached to CTF-116 staff across the road at the boat base. Jerry occasionally flew in the back seat with Black Ponies on coastal surveillance flights in order to get flight time. Ponies enjoyed flying with him, in part because he just loved to fly (especially being chained to the ground job as he was), but also because he was fun to talk to.

Black Ponies had a number of friends they hung around with from outside the ranks of the squadron who lived at Binh Thuy, like Jerry. Some were attached to the CTF-116 staff and some were with the Fleet Air Support Unit (FASU) and some were HAL-3 pilots. The relationship between VAL-4 and HAL-3 was similar to one between two brothers. While it was professional and complementary in the air, on the ground it had its ups and downs.

Being the senior officer around those parts, the CO of HAL-3 began tightening rules and regulations affecting everyone on the aviation side of the road. The Black Ponies' scroungy appearance stood in stark contrast to his squadron, whose pilots wore starched utility covers or black berets. Morale began to deteriorate, especially among VAL-4 enlisted men, when he closed the base to female visitors. That order did nothing but send the men into the Ben Xe Moi bars in droves. From that point on, it seemed as if almost daily some incident or altercation between members of each squadron arose, including a few that actually led to fights.

> When Lt. Rick Tucker, an old friend and fellow flight instructor from Pensacola, reported in to HAL-3, we ran into each other at the admin building. We were really surprised and glad to see each other. I had been on my way to catch a ride to the other side to go fly, so we had only a few moments together. We talked about old friends, and Rick asked about some of our former flight students who now flew in HAL-3. I told him about my former student Buzz Buzzell who was killed. And then I had trouble explaining to him that it was difficult for me, as a Black Pony, to find someone in HAL-3, since the squadron was spread out in nine detachments, and everyone was very busy flying.
>
> Tucker remarked that he would love to go for a ride in an OV-10, and I told him I would like to fly in a Seawolf helo, so we promised each other we would try to arrange the flights. The next time we saw each other was a few days later at the "O"Club. I started to walk over to where Tucker was standing with a number of other HAL-3 pilots, but the uncomfortable expression on his face signaled that this was probably not a good time for this Seawolf to be seen with a Black Pony. We both went back to our tables thinking how dumb this whole thing was. Here we were, half way around the world, fighting a war, and looking at the expressions on the faces of the Black Pony pilots on one side of the room and the Seawolf pilots on the other, one couldn't help but think of two rival street gangs. Fortunately these dark clouds passed over, and I would get know a lot of Seawolves and even fly in their Hueys. And of course, we occasionally would work together.
>
> Kit Lavell, Black Pony

The Fifth Annual Awards Ceremony on Friday 3 December was the most elaborate of all. The festivities began with an irreverent song called "Stewball," by a couple of JOs trying to accompany themselves on the guitar. With Doc as always in charge, the roast continued with his "fond adieu to four of our noble comrades: James Burton, executive officer; John Smalling, safety officer; Howard Hotchkiss, mystery officer; and RPS and general Son of a Bitch officer, Sam Chipps." The evening included the usual pranks and nonsense, as well as a "Shakespearean" play, complete with Roman-style costumes—of sorts—along with apologies to the Bard of Avon.[1] And like the many rivers of the Mekong Delta, life went on.

Black Ponies, like all American servicemen, subscribed to the ritual of counting the time remaining in-country. The count would be the number of days plus "a wake-up," representing the last day in Vietnam. "If I had that many days to DEROS, I'd walk into a prop," a short-timer would advise a newbie.

After a few months in-country, most newbies came down with mild dysentery. Around the squadron, scatological jokes were common, and Doc would say, "Happiness is a formed stool." Bubba expedited his return from a combat mission and even made a straight-in approach to get on the deck quicker, only to have diarrhea overcome him on touchdown. They made him hose out the aircraft.

The hangar was cleaned out again and rumors persisted that the skipper planned to fly a loop through it.

The Song Ong Doc flows along the southern border of the U-Minh, from the Gulf of Thailand to the city of Ca Mau. The Ca Mau Peninsula—the Lobster Tail—was a major VC stronghold. Over the last few weeks of November random Black Pony patrols in the area had been encountering unexpectedly intense 12.7-mm antiaircraft fire. The peninsula was virtually a "free fire zone," so Black Ponies found it routine to get a blanket clearance to fire on anything in the area.

The "Winged Bird Men of the Delta" developed an innovative tactic to quickly identify gun positions that could then be immediately attacked. But the tactic required that the Ponies use themselves as bait, so the practice became known as chumming—or trolling. One aircraft would fly low with lights on, while the other bird with lights out would be perched ready to roll in on the guns when they opened up. The first time a pilot saw it, from the vantage of the bug on the hook, he had to have thought, "This is absolutely crazy." Soon, paradoxically, he was thinking, "This is fun!" One would have thought that, with tracers coming at him from different directions, a pilot's emotions would be very simple at that moment—get the hell out of there! Especially since there were no good guys on the ground who depended on them dueling with antiaircraft guns to help save their lives. And that's what it was. A duel. As simple, as violent, as meaningless as any duel. But it was also as complex, as elemental, as unexplainably alluring as any such one-on-one combat.

On the afternoon of 6 December, Black Ponies flew numerous back-to-back scrambles to that same area, above the Lobster Tail. Most pilots had not been there in the daylight for quite some time, but remembered where the guns were from night. On that day, the army C and C ship identified the same gun positions. The ARVN had reportedly swept the area over the last few days and found nothing. With all the enemy activity Ponies would see in this area in the coming months, many thought there must have been a vast underground tunnel complex, because the enemy could disappear in an instant from one location, phantom-like, and reappear so easily in another. And the ARVN could never find a trace of them. But some would also assert that the ARVN rarely advanced immediately to take an area just abandoned or won from the enemy. And of course there were those who believed they never advanced at all.

The C and C ship radioed that the Black Ponies were taking a lot of fire, so they made two runs apiece. They pickled twice on each run. Each time a pilot pressed the button, five Zunis left the aircraft, the combined equivalent in cost at that time of a Cadillac.

This could have been one of those days when everything was so mechanical; when for the pilot it is a set of coordinates, an altitude, a distance, the flipping of a switch, all those things that are so abstract. Even the bullets coming up at a pilot from the ground could be abstract. He tends to focus on himself. He would depersonalize the enemy and depersonalize the civilians. He would depersonalize the whole war—he almost had to. It was a game almost, and that's how it was sometimes viewed. It was hard to imagine there was actually a man down there shooting those bullets up. A pilot rarely sees the effect of what he does. Except the closer he gets to the ground, the more that changes.

A few nights later the bunker crew scrambled to the same area in support of the 31st Regiment. No need to troll that night. They knew where the guns were. The trick was to avoid them. When the ceilings were low, as they were that night, the only game that mattered was survival, so it was find them, shoot them, destroy them, and forget them.

As Lt. (jg) Pete Wylie returned from the scramble, the weather had deteriorated so badly back at Binh Thuy that his flight had to shoot a "Bassac One" approach. After landing, everyone was tired, so they skipped the movie and hit the rack. They were lucky to grab the sleep because they were awakened a few hours later with another scramble to the Song Ong Doc, although they probably did not fully wake up until they got to the target.

The bad weather had passed through and everything looked good on the return home at sunrise. Just as the sun sets rapidly that close to the equator, the sun also rises very quickly. Flying eastward at a few thousand feet, the pilots watched the stars fade out and the purple ink of the horizon run blood red, then bleed orange, before the sun burst this prism with a blinding white light that washed the violet sky to blue.

The shadow below them receded in synchronization with the rising sun, revealing not the expected and familiar terrain, but rather a monotonously homogeneous expanse of nothingness. Approaching what they knew by dead reckoning to be the field, they saw that low fog covered the entire area. On the ground, it was "zero zero," and from the air, the top of the fog at thirty to forty feet gave the appearance of snow covering the entire Delta as far as could be seen, with only the tops of a few trees sticking through the surface.

For most pilots, flying above an undercast usually engenders a strange amalgam of feelings. Ranging from serenity as they bask in the warmth of the sun beaming down and reflecting back up from the cloud tops, to apprehension, knowing that eventually they must pass from this placid state through the weather before they can safely land. Apprehension can turn to anxiety in proportion to how close to the ground the base of the clouds really is. When the woolly clouds sit on the ground, "ceiling zero" and "zero visibility," the pucker factor comes into play, since the beautiful white blanket is in reality granite in sheep's clothing.

Since the wing aircraft had much less fuel than the flight leader's, he gave wing the lead on the way home. Tired, and low on fuel, they attempted a "Shit Ditch One" approach to Runway 6. They flew up a canal to a "squiggly," or river tributary, and followed it until it turned into the ditch that ran into the base and eventually past the latrine. Where the ditch met the base perimeter, the flight should have been able to see the approach end of the runway. Flying in formation, at what they knew to be the approach end of the runway, the wingman was unable to spot it. From the lead's vantage point, however, just a few feet stepped up from him, he could look down through the fog and see the runway numbers.

The lead kept the other OV-10 on his wing while he poured the coals to it, and made a tight circle at about seventy-five feet of altitude. Looking over his shoulder, he saw that he literally cut a swath through the fog. He pointed that out to his wingman, "kissed" him off, and then the wingman landed before the fog filled in again. The flight leader made a tight turn and landed, to be enveloped by the fog as soon as he touched down. It took him so long to inch his way down the runway and taxiway that he was afraid the aircraft was going to flame out before reaching the revetments. Then suddenly the fog cleared. Then the flight refueled and rearmed, taking off and returning to the area for a third and even a fourth time, until the first scheduled flight of the morning arrived at the bunker to relieve them.

25

The Last Christmas

Include me out.

—Samuel Goldwyn

A Trip to the Boonies

I got a two-day break from paperwork, if not from the war, when I went on a ground visit to the 31st Regiment forward fire base near Song Ong Doc with Ray Morris, two weeks before Christmas. We caught a ride on a Seawolf helo and we visited with Colonel Kim, his ARVN soldiers, and the American advisors for whom we flew close air support. We brought with us a bottle of Johnny Walker Scotch to give to the colonel, and he invited us to share a midday meal with him. From our reception, we realized that he considered it a special occasion and we felt very honored, if not uncomfortable, what with a lieutenant and a lieutenant (junior grade) being treated like flag rank.

We sat on cushions around a low table that was filled with small plates of what turned out to be appetizers, small shrimp and crawfish, dried and highly salted, which everyone ate like peanuts, and some kind of cabbage, as well as salted vegetables. Our host served *nuoc mam,* the traditional, strong fish sauce, to dip our fish and vegetables in. He offered us warm beer, or a shot of something from an old Johnny Walker bottle that we learned was Scotch mixed with *ba xi da,* a rice wine. But in the bottle we could also see what looked like rocks, twigs, and other unrecognizable items. As we sat around the table engaged in pleasant conversation, servants brought in other dishes. A small partial loaf of crusty bread sat on a large plate. I didn't think they served it for its symbolism, but I took it as such, and broke it with our hosts and friends.

The staple food in the country was rice, of course, to which might be added sweet potatoes, corn, taro, manioc yams, arrowroot, eggs, soybeans, and whatever fish and seafood were found locally. In that area it meant carp, catfish, gobies, spiny eels, snakesheads (definitely an acquired taste), killifish (delicious), and crabs, as well as frogs and snakes. We received a wonderful sampling of these local delicacies, and custom as well as hospitality required us to try everything, which I did not mind until the next dishes arrived. What we tasted would have been considered a feast in any Vietnamese home, I am sure. And I knew that normally a Vietnamese host would not kill a chicken, duck, or pig, except for a special occasion, such as a birth, wedding, or death. To which I guess I could now humbly add—a visit from Black Ponies. The roasted chicken was great. The pig intestines and cooked rat took a lot of . . . well, I was reminded of the Stephen Crane phrase— "a temporary but sublime absence of selfishness" —that he used to define "courage." There was no doubt about it . . . it took raw, gutsy courage!

Tea was served along with rice cakes, in several varieties, which were made with glutinous rice, soybeans, and cane sugar and served with various kinds of fruit. I found the "buffalo horns" —sweet, crisp, white nuts picked from water lilies grown in ponds nearby—to be an especially tasty treat. A lot could be hidden underneath a rice cake, I discovered.

Everywhere we went on our visit to these bases, our hosts treated us royally, and we knew virtually everyone we talked to, even if we had never met them on the ground before. We recognized their voices from the radio, just as they knew us by our voices and our call signs. They were eager to show us around their fort, of which they were very proud. The walls of the triangular base were a few hundred feet in length, built out of concrete, mud, and what looked like wooden rocket boxes. Walkways, walls, and small bridges that crossed dikes, all made of wood, showed the work of fine craftsmen. Inside the compound, we saw the living quarters of the soldiers. Construction was bunker or blockhouse-type, designed to withstand B-40 rocket and mortar rounds. Outside the compound, lots of accordion wire surrounded the outer walls. Concealed in the wire we saw Claymore mines that were designed to blow fragments outward, in one direction, toward the enemy, when detonated electronically from within the fort. A battery of "nickel-dimes," 105-millimeter howitzers, had just finished firing "H and I" (harassment and interdiction). We accompanied some ARVN and advisors beyond the perimeter, where a half-dozen VC had been captured, and watched the interrogation.

We later heloed to the outpost I had flown in support of on 26 November, and we then stayed overnight at the 31st's command post there. I found myself on the roof of the CP around midnight drinking *ba xi da* with an ARVN 1st lieutenant who insisted on talking politics. After unsuccessfully trying to change the subject, I listened to him politely, until, while grinning, he told me that he was a VC. I grinned back at him, until his smile dissolved into a stare. Silhouetted against the flare-lighted night sky, he was the Cheshire cat. He turned his back to me, looked out to the horizon and was swallowed up by the eerie shadows. I used the opportunity to bid him a good night and slipped down off the roof to look for someone else to talk to. With everyone asleep, I propped myself up against the wall next to my hootch, with an M-16 in my lap. I got no sleep that night.

The next morning, Colonel Franklin flew his own C and C ship into the base, had breakfast with us, and took us to Ca Mau, where he showed us all around the TOC, briefed us on operations, and treated us as VIPs. We met Major General Nghi, the Commanding General of the 21st ARVN Division. Franklin then flew us to the area where all the enemy contact had been in recent days and coordinated a Black Pony air strike himself. It's amazing how something with which you are very familiar can be so strange when viewed from a new angle. From our helicopter position just above ground level, we found the Black Pony strike to be almost surrealistic. We were so close to the action that, above the *wop wop* of the rotor blades and the high-pitched whine of the turbine behind us, I thought I could even hear the *crack* of the Zuni rockets after they left the OV-10s and broke the sound barrier. I had previously been told that, until the troops on the ground got used to the Zunis (shortly after the squadron first arrived in-country), they would often report secondary explosions to the Black Pony pilots. Apparently they mistook the Zuni's *crack* for a secondary, the two sounds coming so close to each other, just before the rocket's impact. I could understand why. After the air strike Colonel Franklin flew us back to Binh Thuy.

Kit Lavell, Black Pony

A new officer in the Maintenance Department was a rather heavy-set fellow who was not a pilot and who in fact disliked them, especially the junior officer variety. Max Britton worked with him. The new guy, or "Jellybelly," as the JOs called him, wanted to run a tight ship, so he got the idea to make all the pilots working for him be in the maintenance office at 0800 to read the message traffic. Since pilots flew around the clock, this quickly turned into a near mutiny. He also banned the "air shows" that maintenance check pilots used to put on for the troops when they returned from a maintenance check flight.

Max Britton finally had it with Jellybelly after he stole Max's Plexiglas desktop one morning. Wanting a view of the flight line from his second-story office, Jellybelly had the troops cut a hole in his door and insert the Plexiglas as a window. Max decided to get even, and when he returned from a maintenance check flight one day, lined up his descending aircraft with Jellybelly's window, and in a colorful display of airmanship, hit his smoke generator as he roared a few feet past it. Jellybelly ran coughing out the oil-streaked door, poured into his jeep, and careened through the revetments to await Max's landing. Max taxied into the revetments and sat in his aircraft, refusing to shut down as long as the Jellybelly sat in his jeep next to the aircraft. The standoff ended only when Jellybelly finally gave up to go have lunch.

When Jellybelly returned, he caught the skipper before he got into his aircraft, and in front of Max and all the other JOs, told the skipper what he had been doing to bring discipline to his little corner of the world. The skipper pointed to the JOs and asked Jellybelly if he had threatened any of them with bad fitness reports. He replied that he had. The CO looked him squarely in the eye and said, "These guys no longer work for you." The aviators didn't see much of him after that.

As Christmas approached, the only clue was that the allied side pro-claimed a unilateral truce and brought in Bob Hope for a USO show in Saigon. Black Ponies made the effort to get into the seasonal spirit by decorating a small tree in the bunker and sending some of their people to Saigon for the USO show. Lieutenant Lavell would rather fly anyway and the schedules officer must have known, so on Christmas Eve, he went on a three-and-three-tenths-hour coastal surveillance flight with Lt. Cdr. Joe Port.

Before sunset they flew to Long Phu, near the SEAL base at the mouth of the Bassac, and put on an air show for Jerry Fogel to raise his spirits on that holiday so far from home. They then flew along the coast, down to and around the Lobster Tail to the U-Minh. They spotted a couple of large sampans on the beach and went down for a close look, whereupon the sampans opened fire on the OV-10. Since this was during the truce, and VAL-4 had no other scheduled flights airborne with which to form a Fire Team anyway, they had to watch them *didi mau* out to sea. Later that night the bunker crew scrambled out to Phu Quoc Island, where the VC had killed an American and wounded four others in a sapper attack.[1]

The sparse radio traffic gave the Black Ponies standing scramble duty the hope, though not necessarily the expectation, that they would spend a quiet night in the bunker. Christmas or not, this was still bunker duty, and the pilots would just as soon fly. Since the allies were under a truce, the Black Ponies would go on no scheduled random patrol, so the only chance they would have to fly would be if they got a scramble.

Sure enough, the scramble horn went off, and minutes later they were headed out to the U-Minh to deliver Christmas presents to the defenders of a forward firebase and the Grinches who were trying to steal their lives.

On Christmas day, a number of Black Ponies and Seawolves visited the orphanage. One of the men dressed as Santa Claus and distributed presents of clothing and toys that wives and family from the States had sent. One of the Black Ponies delivered to Angéle a letter from Sloan. He did not know its contents. She was nervous at first, then happy when he gave her the letter.

Angéle had sent a letter to Sloan the week after he left. Writing in French, she had explained her actions on the night of the benefactor's dinner:

> Don't you know that "to part is to die a little," and it's true, I cannot tell you how much your departure has made me suffer, anyway, you know the reason for it. . . .
>
> In seeing all that you had given the orphanage, your clothes, all the supplies and things. . . . I was unable to hold back my tears, as if my Sloan had been buried! Hasn't it been said "to love is to suffer?!" Who knows what is on my mind at this moment . . . because it is the first time that I love, but it is also the last time! Believe me . . . what's the good of living when losing you. . . . I die minute by minute, living far away from you. . . .
>
> I saw you pass my room many times where I had hidden myself to watch you because I did not have the courage to say goodbye to you. And I did not want to appear weak to you when you had to leave for duty. I did not have the courage to tell you "goodbye" . . . because I was not separated from one who is dead, but from one who is living; not from an enemy, but from the one I love! I have cried a lot, loneliness has hung heavily on my heart. . . .
>
> Again the noise of your airplane—it pierces the air as it pierces my soul!—and each day, even at night, I awaited its passage through the orphanage to remind me of you. . . .
>
> All that you left me, dear Sloan, I kept preciously as my soul, that is to say how much I cherish them. And in seeing them and pressing them to my lips (I do this a dozen times a day), I have the impression of kissing not a piece of metal or a bit of paper, but you. . . . I wanted to call your

name aloud, because you alone could assuage this suffering! That moment was very painful to me, to think perhaps you have left me forever, and therefore only in heaven will we see each other again.[2]

In his letter, delivered on Christmas day, Sloan told Angéle he wanted to return to Vietnam to bring her back to America with him.

Commander Pickett, the new XO, wanted to see how the Black Ponies flew night scramble missions, so he volunteered himself for the bunker duty. The fact that senior officers did not stand bunker duty was not lost on the JOs who were scheduled with the XO for his little experiment, but that didn't stand in the way of having a little fun at Cdr. Ron Pickett's expense. When the XO showed up for the brief, the JOs were all decked out in G suits, wearing them probably for the first time in-country. After the scheduled night random patrol, the bunker crew normally peeled down to flight suits until retiring to the bunkroom for the night. This evening, however, the JOs kept all their flight gear on, torso harnesses, survival vests, and G suits included. The XO, not wanting to show how uncomfortable he was, acted as if he knew this was SOP, and just grinned but did not bare it. Even when it was time to hit the rack. The JOs cinched up their flight gear and crawled into their bunks, lugging their helmets with them. The XO followed suit, acting as if he did this every night. After twenty minutes of snickers in the darkness, the XO flipped on the light.

"Got ya, XO!" the JOs yelled in unison, tossing their flight gear into a heap on the deck.

Black Pony pilots looked forward to the occasional administrative run to Saigon as a way to unwind. On these flights Black Pony pilots often would fly an enlisted man to R and R and then run an errand at ComNavForV. The current need was to check into why the navy was continually delaying shipping Zuni rockets to VAL-4, and to find out why very few awards found their way out of ComNavForV headquarters, especially for Black Pony enlisted men.

How to Implement a Directive

I carried with me a list of almost two hundred recommendations for awards and medals that had been approved by the local commands and were submitted to Saigon, some going back to 1969, when the squadron was formed. Admiral Zumwalt, just after his appointment as chief of naval operations in 1970, sent out one of his famous "Z Grams" in which he stressed how important it was for morale that awards and medals be processed in a timely manner, and set strict time guidelines. That was more than a year ago.

Since my last time in Saigon several months before, newly promulgated regulations required wearing a uniform while in the city. And that meant no fatigues, much less flight suits. Two MPs stopped us as we drove a borrowed jeep in our grungy flight gear. Only because one of the two soldiers had recently rotated from the bush was he able to convince the other MP that we were dressed that way because there really was a war going on. We had business to do, he said, and they should get out of our way!

Among a sea of brass at ComNavForV the lowest rank we saw was a navy commander, and most everyone looked upon us as poopey-suited intruders. I waited almost an hour in the awards officer's office, when one of the staff go'fers, a navy lieutenant, finally swaggered through the door. No sooner had I begun to tell him why I was there than he interrupted me.

"Uh . . . I don't quite understand why all these awards are continually being submitted from this unit down in the Delta. . . . Just what exactly do you guys do down there, anyway?"

"We're the only fixed-wing U.S. squadron south of Saigon," I answered. "Among others, we support the *navy* in the Delta. We fly combat missions."

"Yeah . . . but all the riverine forces have been Vietnamized," he said, as if his ignorance that a war that was going on would somehow legislate a new reality, or make these apparent oversights all disappear. "And we here at ComNavForV have been . . . *implementing directives* . . . to wind down the U.S. effort."

As I sat there stunned, an attractive blond woman in civilian clothes appeared at the door. The lieutenant jumped up to greet her with a long embrace and kiss. Before he pulled her around the corner to grope at her some more, out of my sight, I could see she was braless under a thin white sweater. And she was the first American woman I had seen in a long, long while.

I sat there for a few minutes fingering my .45, the one in its holster at my side. In front of me, on the corner of a desk, I spotted three stacks of folders with a piece of paper marked "BS-Priority" on top of them. Rifling through them, I discovered they were end-of-tour "meritorious" Bronze Stars for staff people in Saigon, for . . . implementing directives . . . paper pushing! So—I did my own paper pushing. I shoved the pile off the desk where the fan scattered them to the winds, giving new meaning to the phrase, "when the shit hits the fan."

As I headed for the door, I overheard the lieutenant agree to meet the woman at the swimming pool. When we met at the door, I backed him up against the wall with my face inches from his, but never touching him.

With my hand on my hip just above my sidearm I said, "If our backlog doesn't get taken care of, I am coming back here to personally give you a priority end-of-tour award." I walked out, hoping he would say or do something. He didn't. But, then again . . . he was in a hurry to do some . . . well, implementing! I now understood the term "REMF."

Kit Lavell, Black Pony

One of Cdr. Ron Pickett's first duties as the new XO was to prepare a response to a suspicious NavForV directive to "register" all the squadron's "maverick" vehicles.[3] This would be a test, not only of Commander Pickett's ingenuity, but also of his creative writing abilities. Just responding to the official naval message from some REMF at the staff in Saigon would be admitting that the Black Ponies possessed "maverick" vehicles.

After a huddle and a game plan, Pickett wrote the response. "While conducting the review required by (your directive) a number of maverick vehicles were discovered." The Ponies figured they had to fess up to having some cumshawed vehicles, so five seemed to be a good number. No sense in admitting to any more. Besides, you can only "discover" so many before you sound more like a car theft ring and less like an attack squadron. "Subsequently the vehicles have been given an inspection to determine their safety and maintainability." The Ponies didn't want to worry the REMF who was so concerned for the safety of these young drivers.

Then Commander Pickett had to actually justify keeping the vehicles, using phrases like "the tempo of operations" and the separation of the airfield from the living spaces. Just in case the REMF thought Binh Thuy might have a metro bus system or commuter train or rapid water buffalo transit, he also cited "insufficient suitable alternative forms of transportation." Then the closer: "The possibility of operating with fewer vehicles has been thoroughly explored, and it has been determined that a reduction in the number of vehicles would lead to a degradation of the squadron's effectiveness because of the logistical environment and the quick reaction time required for the squadron's assigned mission." There's a war going on, buddy. And to make this staff puke's day, the reply included a graph with usage categories, frequencies of trips, etc., and ended with, "Each of the vehicles listed above is shared and is driven only by qualified, responsible personnel."[4] Right.

As January came to a close, Max Britton, Jim Arthur, Neil Salmi, and Kit Lavell stood the afternoon scramble duty when, during what was supposed to be a stand down in preparation for the Tet truce, they were called out to the U-Minh. On the way to the target, they diverted to a small sliver of land just off the west coast of the Delta where the VC, in five boats, were attacking a small communications station. The enemy had landed on a spit of land next to the small island, where they were launching B-40 rockets at the friendlies. Because of low ceilings the Black Ponies orbited below two thousand feet but several hundred meters north, just out of small-arms range, watching this incredible scene and describing it to everyone they could raise on the radio.

They couldn't get a clearance, even from the TOC that initially called them. The good guys abandoned the island, trying to escape in a boat motoring parallel to the coast, but the VC spotted them and headed out to cut them off. The Ponies made low passes over the enemy boats, but the enemy continued their pursuit of the friendlies. The pilots were convinced the VC must have been listening on the radios because, despite the Ponies' obvious presence, the VC acted with impunity, as if they knew the ROE prevented the Ponies from firing on them. A big mistake for them.

As they approached within B-40 range of the good guys, the Ponies pleaded for clearance to shoot. Unable to get permission, the weather deteriorating, the sun setting, and their aircraft running out of fuel, they reluctantly attacked the boats anyway. As soon as the Ponies rolled in on them, the enemy opened fire on the OV-10s. The Black Ponies blew them away, with Max and Jim each firing a pod of rockets virtually simultaneously from different directions at the VC and then attacking the enemy positions on the island, getting a couple of good secondary explosions.

For saving the defenders the skipper was quite pleased with what the pilots did, then had a change of heart the next morning when Saigon (the Seventh Air Force) informed him that they wanted to court-martial the Black Pony pilots for violation of the rules of engagement. The Black Ponies eventually got them to drop that idea. (Three months later Gen. John D. Lavelle, commanding officer of the Seventh Air Force, was relieved of command for making his own rules, albeit on a somewhat grander scale.)

A few days later, Bubba had a run-in with the new safety officer over a misplaced SOI, a code book called *Standard Operating Instructions*. The new safety officer had developed a reputation of being a very conservative pilot, and some aviators questioned his airmanship. He was very defensive about this, and reacted by using his position as safety officer to aggressively attempt to enforce the "letter of the law" on all the minor procedures that he believed the squadron routinely violated. The major things proved to be beyond his ability to change, but he was openly critical when he was among the junior officers, especially of the "flathatting." He tried to crack down on the commonly violated regulations prohibiting the wearing of army two-piece flight suits, which were cooler and whose top could be quickly removed, and the even more common practice of flying without Nomex flight gloves.

The safety officer would also sneak into the revetments to unscrew fuses on rockets that were loaded on waiting aircraft and deposit them at the door of the maintenance control shack where pilots went to check out aircraft, as his way of showing up "lax" procedures. He stopped when he learned that fuses were supposed to be screwed on hand-tight.

Doc received a letter from Sloan in which he asked Doc to help him plan his return to Vietnam in order to bring Angéle back to the U.S. to get married. Those who knew Angéle recognized how sad she looked, but did not know the reason why. It took Doc a month to reply to Sloan's request.

26

We Gotta Get Out of This Place

It is in order to play the game that our men die.

—Antoine de Saint-Exupéry, *Flight to Arras*

The last replacement pilots joined the Black Ponies in January, 1972: Lts. Bob Lutz, Mike Parkes, and Dennis Gilleran; and Lts. (jg) Larry Brown, Mel Etheridge, and Chuck Karlan. Despite rumors of the squadron being disestablished, flight operations continued at a hectic tempo. Intelligence sources predicted an enemy offensive during the upcoming Tet holidays.

The dry season in the Mekong Delta extends from December to April. Some pilots looked forward to the clear skies it would bring. Some may have thought that flying would be a lot easier, but couldn't have been more wrong. They found it to be not really a dry season, but rather a northeastern monsoon that brought damp trade winds and the so-called *crachin,* a dense, damp fog that often covered the country in a prolonged drizzle. But even the clear weather brought its own unique hazard. After farmers harvested their crops during the dry season, they burned the stubble. While the skies would be virtually cloudless, the smoke and haze often reduced visibility to less than half a mile. Daytime navigation was difficult. Nighttime flying was treacherous.

For a week straight in early February, virtually every bunker crew had a scramble, most of them to the U-Minh, in support of operations near the hump. Even over the U-Minh, away from most of the burning fields, smoke would drift over the area, and only a strong onshore breeze would improve the visibility. But that seemed to be rare. After launching a paraflare the glare against the haze was as if the pilot were inside a milk bowl, with no way to tell up from down.

On 9 February Lts. Bubba Segars and Kit Lavell flew to Ca Mau to present Colonel Franklin and Major General Nghi, the commanding general of the 21st ARVN Division, with Black Pony plaques and hand-carved models of the OV-10, complete with all the details and Black Pony markings.

The Black Ponies shared a discomfort at the violation of protocol. It was very unusual for two lieutenants to perform this courtesy, but the idea for the presentation to the general and colonel was actually Bubba's. Besides, the skipper was unavailable. Bubba was always thinking of ways to improve the effectiveness of the squadron, and strengthening our relationship with the 21st accomplished this. Colonel Franklin was not one to stand on protocol, and as it turned out, neither was General Nghi. They felt that the Black Ponies had served them well, and their enthusiasm at receiving the gifts presented on behalf of VAL-4 during a formal ceremony appeared genuine, which put the lieutenants at ease.

When Lavell and Segars took off for the return flight home they heard an unmistakable shriek over the radio. It was an emergency locator transmitter signaling from somewhere toward the coast. They tried to get a fix on it, but it ceased as soon as they turned toward the initial heading it gave them. They reported what they heard and then monitored several of the area frequencies as they motored back home. They didn't have the fuel to loiter in the area to find out if it was indeed an aircraft emergency.

After landing at Binh Thuy, they learned a Black Pony had gone down. Details were sketchy. Lt. Bob Lutz was missing. First Lt. Eugene Brindle, the marine observer in his back seat, was medevacked to Binh Thuy, critically injured. He was to recall that just as the aircraft was passing through 90 degrees angle of bank, the pilot initiated an ejection. It happened so fast that the back seat observer was punched out parallel to the horizon, skimming across the water like a skipping rock, without even enough time for the parachute to fully open. The seven-tenths of a second delay between the firing of the back seat and the front, designed to protect the ejected rear occupant from being burned by the front ejection seat rocket, prevented Bob from getting out before hitting the water. Chief Petty Officer Stanley Chapman from the USS *Albert David* jumped into the water from a motor whaleboat. Aware of the danger from shark attack because of blood in the water, Chapman rescued the critically injured Bronco rear-seat observer from the water.

Bob Lutz's death stunned everyone. Despite a massive search, it took a few days to recover his body, which eventually washed ashore, where several fishermen found it. Doc was his closest friend in the squadron and ended up being the one who had to identify the remains. Despite all of his medical background, the experience would profoundly shake him.

Black Ponies had been working so much with the U.S. Army's 164th Combat Aviation Group—Darkhorse—that they in effect became the tactical air element for the army in the Mekong Delta. Chief Warrant Officer 2d Class Richard L. "Lash" Larew, the lead Cobra pilot, Charlie 16th AirCav (call sign "Darkhorse 39"), remarked:

> Darkhorse and Black Ponies worked together as alternate TacAir. Towards the end of the war we quit running our scouts out there, because you didn't have to have scouts to find them because you knew where they were. It was like battle lines being drawn. We basically quit running the AirCav mission as it was defined. We became a limited TacAir like you guys (Black Ponies) were . . . an aerial fire mission. . . . We did more and more of that. . . . Towards summer things got so hot in the U-Minh. . . . We started having outposts overrun out there, and frontal assaults coming with us on station. . . . It was like World War II now. . . . The scouts stayed home.[1]

Capt. Hugh Mills was the scout platoon commander ("Darkhorse 16") in February 1972. He was on his second tour as an aeroscout pilot and had been shot down sixteen times and wounded three times.

The first time Mills worked with the Black Ponies was on 20 February 1972. He was standing Scramble One duty at Can Tho with his friend Capt. Rod Willis as Scramble Two. An urgent call came in that another Loach pilot, Mike King, had been shot down while checking out some bunkers along a nipa palm line not too far south of Can Tho. King's Loach crashed twenty-five yards from the enemy bunker.

> The second little bird, piloted by 1st Lt. Drew Scheele ("Darkhorse 15") went in to get him out and he got shot down. We were then scrambled off of Can Tho along with our two Cobras. The 164th Group commander, Col. Jim Mapp and his XO, Col. Bobby Joe Maddox, went out and jumped into their own Cobra. That Cobra wasn't on anybody's books. And Mapp was not officially Cobra rated. Maddox in the front seat was not Cobra rated at all. Mapp was the kind of guy that just liked to get into things. . . . Ken Schriver ("Darkhorse 38") lead the flight and Mapp and

Maddox tied on as number three. I took off as scout lead (Darkhorse 16) with Willis ("Darkhorse 13") right behind me as my wingman.

In the Delta we needed a wingman. The area was so wide open that you could take fire from all directions and never know it.

I made a turn over King and he looked up at me and waved, so he wasn't terribly concerned. So as I turned over the bunker I put a red smoke on it. My crew chief was a kid named Jim Christy, a Spec 4. We put a mark down and then the Cobras went in, one, two, three, and shot rockets. Then I went in to do a little BDA and got fired at again. As I turned out and called, "Taking fire," everybody rolled again. When Mapp pulled off the target—he was number three—Maddox sprayed his minigun to cover the break, not realizing there were two scouts below him. He hit Willis's aircraft and mine. That's the only time I'd ever been under the direct fire of a minigun. At that point the OV-10s arrived.[2]

Hugh Mills, army Darkhorse pilot

A Black Pony Light Attack Fire Team had launched on a random patrol and had just gotten clearance to place a strike for Vinh Long Province TOC when Black Pony base received an urgent call from Darkhorse on the Black Pony FM frequency, requesting assistance. Black Ponies and Darkhorse worked so much together that they would often bypass normal channels and talk directly with one another. As in this case, dealing directly saved time. Black Pony base relayed the request to the flight, and within minutes the Fire Team was on station.

Bubba and I arrived overhead at 1645. We had been monitoring Darkhorse push and I heard the call sign of the first downed Loach, "Darkhorse 17." I had worked with him before, and I was anxious to help get him out of there. We checked in with "Darkhorse 38" (Ken Schriver) who gave us a quick sitrep.

Kit Lavell, Black Pony

As we made the pass over the bunkers we had some guys running up and down the nipa palm line. My door gunner worked on them, as did the Cobras. But when the Black Ponies arrived, Shriver said, "They've got a bigger punch. Let's put them in, up and down the nipa palm line." So I moved out maybe four hundred yards—I wanted to stay in a position that I could watch King—if something happened I was prepared to zip back in there and get him. But I was pretty comfortable with the Ponies.[3]

Hugh Mills, army Darkhorse pilot

The two Loaches sat on the eastern side of the north-south nipa palm line. One faced west, one faced north. King's Loach had its engine shot out. The other had systems failure when it got shot up. The four crewmen had set up a mutual defensive position on the ground with their two dismounted 60s and waited for the enemy to come at them. They were out in the middle of a field where nobody could get at them without drawing fire from their M-60s. The crashed Loaches were between them and the nipa palm. And they had lots of ammo. Besides the M-60s, they had two CAR15s, two M-16s, two M-79 grenade launchers, and two12-gauge shotguns.

The Black Ponies raked the nipa palm with 5-inch Zuni rockets, busting the bunkers and obliterating the machine gun positions. There was a bunker in the "V" of the tree line and dogleg stand of trees. The scout crews had been getting fire from their rear as well as from their front from the bunker.

Darkhorse 38 reported antiaircraft fire but it was quickly suppressed. Mills watched from close by as the Zuni rockets uprooted whole stands of trees and the VT fused ones sprayed shrapnel hundreds of feet into the air.

> That was the first time I flew with Black Ponies. When I saw the Zuni go off in the nipa palm line I thought, "Holy mackerel, it looks like a 105 round." I was very impressed. We tended to hold away from the target but remain on the deck, and I remarked that in the future I would hold slightly further away.[4]
>
> Hugh Mills, army Darkhorse pilot

While the Loaches made another pass over the tree lines, the Black Ponies sat on a perch overhead, just above the Cobras, ready to roll in to protect the scouts, if the remainder of their heavier ordnance was required.

> After the Ponies had expended we went back in and made a run and there were several bunkers, cooking pots, fish traps, and several bodies that we could see. Once we were fairly secure and didn't have a problem with machine gun or ground fire, Capt. Joe Eszes (the mission commander in the UH-1H Huey slick) came out of altitude following Willis and me.
>
> Eszes came in from the east, down on the deck from about a kilometer out, Willis and I led him in, on both sides of the Huey, slightly ahead of him. We overflew the position and my comment to him was, "Here's your crew, mark, mark, mark." He decelerated into the landing zone and Willis and I split left and right. We then flew ovals around the zone and did some shooting to suppress but didn't receive any fire after the Ponies had worked the area over.
>
> The Black Ponies were the only non-AirCav aircraft that we would allow to cover the Loaches when our Cobras were gone. They understood helicopter tactics and they were damned pinpoint when they fired. On many

occasions we scouts would stay on target when the Cobras went back to refuel and rearm as long as I had Ponies. We could talk to each other and they could support me just like a Cobra could and I was very comfortable with the firepower and their ability to put it on target almost immediately.[5]

Hugh Mills, army Darkhorse pilot

Great Balls of Fire

Americans hold many myths about the Vietnam War, the Vietnamese fewer. One of the most widely believed is that Asians don't hold life as sacred as westerners. As proof, many would point to sapper attacks and assaults on forts not as the courageous acts of a determined enemy, but as nothing but using human beings as cannon fodder. When the enemy removed wounded and dead from the battlefield, some would say they were practicing deception by withholding the extent of their casualties from the Americans. On the other hand, many Vietnamese were amazed by Americans' willingness to risk so many lives to retrieve a downed pilot (for the enemy invariably counted on it, much to their success and U.S. misfortune), when Americans often lost several others in the rescue process. The U.S. Air Force and Navy determinedly flew hundreds of sorties against the elusive Than Hoa Bridge in North Vietnam, and lost scores of planes, at a cost of hundreds of millions of dollars—and many lives. From the North Vietnamese perspective, brave and determined U.S. pilots may too have looked like cannon fodder. The enemy turned this American determination against the U.S. by ringing the bridge with some of the most deadly antiaircraft fire and missile defenses in the history of aerial warfare. When smart bombs finally dropped the bridge in 1972, what some suspected would happen, did indeed—the enemy simply forded the river nearby, not even bothering to repair the bridge.

The Vietnam War was to be a test of the American Technocracy. In the final analysis it would be a test America didn't expect—a test not only of character, resolve, and values, but also of who had the clearest objective. As Black Ponies would see in this so-called technological war, oftentimes one bullet was all the technology the VC needed. And all the sophisticated gadgetry at America's disposal was frequently not enough to prevail against a few determined human beings.

American preparation to take that test proved inadequate in some respects, not the least of which was the failure to learn more about the enemy. But then again, America didn't even know its friends that well.

The U.S. military did make attempts to learn the Vietnamese culture and customs, and educate American servicemen. But the efforts were not so much to understand the Vietnamese and better adapt American efforts to help them, some would claim, as it was to smooth the way for the U.S. to run the war the way it wanted.

All of Vietnam's people, regardless of religious or social background, celebrated the country's most important cultural event and holiday of the year, Tet, the Lunar New Year. United States Military Assistance Command, Vietnam (USMACV) presented a pamphlet to all servicemen that described Tet as "a combination of All Soul's Day, a family celebration, a spring festival, a national holiday and an overall manifestation of a way of life." While some bureaucrats may have thought they defined it with the quantifiable accuracy of the systems analysts at the RAND Corporation and in the Pentagon, most missed the significance of some important historical and military elements associated with it.

The Vietnamese associated with the Tet holiday three symbolic military events in their legends and history.[6] The first took place in 1789 during Tet, when Vietnamese emperor Quang Trung made a surprise attack on Hanoi, which had been occupied by the Chinese that year. His army of one hundred thousand troops and hundreds of elephants defeated the unsuspecting and unprepared Chinese, who were celebrating their occupation of Vietnam on this holiday. In 1944 Ho Chi Minh's Vietnamese forces, led by General Vo Nguyen Giap, surprised the French on Christmas Eve, launching the First Indochina War. In 1960, the Vietcong's surprise attack on Tay Ninh in the Mekong Delta during Tet marked the first large-scale engagement of the Second Indochina War. Then, in what proved to be the boldest military action and the pivotal event in the current war, history repeated itself. The communists launched a simultaneous surprise attack on every major military installation and urban area in South Vietnam during Tet in 1968, catching the South Vietnamese and Americans off guard, despite the allies possessing accurate intelligence predicting the offensive. The allies turned back every enemy thrust. The communists suffered substantial casualties and lost credibility and power among the antigovernment movement in the South. But the "TET" offensive, as it came to be called, proved to be a victory from which the South Vietnamese and the Americans would never recover.

In the United States, the shock of the massive TET offensive destroyed the already eroded credibility of political and military leaders who had been proclaiming they saw the light at the end of the tunnel, but who nevertheless allowed themselves to be ignominiously blindsided. American public sentiment turned, and never again would a majority support the war. Richard Nixon won the presidency in 1968 in large part because he had a "secret plan" to end the Vietnam War. The plan turned out to be the imposition of new limits on U.S. involvement in the war, the gradual removal of American forces under the Vietnamization program, and the search for an opportunity to get out completely while still being able to proclaim "peace with honor."

Four years later, with another Tet approaching, American and Vietnamese military leaders openly predicted a major offensive like TET of 1968. Intelligence reports provided to the Black Ponies increasingly pointed to an enemy buildup in the Delta, with several new NVA units identified in the province.

The night after Bob Lutz's death, as a flight was taxiing from the hold-short line to take the runway for takeoff on a nighttime scheduled random patrol, the VC fired at the lead OV-10 from near the Tacan (tactical navigation) building at the western perimeter of the field. As aviators who were still on the ground, the lead pilots' minds initially dismissed what their senses were telling them. When the other aircraft made its turn, sure enough, there was a sniper. The pilots quickly turned out their lights and took off in the dark. After that night Black Ponies changed squadron SOP to require that pilots turn off external lights when leaving the arming area in the darkness, then make a quick turn onto the runway, not stopping on the takeoff roll, hopefully making it more difficult for "Chuck the Sniper" to nail them.

A year before that night, Lt. Don Hawkins had been on final approach to that runway when he casually and unexpectedly glanced out the side of the cockpit to see an old man next to a hootch aiming a rifle at him. Hawkins was so startled he was tempted to raise his gear, make a turn, and fire back. After he got on the ground he mentioned to the skipper what he had wanted to do. The CO quickly retorted, "You don't want to go and do that." Hawkins asked, "Why not?" The skipper replied very seriously, "That guy's been doing that for ages. We wouldn't want them to replace him with somebody who really knows how to shoot, would we?"[7]

Apparently the old guy had been replaced.

Over the next several nights the enemy attacked several outposts in the surrounding area. During those weeks before Tet, the VC also launched a couple of rockets and lobbed a few mortar rounds at the VNAF airfield, none of them causing much damage. The closest one landed harmlessly in the mud outside the revetments. The Ponies all joked about it, sort of whistling past the graveyard, the humor designed more to relieve the tension than anything else.

The Vietnamese prepared weeks ahead of time for the Lunar New Year celebration, so the military began restricting servicemen to the navy base, not wanting to cause an incident or make them targets for VC terrorists. Everyone expected a sapper attack on the base before Tet arrived. Workers rushed to complete a new building on the aviation side of the road which housed the new officers' club on one end and a chiefs' club on the other, with a shared stage in the middle. The new club would get a lot of use by its newly captive clientele.

One of the favorite distractions at the club was playing liars' dice, a game of bluff whose execution Black Ponies would finesse to the nth degree. About a dozen Black Ponies sat around the table one evening taking quite a bit of money from the skipper, who was not in the best condition that night to be playing such a game. None of the other players was in much better shape, but none was trying quite so hard and so obviously to bluff his way out of each hand, especially when he didn't have to.

By the time the dice came to Afterburner Bob, he accepted what was a sure bluff, rolled the dice, and declared that he had a full house. Without hesitation, the JO next to him reached for the cup to uncover his foolhardiness, but the skipper wouldn't let him. He insisted on raising the stakes, which he upped several times as the JO laughingly increased his skepticism in response. Everyone around the table shouted his encouragement for the JO to call him on it, and when he hesitated, they insisted the skipper write the hundred-to-one odds that he gave the JO on the back of a ten-dollar MPC note. Pandemonium ensued when the JO called the skipper's bluff—and he reneged. That was the last time anyone played liars' dice.

A few nights later most of the Black Pony pilots were in the club late one night when a door, unused because no steps led up to it from the ground five feet below, suddenly flew open. A grenade sailed over the crowd and hit the wall behind a group of Ponies, bouncing under their table, where they were playing cards. Backed into a corner, one Black Pony was farther from the nearest exit than anyone else. He had always wondered how fast he could react in such a situation, and was soon disappointed that it was much slower than he ever anticipated. All his memory from that moment on was in slow motion, as his thoughts were . . . as his actions were . . . in agonizingly slow motion . . . in a not so graceful adagio of adrenaline, anxiety, and angst . . . he was the last one headed for the door . . . when the grenade went off. He cringed . . . anticipating the pain in his back. In the instant he realized that it was a smoke grenade . . . he felt incredible relief. But his emotions were quickly yanked to the other extreme . . . as if his neck had snagged a clothesline, when he couldn't see . . . he couldn't breathe. Acrid smoke was filling up the room and displacing all the oxygen. The lights were fading . . . He stumbled toward the door . . . then realized . . . he would make it outside before his lungs burst . . . behind the crush of scurrying bodies ahead . . . elation then overcame him. Bam. Hit by panic, he stumbled to his knees as he remembered that, four years before, in Can Tho, a similar smoke grenade thrown into a room of pilots during TET precipitated a mass slaughter when VC gunned them down as they ran out the door.

Luckily that night the sentries spotted the infiltrator and chased him to the perimeter, but lost him when he escaped under the fence into the darkness.

The skipper ordered the hangar cleaned out, and again rumors persisted that Afterburner Bob was preparing to fly a loop through it.

Everyone gathered outside the bunker one day when the CO's flight returned. As the skipper headed for the hangar in his dive, pilots scattered for the revetments, only to be disappointed when the aircraft roared a few feet next to the hangar for one of the usual pop-up fan breaks.

Returning late one afternoon from a coastal surveillance flight, Bubba's dialing for ballgames produced a frequency being used by an army Air-CavPac rescuing a downed helo crew. Ponies had seen too many helos explode and burn in a white-hot, magnesium-melting incandescence. Ponies never got used to nervously watching and listening while maintaining radio silence until hearing that the crew had been safely picked up. So many army helos had been lost in the war. And the Ponies had seen many, as close as they worked with them. Black Ponies knew that few Loach pilots DEROSed on their scheduled date. Most had been wounded, or killed, or had asked to be transferred before their tour was complete. Bubba joined the army helos and provided cover until he ran low on fuel.

He landed at Soc Trang after darkness, almost flaming out on landing. Unable to find jet fuel, he used automotive gas, and got a hot start on one of the engines. He restarted it, and once safely airborne, had to shut it down when it began overtemping again. The OV-10 flew fine on one engine, as long as you had the airspeed and punched off all the full rocket pods in the instant you lost the engine. Losing an engine on takeoff, fully loaded in the heat, however, was a serious matter, and could ruin your whole day. During a typical one-year tour of duty, some Black Ponies would have lost several aircraft to mechanical failure or ground fire had not the Bronco been twin-engined. On this day, Bubba would make it home safely on one engine, and when he learned that Darkhorse pilots were waiting at the "O"Club, his grateful mood turned to euphoria.

We had invited some of the Darkhorse guys up to our new club and we had an Aussie band with a female singer—one of the few round-eyed women most of us had seen in ages. The band was great and they didn't once sing "Lolling, lolling on the leeeeeeeever." Bubba arrived four sheets to the wind just about the time the group started singing the Animals' classic, "We Gotta Get Out of This Place." The place just went berserk. Bubba started taking off his flight suit to get naked and had climbed up on the stage when the Darkhorse pilots rushed to join him. Several onlookers restrained them before Bubba could grab the Aussie singer. Lt. Cdr. Steve Chappell threw them all out of the club. We all ended up over at the BOQ where someone started a fire extinguisher fight. The Darkhorse guys were getting hosed, then jumping from the second deck into the volleyball court sand yelling, "If you ain't Cav you ain't shit." The next day Bubba was thrown in hack. Doc Rodgers also got thrown into hack as the one who instigated the fire extinguisher fight. He was blamed because, by the time it was over, he was the only one who was not there. He would have been, but he got a call that they were rushing someone into the dispensary who had been hit in the head by a helo rotor blade. To add insult to injury for Doc, the poor guy had been tying down the helo for the night and had pulled too hard on the stationary rotor blade, which banged him in the head. Doc thought a rotating blade had hit the poor guy.

Kit Lavell, Black Pony

I think there were five Cav guys. . . . I remember three, J. R. "Rabbit" Leskovec, myself, and 1st Lt. S. S. "Stormy" Jones. We stole a three-quarter-ton truck and went up there because you all had an Australian floorshow. And Bubba got naked. This guy Rabbit kept yelling, "Show us your tits!" We really got wasted. Then they threw us out of the club. Then we just ravished the place. Like sacking Rome. It was really fun.

The next day our CO, Tom Woods, called me in. He said, "Captain Leandro, were you at Binh Thuy?" I said, "I don't remember. It wasn't me. It was my evil twin." I had to go see the group commander, a colonel, and he asked me if I was there, and I said I thought I was. He told me I could never go back again, ever. He said the navy was really pissed off and they were looking to hang somebody. . . .

Bubba later flew with us. . . . My roommate was the scout platoon leader, Bob Todd. He flew back seat with the Black Ponies. I was supposed to but then we had the Binh Thuy thing. That was one of the most memorable things, two tours in Vietnam and that was one of the take home ones. That was a keeper.[8]

John Leandro, army Darkhorse pilot

When they got back to the BOQ from flying, several pilots saw Jim Arthur between the buildings furiously pumping iron at the weight bench. He was obviously very angry. When he calmed down, he told them that while returning from a combat mission a few hours earlier, he had tried to relax by attempting to tune the high frequency radio to pick up a U.S. radio broadcast. Finding one, he heard an interview with Jane Fonda in which the actress told of her plans in July to visit Hanoi. While the Bronco HF had transmitting capability, Jim knew its range was short. He nevertheless made a valiant try by climbing as high as he could, and probably set an all-time altitude record for the OV-10 as he broadcast his outrage to the world. The only ears on which his radio waves likely fell were not in Hanoi or Los Angeles.

After chow, pilots religiously checked the flight schedule for the next day, which had been dutifully posted in the head. One night Black Pony pilots were surprised to see that some staffers in Saigon had fragged the squadron for their version of an "alpha strike," with all available aircraft to launch on a single mission just before dawn. Black Ponies were to join Vietnamese Air Force A-37s and A-1s for a massive strike on suspected enemy staging areas for a possible TET offensive.

Because the briefing was scheduled for 0300, the normal late-night revelry ended somewhat early. At the briefing pilots peered with bleary eyes in amazement at the guys heading for their aircraft, knowing they had been up most of the night. The normal prohibitions of "twelve hours bottle to throttle" and no smoking within fifty feet of an aircraft sometimes became confused: *no smoking twelve hours before flying and no drinking within fifty feet of the aircraft.* As it turned out, this dawn patrol was a farce, not because of the condition of the pilots flying in the mass gaggle, but because the intelligence was all screwed up. The planners also assigned wrong frequencies, and the VNAF didn't show up until sunrise, giving further credence to the often-expressed belief that they did not like to fly at night.

Just before the stand-down for the TET truce, I led a flight to the area of the Song Ong Doc. Because of increased enemy infiltration of weapons and supplies along the coast of the U-Minh, the powers that be recently changed the ROE, designating as free fire zones supposedly unpopulated areas around the small rivers and canals that emptied into the Gulf. Working with an army C and C ship, our Black Pony Fire Team received clearance to attack a large, heavily loaded sampan trying to evade the helo. We had made a low pass over it, when the helo radioed that we were were taking fire from the boat.

Passing over it I had seen about a half dozen men on the vessel swing around with what looked like automatic weapons. The wingman confirmed muzzle flashes, and since I had plenty of airspeed but little altitude, I rolled the aircraft up into the beginning of a loop. With the nose about 60 degrees up, I shoved the stick to the left and stomped left rudder, skidding the plane into a reversal. Coming down the backside, I selected all three pods of Zunis, and without hesitation began firing three at a time as the bird settled into a shallow dive. The first set impacted short of the boat, but sent a "crescent" pattern of fragmentation through the path of the sampan. Two quick blips of the pickle button then blew the craft away in a spray of water, splinters, and body parts.

The next day we were informed that, once again, someone was looking to court-martial us, even though we had obeyed the ROE, and had proper clearances. But this time higher authorities said we had killed thirteen innocent women and children. An investigation ensued, and word came back that a ground sweep definitely found thirteen bodies of women and children at the site. I had gotten a close look at the boat, so close that I thought our flight would be hit when they opened up on us. I saw only about half a dozen men on the sampan, so I knew there must have been some mistake, but I couldn't help but feel depressed, deeply depressed.

Investigators eventually located the army pilots who confirmed that the sampan had no women and children and was definitely hostile. We had proper clearances, and fired only after the men in the sampan fired upon us. The XO, Commander Pickett, got involved in the investigation, and when other ground units in the area reported that the VC had planted the bodies, he reported that they closed the matter.

Kit Lavell, Black Pony

27

Great Balls of Fire

But how many villages have we seen burnt down only that war may be made to look like war?

—Antoine de Saint-Exupéry, *Flight to Arras*

He not only acted like B. D., Bubba looked like B. D.—the character from the comic strip *Doonesbury,* the guy who had traded his football helmet in for a real one, something a bit more bullet resistant. Recently B. D. found himself at the fictitious "Firebase Bundy in the Delta," which just could have been the VAL-4 bunker in the Mekong Delta. Some Black Ponies insisted it was their bunker! Black Pony pilots had begun driving back and forth between it and Binh Thuy in heavily armed trucks, wearing flak jackets and helmets. In the days leading up to the 15 February start of the three-day Tet celebration, as the intelligence reports became ever more ominous, VAL-4 increased its defensive preparations. The skipper worried that a sapper attack would wipe out most of the squadron because the hangars and ordnance build-up area at the airfield sat exposed and relatively unprotected. He must have even dreamed it, because he was so obsessed with the possibility—he knew it would happen.

Responsibility for base security rested in the hands of the Vietnamese, which Afterburner Bob said concerned him even more. Scores of VAL-4 enlisted men worked in the area, just outside the revetments, which was open to the runway and the perimeter just beyond. Sappers could easily penetrate the perimeter, either next to the runway to the north, or from the tall elephant grass to the east, which grew all the way to the river.

For weeks the skipper had harangued Saigon for a contingent of marines, and VAL-4 finally got them. As soon as they arrived he had them set up a fortified perimeter around the revetments, hangars, bunker, and maintenance area, and they began instructing Black Ponies in small-squad tactics and self-defense. The once-occasional rocket or mortar round now became a more frequent occurrence. Expecting a sapper attack, Black Ponies put in air strikes just on the other side of the airfield after snipers opened fire a couple of times.

I had the bunker duty on the night of 15 February and had just returned from flying the random patrol. I was helping the duty officer, Lt. (jg) Lance Mayhew, change the codes in the aircrafts' KY-28 scrambler radios, which had to be done before midnight, when the sentries dutifully relayed the word that the skipper's Ponymobile had entered the flight line.

We heard the CO open the bunker door as quietly as he could, but given the fact that it weighed a hundred pounds and had a big spring, it sounded more like the old radio show *Inner Sanctum*. Trying to beat the clock, we did not bother to turn around to greet him, as he continued to sneak up on us.

"Bang, bang, you're dead," he yelled, as he aimed his M-16 at us while we were bent over the desk setting the scrambler device.

I turned around to see him pull the butt of the rifle back around to his side as if preparing to hit me with it. I jumped up to defend myself and he aimed the muzzle of the weapon back and forth at each of us.

"I could have killed you! No one challenged me!"

Quickly assessing the situation, I threw my arms up in the air and turned to finish the job of setting the scrambler device.

"Give us a break, Skipper, we knew you were coming— "

"No, you didn't!"

"Aw, sure we did, Skipper— "

"No, you didn't!"

"Sir, he's telling the truth— " Mayhew interjected.

But quicker than he arrived—he was gone.

"What do you think?" Mayhew asked.

"I think we better finish this job," I said, fumbling with the codebook to see where we had gone wrong. The maintenance control chief then phoned, too late of course, to warn us that the skipper was heading our way.

"I think . . . I think . . . he may have been drinking, Mr. Lavell."

The SDO called the hangar to alert the troops there. About ten minutes later a young petty officer, qualified both as a corpsman and an ordnanceman, came running in.

"Sir, you've got to stop the CO!"

"Calm down—what's going on?"

He reported that the skipper had ordered the enlisted men to fill up all the available fire extinguishers with jet fuel and hose down the area next to our revetments, where the elephant grass grew more than ten feet tall. The skipper's obsession had finally gotten the better of him. He was convinced sappers would sneak through this grass and blow away the Black Ponies that very night. He vowed to stop them—by burning it down first. "Kind of like destroying us in order to save us," I seemed to be hearing.

The ordnance build-up area was immediately adjacent to the water-filled ditch into which the latrines emptied, commonly referred to as "The Shit Ditch"; all Ponies knew that dozens of rockets, shells, flares, and various kinds of ammunition had accidentally rolled into the ditch over the years. And the skipper was hosing down the ditch—with volatile jet fuel!

I sauntered out the door, casually walked up to the CO, and asked him what he was planning to do. Someone would have thought I was a sapper judging from his reaction

"Get the hell out of here," he screamed.

Quite a good description of what I was hoping to avoid, I thought, as I retreated with discretion.

Back in the bunker, I called Navy Binh Thuy and had the enlisted watch go wake up the XO and get him to the airfield immediately. After the skipper, I was the senior man at the airfield. The corpsman ran into the bunker again to tell us that the skipper ordered Frenchie, the fuel truck driver, to back the truck up to the ditch and start pumping. Apparently, the skipper thought the fire extinguishers contained insufficient fuel for the job at hand.

I threw open the door and ran at full speed to where I saw the skipper off in the distance swinging a flaming rag in a circle.

"Ready on the right, ready on the left, fire in the hole," he yelled, as I ran toward him.

When I was about fifty feet away, the skipper let loose with the torch and it arced skyward at least twenty feet, then dropped about an inch. A huge explosion sent a fireball hundreds of feet into the air. The concussion blew everyone back against the revetments.

As luck would have it, the last-go was just entering the break overhead when the fireball went up. Lt. (jg) Tony Colantoni and the others in the flight were convinced that the sappers had done their job, and broke out of the pattern to radio the base.

All available hands were now outside trying to put out the fire, and no one heard the first frantic radio calls. Almost immediately, rounds in the ditch began cooking off, ricocheting against the revetments. Since the tails of the aircraft stuck up above the revetments by about six feet and were in danger of being damaged, men began pulling the planes out of the revetments as quickly as they could. A half-dozen men would yank a Bronco from its stall until the tail was safe from flying bullets, then scurry to the next one. The CONEX box next to the ditch containing all the ordnance was cooking, and men were dousing it with all the available water—wishing of course that they had fire extinguishers to help.

I finally made it back into the bunker, just when Colantoni called again. "Everything is okay," I radioed, "The skipper is just burning weeds."

In the confusion, the CO slipped away. Fortunately, the Vietnamese fire trucks arrived quickly and put the fire out.

No one saw the skipper for a couple of days.

Afterburner Bob quickly acquired the additional moniker of "Pyropony," and the episode became known as "The Great Shit Ditch Fire."

Kit Lavell, Black Pony

Over the next few days the Black Ponies relaxed, at least somewhat secure in the thought that the bad guys wouldn't be attacking them through the elephant grass. However, they flew numerous scrambles, all within fifteen minutes of the airfield, in Dinh Tuong, Vinh Long, and their own Phong Dinh Province.

After takeoff one afternoon, on what was scheduled as a naval gunfire spotting mission, a pilot instead joined a scramble to the river's shore just across the Bassac, within mortar range of our airfield, and was back on the deck within fifteen minutes.

After a flight a pilot routinely fills out a "yellow sheet" with all the data from the hop, including a flight purpose code to describe the mission: night or day, visual or instrument flight conditions, attack, reconnaissance, and so on. Friday night, 25 February 1972, Black Ponies would fly a mission with the most unusual flight purpose code they had in their Aviators Flight Log Books: 3W1— "NIGHT, VISUAL, AIR DEFENSE OF OWN BASE."

Lt. (jg) Mel Etheridge, in the back seat of the lead aircraft, got a call on the secure radio thirty minutes after takeoff which diverted him to a set of coordinates he didn't recognize immediately—but with which every Black Pony was very familiar—VNAF Binh Thuy. The Vietcong had ambushed an ARVN patrol along the northwest perimeter of the airfield, in the area where Chuck the Sniper regularly took potshots at taxiing aircraft. The bunker crew had just returned, but needed to refuel and rearm before joining Etheridge's flight as it rolled in on the enemy positions at the end of the runway. They couldn't use their proximity-fused Zunis because the ARVN troops were too close to the enemy, but fortunately they had a working 20-mm cannon.

Later, they joked that the bunker crew that followed them really didn't need to get airborne. If someone outside the aircraft would have flipped the Armament Safety Disable Switch in the left main landing gear wheel well, which prevented ordnance from being fired while on the deck, they could have launched rockets from the hold-short line at the end of the runway. The aircraft would have been pointed right at the bad guys! After the hop, instead of landing on Runway 6, which meant over-flying the target on the approach, they landed on Runway 24. They used reverse thrust on touchdown and then turned around on the runway, to stay as far away from the western perimeter as possible. For days afterward, no one made straight-in approaches to Runway 6 for fear the area west of the airfield was not really secure.

When Tet passed, the Black Ponies expected the tempo of activity to slow. It did somewhat, but they continued to get scrambles to support numerous neighboring provincial outposts. It seemed as if the enemy was testing the defenses with quick forays, then withdrawing just as rapidly. It was a pattern that, in retrospect, provided an ominous warning for one of the biggest offensives of the war.[1]

28

Prelude to an Easter Offensive

What have I learned by this swing round the sky except a slightly
better right to sit down at their table and be silent with them? The
right is dearly bought; but it is a dear right. It is the right to be, and
thus to escape non-being.

—Antoine de Saint-Exupéry, *Flight to Arras*

Some of the first Black Pony operations—and some of the
last—involved flying boat cover in the Rung Sat, the strategic area surrounding the Long Tau River, which connects
Saigon to the South China Sea. The shipping channel into
Saigon was particularly vulnerable to enemy mining. River
patrol boats escorted boat convoys while Seawolf helicopters
from the detachment at Nha Be provided air cover, with occasional support from the Black Ponies. Black Pony boat cover
missions would often last three to four hours and were the
most boring and uncomfortable hops they would fly. Sitting
on the hard ejection seat for any more than two hours or so
got to be a real pain in the butt. The seat could not be padded
because any compression during a multi-G ejection, however
slight from the thinnest of cushions, would be magnified
tremendously in a spine-shattering shock wave.

Black Ponies would drill endless circles in the sky, very
slowly, at low altitude above the boats. Pilots found it impossible to shade themselves from a sun that relentlessly beat
down on them. The sun bleached out the shoulders and upper
arms of flight suits, and the effects of sweat and rubbing
against the torso harness quickly rotted away the areas above

the breast pockets. Occasionally, one aircraft would climb to altitude to cool off the pilots, who would make radio calls back to the base. A few Ponies would bring along books to read as the other pilot would fly the aircraft.

Light Attack Squadron Four flew few of these missions over the last six months, and the enemy rarely attacked the boats. Whatever satisfaction they got was from the hope that the Black Pony presence made a difference. Usually the most exciting thing that ever happened on one of these flights was when another aircraft "jumped" a Black Pony that was orbiting very slowly above the boats. Often the "attacker" was a U.S. Air Force O-2B Super Skymaster FAC aircraft, the military version of the Cessna 337, whose pilot was apparently, like the Black Pony, bored stiff and looking for a "hassle" or dogfight.

On a boat cover flight in March, however, a Vietnamese Navy radioman broke up the normal boredom. He spoke excellent English, and insisted on providing Black Ponies and the other air cover with a descriptive and funny travelogue of his journey through the marshland maze of the shipping channel. But in the middle of a conversation with a helo that was flying just overhead the boat, static cut short his constant radio chatter. Static—then silence—then a tremendous explosion erupted. The Black Ponies saw the shock wave roll upward through the air toward them before they heard and felt the explosion that blew several of the boats out of the water. Apparently, a command-detonated water mine blew up the vessels. No one spotted any enemy, and no one talked to the radioman again, whose fate was unknown. The OV-10s helplessly orbited, as debris seemed to rain down for minutes. Eventually the helicopter began firing at mangrove trees along the bank and asked the Ponies to do the same, but they had no idea what they were shooting at.

On a flight to Saigon, with an enlisted man in the back of the aircraft, one of the more experienced JGs lost an engine. He feathered the propeller on the bad engine and set up for a single-engine approach, but forgot to lower his landing gear and made a gear-up landing. The landing was otherwise so smooth that the enlisted man, grateful for the ride, quickly disappeared, no doubt eager to catch the freedom bird back to the World, now armed with a colorful story. On a cluster bomb unit (CBU-55 FAE) flight with the CO, the same JG had a hung bomb that did not come off on target. Standard procedure called for a straight-in approach to the runway at home, where the ordnancemen would safe the bomb at the end of the runway. Instead, the skipper kept the hapless JG on his wing and performed one of his usual pop-up fan breaks. Ground crews and pilots watched in horror as the bomb flew off the wingman's aircraft in the break, sailed toward them, and landed at the end of the runway, near the base ammunition storage area. Fortunately, it failed to explode.

Scuttlebutt soon had it that ComFAirWestPac in Japan planned to send a team of safety inspectors to investigate VAL-4. When they did come over, most of the pilots were unaware of the visit, including Max Britton, who, returning from a maintenance check flight, put on an air show for the troops above the volleyball court, performing low-altitude aileron rolls as the safety inspectors watched.

Even though the rumors of the squadron's departure had been floating around for months, most Black Ponies felt the time indeed was approaching when they would be receiving orders to pull out. But no one knew for sure. Scuttlebutt then had it that VAL-4 was not decommissioned in its last few months because it had been working so closely with the army that advisors in the field and Gen. Creighton Abrams wanted to keep it there.

That's correct. They did. General Abrams by that time was very high on our whole operation and he saw it as the first real pacification of the Delta. . . .When he came back to be chief of staff he told me that. He personally thanked me for what we had accomplished in the Delta. He told me that he felt that the navy brown water contribution had made it possible to truly pacify the Delta and he particularly commented on the importance of the air operation, both helo and fixed wing. . . . He said, "Those little aircraft [Black Pony OV-10s], when you get away from all that ROE and control crap, they are there when we need them. I'm very high on them."[1]
Adm. Elmo R. Zumwalt Jr., USN (Ret.)

The navy kept sending replacement pilots to the squadron. But when the army kept pulling so many aviation units out of the Delta, VAL-4 knew it would soon be its turn to go home. Most pilots tried to avoid a "short-timer's attitude," if for no other reason than to forestall diverting attention from the job at hand, foremost being surviving to make it home. Pilots purchased life insurance by putting out the maximum effort. Just as in playing football, they knew they must guard against relaxing, no matter how far ahead they thought they were, for injuries result when a player—or pilot—gives less than 100 percent.

The skipper did a lot to keep the squadron focused, with rigorous emphasis on the fundamentals of flying and by keeping up the tempo of operations. Flying as if there were no tomorrow, Black Ponies may have been taking risks that some may have felt were not warranted at this stage of the war, if at all, but to slack off would have invited complacency—and perhaps disaster. The competitiveness, and even the controversial flying practices, may have saved lives in the final analysis. The intensity with which every pilot approached each mission became the premium paid on his insurance policy. And there were plenty of men on the ground who were grateful that the Black Ponies did not let up down the stretch.

Sloan had written to Angéle from the U.S. asking if she and her mother would return to the States with him. Angéle replied in French that she would

> answer your questions which are so important and which torment me greatly. First of all, about my mother: I am sure that she will never leave Vietnam, a land she loves so much and where she wishes to be buried next to her brothers. As for me, how could I leave her when she is so near the grave? Please understand, I beg of you . . . I find myself torn between two loves, one of which is as strong as the other.[2]

Yet in the same letter, Angéle asked Sloan to return to Vietnam.

Past the Point of No Return

Enemy activity increased dramatically all over the Delta in early March, especially in the provinces south of Binh Thuy and in the southern part of the U-Minh Forest. After returning from flying on the skipper's wing one morning, while filling out spotreps in the bunker, Bubba Segars overheard an urgent radio transmission. Antiaircraft guns were shooting up an army AirCavPack working an area the Black Ponies called "The Hatchet." Named because of the outline of the large stand of mangrove trees, the area just above the Song Ong Doc, west of Ca Mau, would become an intense battleground over the next few days.

> Without waiting for a scramble call, Bubba talked the skipper into allowing himself and me to go on an unscheduled flight. At the target, we learned that at least three antiaircraft gun positions, a 12.7-mm and probably the larger, 14.5-mm ZPU, had been holding the helos away from extracting ARVN troops and their American advisors from a position where they were threatened with being overrun by the enemy.
>   Bubba rolled in on the first of what we decided would be only two attacks. I stayed close to his roll-in and watched as the antiaircraft fire opened up. It was so intense we had no trouble seeing the tracers in broad daylight.
>   "You're taking heavy fire, Black Pony," the C and C ship radioed to Bubba as he pulled off target. I was already committed to my run and was

thinking, at least my roll-in heading was about 45 degrees off Bubba's, when tracers and smoke streamed past and swirled over my canopy. I let loose half my Zuni rockets and pulled out. I pushed the stick over to the right and then instinctively thought better of it. I reversed the stick and slammed it to the left, banking the aircraft and climbing steeply off target. The helos spotted at least three gun positions under where I would have pulled off.

Bubba and I agreed on the headings we would use for our last runs and then pressed the attack. As we pulled off target on the second and final run, the helo pilots told us we had silenced at least one of the guns. Over the radio on the way home, we briefed another Black Pony flight that was headed for the same target, and cautioned them not to roll in on the same heading we had used for our last run. Facing interlocking fields of fire, it would be difficult enough to avoid the antiaircraft gunners' aim.

Kit Lavell, Black Pony

On the next flight's first attack, the enemy gunners pummeled the wing aircraft as it pulled off target. When Lt. (jg) Nick Harroun attempted to turn the aircraft as it climbed steeply on its pull out, deflecting the control stick brought no response from the aircraft that continued to roll in the opposite direction. Unable to stop the roll with the stick, Harroun instinctively thought about ejecting, but since he was still over the target, he struggled to regain control. Using rudder and the electric trim tabs Harroun managed to get the Bronco level, compensating for the aileron controls which had been shot away. Fuel was streaming from a gaping hole in the wing, but it had not caught fire.

Nick Harroun was able to keep the aircraft under control and flew back to Binh Thuy, where the squadron safety officer and operations people decided to divert him to Tan Son Nhut. Even though it was ninety miles farther away, landing at Saigon would be safer, they theorized, because Binh Thuy's shorter, narrower runway and a crosswind made an attempted landing there even more precarious.

At Saigon, the Vietnamese tower controllers cleared him for a landing. Then, despite Harroun declaring an emergency, they cleared another aircraft to land in front of him at the last minute.

"What the hell are you doing?" the flight leader angrily radioed to the tower, as Harroun struggled to retain control of the aircraft while making a go-around. "If you pull another stunt like that, I'll blow you out of that tower. Understand?" Harroun made it on the next attempt.

Nick Harroun's airmanship got him and the backseater safely on the deck. The aircraft, however, was so badly damaged that it would remain at Saigon.[3]

The sight of Nick Harroun getting hit over the U-Minh shook Capt. David Hendrix, "Darkhorse 36," who had been flying a Cobra as platoon leader. "I had used to think the Black Ponies were invulnerable," he would later remark. "There's no doubt in my mind, there are names on the list of Darkhorse pilots who would not be here today without the Black Ponies. If the Ponies hadn't been there to do it, we would have had to do it. And the Black Ponies were better equipped to do it. Particularly toward the last when we were getting more .51-cals."[4]

As the end was apparently nearing, most Black Ponies realized that the squadron could literally be ordered out of Vietnam overnight. Word quickly spread that an American television crew would be spending the day with the squadron and possibly even flying with the Black Ponies. When the TV crew arrived, they appeared to be in a huge hurry. While waiting to go out flying with the skipper, the correspondent made a big deal about how valuable his time was and demanded to interview a few pilots and ground personnel while waiting for his flight. He had his pick of just about everyone, since they were all assembled at the flight line. He walked directly up to the only pilot not wearing a black cowboy hat, one who happened to have a wide grin on his face. No wonder, for as soon as the Black Pony saw the reporter—in his Saigon-bought, Tu Do Street–tailored, flapped, slitted, slatted, cargo-pocketed safari suit that looked like it could carry the contents of a C-130, and the Aussie bush hat he was wearing—the absurdity of the situation commanded a twenty-one-gun grin.

"How is the war going?"

"I don't know about the war, but we're doing a good job."

"Oh? Sure, tell me about it."

"Well, we're saving lives with our close . . . "

"Aw come on . . . give me a break."

" . . . with our close air support. We perform a mission that. . . ."

"Hey, you can cut the flak with me, I've heard it all before."

It so happened that the Black Pony had done his homework and had been assigned to brief the man. He was armed with a lot of facts, having just completed the squadron history. He was proud to be a Black Pony, proud of the job they were doing, and saw this as an opportunity to get the story out. But for someone who probably got a much better "briefing" than the Black Pony JO could possibly ever dream of giving him—at the daily "Five O'clock Follies" in Saigon by MACV—the reporter wasn't about to listen to a piker.

"Are you going to film us?" the Black Pony asked, wondering what was the reporter's purpose, since it became apparent that he had no intention of asking his cameraman, who was standing just behind him, to turn on his equipment to film this or any other interview before going flying. In fact, the only pencils or notebooks within sight were in the Black Pony's hands.

The correspondent spent the next five minutes bragging to the Black Pony how smart he was, that he knew what to expect from this ragtag outfit, and that he knew they were going to fire flak his way—that was his favorite word—flak. The Black Pony could have told him to go to hell, but he knew the trip would have been shorter than the one the skipper planned for him. Besides, the correspondent probably didn't know what to do with an ad-lib in an otherwise pre-scripted story he had obviously written in his mind, and no doubt filmed anyway.

As Black Pony pilots were fond of saying at the time, what goes around, comes around. Later, the correspondent would climb out of the skipper's plane, ashen-faced. They managed to bring back a few bullet holes. The flak that he fired was only exceeded by what was sent his way. In the end the Black Ponies were probably as much a caricature to him as he was to them.

Doc finally replied to Sloan's month-old letter:

> I just couldn't formulate much of a letter, your missive was pretty disturbing. . . . Obviously, I'll work with you to communicate with Sister Angéle, but I'll be frank—I don't think it's a good idea to want to marry a nun in a country that's impossible to get out of. The difficulties would be insurmountable.
>
> I think you really should drop the idea—it's just too impractical—it's hard going to marry a U.S. nun. What a fantastic struggle. I'd probably bet it would be easier to marry a giraffe than a VN nun. I think it's noble for you to love her so much, but love is not inevitably to result in marriage. There's all sorts of love.

Except for the increased enemy activity in the Mekong Delta, and despite the ominous intelligence reports and memories of the 1968 TET offensive, the massive nationwide offensive during the Tet holidays that the military had predicted never materialized. When it did not occur, the media criticized American and Vietnamese leaders almost as severely as they rightfully did in 1968 for ignoring the early warnings of that offensive.

But only weeks later, on 30 March, the Thursday before Easter, the Communists launched a major offensive across the DMZ, through Laos into the Central Highlands, and through Cambodia into the area above Saigon. The U.S. and South Vietnam governments had again been caught by surprise. The United States had withdrawn so many units from Vietnam during the last few months that only seventy thousand Americans remained, less than six thousand of them combat troops.

The Black Ponies flew their last combat mission on 31 March, appropriately, in support of the 21st ARVN Division in the U-Minh. The action in the Delta would be light compared with the massive thrusts the NVA made along these three fronts. But the enemy knew that the real prize in the war was the heavily populated, food-producing Mekong Delta.

The 5th VC/NVA Division and units of the 203d Tank Regiment sprang out of Cambodia in the early morning hours of 5 April. They attacked and overwhelmed the ARVN outpost at Loc Ninh at the northern end of Highway 13, which led twenty-five miles south to An Loc, the capital of Binh Long Province. Farther south along the highway lay Saigon, where President Thieu and Lt. Gen. Nguyen Van Minh, commander of III Corps, ordered the military to hold An Loc at all costs. Thieu pulled the 21st ARVN Division and the 15th Regiment of the 9th Division out of the Mekong Delta and sped them to Lai Khe, a base between Saigon and An Loc where they would form a second line of defense for the capital.

The 5th VC/NVA Division, joined by the Seventh and Ninth, effectively surrounded An Loc by 13 April and staged a siege that lasted until 14 May. The 21st ARVN Division and Colonel Franklin moved north from Lai Khe to relieve the beleaguered city, but the division faltered because the new inexperienced commander who had replaced Major General Nghi proved incapable of leading his troops. The Fifteenth Regiment then swung around the bogged-down 21st Division and pushed toward the highway, only to be trapped by the enemy and virtually wiped out. Massive "Arc Light" strikes (code for B-52 bombing strikes), AC-130 Specter gunship support, USAF F-4s, U.S. Marine A-4Es, and attack missions flown by A-4F Skyhawks from the USS *Hancock* and by A-7E Corsairs from the USS *Constellation* broke the siege. The surviving enemy soldiers slipped into Cambodia and the Mekong Delta. The VC quickly filled the vacuum created when the ARVN units moved to An Loc. By the end of May the VC overran or occupied more than one hundred abandoned or lightly defended outposts in the Mekong Delta, and pacification programs in the most strategic areas simply fell apart.[5]

In the aftermath of the Easter offensive it became apparent, if it had not been before, that despite all the planes and equipment that the U.S. had given the South Vietnamese, America couldn't give them the will to fight. While many individual units and soldiers would distinguish themselves, military leadership was as lacking as the political kind.

Light Attack Squadron Four would pull out of Vietnam on 4 April, the Tuesday after Easter. Only days before did the Black Pony officers and men receive orders to stand down and decommission the squadron. Commanders Porter and Pickett had carefully planned the end of VAL-4. (Interestingly, Spad drivers were around for the beginning and the end of the squadron. Commander Pickett had flown A-1 Skyraiders on a previous combat tour.) Everything had been kept secret from the Vietnamese until the last moment; VAL-4 had minimal time to execute a plan to "fly-away" all the aircraft, and get the ground personnel and equipment transported to Saigon, then to the U.S.

> Back in January it became obvious that the squadron was going to be decommissioned, although the actual date was held very closely. Discovering how to decommission a squadron was an interesting process. The flying kept up to the last day, and the last couple of weeks were a lot of fun. Getting all of the paperwork done, deciding who was going to fly the airplanes away and where they were supposed to be taken, and getting rid of the cumshaw and contraband kept me busy. Contraband ranged from air conditioners to jeeps and cars. As the XO, I had inherited the CO's Australian Holden with black and white paint job and a big Black Pony patch painted on the side. How do you dispose of something like that? We also had a cache of illegal weapons ranging from AK-47s to a beautiful Swiss 9-mm submachine gun that I lusted after. We knew that the threat of smuggling drugs and gold out of Vietnam was so big that everything was going to be very thoroughly inspected. So most people were careful about what they took with them. The market for selling things had totally collapsed since so many U.S. forces were leaving at the same time. And there was no hope of trading the once highly valuable items.[6]
>
> Ron Pickett, Black Pony

Packing their belongings surprisingly brought a deep sense of pre-parting blues for most Black Ponies. Everyone was ready to go home. But many also wanted to stay. Looking in the faces of the Vietnamese who worked at Navy Binh Thuy, Black Ponies saw the look of impending doom. The navy gave the usual orders not to sell anything to the Vietnamese for fear it would end up in the hands of the VC or the black market. But some gave away their refrigerators and air conditioners to Co Lang and the other women who worked at the base, and their families. The Black Ponies auctioned off some of the squadron memorabilia for cash, which they then gave to the orphanage.

While overtly the situation was nothing like it would be three years later when the Saigon government collapsed, Black Ponies sensed the quiet desperation of the Vietnamese with whom they had worked and whom they had come to know as friends. But, in this land of contrasts, some Black Ponies would never forget watching a VNAF pilot, his wife, and their children leisurely getting into an O-1 Bird Dog with a picnic basket on the day before Easter, with the offensive raging on, obviously flying somewhere for a family outing. This sight was not unlike others that Americans would witness in the months ahead.

The National Museum of Naval Aviation in Pensacola, Florida, houses a relic that evokes similar incongruities. A Vietnam Air Force O-1 sits curiously on display on the museum floor. A placard tells the story of its VNAF pilot, a Major Buong, who, with his wife and five children aboard, circled the aircraft carrier USS *Midway* in the plane on 30 April 1975 during the evacuation just before Saigon fell. Skosh on fuel, he made three low passes over the ship, dropping notes unsuccessfully until the following message landed on the deck: "Can you move those helicopters to the other side? I can land on your runway. I can fly one more hour. We have enough time to move. Please rescue me." He and his family landed safely.

The Black Ponies assembled all the airworthy aircraft for the flyaway and said their good-byes to the officers and men who would remain behind to catch transport flights to Saigon and then the States. The entire squadron joined up in formation after takeoff to make a low pass over the tower, and then the navy base. As they passed over Navy Binh Thuy, from their vantage near the rear of the formation, "tail-end Charlie" pilots saw the ammunition dump blow up as they flew over it. There was no turning back now. During the entire flight to the airfield at Cam Ranh Bay, Black Ponies could not help but think about the fireball that receded in their rearview mirrors as they left Binh Thuy—the last view of the base they would have. Was anyone hurt?

Approaching Cam Ranh, the Black Ponies were struck by its incredible beauty. Wide, white sandy beaches reached out to turquoise waters, and colorful coral formations just offshore protected the waters of one of the most beautiful bays in the world. Overlooking these not always tranquil waters, on spits of land surrounded by lush green vegetation, the men spotted promontories on which a Hilton might someday sit. Where else in the world could opening your eyes fill you with more wondrous beauty than you could ever possibly imagine, or fill you with more terror than you could dream of?

The Black Ponies learned after landing that sappers had attacked the base at Binh Thuy, wounding several Americans including CWO Wayne Beasley of FASU.

After refueling, they flew to the Philippines and landed at Cubi Point, where they turned over all but two of the aircraft to the U. S. Marines who owned them. Some of the pilots carried back war trophies (some permitted, some not) they hoped to give to friends aboard aircraft carriers that put in to the Philippines on the way back to the States.

The squadron's pilots made hurried plans to catch airline flights back to the States until the skipper got an urgent message suggesting the squadron be kept together, in case it would be recalled to Vietnam because of the offensive. But believing the die had been cast, Cdr. Bob Porter, the CO, allowed the pilots to continue on their way back to the U.S., and no recall occurred. Had they remained in-country one day longer, they probably would have been flying close air support at An Loc, working with the 21st ARVN Division again.

Flying combat missions by the seat of the pants in unsophisticated propeller-driven planes with no electronic gadgetry, weapons, or defenses may have been outmoded even when the Black Ponies were doing it. But as soon as the last propeller stopped spinning, a chapter in aviation history definitely and swiftly came to a close. The events of the next few weeks presaged significant changes in the use of air power, with the introduction on the battlefield of new weapons like the Soviet SA-7 hand-held missile and U.S. laser-guided bombs and other smart technology. In the Delta the Black Ponies had been operating in a relatively permissive air environment and it would have been challenging to go against the SAMs and heavy AAA at An Loc.

After the squadron's departure and the increased enemy activity throughout the Delta, Angéle wrote Sloan:

> I can no longer send letters easily because the Americans don't come as frequently to the orphanage because of the recent events. Say which month, which week you are coming to look for me.

Two aircraft had to be ferried to Taiwan, and Jim Arthur and Kit Lavell volunteered to fly one of them, with one of the lieutenant commanders flying lead.

After getting the weather briefing, I recommended that we delay the flight for a day because of a nasty frontal system between Taiwan and us. The flight leader needed to make a commercial flight connection and insisted on leaving immediately. After we obtained a late update on the weather, and discovered all navigation equipment in the wing bird inoperative, Jim and I told the flight leader that it was foolish to fly. He ordered us to go, and we went.

We found the weather to be as advertised and had to descend to just a few hundred feet above the water to stay out of it. This caused the lead aircraft to lose navigational lock-on and both of us to lose radio communication, as well as dramatically increase our fuel consumption. Well past the point of no return, we found ourselves dead reckoning over open ocean, where, if we missed by a few degrees, we would have ended up in Red China instead of Nationalist China. Fortunately, we spotted the southern tip of Taiwan, but could not fly near Tainan because of the weather. We navigated up the eastern side of the island, still without radio communication. With only minutes of fuel remaining the flight leader decided to fly up a blind valley shrouded by clouds to reach Taipei. We thought that would be insane, so we broke off from his wing and turned down the coast. He turned around and followed us.

Jim and I were preparing to flame out just over the beach and had decided we would eject rather than ditch the plane, when we spotted a runway. No airport showed on the map. Workers were constructing the runway, and only about fifteen hundred feet of it appeared to be paved, the rest had men and equipment on it. The flight leader dashed for the runway first, while we circled, a hydraulic failure forcing us to lower our flaps manually. After we landed, armed Chinese soldiers surrounded us. They escorted us away from the aircraft at gunpoint, but not before I persuaded Jim not to take the flight leader apart limb by limb. While our OV-10s had all their markings painted out, and none of the soldiers spoke English, we thought they would surely recognize us as Americans. Judging from the security they imposed however, we could have been convinced that we had landed in Red China.

As it turned out, the base was a Republic of China Air Force installation under construction, and the Chinese major in charge, to whom we were taken, spoke fluent English. No surprise, I found out, since he graduated from the University of Illinois, my alma mater. He attended when I did (although we had never met) and had been a drama major, performing in several of Shakespeare's plays.

He refueled us by hand, repaired our broken hydraulic line, and sent us on our way to Tainan where I landed 155472, side number 107, on what would be the last flight of U.S. Navy OV-10s.

Kit Lavell, Black Pony

Sloan finalized plans to fly to Vietnam on 1 June. Just before leaving, he received a letter from Angéle:

I cannot give you my brother's address, for he was recently killed in the attacks on Thua Thien.

But when I can, I will give you another address. Come June and July I will no longer be at Can Tho, but will be moved elsewhere, my situation is so unstable. In that event, I will let you know. But you must not come to Can Tho, but wait for my next letter in which I will tell you what to do. . . .

Next, I will tell you straight away, that I am actually free to get married . . . well, what do you think of that! Will you come or not? However, wait for me still, especially my next letter.

Sloan never received another letter. He canceled the flight. It was never rescheduled.

Epilogue

> War is theater, and Vietnam had been fought without a third act. It is a set that hadn't been struck; its characters were lost there, with no way to get off and no more lines to say.
> —William Broyles Jr.

When the last prop unwound in the breeze and spun to a stop, after the last bullet was fired in anger, and sixty days after the last Black Pony gave his life, a significant chapter in naval aviation history came to a close. The navy decommissioned Light Attack Squadron Four on 10 April 1972 and relegated to history the set, the props, and an unfinished script.

Bernard Fall, the French-born American professor and author, delivered a lecture at the Naval War College in 1966, the year before he died in Vietnam. He told the assembled:

When one examines the history of Vietnam, he is struck by its resemblance to a Greek tragedy. In Greek tragedy, and in some of Shakespeare's plays, it seems as though everyone is murdered or betrayed, the best of intentions fall by the wayside, and the entire plot eventually collapses in gloom and doom. The vicissitudes of Vietnamese history unfortunately bear a resemblance to these woeful tales.

It has been said that we Americans have yet to come to terms with the Vietnam War, primarily because we cannot agree on what happened to us in Vietnam and why. Whether or not we agree that Vietnam was America's "tragedy," we can agree that not all our players on the stage were tragic characters. While tragedy was known, our players displayed courage, dedication, resourcefulness, loyalty, romance, gentleness, and humor. The players in this unfinished script may be stuck without an ending, but that in no way detracts from the quality of their performance.

For their part, the Black Ponies would earn numerous individual and unit awards, including the Presidential Unit Citation. In its short history VAL-4 flew more than twenty-one thousand combat sorties, amassing more than forty-two thousand flights, a U.S. Navy record for fixed-wing aircraft.[1] By any standard of achievement—in its ability to destroy the enemy on the ground—VAL-4 set the record for close air support squadrons during the Vietnam War. But more than anything else, the Black Ponies demonstrated how close air support could and should be used to save the lives of U.S. and allied ground troops and riverine forces.

Appendix A
Bureau Numbers (BUNO) of Light Attack Squadron Four (VAL-4) OV-10 Aircraft

155393 Replacement aircraft arrived in Vietnam Feb 70. Shot down 30 March 70. Lt. Cdr. Westerman and Lt. (jg) Ford WIA.

155394 Replacement aircraft arrived in Vietnam Jan 70. Shot down 29 Oct 71. Lt. Segars and Lt. Smith WIA. Side No. 111.

155405 Replacement aircraft. Currently with the California Department of Forestry.

155417 Replacement aircraft. Currently with the Department of State.

155427 Replacement aircraft. Currently with the California Department of Forestry.

155458 Replacement aircraft arrived in Vietnam 22 Jun 70. Lt. Hotchkiss WIA 5 Apr 71.

155460 North Island NAS RAG, struck, aircraft crashed, killing Lt. Leebern. Side No. 101.

155461 Original contingent Vung Tau. Crashed 9 Feb 72. Lt. Lutz KIA and 1st Lt. Brindle WIA. Side No. 102.

155462 North Island NAS RAG. Side No. 103.

155463 Original contingent, NSA, Binh Thuy. Side No. 104.

155470 North Island NAS RAG. Side No. 105.

155471 Original contingent, NSA, Binh Thuy. Currently with the California Department of Forestry. Side No. 106.

155472 Original contingent, VNAF Binh Thuy. Lt. Pete Russell KIA 23 May 69. Side No. 107. Lt. Lavell and Lt. Arthur flew this aircraft from Vietnam to the P.I. when squadron decommissioned. This aircraft is on a long-term loan by the Marine Corps to the Carolina Historic Aviation Commission and Museum, Charlotte/Douglas International Airport <http://www.coastcomp.com/av/chac/index.htm>.

155473 North Island NAS RAG. Side No. 108.

155474   Original contingent, VNAF Binh Thuy. Side No. 105. Currently with the Department of State. Side No. 109.

155475   Original contingent Vung Tau. Currently with the California Department of Forestry. Side No. 110.

155479   Replacement aircraft.

155480   Replacement aircraft. Currently with the California Department of Forestry.

155490   Original contingent, VNAF Binh Thuy, shot down 12 Jul 69. Lt. Martin KIA and Lt. (jg) Sikkink KIA. Side No. 111.

155491   Original contingent Vung Tau. Side No. 112.

155493   Original contingent, VNAF Binh Thuy. Side No. 115.

155494   Original contingent Vung Tau. Currently on static display at MCAS Miramar. Side No. 114.

155495   Original contingent, VNAF Binh Thuy, shot down 7 Jun 70. Lt. Cdr. Barton KIA and Lt. Cdr. Hanks WIA. Side No. 113.

155496   Original contingent Vung Tau. Currently with the California Department of Forestry. Side No. 116.

155497   Original contingent, VNAF Binh Thuy. Shot down 29 Sep 70. Lt. (jg) Bastarache WIA and Lt. (jg) Ford WIA.

155503   Original contingent Vung Tau. Shot down 20 Dec 69. Lt. (jg) Sandberg KIA and Capt. Long KIA.

Appendix B
Statistics[*]

	1969 (Apr-Dec)	1970	1971	1972 (Jan-Mar)	Total
Total Flight Hours	9,613	15,268	14,250	3,731	42,862
Sorties	5,395	7,354	7,004	2,049	21,802
Confirmed KBA	751	1,090	2,425	265	4,531
Structures Destroyed	1,136	1,248	1,969	410	4,763
Sampans Destroyed	307	311	347	71	1,036
SL-8 Trawler Sunk			1		1
VAL-4 KIA	4 + 1 observer	1	—	1	7
VAL-4 WIA	—	5	3	1 observer	9

7 OV-10 aircraft lost in combat
1 OV-10 aircraft lost in a RAG accident
Approximately 650 men assigned to VAL-4
123 Black Pony pilots

[*] Does not include NOGS detachment statistics.

Notes

Chapter 1. Setting the Stage
1. Lt. Cdr. Thomas J. Cutler, USN, *Brown Water, Black Berets: Coastal and Riverine Warfare in Vietnam* (Annapolis, Md.: Naval Institute Press, 1988), 139.

Chapter 2. For the Want of a Pony
1. John Forbes and Robert Williams, *Riverine Force* (New York: Bantam, 1987), 37–39; Cutler, *Brown Water*, 82–84.
2. Forbes and Williams, *Riverine Force*, 52–53.
3. Cutler, *Brown Water*, 154–58.
4. Cutler, *Brown Water*, 192–94; Forbes and Williams, *Riverine Force*, 68.
5. Forbes and Williams, *Riverine Force*, 83.
6. Cutler, *Brown Water*, 236; Forbes and Williams, *Riverine Force*, 84.
7. Adm. Elmo R. Zumwalt, USN (Ret.), *On Watch: A Memoir* (New York: Quadrangle, 1976), 37.
8. Ibid., 40.
9. Ibid., 36–42.
10. Cecil Martin, telephone interview by author, 3 March 1999.
11. ComNavForV message 030145Z November 1968 Re: Game Warden A/C Requirements, Naval Historical Center, Washington, D.C. (cited hereafter as NHC).
12. Martin, telephone interview.

Chapter 3. Making It Up as You Go Along
1. Zumwalt, *On Watch*, 38.
2. Cdr. R. L. Schreadley, USN (Ret.), *From the Rivers to the Sea: The U.S. Navy in Vietnam* (Annapolis, Md.: Naval Institute Press, 1992), 164.
3. Admiral Zumwalt, telephone interview by author, 25 May 1999.
4. Rene J. Francillon, *Tonkin Gulf Yacht Club: U.S. Carrier Operations off Vietnam* (Annapolis, Md.: Naval Institute Press, 1988), 59–60.
5. Peter B. Mersky and Norman Polmar, *The Naval Air War in Vietnam* (Baltimore: The Nautical and Aviation Publishing Company of America, 1986), 121–24.
6. Throughout 1968 message traffic circulating between the commanders of Naval Forces Vietnam, Pacific Fleet, Naval Air Pacific Fleet, Fleet Air Western Pacific, and the chief of naval operations, debated what kind of aircraft would be used to support Game Warden. A 27 October 1968 message from CinCPacFlt to the CNO summarized the situation by acknowledging that the OV-10 was selected as an interim measure, with the number one choice being the Cobra helicopter and the second choice being the UH-1G Huey gunship. But before the OV-10 was

selected as an interim aircraft, another aircraft had been chosen as a stop gap—the OV-12A. Fairchild Hiller recently had modified the Pilatus PC-6 Turbo-Porter and called it the AU-23A. It carried either a single General Electric XM-197 three-barrel 20-mm Gatling gun, or two G.E. 7.62 MXU-470 minigun modules. It was also to have dropped napalm (ComNavForV Message 241721Z Feb 68). Fairchild planned to build under license a similarly equipped aircraft for VAL-4 designated the OV-12A. There was also a float plane version that could tie up to a PBR (CNO Message 201734Z February 1968). The rear admiral in charge of Plans and Requirements in the CNO's office wrote to the deputy commander, Naval Forces Vietnam on 12 March 1968, "Also greatly appreciate your comments on your readiness to handle any additional gunships we can get into the Game Warden area. This is still one of the most ridiculous programs ever seen, from a Washington point of view (including the F-111B). The SecDef memorandum which directed the Army to give us 19 HU-1/Cobra helicopters for 'Market Time' was obviously a 'bust.' There is no such thing as an HU-1 Cobra. They have no intention of giving us Cobras. What he meant was straight UH-1B gunships for Game Warden. The latest wrinkle is that the Army doesn't have helicopters to give us. As soon as McNamara left office, the Secretary of the Army signed a reclama to OSD, requesting that the decision be reversed. I have no idea what will happen, but I know the Army is going to drag its feet and I don't blame them. I doubt seriously if we'll see any more 'loan' helicopters from the Army unless things improve a great deal in Southeast Asia. Therefore, it becomes even more mandatory that we get some substitute such as the OV-12A. In that regard, we're slugging it out, waiting on the Secretary of the Navy to cool down from his 'mad on' that he has because we oppose him on the F-111B. At the moment we can't approach him on any subject, including nuclear powered carriers, but we hope that he'll cool off in the next few days and we can again approach him with such great problems as the OV-12A. Our current hope is that he will authorize sole source procurement and we can go ahead and get the Congress to finish up the approval action. Specifically, I don't think we can get the full 19 by 30 June. There are long lead items for armor plating, etc. as well. But hopefully we could get them sometime soon. The messages you have sent have been wonderful in support. Our objective is to get 19 loan helicopters, plus 19 OV-12As. Then as a long-range solution, we want to get all 57 birds replaced with Cobras. But I can't see any Cobras coming to Game Warden for some time." When the Congress balked at a sole source contract, at the last minute the U.S. Navy cancelled the order for twenty of these aircraft and instead borrowed OV-10A aircraft from the Marine Corps.

7. The information was the type contained in the OV-10A (Black Pony) Information Sheet for PBR Drivers, Swifties, SEALs, Staff Planners, Etc., page 3. Officers in the VAL-4 Operations Department wrote it in 1969 and had it duplicated for the benefit of those for whom Black Pony pilot flew close air support.

8. The BDM Corporation, *A Systems Analysis View of the Vietnam War: 1965–1972* (Washington D.C.: National Technical Information Service, 1980), 6.16–6.19.

9. Gil Winans, telephone interview by author, 12 June 1999.

10. Ken Russell , telephone interview by author, 1 February 1999.

11. Dick Davis, *Spads,* on-line posting SpadNet [associated with an electronic Web site] [cited 29 Mar 1999].

12. Marty Schuman, telephone interview by author, 23 March 1999.
13. "Light Attack Squadron Four Command History," 26 March 1969 to 31 August 1969, NHC, 1 November 1969.
14. Graham Forsyth, interview by author, San Diego, Calif., 30 August 1997.
15. Bob Scholl, telephone interview by author, 23 March 1999.
16. Robert Campbell, telephone interview by author, 12 May 1999.
17. John Stevens, "North American Rockwell OV-10A Technical Representative Reports," January 1969 to April 1970. Stevens wrote the field reports to North American Rockwell, Columbus, Ohio. One or more tech reps (unidentified) added notes to the reports through September 1970. The reports were made available on the Black Pony Web site (http\\www.blackpony.org/techlead.htm [cited 16 June 1999]).
18. Don Florko, telephone interview by author, 5 February 1999.
19. ComFAirWestPac message 010859Z October 1968 Re: Game Warden Aircraft, NHC.

Chapter 4. Aftermost Milking Station

1. ComFAirWestPac message 160815Z November 1968, NHC.
2. 338th Aviation Detachment (OP) Department of the Army, "Army Airfield Survey (RCS AVHAV-1)," 18 July 1968.
3. Charlie Sapp, telephone interview by author, 30 May 1999.
4. Don Florko, telephone interview.
5. Adrian Wilson & Associates Architects & Engineers, "Master Plan: Binh Thuy Air Base, Republic of Vietnam," Contract No. AF 64 (605)-3933 (Los Angeles, September 1966), sheets 2–3. This huge book of engineering drawings and plans for the construction of VNAF Binh Thuy was found in a used book store in Santa Monica in the late 1970s by Howard Hotchkiss's sister, who bought it. They presented it to the author. It may be the only set of plans, schematics, diagrams, and specifications remaining for the base. The Vietnamese no doubt could have used it.
6. "Light Attack Squadron Four Command History," 26 March 1969 to 31 August 1969, NHC, 1 November 1969.
7. Gil Winans, telephone interview by author, 2 February 1998.
8. Zumwalt, telephone interview.
9. "Light Attack Squadron Four Command History," 26 March 1969 to 31 August 1969.
10. Seawolf Association, "Shot Down in Cambodia," on-line posting (http://www.seawolf.org [electronic Web site] [cited 30 June 1999]).
11. Mike Quinlan, telephone interview by author, 29 September 1998.

Chapter 5. Wake-Up Call

1. Gary Rezeau, telephone interview by author, 7 July 1999.
2. John Butterfield, telephone interview by author, 17 May 1999; Bob Wilson, telephone interview by author, 22 February 1999.
3. Schreadley, *From the Rivers to the Sea*, 185.
4. Jimmy R. Bryant, letter to author, 10 January 1999.

5. Winans, telephone interview by author, 12 June 1999: Schuman, telephone interview by author, 23 March 1999; Robert Stoddert, telephone interview by author, 26 June 1999.
6. Campbell, telephone interview.
7. Gerald D. Cole, telephone interview by author, 12 June 1999.
8. Winans, telephone interview, 12 June 1999
9. Jeff Johnson, telephone interview by author, 28 September 1998.

Chapter 6. Paying the Price

1. Schuman, telephone interview.
2. Sapp, telephone interview.
3. Russell, telephone interview.
4. Stevens, "Reports."
5. Ibid.
6. Ibid.
7. Dave Wallace, telephone interview by author, 19 December 1998.
8. Ibid.
9. Bill Lannom, telephone interview by author, 26 December 1998.
10. Ibid.
11. Wayne Clarke, telephone interview by author, 18 January 1999.
12. Reba Sikkink, telephone interview by author, 14 June 1999.
13. Winans, telephone interview, 12 Jun 1999; Clarke, telephone interview; Cdr. G. L. Winans, Letter to Graves Mortuary, Can Tho, from CO, VAL-4, Serial 322, 21 July 1969, NHC (sources are listed in two ways, as civilians and with their military ranks at time they wrote documents); VAL-4 message 191748Z July 1969, NHC; VAL-4 message 201336Z July 1969, NHC.
14. Johnson, telephone interview.

Chapter 7. Establishing a Reputation

1. Larry Hone, telephone interview by author, 24 September 1998.
2. Richard Marcinko, *Rogue Warrior* (New York: Pocket Books, 1992), 229; John Butterfield, telephone interview.
3. 1st Lt. Bruce M. Freeman, USAF, letter to VAL-4 CO from Air Liaison Office ARVN Airborne Division, 26 August 1969, NHC; Lt. C. P. Metzier, USN, CTF 194.9.5.1, Distinguished Flying Cross Award Lt. Cdr. Don Florko [the flight leader] and Lt. Cdr. John Butterfield [his wingman], Recommendations for, 26 August 1969, NHC; Florko, telephone interview; Butterfield, telephone interview.
4. Stevens, "Reports."
5. Winans, telephone interview, 12 June 1999.
6. Rezeau, telephone interview.
7. D. L. Schaible, "SEAL Operations Retrieval System (SORS)" NHC, 9 December 1971.
8. Edward J. Marolda et al., *The United States Navy and the Vietnam Conflict* (Washington D.C.: Naval Historical Center, Department of the Navy, 1986), 103–21.
9. Bill Fawcett et al., eds., *Hunters and Shooters: An Oral History of the U.S. Navy SEALs in Vietnam* (New York: Avon Books, 1995), 357.

10. Marolda, *United States Navy and Vietnam,* 303–5.

11. Ibid., 148.

12. Ibid., 338–39.

13. Fawcett, *Hunters and Shooters,* 357.

14. T. Y. Baker, "Thy Neighbor's Keeper," in a letter to author, 1 September 1997; Charles "Sandy" Prouty, telephone interview by author, 5 October 1998.

15. John Skwara, telephone interview by author, 30 September 1998.

16. George J. Veith, *Code-Name Bright Light: The Untold Story of U.S. POW Rescue Efforts During the Vietnam War* (New York: The Free Press, 1998), 229.

17. Veith, *Bright Light,* 261; CWO-2 John A. F. Macdonald, "Operations," in *Annual Supplement, History of the 73D Aviation Company, 1969,* on-line posting (http://www.OV-1.com/73d_AVN/73d-history69.html [electronic Web site] [cited 6 February 1997]).

18. Roy "Bubba" Segars, interview by author, St. Louis, Mo., 20 October 1989; Edward A. Smith, telephone interview by author, 2 June 1999.

19. Veith, *Bright Light,* 312; Smith, telephone interview; Lieutenant Commander Graf escaped and was reported (by the Vietnamese) to have later drowned. His pilot, then-Major White, was repatriated during "Operation Homecoming" in 1973. Graf had possessed specialized knowledge about East European intelligence operations and would have been invaluable to the Soviets. At least one U.S. intelligence officer speculates that Graf may have been taken to the USSR.

20. Baker, "Thy Neighbor's Keeper," in letter to author.

Chapter 8. Changing Direction

1. Stevens, "Reports."

2. "Light Attack Squadron Four Command History 1969," NHC, 5 March 1970.

3. Stevens, " Reports": *Navy Times* reported monthly throughout the war BDA statistics for all navy squadrons. Consistently, VAL-4 was reported to have inflicted more casualties and damage on the enemy than all the squadrons combined. At various times it was reported that VAL-4 inflicted more casualties and damage on the enemy than any air unit in Vietnam, for example, in September 1971.

4. Gerry Mahoney, telephone interview by author, 30 May 1999.

5. Campbell, telephone interview.

6. Mahoney, telephone interview.

7. Stevens, "Reports"; Cdr. L. Zagortz, USN, VAL-4 messages to ComNavForV, archived at NHC: Message O 201240Z December 1969, message O 201400 December 1969, message O 210942Z December 1969, message O 211056Z December 1969, message O 220754Z December 1969, message O 222057Z December 1969, message P 241040Z December 1969.

8. Mahoney, telephone interview; Charlie Fail, telephone interview by author, 22 April 1999.

9. Bob Peetz, telephone interview by author, 29 December 1998.

Chapter 9. Farewell to the Plankowners

1. *Family Grams* were written by the public affairs officer (a JO/pilot) with input from others and sent out monthly over the CO's signature. Lt. (jg) T. Y. Baker,

whose collateral duty was PAO, wrote the first Christmas *Family Gram* quoted in the excerpt, from copy in author's files.

2. Larry Hone, telephone interview, 24 September 1998.
3. Scholl, telephone interview.
4. Stevens, "Reports."
5. Zumwalt , telephone interview.
6. Schuman, telephone interview.
7. Zumwalt, *On Watch*, 36.
8. Vice Adm. Emmett H. Tidd, USN (Ret.), e-mail to Marty Schuman, 11 August 1999.
9. Larry Hone, "The JO Jeep," letter to author, 30 August 1997.
10. Tim Sikorski, telephone interview by author, 21 April 1999.
11. Lt. Cdr. Jere Barton, USN, VAL-4 message P 300600Z March 1970, NHC; message P 310809Z March 1970, NHC; John Westerman, telephone interview by author, 10 May 1999; Pete Ford, telephone interview by author, 22 April 1999; Ford, interview by author, San Diego, Calif., 30 August 1997; Ross Hanover, telephone interview by author, 17 June 1999; Larry Hone, telephone interview, 24 September 1998; Hone, interview by author, San Diego, Calif., 30 August 1997.

Chapter 10. SEALs and Ponies

1. Ed Sullivan, e-mail to author, 8 February 1999.
2. Jim Hardie, telephone interview by author, 21 April 1999.
3. Hardie, telephone interview.
4. Cdr. D. L. Schaible, USN, "Report on the Fitness of Officers for Lieutenant Boyhan, 25 September 1970," copy in author's files from Tom Boyhan.
5. Lt. Tom Boyhan, USN, and CGM Barry W. Enoch, SEAL Team One, Charlie Platoon, barndance card C-49 P090615Z April 1970, copy in author's files from Tom Boyhan.
6. Enoch, telephone interview by author, 29 September 1998; Barry W. Enoch with Gregory A. Walker, *Teammates: SEALs at War* (New York: Pocket Books, 1996), 278–87; *The Navy Cross, Vietnam* (Forest Ranch, California: Sharp-Dunnigam, 1987); Mahoney, telephone interview; Ed Sullivan telephone interview by author, 31 December 1998; Larry Hone, interview by author, San Diego, Calif., 30 August 1997; Hone, telephone interview by author, 24 September 1998; Tom Boyhan , telephone interview by author, 11 October 1998; T. Y. Baker, telephone interview by author, 29 September 1998; ComNavForV, Monthly Historical Summary, April 1970, NHC; Lt. D. R. Moran, USN, NILO Soctrang Information Report, SEAL Operations 18 February to 14 June 1970, 22 June 1970, NHC; B. P. Dyer, End of Tour Report, O-in-C SEAL Detachment GOLF, 25 August 1970, NHC.
7. Hone, telephone interview.
8. Enoch with Walker, *Teammates: SEALs at War*, 108–09.
9. John Leandro, telephone interview by author, 18 January 1999.

Chapter 11. Consolidation

1. Tom Thomson, telephone interview by author, 6 April 1999.
2. Bob Wilson, telephone interview by author.

3. Forsyth, interview.
4. Tom McCracken, telephone interview by author, 22 April 1999.
5. Baker, "Thy Neighbor's Keeper," in letter to author.
6. Pete Ford , telephone interview by author, 22 April 1999.
7. Ford, telephone interview.
8. Sikorski, telephone interview.
9. Bruce Turner, telephone interview by author, 22 April 1999.
10. Turner, telephone interview.
11. Sikorski, telephone interview.
12. Mahoney, telephone interview.
13. Stephen Coonts, *The Cannibal Queen: A Flight Into the Heart of America* (New York: Pocket Books, 1992), 58.
14. Jimmy Hanks, telephone interview by author, 22 April 1999.
15. Ibid.
16. Lt. J. C. McColly, USN, VAL-4 message P 071400Z June 1970, NHC, and VAL-4 message P 081022Z June 1970, NHC; Hanks, telephone interview; Larry Hone interview by author, San Diego, Calif., 8 June 1999.
17. Hone, interview by author.

Chapter 12. Bucking Broncos

1. McCracken, telephone interview.
2. Baker, telephone interview.
3. Lt. Cdr. J. Hardie, USN, VAL-4 spotrep 00832 16 August 1970, NHC; Hardie, telephone interview.
4. "Light Attack Squadron Four Command History," 1 January 1970 to 31 December 1970, NHC, 24 August 1970; T. L. Bosiljevac, *SEALs: UDT/SEAL Operations in Vietnam* (New York: Ivy, 1990), 146.
5. Lt. Cdr. J. Westerman, VAL-4 spotrep 01445 29 September 1970, NHC.
6. Rob Mott, telephone interview by author, 22 February 1999.
7. Ibid.
8. Ed Bastarache, telephone interview by author, 5 January 1999.
9. Pete Ford interview by author, San Diego, Calif., 30 August 1997; Ford, telephone interview by author, 22 April 1999.
10 Bastarache, telephone interview.
11. Ford, interviews.
12. Ibid.
13. Westerman, telephone interview, 10 May 1999.
14. Ford, interviews.

Chapter 13. Father Mac, the Warrior Priest

1. Joe DeFloria, interview by author, San Diego, Calif., 29 September 1998.
2. Fr. Ed McMahon, telephone interview by author, 2 October 1998.
3. Harry Constance, interview by author, San Diego, Calif., 20 October 1998; Father McMahon, telephone interview by author; Harry Constance and Randall Fuerst, *Good to Go: The Life and Times of a Decorated Member of the U.S. Navy's Elite SEAL Team Two* (New York: Avon Books, 1997), 332–42.

4. Schreadley, *From the Rivers to the Sea,* 221.
5. Edward J. Marolda, Chapter 4 in *By Sea, Air, and Land: An Illustrated History of the U.S. Navy and the War in Southeast Asia,* paperback (Washington D.C.: Naval Historical Center, 1994) [Web site on-line] http://www.history.navy/mil/seairland/chap4.htm [cited 8 Nov 1997], available from NHC.
6. "Light Attack Squadron Four Command History," 1 January 1970 to 31 December 1970; Ross Hanover, telephone interview by author, 17 June 1999; Schreadley, *From the Rivers to the Sea,* 318–19.
7. McCracken, telephone interview.
8. Lt. T. McCracken, VAL-4 spotrep 01525, 29 November 1970, NHC.
9. "Light Attack Squadron Four Command History," 1 January 1970 to 31 December 1970.
10. Father McMahon, telephone interview.
11. Thomson, telephone interview.
12. Charlie Moore, telephone interview by author, 23 March 1999.
13. Cdr. R. W. Porter, USN, Personal Award Recommendation Lt. (jg) C. Moore, Distinguished Flying Cross for, 24 April 1971, NHC.
14. Father McMahon, telephone interview.
15. Joe DeFloria, interview.

Chapter 14. SEAL Extractions

1. *The Navy Cross, Vietnam,* 21–22; ComNavSupPac Saigon message 220318Z December 1970, NHC; ComNavForV, "Monthly Historical Summary," December 1970, 14, NHC; "Light Attack Squadron Four Command History," 1 January 1970 to 31 December 1970; Tom McCracken, telephone interview.
2. Constance, interview; Ken Williams, telephone interview by author, 31 May 1999; Constance and Fuerst, *Good to Go,* 328–29.
3. Constance, interview; Constance and Fuerst, *Good to Go,* 329–31.
4. Sikorski, telephone interview.
5. From 1969 to 1971 the squadron used aircraft side numbers for identification: Black Pony 102 referred to the pilot in No. 102 as well as to the aircraft. In 1971 pilots were assigned personal "Pony" numbers corresponding to seniority in the squadron (the CO was "Black Pony 1," the XO, "2," and so on).
6. Sikorski, telephone interview.

Chapter 15. Hunter Killers

1. Thomson, telephone interview; Adm. B. A. Clarey, USN, Silver Star Medal Citation for RD1 Warren K. Thomson, 28 February 1971.
2. Sikorski, telephone interview.
3. Maj. Thomas N. Turk, USA, and Lt. John D. Rausch, USN, Letter to ComNavForV from Senior Advisor and Naval Intelligence Liaison Officer, Phu Quoc/An Thoi, 20 July 1971, NHC; Jim Dearborn, telephone interview by author, 13 July 1999.
4. Danny Miller, telephone interview by author, 14 January 1999.
5. Jim Wood, telephone interview by author, 18 January 1999.

6. Wayne Burk, telephone interview by author, 25 February 1999.

7. Ibid.

8. Lt. (jg) D. Hawkins, USN, VAL-4 spotrep 00531, 22 March 1971, NHC; Don Hawkins, telephone interview by author, 31 May 1999.

9. Ibid.

10. Delta Regional Assistance Command Advisory Team 51, "The U-Minh Campaign December 1, 1970 – November 26, 1971," November 1971, author's files, 22.

11. Wood, telephone interview.

12. Advisory Team 51, "U-Minh Campaign," 20–23.

Chapter 16. The Trawler

1. Vice Adm. S. Robert Salzer, USN, "Reminiscences of Vice Admiral Robert S. Salzer," U.S. Naval Institute Oral History Collection (Washington, D.C., November 1977), 476.

2. Schreadley, *From the Rivers to the Sea*, 97.

3. Salzer, "Reminiscences," 596–98.

4. ComNavForV, "Monthly Historical Summary," Box 266, NHC, April 1971, 77; ComNavForV Daily Narrative, 11 April 1971, NHC.

5. Ernie Wells, telephone interview by author, 29 December 1998; Brig. Gen. George Walker, telephone interview by author, 4 February 1999.

6. Richard Osborne, telephone interview by author, 19 March 1999.

7. Bruce Turner, telephone interview by author, 30 December 1998; Turner, telephone interview by author, 22 April 1999.

8. The P-3 patrol aircraft recorded the internal communications on the aircraft and the UHF frequency radio transmissions between all U.S. participants from approximately 0027 H to 0102 H. The author has a copy of that tape.

9. Osborne, telephone interview.

10. Charlie Moore, telephone interview by author, 16 March 1999; Moore, telephone interview, 23 March 1999.

11. Lt. Bruce Turner, USN, VAL-4 spotrep 00659, 12 April 1971, NHC; Turner, telephone interview; Bastarache, telephone interview by author, 30 December 1998; Bastarache, telephone interview by author, 5 Jan 1999; Moore, telephone interview; Joe Keller, telephone interview by author, 23 March 1999.

12. Historical accounts written about this trawler incident, especially Coast Guard treatments of the action, rely on incomplete and selective data. Regarding the authors of these accounts, no one interviewed the Black Pony pilots. No one interviewed the YO3A pilot, or the detachment commander, or the army's G2 Air. No one interviewed the P-3 crew or listened to the audio tape of the events of that night. No one cites the VAL-4 spotrep or the NavForV Daily or Monthly Summaries, or other available documentation. The Coast Guard versions do not include interviews of the *Antelope*'s crew or the navy patrol boat's after-action report. Most accounts do not mention the Black Ponies, or if they do, minimize their role (some refer to them as helicopters, some as marine aircraft). Alex Larzelere's *The Coast Guard at War: Vietnam, 1965–1975* (Annapolis, Md.: Naval Institute Press, 1997) does not mention the Black Ponies, the P-3, the YO3A, or the Vietnamese patrol boats. (While the Coast Guard and U.S. Navy

disregard their role, no one can say how close to the action the Vietnamese vessels were, whether or not they fired, or whether or not they may have added to the confusion when the ships opened fire on the trawler, and possibly on each other, according to one observer). Larzelere says the *Antelope* took the trawler under fire and the trawler headed for open sea where the *Rush* and *Morganthau* engaged it with their 5-inch guns. Larzelere then quotes the *Rush's* press release: "As *Antelope* closed the trawler, a devastating explosion was observed after which the trawler disappeared from all radar scopes. No survivors were observed in the area following the sinking."

Lt. Eugene Tullich, operations officer aboard the *Morganthau*, is the Webmaster for the *Morganthau* Web site: http://198.216.5.20/eugenet/Morgenthau.html. He includes the ComNavForV press release on his Web site that mentions all the participants. Tullich heard the Black Ponies come in but recalls, "They made a few approaches and then due to the very heavy antiaircraft fire coming from the trawler, they backed off as well from that engagement, the fire was so intense" (telephone interview by author 30 December 1998). But the *Morganthau* and the *Rush* were three to seven miles from the trawler, according to Tullich (eight thousand to twelve thousand yards when the Ponies engaged the trawler according to other sources), and never at any time closer than three miles. It would have been impossible for anyone to understand what was going on during a nighttime air attack, let alone see it, from that distance.

The *Antelope* was somewhat closer to the trawler than the cutters at this point, but with only a slightly better vantage to observe the air attack. EM3 Duane Fredendall, the starboard machine-gunner manning the twin .50s on the *Antelope*, recalls seeing the OV-10s shooting and the trawler shooting back while the *Antelope* stayed out, not getting close (telephone interview by author 8 February 1999). Gary Wentworth was in the engine room listening on the headphones. He heard the Ponies attack the trawler as the *Antelope* was remaining outside of gun range (telephone interview by author 8 February 1999). Lt. Cdr. Frank Lugo, the CO of the *Antelope*, talked to the Black Ponies but did not see the attack (telephone interview by author 11 February 1999).

After the Black Ponies left the trawler listing and in a continuous port turn, the *Rush* instructed the *Antelope* to close on the North Vietnamese ship. Tullich believes the trawler then destroyed itself with a self-destruction charge. John Hawkins, an RD3 in the CIC aboard the *Rush* agrees, "I had jumped out of the CIC to use the head. The trawler was off to our port side. I saw the *Antelope* go in. I saw her begin to fire. I saw the trawler explode. The amount of fire the *Antelope* put into her was not sufficient to have caused the explosion" (telephone interview by author, 6 February 1999). Fredendall, who was aboard the *Antelope*, also believes the trawler later blew itself up. Captain (now Brigadier General) Walker, the CO of the YO3A detachment at Binh Thuy, also agrees, "At some point the damn thing blew up . . . the general consensus of my pilots was that they probably scuttled the damn thing" (telephone interview by author 4 February 1999).

Frank Lugo, the CO of the *Antelope* disagrees, "At that point (when the trawler blew up), I would have to say they (*Rush* and *Morganthau*) were several miles away because we were in something less than ten feet of water. . . .We had a draft of less than seven feet and I was a little bit nervous because we were in that shallow of water." The *Antelope* had been hit sometime during the engagement, sustaining what looked like a 20-mm round in the hull just above the water line at the galley. Lugo estimates the *Antelope* was six hundred yards away when the trawler blew up. "It was the 40 mm that did the trick." Engineman 3d Class Steve Moor recalled, "I watched the 40-mm round go right into that baby and saw it blow . . . it was instantaneous (telephone interview by author 7 February 1999).

What happened at the very end is unclear. What is clear, however, is the role the Black Ponies played in sinking the trawler. Rolling in at from three thousand to five thousand feet above the trawler, facing intense antiaircraft fire in such a small, lightly armored aircraft, unleashing thirty-eight devastating Zuni rockets with accuracy, pulling out barely fifteen hundred feet above the guns, no one was closer to the action, and no one was braver.

The fact that this story had to wait until now to be fully told underlies the reason for writing this book. Outside the circle of those for whom the Black Ponies flew, around the clock, seven days a week, few know who the Black Ponies were or what they did or how they did it.

Chapter 17. Battle for the Forest of Darkness

1. Advisory Team 51, "U-Minh Campaign," 28.
2. Schreadley, *From the Rivers to the Sea Vietnam*, 240.
3. "Light Attack Squadron Four Command History 1971 to 1972," 1 January 1971 to 10 [sic] April 1972, Box 3, NHC, 5 April 1972 (VAL-4 was officially decommissioned on 10 April, but this document was "postdated" as of the 10th and written on 5 April since the squadron left Vietnam in a hurry on that date).
4. CTG 116.8 [CO of VAL-4], VAL-4 spotrep 01132 BDA follow-up from Bac Lieu TOC, 24 June 1971, NHC.
5. Scholl, telephone interview.

Chapter 18. The September Battle

1. "Light Attack Squadron Four Command History," 1 January 1971 to 10 April 1972, NHC, 5 April 1971–1972; Advisory Team 51, "U-Minh Campaign," 41–42.
2. Lt. (jg) M. Lamberto, USN, VAL-4 spotrep 01763, 16 September 1971, NHC; Cdr. R. W. Porter, Personal Award Recommendation—Distinguished Flying Cross for Lt. (jg) M. Lamberto, 13 December 1971, NHC.
3. Lt. J. Arthur, USN, VAL-4 spotrep 01779, 17 September 1971, NHC.
4. Ross Franklin, telephone interview by author, 4 February 1999.
5. Bruce Turner, telephone interview by author, 22 April 1999.
6. Col. Joseph R. Franklin, USA, Letter of Commendation for all Black Ponies, to be included in service records (MACDRAC-51-SA), 23 September 1971, NHC.

Chapter 19. Orphans of the Storm

1. Sloan's and Marie Angéle's names have been changed from their real ones.
2. Scholl, telephone interview.

Chapter 20. Hail and Farewell

1. Doc Rodgers, with input from J. K. Pell, D. K. Sheldon, Ben LoBalbo, Mike Despain, and others, composed these skits.

Chapter 21. Riders on the Storm

1. VAL-4 conducted extensive operational evaluation of the CBU-55 FAE for the Naval Weapons Center, China Lake. Ground combat units provided extensive bomb damage assessments in after-action reports for the CBU-55 FAE. Considering the delivery limitations (lay-down delivery at one thousand feet being the most accurate), the weapon proved useful for LZ prep in a relatively permissive (small arms, automatic weapons) air environment, where pinpoint accuracy was not important.

Chapter 22. Light Attack Quack

1. Smith, telephone interview by author.
2. Segars, interview.

Chapter 23. Change in the Air

1. See Appendix A for a list of all the VAL-4 OV-10 Broncos.

Chapter 24. Trolling

1. Written by Doc Rodgers with assistance from the usual cast of characters.

Chapter 25. The Last Christmas

1. "Light Attack Squadron Four Command History," 1 January 1971 to 10 April 1972, NHC, 5 April 1971–1972.
2. Letter to "Sloan" from "Marie Angéle" in author's files.
3. ComNavForV message 230323Z December 1971, Code N471 NHC.
4. Cdr. R. B. Pickett, USN, "Maverick Vehicles; Request for Registration of," Serial 3-72, Box 3, NHC, 4 January 1972.

Chapter 26. We Gotta Get Out of This Place

1. Richard L. "Lash" Larew, telephone interview by author, 13 January 1999; Larew, telephone interview by author, 26 January 1999.
2. Hugh Mills, telephone interview by author, 26 January 1999.
3. Ibid.
4. Ibid.
5. Ibid.
6. Don Oberdorfer, *Tet!* (New York: Avon Books, 1971), 87–88.
7. Don Hawkins, telephone interview.
8. John Leandro, telephone interview.

Chapter 27. Great Balls of Fire

1. "Light Attack Squadron Four Command History," 1 January 1971 to 10 April 1972.

Chapter 28. Prelude to an Easter Offensive

1. Zumwalt, telephone interview.
2. This and following letters to "Sloan" in author's files.
3. Lt. K. Lavell USN, VAL-4 message P 120753Z 12 March 1972, NHC; "Light Attack Squadron Four Command History," 1 January 1971 to 10 April 1972; Segars, interview.
4. David Hendrix, telephone interview by author, 24 February 1999.
5. David Fulghum and Terrence Maitland et al., *South Vietnam on Trial,* The Vietnam Experience, vol. 16 (Boston: Boston Publishing Company, 1984), 150–54.
6. Ron Pickett, interview by author, San Diego, Calif., 26 April 1999.

Epilogue

1. "Light Attack Squadron Four Command History," 1 January 1971 to 10 April 1972.

Bibliography

Airmobility Handbook. Headquarters, Delta Regional Assistance Command. 27 November 1971. Author's files.

Arthur, Lt. J., USN. VAL-4 spotrep 01779, 17 September 1971. Naval Historical Center.

Baker, T. Y. "Thy Neighbor's Keeper." Letter to author, 1 September 1997.

———. Telephone interview by author, 29 September 1998.

Barton, Lt. Cdr. Jere, USN. VAL-4 message P 300600Z March 1970. Naval Historical Center, Washington, D.C. (Cited hereafter as Naval Historical Center.)

———. VAL-4 message P 310809Z March 1970. Naval Historical Center.

Bastarache, Ed. Telephone interview by author, 30 December 1998.

———. Telephone interview by author, 5 January 1999.

The BDM Corporation. *A Systems Analysis View of the Vietnam War: 1965–1972.* Washington D.C.: National Technical Information Service, 1980.

Becker, Jim. Interview by author, San Diego, Calif., 26 March 1999.

Bosiljevac, T. L. *SEALs: UDT/SEAL Operations in Vietnam.* New York: Ivy, 1990.

Boyhan, Tom. Telephone interview by author, 11 October 1998.

Boyhan, Lt. Tom, USN. End of Tour Report, O-in-C, SEAL Team Detachment Golf, Charlie Platoon, 28 Jul 1970. Copy in author's files.

Boyhan, Lt. Tom, USN, and CGM Barry W. Enoch. SEAL Team One, Charlie Platoon. Barndance card C-49 P090615Z, April 1970. Copy in author's files.

Bryant, Jimmy R. Letter to author, 10 January 1999.

"Bucked From a Bronco." *Approach.* October 1970.

Bunton, Ray. Telephone interview by author, 24 June 1999.

Burk, Wayne. Telephone interview by author, 25 February 1999.

Butterfield, John. Telephone interview by author, 17 May 1999.

Campbell, Bob. Telephone interview by author, 12 May 1999.

Clarey, Adm. B. A., USN. Silver Star Medal Citations for RD1 Warren K. Thomson, 28 February 1971.

Clarke, Wayne. Telephone interview by author, 18 January 1999.

CNO message 281635Z December 1968: Establishment of VAL-4, 28 December 1968. Naval Historical Center.

Cole, Gerald D. Telephone interview by author, 12 June 1999.

ComFAirWestPac message 010859Z October 1968 Re: Game Warden Aircraft. Naval Historical Center.

ComFAirWestPac message 160815Z November 1968. Naval Historical Center.

ComNavForV. Daily Narrative, 11 April 1971. Naval Historical Center.

ComNavForV. Daily Operational Narrative, 1969–1972). Naval Historical Center.

ComNavForV message 030145Z November 1968 Re: Game Warden A/C Requirements. Naval Historical Center.

ComNavForV message 230323Z December 1971. Code N471: Naval Historical Center.

ComNavForV. Monthly Historical Summary, April 1970. Naval Historical Center.

ComNavForV. Monthly Historical Summary, December 1970. Naval Historical Center.

ComNavForV. Monthly Historical Summary, April 1971. Naval Historical Center.

ComNavSupPact Saigon message 220318Z December 1970. Naval Historical Center.

Constance, Harry. Interview by author, San Diego, Calif., 20 October 1998.

Constance, Harry, and Randall Fuerst, *Good to Go: The Life and Times of a Decorated Member of the U.S. Navy's Elite SEAL Team Two.* New York: Avon Books, 1997.

Coonts, Stephen. *The Cannibal Queen: A Flight Into the Heart of America.* New York: Pocket Books, 1992.

CTG 116.8 [CO of VAL-4]. VAL-4 spotrep 01132 BDA follow up from Bac Lieu TOC, 24 June 1971. Naval Historical Center.

Cutler. Lt. Cdr. Thomas J., *Brown Water, Black Berets: Coastal and Riverine Warfare in Vietnam.* Annapolis, Md.: Naval Institute Press, 1988.

Davis, Dick. *Spads.* On-line posting SpadNet [associated with an electronic Web site] [cited 29 March 1999].

DeFloria, Joe. "Joe DeFloria." In *The Men Behind the Trident.* Edited by Dennis J. Cummings. New York: Bantam Books, 1997, 222–23.

———. Interview by author, San Diego, Calif., 29 September 1998.

Delta Regional Assistance Command Advisory Team 51. "The U-Minh Campaign December 1, 1970–November 26, 1971." November 1971. Author's files.

"Disestablishment of VAL-4; Historical Significance." VAL-4/SWJ:rn 1650 Ser:513. 7 April 1972. Naval Historical Center.

Doyle, Lt. Robert C., USN. Naval Intelligence Liaison Officer (NILO) Ben Tre End of Tour Report, March 1970 to March 1971. Copy in author's files.

Dyer, B. P. End of Tour Report, O-in-C SEAL Detachment GOLF, 25 Aug 1970. Naval Historical Center.

Enoch, Barry. Telephone interview by author, 29 September 1998.

Enoch, Barry W., and Gregory A. Walker. *Teammates: SEALs at War.* New York: Pocket Books, 1996.

Fail, Charlie. Telephone interview by author, 22 April 1999.

Fawcett, Bill, et al., eds. *Hunters & Shooters: An Oral History of the U.S. Navy SEALs in Vietnam.* New York: Avon Books, 1995.

Florko, Don. Telephone interview by author, 5 February 1999.

Forbes, John, and Robert Williams. *Riverine Force.* New York: Bantam, 1987.

Ford, Pete. Telephone interview by author, 22 Apr 1999.

———. Interview by author, San Diego, Calif., 30 August 1997.

Forsyth, Graham. Interview by author, San Diego, Calif., 30 August 1997.

Francillon, Rene J. *Tonkin Gulf Yacht Club: U.S. Carrier Operations off Vietnam.* Annapolis, Md.: Naval Institute Press, 1988.

Franklin, Col. Joseph R., USA. Letter of Commendation for all Black Ponies, to be included in service records (MACDRAC-51-SA), 23 September 1971. Naval Historical Center.

Franklin, Ross. Telephone interview by author, 4 February 1999.

Fredendall, Duane. Telephone interview by author, 8 February 1999.

Freeman, 1st Lt. Bruce M., USAF. Letter to VAL-4 CO from Air Liaison Office ARVN Airborne Division, 26 August 1969. Naval Historical Center.

Fulghum, David, and Terrence Maitland et al. *South Vietnam on Trial*, The Vietnam Experience, vol. 16. Boston: Boston Publishing Company, 1984.

Gaylien, Dan JO3. "One of a Kind." *Naval Aviation News*, June 1971.

Gorman, PHC John, and PHC Arthur Hill. "The Bronco After One Year." *Naval Aviation News*, September 1969.

Hanks, Jimmy. Telephone interview by author, 22 April 1999.

Hanover, Ross. Telephone interview by author, 17 June 1999.

Hardie, Lt. Cdr. J., USN. VAL-4 spotrep 00832, 16 August 1970. Naval Historical Center.

Hardie, Jim. Telephone interview by author, 21 April 1999.

Hawkins, Don. Telephone interview by author, 31 May 1999.

Hawkins, Lt. (jg) Don, USN. VAL-4 spotrep 00531, 22 March 1971. Naval Historical Center.

Hawkins, John. Telephone interview by author, 6 February 1999.

Hendrix, David. Telephone interview by author, 24 February 1999.

Hone, Larry. Interview by author, San Diego, Calif., 30 August 1997

———. "The JO Jeep." In letter to author, 30 September 1997.

———. Telephone interview by author, 24 September 1998.

———. Interview by author, San Diego, Calif., 8 June 1999.

———. Telephone interview by author, 10 June 1999.

Johnson, Jeff. Telephone interview by author, 28 September 1998.

Keller, Joe. Telephone interview by author, 19 March 1999.

Lamberto, Lt. (jg) M., USNR. VAL-4 spotrep 01763, 16 September 1971. Naval Historical Center.

Lannom, Bill. Telephone interview by author, 26 December 1998.

Larew, Richard L. "Lash." Telephone interview by author, 13 January 1999.

———. Telephone interview by author, 26 January 1999.

Lavell, Lt. K., USN. VAL-4 message P 120753Z March 1972. Naval Historical Center.

Leandro, John. Telephone interview by author, 18 January 1999.

LIGHT ATKRON FOUR, Binh Thuy, Vietnam, 1971–1972 "cruise book." 1971.

"Light Attack Squadron Four Command History." Monthlies. Box 3: Naval Historical Center.

"Light Attack Squadron Four Command History 1969." Partial, 26 March to 31 August. Naval Historical Center, 1 November 1969.

"Light Attack Squadron Four Command History 1969." Naval Historical Center, 5 March 1970.

"Light Attack Squadron Four Command History 1970." 1 January to 31 December. Naval Historical Center, 24 August 1971.

"Light Attack Squadron Four Command History 1971." Partial, 1 January to 10 April. Naval Historical Center, 5 April 1972.

"Light Attack Squadron Four Command History." 1 January 1971 to 10 April 1972. Naval Historical Center, 5 April 1971–1972.

"Light Attack Squadron Four Command History 1971 to 1972." 1 January 1971 to 10 [sic] April 1972. Box 3: Naval Historical Center, 5 April 1972.

"Light Atkron Four Standard Operating Procedures,. VAL-4 INST 3000.1 CH-1. 30 September 1971. Copy in author's files.

Lugo, Frank. Telephone interview by author, 11 February 1999.

Macdonald, CWO-2 John A. F. "Operations." In Annual Supplement, History of the 73D Aviation Company, 1969 http://www.OV-1.com/73d_AVN/73d-history69.html [online posting] [cited 6 February 1997].

Madden, Ed. Telephone interview by author, 5 January 1999.

Mahoney, Gerry. Telephone interview by author, 30 May 1999.

Marcinko, Richard. *Rogue Warrior.* New York: Pocket Books, 1992.

Marolda, Edward J. Chapter 4. In *By Sea, Air, and Land: An Illustrated History of the U.S. Navy and the War in Southeast Asia.* Paperback. Washington D.C.: Naval Historical Center, 1994. [Web site on line] http://www.history.navy/mil/seairland/chap4.htm [cited 8 Nov 1997]. Available from NHC.

Marolda, Edward J., et al. *The United States Navy and the Vietnam Conflict.* Washington D.C.: Naval Historical Center, Department of the Navy, 1986.

Martin, Cecil. Telephone interview by author, 3 March 1999.

McColly, Lt. J. C., USN. VAL-4 message P 071400Z June 1970. Naval Historical Center.

———. VAL-4 message P 081022Z June 1970. Naval Historical Center.

McCracken, Lt. T., USN. VAL-4 spotrep 01525, 29 November 1970. Naval Historical Center.

McCracken, Tom. Telephone interview by author, 22 April 1999.

McMahon, Father Ed. Telephone interview by author, 2 October 1998.

Meritorious Unit Citation for VAL-4. 1969.

Mersky, Peter B., and Norman Polmar. *The Naval Air War in Vietnam.* Baltimore: The Nautical and Aviation Publishing Company of America, 1986.

Metzier, Lt. C. P., USN. CTF 194.9.5.1. Distinguished Flying Cross Award Lt. Cdr. Don Florko and Lt. Comdr John Butterfield, Recommendations for, 26 August 1969. Naval Historical Center.

Miller, Danny. Telephone interview by author, 14 January 99.

Mills, Hugh. Telephone interview by author, 26 January 1999.

Moor, Steve. Telephone interview by author, 7 February 1999.

Moore, Charlie. Telephone interview by author, 16 March 1999.

———. Telephone interview by author, 23 March 1999.

Moran, Lt. D. R., USN. NILO Soctrang Information Report, SEAL Operations 18 Feb to 14 Jun 1970. Naval Historical Center, 22 June 1970.

Morris, Ray. Telephone interview by author, 31 May 1999.

Mott, Rob. Telephone interview by author, 22 February 1999.

NATOPS Flight Manual–OV-10A. Chief of Naval Operations, May 1969.

The Navy Cross, Vietnam. Forest Ranch, Calif.: Sharp-Dunnigam, 1987.

Navy Unit Citation for VAL-4, 1969–1971.

Oberdorfer, Dan. *Tet!* New York: Avon Books, 1971.

Office of the CNO, Aviation Plans and Requirements Division. Letter to deputy commander, NavForV, 12 March 1968.

Osborne, Richard. Telephone interview by author, 19 March 1999.

OV-10A (Black Pony) Information Sheet for PBR Drivers, Swifties, SEALs, Staff Planners, Etc. VAL-4 Operations Department. Duplicated material, 1969.

"OV-10A Fleet Replacement Pilot and Instructor Under Training Syllabus." VS-41 INST 1542.1A CH-1. 14 May 1970. Copy in author's files.

P-3 patrol plane assigned to Market Time. Audiocassette tape of internal communications and external UHF frequency radio traffic concerning the sinking of the NVA SL-8 trawler, 11–12 April 1971. A copy is in the author's possession.

Peetz, Bob. Telephone interview by author, 29 December 1998.

Pickett, Cdr. R. B., USN. "Maverick Vehicles; Request for Registration of," Serial 3-72. Box 3: Naval Historical Center, 4 January 1972.

Pickett, Ron. Interview by author, San Diego, Calif., 26 April 1999.

Porter, Cdr. R. W., USN. Information Concerning VAL-4 Operations for Possible Army Valorious Unit Citation, Serial 010. Naval Historical Center, 7 April 1972.

———. Personal Award Recommendation Lt. (jg) M. Lamberto, Distinguished Flying Cross for, 13 Dec 1971. Naval Historical Center.

———. Personal Award Recommendation Lt. (jg) C. Moore, Distinguished Flying Cross for, 24 April 1971. Naval Historical Center.

———. Presidential Unit Citation Light Attack Squadron Four, Recommendation for, Serial 026. Naval Historical Center, 4 December 1971.

———. Presidential Unit Citation Light Attack Squadron Four, Request for Extension, Serial 09. Naval Historical Center, 6 April 1972.

———. Republic of Vietnam Armed Forces Presidential Unit Citation Light Attack Squadron Four, Recommendation for, Serial 018. Naval Historical Center, 21 September 1971.

———. Republic of Vietnam Armed Forces Unit Citation (Gallantry Cross) Light Attack Squadron Four, Serial 013. Naval Historical Center, 23 August 1971.

Presidential Unit Citation for VAL-4, 1969–1970. Naval Historical Center.

Presidential Unit Citation in the case of Light Attack Squadron Four, Recommendation for, 4 December 1971. Naval Historical Center.

Prouty, Charles "Sandy." Telephone interview by author, 5 October 1998.

"Qualification of Newly Assigned Pilots for Fire Team Wingman/Leader; Procedures for." LT ATKRON FOUR INSTRUCTION 3740.1C., 18 September 1971. Copy in author's files.

Quinlan, Mike. Telephone interview by author, 29 September 1998.

Rezeau, Gary. Telephone interview by author, 7 July 1999.

Robertson, Bill. Telephone interview by author, 18 January 1999.

Russell, Ken. Telephone interview by author, 1 February 1999.

Salzer, Vice Adm. Robert S., USN. "Reminiscences of Vice Admiral Robert S. Salzer, U.S. Naval Institute Oral History Collection." Washington, D.C., November 1977.

Sapp, Charlie. Telephone interview by author, 30 May 1999.

Schaible, Cdr. D. L., USN. "Report on the Fitness of Officers for Lieutenant Boyhan, 25 September 1970." Copy in author's files.

———. SEAL Operations Retrieval System (SORS). Naval Historical Center, 9 December 1971.

Scholl, Bob. Telephone interview by author, 23 March 1999.

Schreadley, Cdr. R. L., USN, (Ret.). *From the Rivers to the Sea: The United States Navy in Vietnam.* Annapolis, Md.: Naval Institute Press, 1992.

Schuman, Marty. Telephone interview by author, 23 March 1999.

Seawolf Association. "Shot Down in Cambodia." On-line posting http://www.seawolf.org [electronic Web site] [cited 30 June 1999].

Segars, Roy "Bubba." Interview by author, St. Louis, Mo., 20 October 1989.

Sheehan, Lt. Cdr. Daniel B., USN (Ret). "The Black Ponies." U.S. Naval Institute *Proceedings* (April 1988): 84–88.

Sikkink, Reba. Telephone interview by author, 14 June 1999.

Sikorski, Tim. Telephone interview by author, 21 April 1999.

Skwara, John. Telephone interview by author, 30 September 1998.

Smith, Edward A. Telephone interview by author, 2 June 1999.

Stevens, John. "North American Rockwell OV-10A Technical Representative Reports" January 1969 to April 1970. Field reports to North American Rockwell, Columbus, Ohio. On-line posting http//www.blackpony.org/techlead.htm [Black Pony electronic Web site] [cited 16 June 1999].

Stoddert, Robert. Telephone interview by author, 26 June 1999.

Sullivan, Ed. E-mail to author, 8 February 1999.

———. Telephone interview by author, 31 December 1998.

The Teams: An Oral History of the U.S. Navy SEALs. Edited by Kevin Dockery and Bill Fawcett. New York: William Morrow, 1988.

Thomson, Tom. "Telephone interview by author, 6 April 1999.

338th Aviation Detachment (OP) Department of the Army. "Army Airfield Survey (RCS AVHAV-1)." 18 July 1968.

Tidd, Vice Adm. Emmett H., USN (Ret.). E-mail to Marty Schuman, 11 August 1999.

Tullich, Eugene. Telephone interview by author, 30 December 1998.

Turk, Maj. Thomas N., USA, and Lt. John D. Rausch, USN. Letter to ComNavForV from Senior Advisor and Naval Intelligence Liaison Officer, Phu Quoc/An Thoi, 20 July 1971, Naval Historical Center.

Turner, Lt. B., USN. VAL-4 spotrep 00659, 12 April 1971. Naval Historical Center.

Turner, Bruce. Telephone interview by author, 30 December 1998.

———. Telephone interview by author, 22 April 1999).

VAL-4 message 191748Z July 1969. Naval Historical Center.

VAL-4 message 201336Z July 1969. Copy in author's files.

VAL-4 Brevity Codes, 1971. Copy in author's files.

VAL-4 *Commissioning Ceremony Pamphlet,* 3 January 1969. Naval Historical Center.

VAL-4 Delta UHF & FM Frequency/Call Sign Cards, 1971. Copy in author's files.

VAL-4 *Family Grams,* 1970. Naval Historical Center. Also several in author's files.

VAL-4 Flyaway Instructions, 1972. Copy in author's files.

VAL-4 *Honors-Awards Ceremony Pamphlet.* 3 April 1972. Naval Historical Center.

VAL-4 Insignia File, 1969–1972. Naval Historical Center.

VAL-4 OV-10A Aircraft Monthly Activity by Bureau Number, 1969–1972. Naval Historical Center.

VAL-4 Press Releases, 1969–1970. Naval Historical Center.

Veith, George J. *Code-Name Bright Light: The Untold Story of U.S. POW Rescue Efforts During the Vietnam War.* New York: The Free Press, 1998.

Walker, Brig. Gen. George. Telephone interview by author, 4 February 1999.

Wallace, Dave. Telephone interview by author, 19 December 1998.

Wells, Ernie. Telephone interview by author, 12 December 1998.

Wentworth, Gary. Telephone interview by author, 8 February 1999.

Westerman, Lt. Cdr., J. VAL-4 spotrep 01445, 29 September 1970. Naval Historical Center.

Westerman, John. Telephone interview by author, 10 May 1999.

———. Telephone interview by author, 21 April 1999.

Williams, Ken. Telephone interview by author, 31 May 1999.

Wilson, Adrian & Associates Architects & Engineers. "Master Plan: Binh Thuy Air Base, Republic of Vietnam. Contract No. AF 64 (605)-3933. Los Angeles: September 1966. Copy in author's files.

Wilson, Bob. Telephone interview by author, 22 February 1999.

Winans, Cdr. G. L., USN. Letter to Graves Mortuary, Can Tho, from CO, VAL-4, Serial 322, 21 July 1969. Naval Historical Center.

Winans, Gil. Telephone interview by author, 2 February 1998.

———. Telephone interview by author, 12 June 1999.

Wood, Jim. Telephone interview by author, 18 January 1999.

Zagortz, Cdr. L., USN. VAL-4 message O 201240Z December 1969. This and following are archived at the Naval Historical Center.

———. VAL-4 message O 201400Z December 1969.

———. VAL-4 message O 210942Z December 1969.

———. VAL-4 message O 211056Z December 1969.

———. VAL-4 message O 220754Z December 1969.

———. VAL-4 message O 222057Z December 1969.

———. VAL-4 message P 241040Z December 1969.

Zumwalt, Adm. Elmo. Telephone interview by author, 25 May 1999.

Zumwalt, Adm. Elmo R., USN (Ret.). *On Watch: A Memoir.* New York: Quadrangle, 1976.

Index

About the Author

As a naval aviator Kit Lavell flew 243 combat missions with the Black Ponies and was awarded the Distinguished Flying Cross, twenty-one Air Medals, five Navy Commendation Medals, a Navy Achievement Medal, and a Combat Action Ribbon.

After returning to the states, he flew as a commercial pilot and was the owner of an engineering and construction company that specialized in alternative energy projects. Mr. Lavell recieved the California Affordable Housing Competition Award for housing he developed for the handicapped and the elderly. Currently living in California, he is a produced playwright and screenwriter.